PRAISE FOR

The Nationalist Revival

"Methodically and with data widely drawn, Judis points the finger at a globalization that has seen once well-rewarded jobs shipped overseas; at immigration and the cultural and economic resentment it stirs; and at terrorism and the fear of the other it provokes. He also reminds us that ethnic nationalism is hardly new in the United States—that the melting pot self-conception of the American nation is relatively recent and that for more than a century the American people conceived their country in strictly white, northern European and Protestant terms. Wisely, he argues that nationalism does not have an innate political color, that it can shade right or left depending on the ideological pigment with which it is combined."

JONATHAN FREEDLAND
New York Times Book Review

"John B. Judis, author of *The Nationalist Revival*, does not see a death-match between imperial liberalism on the one hand and nationalism on the other. His book argues that elites have overreached, both in the U.S. and in Europe, in advocating large-scale immigration and trade deals and foreign interventions. As a result, Mr. Judis—a former *New Republic* editor who has long supported progressive and pro-labor economic policies—calls for a synthesis between liberalism and nationalism."

JASON WILLICK
Wall Street Journal

"John B. Judis is the rare left-of-center journalist who takes our populist-nationalist moment seriously. Rather than dismiss the leaders and constituencies of the American and European movements as mere xenophobes, he offers an empathetic balls-and-strikes analysis of the socioeconomic factors that made—and continue to make—such campaigns viable."
The American Conservative

The Politics of Our Time
Populism, Nationalism, Socialism

COLUMBIA GLOBAL REPORTS
NEW YORK

The Politics of Our Time

Populism, Nationalism, Socialism

John B. Judis

United
States

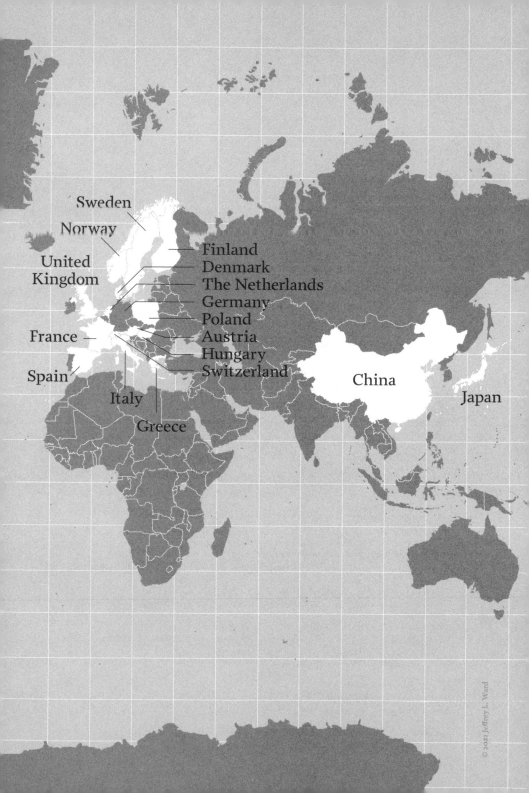

The Politics of Our Time : Populism, Nationalism, Socialism
Copyright © 2021 by John B. Judis
All rights reserved

Published by Columbia Global Reports
91 Claremont Avenue, Suite 515
New York, NY 10027
globalreports.columbia.edu
facebook.com/columbiaglobalreports
@columbiaGR

Library of Congress Cataloging-in-Publication Data
Names: Judis, John B., author. | Judis, John B. Populist explosion. | Judis, John B. Nationalist
    revival. | Judis, John B. Socialist awakening.
Title: The politics of our time / John B. Judis.
Description: New York: Columbia Global Reports, [2021] | Includes bibliographical
    references and index.
Identifiers: LCCN 2020058118 | ISBN 9781735913605 (hardcover)
Subjects: LCSH: World politics--21st century. | Populism. | Nationalism. | Socialism.
Classification: LCC D863 .J83 2021 | DDC 320.56/62--dc23
LC record available at https://lccn.loc.gov/2020058118

Book design by Strick&Williams
Map design by Jeffrey L. Ward
Author photograph by Miranda Sita

Printed in the United States of America

To the memory of James Weinstein

CONTENTS

Introduction
The Crisis of Our Time

All the decades of modern history—beset by the emergence of rival nation-states and imperialisms, the ups and downs of global capitalism, war, and natural disasters—can be described as times of crisis. "Crisis," as the philosopher Nancy Fraser has remarked, is often used through "loose talk" simply to refer to "things going badly." But there have been periods in the last three centuries in which the very foundations of societies have been shaken.

One of these would be the period from the 1770s to 1815 in Europe and the United States, the time of the American and French revolutions, the Napoleonic wars, the rise of the new kind of nation-state and nationalism, and the emergence of Great Britain as the leader of global capitalism. Another would be the period from the early 1900s to 1950, which saw a Great Depression, the collapse of the pound-based gold standard, the rise and fall of fascism, two world wars, the Russian and Chinese revolutions, the growth internationally of communist and anti-colonial movements, and the beginning of a new Cold War.

The current period, which begins roughly in the 1980s and will continue well through the 2020s, if not beyond, bears the markings of a genuine crisis. It began with the collapse of the Soviet Union

16 and its empire, the rise of China as a global power and of East Asia as a center of capitalist production, the formation of the European Union and Eurozone, the expansion of NATO eastward, the creation of the World Trade Organization, and the successful American-led wars in Kuwait and the former Yugoslavia. These were followed by terrorist attacks, disastrous wars, a global financial crash, the beginnings of a heated rivalry between China and the United States, and nature's revenge against global capitalism—climate change and the COVID-19 pandemic.

During this period, public officials and policymakers were initially guided by common assumptions about the domestic and international economy and about the conditions for peace. Policymakers had blamed the slowdown in growth that had begun in the early 1970s on government regulations, punitive taxes on business and the wealthy, and deficit spending that they believed had crowded out private investment. They called for reducing the government presence in the private economy. Internationally, they advocated free trade and the free movement of capital and labor. Companies should be able to move overseas and workers to cross borders. They thought that the spread of free market capitalism would encourage the transformation of authoritarian and state socialist regimes, including those in Russia and China, into liberal democracies.

The first part of this period, which spanned the last decades of the twentieth century, reinforced optimism about the spread of liberal democratic capitalism outward from the United States and Western Europe to former communist states in Eastern Europe and Russia. For the West, the century-old promise of the China market was finally to be kept. The Eurozone would bring the less prosperous southern European countries up to the level of the northern countries. The UN coalition's success in Kuwait and NATO's apparent success in the Balkans lent credence to the view that United States and its allies would be able to snuff out future conflicts. Millions of immigrants from the less-developed countries would ease the burden of aging societies. The computer revolution would fuel rapid

economic growth. The new economics, American Treasury and Federal Reserve officials believed, would tame the business cycle.

The bubbly optimism of this time was evident in two books that appeared in 1999: *New York Times* columnist Thomas Friedman's *The Lexus and the Olive Tree: Understanding Globalization* and *Dow 36,000: The New Strategy for Profiting from the Coming Rise in the Stock Market* by James Glassman and Kevin Hassett from the American Enterprise Institute. The highbrow version could be found in German philosopher Jurgen Habermas's *The Postnational Constellation* and British sociologist Anthony Giddens's *The Third Way: The Renewal of Social Democracy*.

There were hints of trouble beginning with the Asian financial crisis of 1997, but for the United States and Europe, the trouble really began with the bursting of the dot-com bubble in the Spring of 2001 and the al-Qaeda attack on September 11 (which was in part blowback from the first Iraq war in 1991), followed by the Iraq war and the Great Recession that revealed that the combination of footloose American corporations, Chinese mercantilism, and automation had carved out great craters in what had been the industrial heartland of the United States. That had angered the workers and small business people who had staked their and their children's lives on the promise of lifetime employment in factories, mines, and offices. They now felt, in the words of British sociologists Robert Ford and Matthew Goodwin, "left behind." The Great Recession also dashed the dreams of young college graduates who expected to move up the ladder in income and responsibility. And a spate of hurricanes and wildfires raised the specter of uncontrolled climate change.

In Europe, the Great Recession showed how the introduction of the Euro and the budgetary strictures created by the Stability and Growth Pact had not led to convergence but to greater divergence between the northern and southern economies. Germany's trade surpluses had created precarious imbalances with the nations of Southern Europe. The free flow of migrants and refugees stoked a clash of cultures that had been exacerbated by the rise of Islamic terrorism. In Eastern Europe, a burst of post-Communist enthusiasm for neoliberal economics had led to corruption, stagnation, and growing inequality. At the same time, within Europe's nations, the recession highlighted, as it did in the United States, the gap between the boarded up factory and mining towns and the shiny new post-industrial metro centers. In Europe and the United States, these two groups, the left behinds and the disillusioned young college graduates became, respectively, the shock troops of protest on the right and the left.

The new capitalism, it became clear, had created growing inequality within nations and in Europe between nations as well. The system depended on the United States acting as the consumer of last resort for goods from China, which by suppressing consumption, produced and exported far more than it consumed. A similar relationship existed between Europe's debt-burdened nations and Germany. In the United States and in countries like Spain, Italy, and Greece, this arrangement had encouraged rising public and private debt (including in the United States, subprime mortgages and student loans). As spelled out by Matthew Klein and Michael Pettis in *Trade Wars Are Class Wars*, this unstable arrangement, premised on rising debt, was responsible for the Great Recession and will continue to plunge global capitalism into periodic downturns. If you overlay this economic instability with the increasingly fractious geopolitical competition between China and the United States, you have the ingredients for trouble, even war.

Three Phases of Political Reaction

As optimism about capitalism gave way to fear and anger, the political reaction in the United States and Europe went through two phases—call them failed adjustment and populist protest—and now, with the defeat of Donald Trump and the election of Joe Biden in the United States, has entered a third phase. In the first phase of failed adjustment, countries attempted to meet the challenge of the Great Recession, the influx of migrants and refugees, and the onset of Islamic terrorism by refining neoliberal approaches. Governments in the U.S. and Europe initially attempted to revive their economies through monetary and fiscal stimulus programs, but having warded off the worst, reverted to a politics of budget and debt reduction that prolonged the downturn. Rightwing critics of Islam were scorned and in some cases put on trial for hate speech.

As the recovery stalled, politicians, parties, and movements on the left and right challenged the prevailing consensus among Western leaders. In the United States, these included the Tea Party, Occupy Wall Street, the presidential campaigns of Bernie Sanders and Donald Trump; in Europe, France's National Front, Denmark's Peoples' Party, Greece's Syriza, Spain's Podemos, in Hungary, Viktor Orban and Fidesz, in Britain, Jeremy Corbyn's Labour Party and the United Kingdom Independent Party (UKIP), and in Germany, the Alternativ für Deutschland (AfD). Few countries in Europe were spared some kind of counter-hegemonic movement or party.

These politicians and parties were populist in character—that is, they framed their political appeal as being a defense of the people against the elites or establishment. In this second phase, populist protest took a leftwing and rightwing form:

Leftwing populism: Sanders and Massachusetts Senator Elizabeth Warren in the U.S., Corbyn in the UK, Podemos in Spain, Syriza in Greece, and the Five Star Movement in Italy championed "the people," "working people," "the many," against the "billionaire class," "the few," the "caste." They attacked the neoliberal politics of austerity, the power of wealth, and the promotion of globalization. Some, like Sanders and Corbyn, combined populism with democratic socialism, which particularly resonated among younger voters in the great metro centers. Other populists, including Warren, Beppe Grillo of the Five Star Movement, or Inigo Errejon of Podemos, eschewed advocacy of socialism. But the two groups shared the same political base and the same egalitarian objectives.

Rightwing populism: Trump in the U.S. during his 2016 campaign, Le Pen in France, and the Danish People's Party shared the left's

20   opposition to neoliberalism and globalization, but combined it with an exclusionary nationalism that limited who was included in "the people," and charged elites with coddling an outsider group of illegal immigrants, refugees, or Muslims. Some of the rightwing populist groups, such as the Danish People's Party or Finland's Finns, played according to the rules of Western democracy—honoring transitions of power and liberal freedoms—but others, including Viktor Orban's Fidesz and Poland's Law and Justice, sought to bend the rules in order to remain in power indefinitely. The politicians and parties found their base among the "left-behinds" who lived outside of New York City, London, Copenhagen, and Budapest.

Over the first two decades of the twenty-first century, the rightwing populists enjoyed a larger and noisier following than the left-leaning populists. They joined national governments in Europe, built a powerful faction in the European parliament, and won the White House in the United States. Their ascendancy represented, above all, a warning to business and political leaders—to the country's elites—that the policies they had championed had failed and that they had fallen into disrepute among significant parts of the electorate.

As a global pandemic and recession have ravaged the United States and Europe, politics has entered a third phase of tenuous adjustment, highlighted by Trump's defeat in November 2020. While discontent remains high in Trump's middle America, or among the "left-behinds" in Europe, much of the electorate, in response to the threat of the pandemic and to the excesses of rightwing populism, has turned to technocrats like France's Emmanuel Macron, a former economic minister, and Italy's Giuseppe Conte, a law professor and former bureaucrat, and to older established leadership. The German electorate has re-embraced Angela Merkel and the Americans the 78-year-old former senator and vice president Joe Biden. But these political leaders preside over a fractured and unhappy electorate and a deeply flawed political economy. Their attempt at restoring political order, like the prior attempt at adjustment, could usher in a new wave of strident dissent on the left and right.

Donald Trump's Populist Adventure

The swift rise and latter-day decline of rightwing populism during the 2010s was encapsulated in the two presidential campaigns and the presidency of Donald Trump. Trump's 2016 campaign highlighted the failures of neoliberalism. He appealed to middle America and its left behinds. He denounced corporations for moving to Mexico or Asia and past administrations for "bad trade deals" that led to factory shutdowns and trade deficits. He promised to contest China's mercantilist strategy and to close porous borders that had allowed millions of illegal unskilled immigrants into the country. He repudiated conservative Republican advocacy of austerity, promising to protect Medicare and Social Security, replace the Affordable Care Act with a more universal system that charged less, and spend trillions on infrastructure.

Trump mixed these appeals, some of which echoed those of Sanders and leftwing Democrats, with the dark side of rightwing populism. He dismissed experts, meeting with anti-vaccine activists and declaring climate change a hoax. He stigmatized illegal immigrants, a great majority of whom had entered the country in search of work, by identifying them with Mexican "rapists" and drug-dealers. He described asylum-seekers as bringing on an "invasion." He encouraged skepticism about whether Barack Obama had been born in the United States rather than Africa, and he mounted vicious and often unfounded attacks against his Republican opponents in the primary and against his Democratic opponent in the general election. In August 2016, Trump replaced Paul Manafort, a conventional Republican, as campaign manager with populist flamethrower and Breitbart News co-founder Steve Bannon. As he acquired a rowdy and enthusiastic following, he made increasingly extravagant claims—that, for instance, he would force Mexico to pay for a billion-dollar border wall. In response, his followers at rallies chanted back, "Build the wall!"

Populists have trouble winning high office precisely because they rally "the people" against the "establishment" and make demands

22   that the establishment is bound to reject. They provoke the country's leadership to oppose them. Trump faced concerted opposition
from Republican party elites, from many business leaders, and from
the mainstream media and political intelligentsia, including conservative opinion journals like *National Review* and *The Weekly Standard*.
Trump won the Republican nomination in a crowded field because of
his superior name recognition and reputation as a successful businessman and because of his appeal to the left-behinds. Overall, he
remained an unpopular choice, but he won the presidency because
his opponent, Hillary Clinton, ran an extraordinarily inept campaign
(ignoring those areas of the country that had been hard hit by neoliberal neglect). She still got more votes than Trump, but because of the
American electoral system, Trump won the election.

Having run and won as an anti-establishment candidate, Trump
faced an immediate problem when he took office: He could not draw
upon a stock of experienced policymakers who shared his outlook and who would enthusiastically implement his program. They
didn't exist. Trump appointed establishment figures, particularly
from the military, and hoped they would bend to his will. When
they didn't, he fired them. As a result, his administration was a constantly revolving door. As of the November 2020 election, he had
had four White House chiefs of staff, five deputy chiefs of staff, six
communication directors, four National Security Advisors, and six
deputy National Security Advisors.

As a populist, Trump also faced a rhetorical problem. The rhetoric of populism is us vs. them, the good people against an evil
establishment. Rightwing populism is particularly divisive because
it attacks the establishment for favoring an outgroup, which in
Trump's case was illegal immigrants and Muslims. If Trump were
to have acted like a normal President and not like a populist, he
would have sanded off the rough edges of his campaign rhetoric
and have purported to speak as President on behalf of all Americans. That's how Trump's Republican and Democratic predecessors
had conducted themselves. The George H. W. Bush of the vicious

Willie Horton campaign ads in 1988 was not George H. W. Bush the
president.

But after he won the presidency, Trump continued to speak primarily to his core supporters and to frame politics in terms of us vs.
them. "Them" were Democrats who denied his legitimacy, Republicans who defied him, experts who disagreed with him on climate change or the pandemic (he disparaged Dr. Anthony Fauci, the
director of the National Institute of Allergies and Infectious Diseases, as an "idiot"), and above all the mainstream press, whom he
described as "very, very dishonest people" and the purveyors of
"fake news." His language was incendiary, appealing to racial and
ethnic prejudice. He tweeted that four progressive congresswomen
(Alexandria Ocasio-Cortez, Ilhan Omar, Rashida Tlaib, and Ayanna
Pressley) "came from countries whose governments are a complete
and total catastrophe, the worst, most corrupt and inept anywhere
in the world." He urged them to "go back and help fix the totally
broken and crime infested places from which they came." Of them,
only Omar had not been born and grown up in the United States.
Trump also lied continually in his tweets and other public statements about his accomplishments and his enemies' failings—the
Washington Post counted over 22,000 lies in four years. He created a
cocoon of adulation and grievance around himself and his followers,
while offending much of the electorate outside.

As president, Trump was hamstrung getting Congressional
approval for the programs he had advocated in the campaign. The
Senate was dominated by business conservatives. In the House of
Representatives, Tea Party anti-government Republicans exercised a veto within the Republican caucus. His infrastructure plans
never materialized, nor did he get a bill reforming immigration laws.
Trump got some of his agenda through executive orders. He put out
thirteen executive orders altering immigration law, including, most
notably, one that would not grant green cards (allowing employment
and permanent residency) to migrants who were receiving any kind
of public assistance. (The day before the 2020 election, a District

24 Judge threw it out.) He appointed a head of the Federal Reserve whom he repeatedly criticized, but who actually shared Trump's preference for goosing the economy.

His most notable achievements were in trade policy, where he sometimes got support from labor Democrats. He and his United States Trade Representative Robert Lighthizer (one of the few establishment appointees who shared his perspective on the issue at hand) got Canada and Mexico to agree to, and Congress's approval for, a new United States Mexico Canada agreement that made small, but genuine, improvements on NAFTA. The new agreement raised from 62.5 to 75 percent the amount of a car or auto that had to be manufactured in the three countries to enjoy free passage among them. That ruled out, say, Japanese firms that might assemble cars within Mexico with Japanese-made engines to ship without tariffs to the United States. The new agreement also strengthened labor and environmental regulations and added a requirement for a minimum wage in Mexican factories.

Trump's attempts to curb China's mercantilist trade strategy and reduce America's trade deficit were less successful. Trump got Congress to strengthen American oversight on Chinese investments in the United States that could imperil American national security and the American presence in vital industries. He used tariffs to pressure China into negotiations, but the "phase one" agreement he signed in January 2020 with China's Xi Jinping consisted of unenforceable promises to police intellectual property theft and eliminate requirements that American firms transfer technology in order to gain access to China's market; it also included a promise of an additional $200 billion in imports to reduce China's trade surplus with the U.S., but China only imported half of the amount. To Trump's credit, he continued Obama's "pivot to Asia," and drew attention to the unhealthy dependence of American industry on Chinese imports, but he also displayed indifference or even hostility to American allies in the region and in his diplomacy with China mixed bellicosity with fatuous glad-handing.

When it came to major congressional initiatives on healthcare   25
and taxes, Trump abandoned the populist agenda of his campaign.
As Trump's chief strategist in the White House, Bannon had urged a
tax bill that would co-opt the appeal of a Democratic populist challenger in 2020 by raising marginal tax rates for the wealthy as well
as eliminating incentives for American firms moving overseas. But
Bannon met opposition from Republicans in Congress and from
Trump's establishment appointees, National Economic Council
director Gary Cohn and Treasury Secretary Steven Mnuchin. The
final product, applauded by Trump, significantly lowered taxes on
the wealthy and provided new and different incentives for American firms to move overseas to avoid taxes in the United States.
When Bannon complained to Robert Kuttner of *The American Prospect* about being upstaged by Cohn and Mnuchin, Trump, who cared
more about getting a bill passed—which to him meant "winning"—
than about its content, fired him for his disloyalty.

Bannon also lost out in the debate over healthcare reform.
Bannon preferred to put the repeal of the Affordable Care off until
the administration had a genuine replacement for it, and Trump
labeled the first House attempt to repeal the bill "mean," but
Trump and the administration went along with a Senate bill that
would have stripped about 22 million people of their insurance.
Just as it appeared ready for passage, Arizona Senator John McCain
announced his opposition, leading to the bill's defeat, but as Bannon
feared, the very idea that the administration would gut the Affordable Care without providing even a barely adequate replacement was
a grave political error that undermined Trump's appeal.

The first clear confirmation of Trump's unpopularity came in
the 2018 midterm elections. Ordinarily, the party that controls the
White House loses at least several seats in the midterm vote. The
exception is when the economy is growing. In 1998, in the midst of the
internet boom, Bill Clinton and the Democrats picked up five seats in
the House of Representatives. In 2018, the economy was growing at
a rapid 3.1 percent, unemployment was at a forty-nine-year low of

26   3.7 percent, and wages were rising. Yet, Trump and the Republicans
lost forty-one seats and control of the House of Representatives.
The main reason was voter disapproval of Trump's conduct—a highlight being his suggestion there were some "very fine people" among
neo-Nazis marching in Charlottesville, Virginia—and concern that
by repealing the Affordable Care Act, Republicans would deny coverage to people with pre-existing conditions.

Still, with the economy humming, and with the power of
incumbency, and with the Democrats lacking a riveting choice to
run against him, Trump stood a good chance of being re-elected in
2020. But Trump, disdainful of experts, bungled the government
response to the pandemic. Under attack, he became bitter and angry,
culminating in a rude, bullying performance in his first debate with
Biden. He seemed convinced that the ardent following he had created in 2016 would once again carry him across the finish line. But
Trump's base—the people who wore MAGA hats and accepted his
lies as gospel—was never more than 20 to 25 percent of the electorate. The remaining Trump voters were Republicans and independents who had preferred him to the opposition.

This time, Trump's opponent was a likeable everyman who made
voters feel he cared about them. Trump lost the vote among the independents and moderates whom he had won in 2016. Biden also didn't
make the mistake of ignoring the "left behind" voters in the Midwest.
And he parried Trump's exclusionary "America First" with his Lincol-
nian nationalism that stressed national unity. "There will be no blue
states or red states when we win; just the *United* States of America,"
Biden declared. Trump's attempt to portray himself as a populist outsider and Biden as a Washington insider also had the perverse effect
of invoking Biden's experience to govern in the midst of a pandemic
and of comparing his calm and competence with Trump's choleric,
erratic blundering. Trump tried, but failed, to rerun the 2016 campaign, losing crucial states that had carried him to the presidency four
years earlier. But Biden and the Democrats, who lost congressional

seats, failed to win a mandate to govern. The 2020 election was a referendum on Trump, and Trump lost it.

After the election, Trump refused to concede defeat, and attempted to overturn the result through a blizzard of lawsuits and, when these failed, by pressuring legislators and governors of states that had voted for Biden to reverse the outcome. Trump rallied his avid supporters to "stop the steal." Demonstrations and rallies (enflamed by fear and denial bred by the pandemic and by the need to escape social isolation) took place at which speakers spoke of armed rebellion. These culminated in Trump's followers storming the Capitol during the electoral college vote.

Some left-leaning psychologists described Trump as mentally ill, but during these last months, he acted, as commentator Andrew Sullivan suggested, like one of Shakespeare's power-mad kings. His derangement cost his party two Senate run-offs in Georgia and control of the Senate. His contempt for democratic procedure isolated him from his fellow Republicans. And the actions of his avid followers laid bare their own delusions and stalled, at least for the moment, the development of a populist rightwing movement.

Trump's Challenge

It's certainly too soon to assess the impact of Trump's presidency, but there are two widely held beliefs about it that need to be considered. Trump's critics on the left have frequently charged that he was a fascist and his movement was a harbinger of an American fascism. After the election, Trump's critics and admirers compared his supporters' defiance to that of the South prior to the Civil War. There was even a reckless proposal of secession from the chair of the Texas Republican Party. Both historical analogies have some basis, but also fail to get at what was peculiar about Trump's populist adventure and our present moment.

There are certainly resemblances between Trump and the fascists of the 1920s and 1930s. Like them, Trump espoused an exclusive

28   nationalism of us vs. them. Like them, he was attempting to restore an imagined glorious past—expressed in his slogan "make America great again"—and to win not simply votes, but fervent allegiance. He has served for his followers as a strong, charismatic leader with religious undertones of savior and shaman. And in the wake of his loss in the November election, he seemed ready to subvert electoral democracy in order to remain in power.

But the differences between Trump and the interwar fascists are also striking. The interwar fascists arose in the wake of a wartime defeat (Italy was not actually defeated, but it felt it had been cheated out of the spoils of war) and of genuine revolutionary movements inspired by the Russian revolution of 1917 that threatened to seize state power in Italy and Germany. European fascists had their own private armies that clashed with an armed left. When finally seen as the alternative to socialist revolution, the fascists won the support of business and the military in their attempt to seize power and in quick order do away with democratic rights. Trump warded off no similar threat, although at times he and the Republicans tried to convince voters they did with ads warning of the violent takeover of the country by socialists. As a result, he could not command the loyalty of business or military leaders for overturning election results, and he could at best threaten the republic with an army of ad hoc militias and ineffectual lawyers.

European fascism was also militantly expansionist. Hitler dreamed of a Thousand Year Reich and Mussolini of restoring the Roman imperium. Trump and his followers didn't appear to want to take over the world but to some extent to withdraw from it. They didn't want to take over Mexico, for instance, but to build an impenetrable wall between it and the United States. They didn't want to erect or revive global alliances with the United States unequivocally in charge, but to withdraw from those alliances. European fascist movements were centrifugal. Trump's movement (as well as those of Trump allies in Eastern Europe) were centripetal. Nationalism

did not mean imperialism. In other words, it is not helpful to think
of Trump and his movement as fascists.

As for the comparison of Trump's supporters to antebellum
Confederates, there are, indeed, some resemblances between the
present and the pre-Civil War 1850s: the polarization of politics;
the abandonment of democratic norms by one of the major parties,
and the sharp clash of cultures. But the resemblances end there. In
both cases, the clash of cultures has an economic basis, but the economic basis is very different.

Ideological differences between the Union and Confederacy in
the Civil War were rooted in two opposing modes of production—
a capitalism based on wage labor and another based on slavery.
The Civil War represented a clash over the westward expansion
of one of these modes of production over the other. The current
clash of cultures is underlain to a certain extent by a clash over
rival industries—resource extraction, for instance, vs. high technology, including software—but it is not over modes of production. The pro-Trump deindustrialized parts of America, where
the main employers are now Walmart and local hospitals, do not
seek to extend their economy into other parts of the country, but
to enjoy more of the fruits of the post-industrial economy—as
well as to have their culture respected. This is not the stuff of a
new civil war.

If the current political clash resembles anything, it is the clash
from the 1880s through the 1930s that was rooted in differences
between the older agriculture economy, based on small farms and
shops, and the new industrial, urban economy. The Democrats, the
Populists, and the Socialists (whose strength lay more in the rural
West than the urban East) represented the former; the Republicans
the latter. The conflict was finally resolved in the 1930s and 1940s
through a major realignment of the political parties and the introduction of a new political economy. Culturally, economically, that is
much more similar to the conflict that the United States faces today.

30   But Trump remains *sui generis*. The only comparable figure from
the earlier period is William Jennings Bryan, who was untainted
by scandal and corruption, an honorable career politician devoted
to the national interest—which is to say, not comparable to the
self-absorbed, illiberal, and corrupt Trump who left office in dis-
grace. If the analogy with the early twentieth century holds at all, it
means we are still in the mid-stages of transition.

Europe's Rightwing Populists

In Western Europe during the last decade, rightwing populist parties dramatically gained support because of the influx of refugees
from the Middle East and North Africa, the growing incidence of
terrorist attacks from Islamic radicals (which reinforced the fear
of Muslim refugees), and the anger and resentment that the Great
Recession stoked between the more prosperous Northern nations,
which weathered the crash, and the improvident Southern nations.
The rightwing parties in the more prosperous North opposed the
EU aiding the countries in the South. Rightwing parties in France
and Italy blamed the EU's strictures for their failing economies. The
parties at a minimum called for the EU to return to its original limited role as a free trade zone; several of the parties called for their
countries to exit the Eurozone and, in the case of UKIP, the EU itself.

In Finland, Norway, Denmark, Switzerland, and Italy, rightwing
populist parties were part of governing coalitions. In Germany, the
Netherlands, and Sweden, rightwing populist parties came out of
nowhere to unsettle configurations of power. And in France, Marine
Le Pen's National Rally (formerly the National Front) became the
country's second-leading party. But in the last years of the decade,
and during the pandemic and recession, many of these parties have
lost ground. There are three reasons why.

First, as a result of negotiations with Turkey over the disposition of refugees, the war in Syria winding down, and the pandemic
closing borders, the flood of refugees to EU countries has slowed to a
trickle. There is still heated debate in Sweden about what to do about

the refugees who came there, or in France about immigrants and children of immigrants from Muslim North Africa, but there are no longer
widespread protests over the numbers of refugees coming in. Second,
due to the dismemberment of ISIS, and the decline of al Qaeda, the
number of terrorist incidents has gone down. As a result, migration
and terrorism are no longer fused as front burner issues the way they
were in the mid-2010s. Third, the havoc wrought by the pandemic on
public health and Europe's economies has forced countries like Italy
and Spain to look to the EU for aid and the electorate to look toward
technocrats and experienced leaders like Germany's Merkel to govern.
Populists are seen as parties of protest rather than governance.

In Germany's 2017 election, the AfD got 12.6 percent of the vote,
making it the third largest party. With the Christian and Socialist
Democrats forming a coalition government, the AfD became the
leading opposition party in the Bundestag. But the party suffered
a split between its leadership that sought respectability and a faction called "the wing" that sought to contest Germany's "culture
of remembrance" regarding the Holocaust and Hitler. By the fall of
2020, the AfD was running fourth at 8 percent in the polls behind
the Christian Democrats, Social Democrats, and Greens. It was in
danger of becoming a minor party.

The rightwing populist parties that joined governments as
junior partners had to choose between loyalty to their base and loyalty to their senior coalition partner, which invariably involved
taking stands that would alienate their base. Finland's Finns split
when its rank-and-file objected to compromises made by its members in government. Other populist parties suffered the usual fate of
populist parties, going back to the original American Populist Party
of the 1890s. They had their distinguishing demands co-opted by
one of the major parties. That happened most clearly to Britain's
UKIP and to the Danish People's Party.

Britain's UKIP played a large role in winning a majority in the
June 2016 referendum to exit the European Union. In May 2019,
its successor, the Brexit Party of Nigel Farage, came in first in the

32 elections to the European parliament. But in the December elections
for Parliament and prime minister, Boris Johnson's Tories ran on the
Brexit platform. The Brexit Party got 2 percent in the election and no
seats in parliament. It was finished as a party. The Danish Peoples'
Party, buoyed by the refugee crisis in Europe, won 21.1 percent of the
vote in the 2015 elections, making it the second largest party. But
the Liberals and the Social Democrats subsequently adopted much
of the People's Party's hardline stances on migrants. In the 2019 parliamentary election, won by the Social Democrats, the Peoples' Party's vote fell to 8.7 percent.

The only rightwing populist parties that have maintained
their strength have been Orban's Fidesz in Hungary and Jaroslaw
Kaczynski's Law and Justice Party in Poland. Unlike the Western
European parties, they were always major parties that enjoyed support from business. They were part of the establishment. They
used populist appeals against migrants, gays (in the case of Poland),
George Soros (in the case of Hungary) and the EU's bureaucracy to
strengthen their rule. Once in office, both parties have sought to
pack their country's judiciary and stifle the opposition press. They
challenged the EU's commitment to extending liberal democracy
eastward. During the pandemic, they fought attempts by Western
European countries to attach political conditions about adhering to
democratic norms to economic aid.

Shackled by the Euro
Europe's leftwing populists were concentrated in the Southern
nations hit hardest by the Great Recession. Populist parties in
Greece, Italy, and Spain rose to prominence by attacking the major
parties of the center-right and center-left for acceding to the draconian conditions for economic assistance that the EU authorities had
imposed. Greece's Syriza displaced the Panhellenic Socialist Movement (PASOK) and took office in 2015; in the 2015 election, Spain's
Podemos received 21 percent to 22 percent for Spain's Socialist Party
(PSOE) and looked poised to surpass it; in the 2018 Italian elections,

the Five Star Movement (M5S) came in first with 33 percent compared to 19 percent for the center-left Democratic Party. But Syriza is now out of power; M5S is part of a ruling coalition, but has steadily lost support in local and regional elections; and Podemos (having formed a new party Unidas Podemos) is a very junior partner of PSOE in Spain's government, having received only 12.8 percent in the November 2019 election.

Each of these parties had particular difficulties—M5S lacked seasoned leadership, PSOE moved left and stole Podemos's thunder, Syriza overpromised—but they faced a common obstacle: trying to reform and revive their economies while remaining faithful to EU and Eurozone's strictures. By joining the Eurozone, these countries had abandoned the one weapon that countries traditionally used to reduce large trade deficits: devaluing their currency. They also couldn't have recourse to other remedies that countries used during sharp downturns. Their use of deficit spending was limited by the Stability and Growth Pact, and they were barred from using state aid to boost ailing industries. The only weapon they had to reduce trade deficits was to reduce consumer demand by cutting social spending and wages, which is what the European Central Bank (ECB) and the European Commission demanded that the countries do.

In Greece, Syriza, facing a threat of an imminent bank crash, backed down on its threat to leave the Eurozone if the European Central Bank, European Commission, and International Monetary Fund didn't lessen their conditions on aid. In Italy, M5S and its populist rightwing coalition partner, the League, backed down on their threat to defy the EU. And in Spain, Podemos recognized that the country's electorate, eager after the Franco era to be an accepted nation in Europe, would not support Spain leaving or even threatening to leave the Eurozone. That left them with little to offer but the same kind of piecemeal reforms that PSOE was proposing. They were shackled by the economic rules of the EU and the Eurozone—an obstacle also faced by France's National Rally and by Jean-Luc Melenchon's party, La France Insoumise.

34   **Europe's Stasis**

The leftwing and rightwing populist challenges have abated in
Northern and Southern Europe, but that has not led to clear victories by the older, established parties. Instead, in the countries
with multi-party systems, elections have led to tortuous negotiations among the parties to cobble together a majority. The proportion of the vote commanded by what were once the dominant
parties in Germany, Denmark, Sweden, Spain, Norway, Austria, Ireland, and the Netherlands has gone down. In France, where parliamentary and presidential elections are settled by runoffs between
the top two contenders, what had been the major parties of the last
decades didn't even make the cutoff in the 2017 elections.

France's problems are a microcosm of continental Europe's. The
2017 presidential election was won by Emmanuel Macron, who had
created a new party, en Marche, virtually overnight. Macron bears
little resemblance to Trump, but he was elected in similar fluky circumstances. Voters, convinced that the Socialist President François
Hollande had failed to guide France through the Great Recession,
gave up on France's center-left party, and they abandoned the presidential candidate of the center-right Republicans when he was
indicted for embezzlement. That left Macron to face off against Le
Pen, who had benefited in the first round by her hardline on Islamic
radicalism, but was undermined in the runoff by her party's Vichy
past, its Euroskepticism, and by the voters' distrust of a party that
had never really run anything. Macron won easily.

But as president, Macron was hobbled by France's membership
in the Eurozone. Unable to boost France's economy by trade protection, deficit spending, and aid to industries, he adopted a neoliberal strategy, passing legislation that would hold down French wages
by making it easier for firms to fire workers and harder for unions
to bargain collectively, while reducing taxes on the wealthy. He also
attacked climate change by raising gasoline taxes—a measure that
particularly affected French workers in small towns who had to
drive to work. In response to these measures, Macron faced almost

continuous protests from France's working classes, highlighted by
the Yellow Vest movement that began in 2018. His approval ratings have at times been worse than those of Trump, and his party
is in shambles. In the 2020 municipal elections, it failed to win a
single mayoralty in any of the forty-two cities with populations over
100,000.

In France's upcoming presidential election in 2022, a new
party and candidate may emerge from the shadows, as Macron and
en Marche did, but it may very likely be a rematch between the
unpopular Macron and the even more unpopular Le Pen, in which
Macron will again be the victor. If so, France will have once again
weathered the populist challenge from Le Pen, but it will be left, as
will the rest of Europe, with an unpopular leadership that will have
difficulty contending with the nation's unresolved social and economic conflicts.

In Europe, the creaky foundation of the European Union and
the Eurozone stands in the way of a new synthesis. There are two
apparent solutions. One is a United States of Europe or a "sovereign
Europe," as Macron has advocated, that has a collectively elected
leadership and a continental budget capable of taming the business cycle and of reducing inequality among the regions. The other
apparent solution, as several rightwing populist parties have advocated, is the dissolution (at a minimum) of the current Eurozone and
the reversion of the EU to a customs union.

But neither solution is politically feasible. The consolidation
of the EU into a sovereign Europe is blocked by the very conflicts
between North and South (over economics) and between West
and East (over democratic politics) that it is meant to resolve. The
principal event of the last decade was Britain's decision to *leave* the
EU. The abandonment of the Euro is blocked by the fear of financial chaos and of the return of ancient national conflicts. A genuine
solution is simply not yet apparent. Former IMF official Ashoka
Mody, who had warned in the early 2000s of an oncoming financial crash, and who has written an authoritative study of the crash

36 and its aftermath, *Eurotragedy*, said the EU is "in a slow-motion wreck, like an elevator falling from the thirtieth floor and passing the tenth floor blissfully."

Biden's Challenge

Biden's Democratic predecessors Bill Clinton and Barack Obama embraced, in varying degrees, the assumptions of neoliberal economic policy on trade, corporate and financial regulation, taxes, and immigration. Under Clinton, former Goldman, Sachs CEO Robert Rubin dominated the higher reaches of economic policy as head of Clinton's National Economic Council (NEC) and then as Secretary of the Treasury; under Obama, two of Rubin's proteges, NEC head Larry Summers and Treasury Secretary Tim Geithner, played a similar role. There were differences, of course, with the Republican leadership in Congress, but they were of degree. Obama, for instance, wanted a 39 percent rather than a 36 percent marginal tax rate on the very rich. Clinton and Obama had a far more favorable view of unions than House Speaker Newt Gingrich or Senate Majority Leader Mitch McConnell, but faced with Republican opposition, did very little to halt the decline of the labor movement.

Toward the end of Obama's first term, prodded by the Occupy Wall Street movement, the center of gravity of the Democratic Party on economic policy began to shift leftward away from neoliberalism. The key people were Warren and Sanders, both of whom clashed with the Obama administration. Sanders would run for president in 2016 and 2020, and Warren in 2020. Sanders called himself a democratic socialist, and Warren insisted she was a "capitalist to my bones," but both advocated what Europeans would call an advanced form of social democracy—or what I call "shadow socialism"—that would reduce income inequality, strengthen the power of labor, and subject sectors of economy that were not operating in the national interest, including healthcare and energy, to greater public control. During the presidential campaign, Biden differed with them, and particularly with Sanders, on such specifics as Medicare for All, but

he adopted much of their approach to the economy. Biden also took
what was positive from Trump's presidency, including his attempt
to challenge China's mercantilism. After Biden won the nomination,
Sanders said he could be "the most progressive president since FDR."

As campaigner, and as President-elect, Biden has pledged to
arrest the pandemic and speed the recovery. He also announced
ambitious plans to reduce economic inequality, bring free broadband and economic development to rural America, reduce carbon
emissions as part of a massive infrastructure program, encourage
"Made in America" by rewarding firms that produce in the U.S.,
strengthen labor law, and increase tax rates on the wealthy and on
corporations. He nominated former Federal Reserve head Janet
Yellen, a liberal economist without ties to Wall Street, as Secretary of Treasury, former trade unionist and Boston Mayor Marty
Walsh as Secretary of Labor, and appointed labor economists to
the Council of Economic Advisors who understand that growing
inequality is not merely an injustice, but a source of economic instability. Biden's emphasis on economic equality and labor was a version of shadow socialism. His emphasis on "Made in America" also
flew directly in the face of neoliberal economics. Biden, like British
prime minister Boris Johnson and his Labour Party adversary Keir
Starmer, and like Trump himself, was endorsing economic nationalism. And like Trump, he justified his proposals as attempting to
meet the challenge of Chinese mercantilism.

Biden himself has repeatedly compared his situation to that of
Roosevelt after he won the presidency in November 1932 and faced
the challenge of the Great Depression. Biden does face a substantive challenge comparable to that which Roosevelt faced, but he also
faces greater obstacles in getting his program across. Roosevelt won
a landslide and Democrats won huge majorities in Congress. Biden
eked out a win with a total margin of 90,000 votes in Nevada, Arizona, Georgia, and Wisconsin; Democrats lost at least nine House
seats; and the Democrats' margin in the Senate depends on Vice
President Kamala Harris casting a vote to break a 50-50 tie. And the

fifty Democrats include several "blue dogs" who may oppose Biden's more ambitious initiatives.

Roosevelt also benefited from a Republican opposition and a business class that had been publicly discredited by Depression scandals. If the last three administrations are any indication, Republicans will oppose most of what Biden proposes. And even within the Democratic Party, major business donors from high tech and financial firms will oppose some attempts to carry out a "Made in America" policy or to enact radical tax reform or labor law reform to make it easier for workers to unionize.

Finally, Roosevelt didn't have a mandate for specific policies in 1933, but a desperate public and Congress was receptive to almost anything. The traditional American skepticism toward "big government," which goes back to the Revolution, had been tempered by Herbert Hoover's failure to revive the economy. But these sentiments are still strong. The Great Recession brought forth the anti-government Tea Party, and the pandemic brought out deep divisions within the country over personal liberty that Trump exacerbated through his rhetoric. These sentiments—some of them very ugly—could stand in the way of reforms that Biden has said he wants to enact.

But Biden could overcome some of these obstacles. The pandemic and recession have created support for huge government spending programs and an indifference to the deficits that they create. Biden may be able to use this support—and the need for simple majorities to pass government budgets—to put into place some of his program, including the upgrading of the Affordable Care Act to move it closer to being a universal program, large expenditures on infrastructure that will also reduce carbon emissions, the repeal of some of Trump's regressive tax cuts, and government conditions on subsidies to private corporations. He may, in other words, be able to make a down payment on an advanced social democracy and shadow socialism and in the process forestall populist outbursts on either the far right or left.

But Biden will not be able to "heal," as he has proposed, the divisions within the American polity and culture—divisions underlain
by the fracture between the great post-industrial metro centers and
a deindustrialized middle America. He may succeed in reducing the
country's carbon emissions, but he will face continuing opposition
from the oil and gas industry. His new Labor Secretary may be able
to force businesses to pay attention to worker health and safety,
but he is unlikely to reverse the growing imbalance between business and labor. In the United States and Europe, it's likely that the
underlying causes of discontent—growing inequality within and
between nations, the lack of opportunity outside of the great metro
areas, a fractured and unhappy electorate, a warming planet, and
the rising tension with China over trade and control of the Western
Pacific—will persist, and that in these respects, the turbulence of
our times will continue.

Note to Readers
This volume includes in updated and revised form three small books
about American and European politics that I published over the last
five years— *The Populist Explosion, The Nationalist Revival,* and *The
Socialist Awakening.* The three subjects are interrelated. Populism is
the framework that dissent from the prevailing neoliberal ideology
has taken—whether on the right or the left. Both kinds of populism pit the people against the elites, but populism on the right also
targets an outgroup, such as Muslims or illegal immigrants, that it
charges the elites with coddling. Rightwing populists advocate a
militant nationalism that excludes the outgroup from the nation.
By contrast, and in reaction to the right, leftwing populists often
declare themselves in opposition to nationalism. They fail to recognize that a common national identity is the basis for a functioning
democracy and an advanced welfare state. They even cede patriotism to the right.
     A new socialist politics has emerged in the United States and
Europe that eschews the utopian fantasies of orthodox Marxism

40 and the authoritarianism of Soviet or Chinese socialism. Instead, it sees socialism, on the model of advanced social democracy, emerging within capitalism the way capitalism itself arose within feudalism. The new socialists—typified by Bernie Sanders and his supporters—also reject the orthodox view of class conflict rooted in the inexorable growth of a blue-collar working class. Instead, recognizing the growth of an entirely new diversified and stratified labor force, they use the framework of populism, championing "the people" and "working people."

To date, this revival of a new explicitly identified socialism is concentrated among young people who didn't grow up during the Cold War. But many "liberal" or "progressive" politicians like Massachusetts Senator Elizabeth Warren advocate the same kinds of policies, rooted in greater public intervention in the private sector and a commitment to social and economic justice, as Sanders and the young socialists. They also employ the framework of populism. These "shadow socialists" enjoy growing influence, including with the new Congress and the Biden administration. The United States and Europe may eventually come to embrace the new socialism, even if for the time being it does not do so in its name.

The Populist Explosion

Part One

—

What Is Populism, and Why Is It Important?

In the wake of the Great Recession, populist parties and candidates were on the move in the United States and Europe in 2016. Bernie Sanders came in a very strong second to Hillary Clinton for the Democratic nomination; and Donald Trump not only won the nomination, but the presidency. And these candidacies came on the heels of the Tea Party and Occupy Wall Street movements. In Europe, populist parties in France, Sweden, Norway, Finland, Denmark, Austria, Germany, Greece, Italy, Spain, and Switzerland were contending for power or were already part of the government.

In France, the National Front (FN) came in first in the regional elections in December 2015 with 27.73 percent of the vote, but was denied a victory in the regional presidencies because the Republican and Socialist parties joined forces against it in the runoff. In Denmark, the People's Party (DF) came in second in the June 2015 parliamentary elections. In Austria, Freedom Party (FPÖ) candidate Norbert Hofer came in first in the first round of the presidential election in April 2016.

In Switzerland, the Swiss People's Party (SVP) came in first in the parliamentary elections with 29.4 percent of the vote, almost twice the total of the Social Democrats and the Liberals. In Norway,

44 the Progress Party (FrP) has been part of the ruling government coalition since 2013. In the Netherlands, Geert Wilders's Freedom Party
(PVV), the country's third largest party, was well ahead in polls for
the 2017 parliamentary elections. Britain's United Kingdom Independence Party (UKIP), after disappointing results in the 2015 parliamentary elections, bounced back in local elections, ousting the
Labour Party in Wales and was at the forefront of the British campaign to exit the European Union.

In Europe, populist parties also arose on the left and center-left.
In Italy, comedian Beppe Grillo's Five Star Movement won the most
seats in the 2013 election to the Chamber of Deputies. In the June
2016 municipal elections, Five Star candidate Virginia Raggi was
elected Rome's mayor with 67 percent of the vote. In Spain, the
Podemos Party, founded in 2014, came in third in the December 2015
and June 2016 parliamentary elections. In Greece, the decade-old
Syriza Party came in first in two parliamentary elections in 2015, and
took charge of the government. Part One is about how these populist candidates and movements have come about, and why in the
wake of the Great Recession, they proved so successful in mobilizing
support.

Defining Populism
When political scientists write about populism, they often begin
by trying to define it, as if it were a scientific term like entropy or
photosynthesis. That's a mistake. There is no set of features that
exclusively defines movements, parties, and people that are called
populist—from the Russian Narodniks to Huey Long, and from
France's Marine Le Pen to the late congressman Jack Kemp. As with
ordinary language, even more so with ordinary *political* language, the
different people and parties called "populist" enjoy family resemblances of one to the other, but not a set of traits that can be found
exclusively in all of them.

There is, however, a kind of populist politics that originated
in the United States in the nineteenth century and has recurred in

the twentieth- and twenty-first centuries in the United States and
Europe. Whereas populist parties and movements in Latin America
have sometimes tried to subvert the democratic competition for
power, the populist campaigns and parties in the United States and
Western Europe have, with one very recent exception, embraced it. In
the last decades, these campaigns and parties converged in their concerns, and in the wake of the Great Recession, they surged.

First of all, the kind of populism that runs through American
and European history cannot be defined in terms of right, left, or
center. There are rightwing, leftwing, and centrist populist parties.
It is not an ideology, but a political logic—a way of thinking about
politics. In his book on American populism, *The Populist Persuasion*,
historian Michael Kazin gets part of this logic. Populism, he writes,
is "a language whose speakers conceive of ordinary people as a noble
assemblage not bounded narrowly by class; view their elite opponents as self-serving and undemocratic; and seek to mobilize the
former against the latter."

That's a good start. It doesn't describe someone like Ronald
Reagan or Vladimir Putin, both of whom have sometimes been called
"populist," but it does describe the logic of the parties, movements,
and candidates from America's People's Party of 1892 to Marine Le
Pen's National Front of 2016. I would, however, take Kazin's char-
acterization one step further and distinguish between leftwing
populists like Sanders or Podemos's Pablo Iglesias and rightwing
populists like Trump and the National Front's Le Pen. Leftwing populists champion the people against an elite or an establishment.
Theirs is a vertical politics of the bottom and middle arrayed against
the top. Rightwing populists champion the people against an elite
that they accuse of coddling a third group, which can consist, for
instance, of immigrants, Islamists, or African American militants.
Leftwing populism is dyadic. Rightwing populism is triadic. It looks
upward, but also down upon an out group.

Leftwing populism is historically different from orthodox socialist or social-democratic movements. It is not a politics of class

THE POPULIST EXPLOSION   CHAPTER ONE – WHAT IS POPULISM . . . ?

46 conflict, and it doesn't necessarily seek the abolition of capitalism. It is also different from a progressive or liberal politics that seeks to reconcile the interests of opposing classes and groups. It assumes a basic antagonism between the people and an elite at the heart of its politics. Rightwing populism, on the other hand, is different from a conservatism that primarily identifies with the business classes against their critics and antagonists below. In its American and Western European versions, it has also been different from an authoritarian conservatism that aims to subvert democracy. It has operated within a democratic context.

Just as there is no common ideology that defines populism, there is no one constituency that comprises "the people." It can be blue-collar workers, shopkeepers, or students burdened by debt; it can be the poor or the middle class. Equally, there is no common identification of "the establishment." It can vary from the "money power" that the old populists decried to George Wallace's "pointy-headed intellectuals" to the "casta" that Podemos assails. The exact referents of "the people" and "the elite" don't define populism; what defines it is the conflictual relationship between the two—or, in the case of rightwing populism, the three.

The conflict itself turns on a set of demands that the populists make of the elite. These are not ordinary demands that populists believe will be subject to immediate negotiation. The populists believe the demands are worthy and justified, but they don't believe the establishment will be willing to grant them. In 2016, Sanders wanted "Medicare for All" and a $15 minimum wage. If he had wanted the Affordable Care Act to cover hearing aids, or to raise the minimum wage to $7.75, that wouldn't have defined a clash between the people and the establishment. If Trump were to have demanded an increase in guards along the Mexican border, or if Denmark's People's Party had campaigned on a reduction in asylum-seekers, these would not have opened up a gulf between the people and the elite. But promising a wall that the Mexican

government would pay for or the total cessation of immigration   47
does establish a demarcation.

These kinds of demands define the clash between the people
and the establishment. If they are granted in whole or even in part,
as when the Democrats in 1896 adopted the People's Party's demand
for free silver, or if they abandon them as too ambitious, as Syriza
did its demands for renegotiation of Greece's debt, then the populist
movement is likely to dissipate or to morph into a normal political
party or candidacy. In this sense, American and Western European
populist movements have flourished when they are in opposition,
but have sometimes suffered identity crises when they have entered
government.

The Significance of Populism

The second important feature of the populist campaigns and parties I am describing is that they often function as warning signs of
a political crisis. American populist movements have arisen only
under very special circumstances. In Europe, populist parties have
endured on the fringes at times, because the European multi-party
systems tolerate smaller players. But like American populists, they
have won success only under certain circumstances. Those circumstances are times when people see the prevailing political norms—
put forward, preserved, and defended by the leading segments in
the country—as being at odds with their own hopes, fears, and concerns. The populists express these neglected concerns and frame
them in a politics that pits the people against an intransigent elite.
By doing so, they become catalysts for political change.

On both sides of the Atlantic, the major parties favored increased
immigration, only to find that in the United States voters were up in
arms about illegal immigration and in Europe about immigrant communities that became seedbeds of crime and, later, terror. The populist candidates and parties gave voice to these concerns. In Europe,
the major parties on the continent embraced the idea of a common

48   currency only to find it fall into disfavor during the Great Recession. In the United States, both parties' leaders embraced "free trade" deals only to discover that much of the public did not support these treaties.

The movements themselves don't often achieve their own objectives. They don't necessarily succeed in providing Medicare for All or protecting workers against global capitalism or the European Union. Their demands may be co-opted by the major parties or they may be thoroughly rejected. But the populists roil the waters. They signal that the prevailing political ideology isn't working and needs repair, and the standard worldview is breaking down. That's why Trump and Sanders are important in America, and why the populist left and right are important in Europe.

The Logic of American Populism

From the People's Party
to George Wallace

No one, not even Donald Trump, expected him to get the Republican presidential nomination, let alone to win the presidency, in 2016. Similarly, no one, including Bernie Sanders, expected that up through the California primary in June, the Vermont senator would still be challenging Hillary Clinton for the Democratic nomination.

Trump's success was initially attributed to his showmanship and celebrity. But as he won primary after primary, political experts saw him playing on racist opposition to Barack Obama's presidency or exploiting a latent sympathy for fascism among downscale white Americans. Sanders's success invited less speculation, but commentators tended to dismiss him as a utopian and to focus on the airy idealism of millennial voters. If that were not sufficient explanation for his success, they emphasized Hillary Clinton's weakness as a front-runner. It makes more sense, however, to understand Trump's and Sanders's success as the latest chapter in the history of American populism.

Populism is an American creation that spread later to Latin America and Europe. While strands of American populism go back to the Revolution and the Jacksonian War on the Bank of the United States, it really begins with the People's Party of the 1890s, which

50 set the precedent for movements that have popped up periodically. In the United States, in contrast to Europe, these campaigns have burst forth suddenly and unexpectedly. Usually short-lived, nevertheless they have had an outsized impact. While they seem unusual at the time, they are very much part of the American political fabric.

Two Kinds of Political Events

While the history of American politics is riven with conflicts— over slavery, prohibition, the trusts, tariffs, abortion, intervention abroad—it is also dominated for long stretches by an underlying consensus about government's role in the economy and abroad. If that consensus doesn't always unite the parties, it determines the ultimate outcome of political conflict. Thus, from 1935 to the 1970s, there were occasional debates about the virtues of a progressive income tax, but American policy reflected an underlying consensus in favor of it. Progressive taxation was itself part of a broader world-view sometimes described as New Deal liberalism. It had replaced a worldview that stressed a far more limited role for government in the economy.

The role of underlying worldviews is characteristic of politics in the United States and Europe, and of all countries that are governed primarily by consent rather than by force and terror. In Great Britain, for instance, laissez-faire capitalism, associated with Adam Smith's invisible hand, prevailed for much of the nineteenth century, but after World War II it was superseded by Keynesian economics.

American politics is structured to sustain prevailing worldviews. Its characteristics of winner takes all, first past the post, single-member districts have encouraged a two-party system. Third-party candidates are often dismissed as "spoilers." Moreover, in deciding on whom to nominate in party primaries, voters and party bigwigs have generally taken electability into account, and in the general election, candidates have generally tried to capture the center and to stay away from being branded as an "extremist." American political history is littered with candidates who proved too extreme for

the prevailing consensus of one or the other major parties—think of
Fred Harris or Jesse Jackson among Democrats and Tom Tancredo
or Pat Robertson among Republicans.

As a result of this two-party tilt toward the center, sharp political differences over underlying socioeconomic issues have tended
to get blunted or even ignored, particularly in presidential elections.
Campaigns are often fought over fleeting social issues such as tem-
perance or abortion or subsidiary economic issues such as the minimum wage or the deficit. But there are times when, in the face of
dramatic changes in the society and economy or in America's place
in the world, voters have suddenly become responsive to politicians
or movements that raise issues that major parties have either downplayed or ignored. There are two kinds of such events.

The first are what political scientists call realigning elections. In
these, a party or a presidential candidate's challenge to the prevailing
worldview causes an upheaval that reorders the existing coalitions
and leads to a new majority party. Franklin Roosevelt's campaigns
in 1932 and, even more so, 1936 did this, and so did Ronald Reagan's
campaign in 1980. Such elections are rare. They are usually precipitated by economic depression or war, and by a succession of political
outbursts that challenge, but do not replace, the prevailing worldview. In American politics, these outbursts often take the form of
populist candidacies and movements.

These catalytic populists have defined politics in "us vs. them"
terms—as struggles of the people against the establishment based
on issues and demands that the latter had been sidestepping. The
rise of the People's Party was the first major salvo against the worldview of laissez-faire capitalism. Huey Long's Share Our Wealth
coincided with Franklin Roosevelt's election in 1932 and helped
drive the Roosevelt administration to develop a new politics to sustain its majority. Together, these movements established the populist framework that Bernie Sanders, who described himself both as
a democratic socialist and as a progressive, would adopt during his
2016 campaign.

52   As liberal critics would point out during the 1950s, the People's Party had within it strains of anti-Semitism, racism, and nativism, particularly toward the Chinese, but these were at best secondary elements. Until the movement began to disintegrate, the original People's Party was primarily a movement of the left. The first major instances of rightwing populism would come in the 1930s with Father Charles Coughlin, and then in the 1960s with George Wallace's presidential campaigns. Wallace helped doom the New Deal majority and helped lay the basis for the Reagan realignment of 1980. He created a constituency and a rightwing variety of populism—what sociologist Donald Warren called "middle American radicalism"—that would migrate into the Republican Party and become the basis of Donald Trump's challenge to Republican orthodoxy in 2016.

The People's Party
In May 1891, the legend goes, some members of the Kansas Farmers Alliance, riding back home from a national convention in Cincinnati, came up with the term "populist" to describe the political views that they and other alliance groups in the West and South were developing. The next year, the alliance groups joined hands with the Knights of Labor to form the People's Party that over the next two years challenged the most basic assumptions that guided Republicans and Democrats in Washington. The party would be short-lived, but its example would establish the basis for populism in the United States and Europe.

At the time the populists were meeting in Cincinnati, the leading Republicans and Democrats in the United States were reveling in the progress of American industry and finance. They believed in the self-regulating market as an instrument of prosperity and individual opportunity, and thought government's role should be minimal. Grover Cleveland, who was president from 1884 to 1888 and from 1892 to 1896, railed against government "paternalism." Public

sector intervention, he declared in his second inaugural address,   53
"stifles the spirit of true Americanism"; government's "func-
tions," he stated, "do not include the support of the people." Its principal role was to maintain a "sound and stable currency" through
upholding the gold standard. Cleveland and his rivals quarreled
over the tariff and whether the Democrats were the party of "Rum,
Romanism, and Rebellion," but they agreed on the fundamental relationship between government and the economy.

But during these years, farmers in the South and the Plains
suffered from a sharp drop in agricultural prices. Farm prices fell
two-thirds in the Midwest and South from 1870 to 1890. The Plains,
which prospered in the early 1880s, were hit by a ruinous drought in
the late 1880s. But unsympathetic railroads, which enjoyed monopoly
status, raised the cost of transporting farm produce. Many farmers
in the South and the Plains states could barely break even. The small
family farm gave way to the large "bonanza" farm, often owned by
companies based in the East. Salaries were threatened by low-wage
immigrants from China, Japan, Portugal, and Italy. Farmers who
retained their land were burdened by debt. In Kansas, 45 percent of
the land had become owned by banks.

The farm revolt began in the 1870s with the Farmer Alliances
in the North and South. These were originally fraternal societies,
modeled on the Masons, with secret handshakes that bonded the
members together. The Southern Alliance began in Texas and
spread eastward over the South. In the North, it began in New York,
died out, and then was revived in the 1880s in the Plains states.
The alliances organized cooperatives to try to control prices, which
were increasingly set in distant markets, and they began to pressure
legislators to regulate railroad rates. As they became more deeply
involved in politics, they began to join forces with the Knights of
Labor, the workingman's organization that had been founded in
1869 and that by the early 1880s was the main labor group in the
United States. In 1885, the Texas alliance declared in a resolution

54   that it sought a "perfect unity of action" between itself and the Knights of Labor.

While the Grange, a farm advocacy group that started just after the Civil War, foreshadowed later interest groups like the National Farmers Union, the alliances saw themselves representing the "people," including farmers and blue-collar workers, against the "money power" or "plutocracy." That was reflected in their early programs, which included a demand for the incorporation and recognition of labor unions alongside demands for railroad regulation, an end to land speculation, and easy money (through the replacement or supplementing of the gold standard) to ease the burden of debt that the farmers suffered from. Except for a few scattered leaders, the populists were not socialists. They wanted to reform rather than abolish capitalism, and their agent of reform was not the socialist working class, but the loosely conceived idea of "the people." Daniel DeLeon, the head of what was then the country's main socialist party, the Socialist Labor Party, criticized them as "bourgeois."

Some of the alliance members backed the Greenback Party's presidential slate in 1880 and 1884, but most sought to influence the dominant parties in their region. The Southern Alliance wanted to transform the Democratic Party, and the alliance in the Great Plains wanted to change the Republicans. In December 1889, the alliances began a series of meetings to develop a national program. Besides the demands on currency and land, the program now also included the nationalization of railroads, a graduated income tax, political reform (including the secret ballot and direct election of senators), and a "sub-treasury" plan that would allow farmers to borrow money from the federal government to store their crops until prices rose high enough for them to be profitable.

When the alliance pressured candidates from the Democrats and Republicans to endorse this platform, the demands proved to be too radical and far-reaching for the major parties. In the Plains, Republicans scorned the alliance proposals as utopian moralism.

"The Decalogue and the golden rule have no place in a political campaign," Kansas Republican senator John J. Ingalls wrote. In the South, some Democratic statehouse candidates endorsed the alliance proposals, but once in office they rebuffed them. Alliance leaders concluded the Democrats and Republicans were in the grip of the plutocracy and that the populists would have to organize their own party. Kansas alliance members organized in 1890 a state People's Party that did well in that year's elections. Then, in 1892, the alliances, along with the Knights of Labor and other groups, formed a national People's Party and nominated James K. Weaver, a former Greenback Party presidential candidate, to run for president.

The party held its convention in February in St. Louis, where Minnesota populist Ignatius Donnelly penned a preamble to the platform that won widespread acclaim and became the group's manifesto—what the populists called the nation's "second Declaration of Independence." Donnelly was a former Republican congressman and railroad lobbyist who in the mid-1870s had begun moving leftward and had won acclaim as an author and an orator. In the preamble, Donnelly charged that "the fruits of the toil of millions are boldly stolen to build up the colossal fortunes of a few." Government and the major parties were complicit in this theft. "We charge that the controlling influences dominating both these parties have permitted the existing dreadful conditions to develop without serious effort to prevent or restrain them," Donnelly wrote.

Donnelly's preamble echoed the themes of Jacksonian democracy. "We seek to restore the government of the Republic to the hands of 'the plain people,' with whose class it originated," he wrote. But while the Jackson Democrats wanted to restore popular democracy by *eliminating* the role of government in the economy, Donnelly and the populists—in a challenge to the prevailing laissez-faire worldview—wanted government to actively combat economic injustice. "We believe that the powers of government—in other words, of the people—should be expanded . . . as rapidly and as far as the good

56   sense of an intelligent people and the teachings of experience shall justify, to the end that oppression, injustice, and poverty shall eventually cease in the land."

At the St. Louis convention, Donnelly's platform was enthusiastically endorsed by Georgia's Tom Watson, who had been elected to Congress in 1890 as a Democrat backing the alliance platform. "Never before in the history of the world was there arrayed at the ballot box the contending forces of Democracy and Plutocracy," Watson declared. "Will you stand with the people . . . by the side of the other wealth producers of the nation . . . or will you stand facing them, and from the plutocratic ranks fire a ballot in support of the old parties and their policies of disorganization, despotism, and death?"

There was always a more conservative strain within the populist movement. In the South, some alliance members cooperated with the parallel Colored Farmers' Alliance, but others did not, and racial issues often divided populists from the Plains and the South. Populists also favored the expulsion of Chinese immigrants, whom businesses had imported to provide cheap labor on western farms and railroads. That was understandable, but their support for exclusion was often colored by racist rhetoric. Kansas populist leader Mary E. Lease warned of a "tide of Mongols." And Watson's *People's Party Paper* denounced the Chinese as "moral and social lepers." But in the 1880s and early 1890s, populist politics was primarily directed upward at the plutocrats. As historian Robert McMath recounts, they were repeatedly accused of being "Molly Maguires, Anarchists, and Communists."

In the 1892 election, the People's Party did remarkably well. Their woefully underfunded presidential candidate received 8 percent of the vote and carried five states. Then, in 1893, as Cleveland was taking office, an economic depression took hold, leaving a quarter of Americans unemployed and thousands of farmers bankrupt. Cleveland reaffirmed the gold standard, and to pleas for government aid from farmers, Cleveland's secretary of agriculture, Julius Sterling Morton, responded, "The intelligent, practical, and

successful farmer needs no aid from the government. The ignorant, 57
impractical, and indolent farmer deserves none."

In the 1894 election, the People's Party's candidates for the
House of Representatives won 10 percent of the vote. The party
elected 4 congressmen, 4 senators, 21 state executives, and 465 state
legislators. With their base in the South and the West, and with
Cleveland wildly unpopular, they looked to be on their way to challenging the Democrats as the second party, but the election of 1894
turned out to be the party's swan song.

The populists were done in by the dynamics of the two-party
system. In the Plains states, anger against Cleveland turned voters
back to the more electable Republicans. In the South, Democrats
subdued the People's Party by a combination of co-optation and,
in response to the willingness of some populists to court the negro
vote, vicious race-baiting. Watson said of the opposition to the People's Party, "The argument against the independent political movement in the South may be boiled down into one word—nigger."

In the wake of 1894, Southern Democrats like South Carolina senator "Pitchfork" Ben Tillman commonly combined a patina
of populist economics and political reform with white supremacy.
(Tillman's nickname came from his promise in 1894 that if he
were elected, he would go to Washington and "stick a pitchfork in
Grover Cleveland's old fat ribs.") Watson himself and Texas's James
"Cyclone" Davis, while continuing to support populist economics,
became allies of the Ku Klux Klan.

But the biggest damage occurred on the national stage. In 1896,
the Democrats nominated Nebraskan William Jennings Bryan and
adopted key planks of the populist platform, including monetiza-
tion of silver ("free silver"!), the regulation of the railroads and other
corporations, and a restriction on "foreign pauper labor." At its convention, the People's Party chose to endorse Bryan rather than to
run a candidate of its own. In the 1896 election, the populist vote
migrated to the major parties. To make matters worse, the populists
also lost their blue-collar ally when the Knights of Labor fell apart

58 and was replaced by the interest-group-oriented American Federation of Labor. The People's Party limped along and finally collapsed after the 1908 election when Watson, running as its presidential candidate, received 0.19 percent of the vote.

But during their heyday from 1885 to 1894, the populists of the alliances and the People's Party had a profound effect on American and, as it turned out, Latin American and European politics. They developed the logic of populism—the concept of a "people" arrayed against an elite that refused to grant necessary reforms. In American politics, they were an early sign of the inadequacy of the two parties' views of government and the economy.

The populists were the first to call for government to regulate and even nationalize industries that were integral to the economy, like the railroads; they wanted government to reduce the economic inequality that capitalism, when left to its own devices, was creating; and they wanted to reduce the power of business in determining the outcome of elections. Populism had an immediate impact on the politics of some progressive Democrats like Bryan, and even on Republicans like Theodore Roosevelt and Robert La Follette. Eventually, much of the populists' agenda—from the graduated income tax to a version of the sub-treasury plan—was incorporated into the New Deal and into the outlook of New Deal liberalism.

Huey Long's Share Our Wealth

In the 1920s, while much of Europe suffered from economic and political instability, partly as a result of post–World War I reparations and gold-based finance, the American economy enjoyed a boom. Republican business boosterism and rugged individualism dominated politics. But the stock market crash of 1929 and the Great Depression that followed shattered the public's confidence in the free market, as well as in Republican rule, and helped to bring about a new Democratic majority.

Franklin Roosevelt and the Democrats won a landslide victory in 1932, but not by repudiating the Republicans' overall outlook on

government and the economy. In the campaign, Roosevelt criticized 59
Republican incumbent Herbert Hoover for overspending and promised to cut the government bureaucracy by 25 percent and balance
the budget. Once in office, Roosevelt actually tried to make good
on this promise through the Government Economy Act, which cut
more than $500 million from the budget mainly out of veterans'
benefits and government salaries.

Roosevelt did move aggressively during his first two years to
reform banking and provide jobs through new government programs. He created a National Recovery Administration that was
supposed to work out corporatist arrangements between business
and labor and stem cutthroat price competition. But Roosevelt did
not directly address economic inequality, which had grown during
the years of the Republican majority and which progressive economists believed lay at the heart of the crash and the Depression. It
took pressure from outside to get Roosevelt to do this, and much of
it came from Louisiana politician Huey Long. Long created a populist movement that Democrats feared would threaten Roosevelt's
reelection and possibly even the existence of the Democratic Party.

Long grew up in Winn, Louisiana, a small, poor farming town
that was a hotbed of populist and socialist support. He carried on the
populist tradition, campaigning for governor on the slogan, "Every
man a king, but no man wears a crown," and railing against oil companies and the "money power." Elected governor in 1928, he funded
Louisiana's roads, healthcare system, and schools, while exempting
low-income people from taxes and proposing (and eventually getting) an extraction tax on oil companies. He didn't repudiate racism,
but he didn't actively encourage it either. "Don't say I am working for
niggers, I'm not. I'm for the poor man—all poor men," he declared.
Dictatorial and charismatic, he was an exemplar of the populist who
became the unifying force holding "the people" together. One reporter
wrote of Long's constituents, "They worship the ground he walks on."

Long got elected to the Senate in 1930, and in 1932 he backed
Roosevelt for president. But soon after Roosevelt took office, Long

60 broke with him. He spoke out and voted against the Government Economy Act. He claimed it was the work of "Mr. Morgan" and "Mr. Rockefeller." In February 1934, Long announced on radio the formation of a Share Our Wealth Society. Its centerpiece was a proposal to cap a family's wealth at $5 million and income at $1 million through taxes, and to use the revenue to provide every family a "household estate" that would be enough for "a home, an automobile, a radio, and ordinary conveniences" and a guaranteed annual income to "maintain a family in comfort," as well as an old-age pension.

Long's tax rates on the wealthy were draconian, but they still would not have produced the revenue necessary for what he promised. Roosevelt's allies in the media mocked Long's proposal. The *New Republic* sent Long a mock questionnaire about the details of his plan, asking, "Upon what statistics of economic studies do you base your conclusions?" But the very extravagance of Long's plan established a political divide between him and the powers-that-be that could not easily be bridged. It defined the movement's radicalism the way free silver, the sub-treasury plan, and the nationalization of railroads defined the People's Party.

Long's Share Our Wealth clubs—more than 27,000 had started by the following February—functioned not only as local political organizations but as the basis for a new political party. They were often run out of churches and schools. In addition, Long boasted of a mailing list of more than 7.5 million. Long's most active base, like that of the People's Party and subsequent populist movements, was not among the very poor. It was among the middle class, who feared that they would be cast down by the Depression into the ranks of the very poor. Historian Alan Brinkley wrote of Long's followers:

> Having gained a foothold in the world of bourgeois respectability, they stood in danger of being plunged back into what they viewed as an abyss of powerlessness and dependence. It was that fear that made the middle class, even more than those who were truly rootless and indigent, a politically volatile group.

Roosevelt and the Democrats feared Long's candidacy. In 1935, the Democratic National Party did a secret poll in which they determined that if Long ran on a third-party ticket against Roosevelt in 1936, he could win between three and four million votes and throw the election to the Republicans. That fear was an important factor in Roosevelt and the Democrats joining forces that year to pass what was called "the Second New Deal." Unlike the first, it dealt directly with the issue of economic inequality that Long had repeatedly raised.

On June 19, the Senate passed the Social Security Act, which provided old-age pensions and unemployment compensation. On the same day, Roosevelt surprised Congress by proposing a tax reform measure to encourage "a wider distribution of wealth." He imposed levies on large businesses and raised taxes on the wealthy and on large inheritances. Long criticized the proposals as being weak, but they were widely portrayed as "soaking the rich." Roosevelt also incorporated populist rhetoric in his presidential campaign that year, championing the "average man" against the "economic royalists."

As it turned out, Roosevelt did not have to fear Long's candidacy. In September 1935, the Kingfish was assassinated in Baton Rouge. And in 1936, Roosevelt won another landslide. But Long had a significant influence over the New Deal and over American politics. He and his movement pushed Congress to adopt programs that became pillars of American policy for the next four decades. Long brought the New Deal's outlook into line with the public's underlying concern about the inequality of wealth and power.

George Wallace

The '60s were thought of as an era of ferment on the left. In Europe, there were the May–June 1968 protests in France and the Hot Autumn in Italy in 1969. In the United States, it was the time of civil rights, black power, anti-war, feminism, and environmentalism. But it was also when a rightwing populist, George Wallace, acting in opposition to civil rights rulings and legislation, blew a large

62 hole in the roof that New Deal liberalism had erected over American politics.

The New Deal had rested on a tacit alliance between liberal Democrats and conservative Southern Democrats who resisted any legislation that might challenge white supremacy. As a result, key New Deal legislation, including the Social Security and Minimum Wage Acts, were formulated to exclude southern black people from their benefits. But after World War II, northern Democrats, propelled by the Cold War's ideological struggle, *Brown v. Board of Education*, and a powerful civil rights movement, embraced the African American cause.

As the party of Abraham Lincoln, Republicans had traditionally been receptive to civil rights, and the Republican leadership in Congress supported Lyndon Johnson's Civil Rights and Voting Rights Acts of 1964 and 1965. Barry Goldwater was an early dissenter, but in the 1964 presidential election, Johnson easily defeated him. Johnson's victory did not, however, signal widespread support for his civil rights initiatives, and after he passed the Voting Rights Act and launched the War on Poverty, a popular backlash grew. Wallace turned the backlash into a populist crusade.

Wallace was raised in a rural small town in Alabama. His father and grandfather dabbled in politics. They were New Deal Democrats under Roosevelt's spell. Wallace would eventually make his name as an arch-segregationist, but he was initially a populist Democrat like Long for whom race was strictly a secondary consideration. When he was a delegate to the 1948 Democratic Convention, he didn't join the Dixiecrat walkout in protest of the party's civil rights platform. He initially ran for governor in 1958 as a New Deal Democrat and lost against a candidate backed by the Ku Klux Klan. After that, he pledged, "I will never be outniggered again."

In 1962, Wallace ran again and this time he won as a proponent of "segregation now, segregation tomorrow, segregation forever." In 1963, he gained notoriety when he attempted to block two black students from registering at the University of Alabama. In 1964, he ran in the Democratic primaries against Johnson's surrogates in Wisconsin, Indiana, and Maryland and got about a third of the vote—as high as 43 percent in Maryland, where he carried 15 of 23 counties. In 1968, he ran as an independent against Nixon and Humphrey. In early October, he was ahead of Humphrey in the polls, but in the end, he got 13.5 percent of the vote and carried five states in the South. In 1972, he ran as a Democrat, and stood a chance of taking the nomination when an assassin shot and crippled him while he was campaigning in May for the Maryland primary.

Wallace emphasized his opposition to racial integration, but he framed it as a defense of the average (white) American against the tyranny of Washington bureaucrats. Big government was imposing its way on the average person. Appearing on *Meet the Press* in 1967, Wallace summed up his candidacy:

> There's a backlash against big government in this country. This is a movement of the people.... And I think that if the politicians get in the way a lot of them are going to get run over by this average man in the street—this man in the textile mill, this man in the steel mill, this barber, this beautician, the policeman on the beat ... the little businessman.

Wallace opposed busing—which became a major issue after a 1971 Supreme Court order upheld it as a means to achieve desegregation—because it was breaking up working-class neighborhoods, and he attacked the white liberals who promoted it as hypocrites who refused to subject their children to what they insisted that working- and middle-class kids be subjected to. "They are building a bridge over the Potomac for all the white liberals fleeing to Virginia," he declared.

Wallace was not, however, a political conservative. On domestic issues that didn't directly touch on race, Wallace ran as a New Deal Democrat. In his campaign brochure in 1968, he boasted that, in Alabama, he had increased spending on education, welfare, roads,

64 and agriculture. When he was asked in 1967 who he would appoint to his cabinet if he were elected, he said he would consider either AFL-CIO head George Meany or Leonard Woodcock, the head of the United Auto Workers. He also drew a line between the people and the very rich and powerful. Campaigning in Florida, he said, "We're sick and tired of the average citizen being taxed to death while these multibillionaires like the Rockefellers and the Fords and the Mellons and Carnegies go without paying taxes." Wallace, like Long, was often called fascist, but he was a rightwing populist in the tradition of the post-1896 Tom Watson. When protesters accused him of being a fascist, Wallace, who served in World War II, responded, "I was killing fascists when you punks were in diapers."

Like Wallace, his supporters were a mix of left and right in their convictions. In 1976, sociologist Donald Warren published a study of what he called "middle American radicals," or MARs. On the basis of extensive surveys conducted in 1971—72 and 1975, Warren defined a distinct political group that was neither left nor right, liberal nor conservative. MARs "feel the middle class has been seriously neglected," Warren wrote. They see "government as favoring both the rich and poor simultaneously."

Warren's MARs held conservative positions on poverty and racial issues. They rejected racial busing and welfare agencies as examples of "the rich [giving] in to the demands of the poor, and the middle income people have to pay the bill." They disliked the national government, but they also thought corporations "have too much power" and were "too big." They favored many liberal programs. They wanted government to guarantee jobs to everyone. They supported price (but not wage) control, Medicare, some kind of national health insurance, federal aid to education, and Social Security.

Warren found that MARs represented about a quarter of the electorate. They were on average more male than female; they had a high school but not a college education; their income fell in the middle, or slightly below; they had skilled or semi-skilled blue-collar jobs, or clerical or sales white-collar work. When Warren grouped by income and education the other groups he surveyed into "lower income," "average middles," "high education middles," and "affluents," he found that, of all of them, the MARs were most likely to contemplate voting for George Wallace in 1972. A Gallup study of the demographics of the 1968 Wallace vote found his constituency to be identical to that of Warren's MARs.

In other words, Wallace's base was among voters who saw themselves as "middle class"—the American equivalent of "the people"— and who saw themselves locked in conflict with those below and above. Like Wallace, they remained New Deal liberals in many of their views, but not on matters that bore on race or law and order. In these cases, they adamantly rejected the welfare and busing and affirmative action policies that 1972 Democratic presidential candidate George McGovern and many liberal Democrats favored. They had begun the political journey from Democrat to Independent to Republican that would finally conclude in the 1994 congressional elections.

Wallace, like Long, was a movement unto himself. When he was shot and forced to drop out of the presidential campaign, it ended his attempt to transform American politics. He would run again in 1976 but would be eclipsed by another southern politician, Jimmy Carter. Attempts by conservatives to retain his American Independent Party flopped. He would serve as governor again, and would repudiate and apologize for his own opposition to racial integration. He would end his career much as he began—as a New Deal Democrat. But Wallace and his followers had already had a profound influence on the two-party system.

Wallace's campaigns were the opening wedge in the realignment of the parties in the South. The Republicans would subsequently accommodate Wallace's positions on big government, welfare, busing, and affirmative action. And Nixon had already begun to do that. As Kevin Phillips understood in his prescient 1969 book, *The Emerging Republican Majority*, Wallace's votes would migrate to the Republican Party. In 1972, Nixon's percentage vote against McGovern closely resembled the total of Nixon's and Wallace's

66 votes in 1968 in 45 of 50 states. In 14 states, the percentages were almost identical.

The Democratic and Republican coalitions that would emerge after Wallace's 1968 run and McGovern's 1972 campaign would be significantly different from the coalitions of the New Deal era. From 1932 through 1960, the two parties' support could roughly be arrayed in a pyramid with income and education moving upward. Democrats, as the party of the "common man," took up most of the bottom two-thirds. That allowed the Democrats to win most of the elections.

In 1972, many white voters in the lower and middle segments of the pyramid would begin shifting to the Republicans, while many professionals—from nurses and teachers to engineers and architects—who had been loyal Republicans, but who had been touched by the new left movements of the '60s, and had expected but not found autonomy and satisfaction in their work, would begin voting for the Democrats. They became critics of unregulated capitalism, and their descendants would provide much of Bernie Sanders's support. The Democrats began building an odd coalition of the minority poor with upper-middle-class whites. There would no longer be a clear demarcation between the parties on income and education.

The transformation of the coalitions would be delayed by the Watergate scandal and wouldn't fully come to fruition until 1980 or even 1994, when the Republicans would win both houses of Congress. Wallace's populist candidacies, far more than Goldwater's, set this process in motion. His campaigns would lead to Republicans adopting Wallace's stand on government and state's rights, along with an opportunistic imitation of his own populist anti-elitist politics (directed at "Washington"). But then Pat Buchanan in his 1992 and 1996 campaigns and Trump in his 2016 campaign would draw on the unruly populism of Wallace's middle American radicals and would mobilize it against the Republicans' more traditional supporters.

Neoliberalism and Its Enemies

Perot, Buchanan, the Tea Party, and Occupy Wall Street

New Deal liberalism reigned from 1932 to 1968. The New Deal did not represent, as some critics claimed, a repudiation of capitalism, but an attempt to save and reform it, after the laissez-faire, pro-business policies of Republican administrations had helped to bring about the financial crash and the Great Depression. The New Deal approach, which used government to counter capitalism's tendencies toward unemployment, inequality, monopoly, and environmental pollution, helped produce several decades of post–World War II prosperity.

George Wallace's populist crusade undermined the Democrats' political majority, which depended upon the support of southern states, but it didn't discredit the New Deal liberal worldview of government and the economy. Wallace, after all, was a New Deal liberal himself. That discrediting would happen during the 1970s, as the United States faced economic conditions that appeared to justify a new conception of the relationship between government and the economy. The business community would champion this new conception, and Republicans, many of whom had reluctantly backed the New Deal—Goldwater famously called the Eisenhower administration's budget a "dime store New Deal"—would embrace the new approach.

68   Democrats would initially object to the new conception, but by
the 1990s would in some cases come around to its essentials, or in
others be forced to do so by a powerful Republican opposition. The
approach was initially called "supply-side economics," and that term
fits part of it. Leftwing political scientists have also called it "neoliberalism" and have drawn a connection to similar politics in Europe.
The term is ambiguous, because while liberalism in the United
States refers often to New Deal liberalism, it refers in Europe to classical free-market economics. But I am going to use it because the
result in both cases is equivalent.

In the United States, neoliberalism meant the modification,
but not wholesale abandonment, of New Deal liberalism—support
for the New Deal safety net, but beyond that, priority to market
imperatives—while in Europe, it meant the partial return to an older
free market liberalism. The United States is still in an era dominated by this neoliberal worldview, but it has come under attack
from populist politicians and movements—from Ross Perot and Pat
Buchanan in the early 1990s to the Tea Party and Occupy Wall Street
in the 2010s.

The Triumph of Neoliberalism
The origins of neoliberalism go back to the global challenges that
American business began to face in the early 1970s, as Western
Europe and Japan had rebuilt their factories and were able to compete effectively with American manufacturers. That became evident when, for the first time in the twentieth century, the United
States ran a trade deficit in 1971. With developing nations beginning
to build steel mills as well as textile plants, American producers
were also faced with global overcapacity in key industries like steel,
shoes, textiles, shipbuilding, chemicals, televisions, automobiles,
and refrigerators. (The list has continued to grow over the years.)
The combination of growing competition and global overcapacity
was an important factor in driving down profit rates for American
producers. According to economic historian Robert Brenner, from

1965 to 1973, rates of profit fell 40.9 percent in manufacturing and 23.1 percent in non-manufacturing.

During the decades of postwar prosperity, business had acquiesced in steady wage increases, especially in unionized industries, because they could be defrayed through rising prices, productivity, and sales. But by the early 1970s, businesses were also increasingly worried about wage pressure from below that was threatening their rates of profit. A major strike wave had occurred from 1965 to 1973, almost doubling the number of strikes that had occurred in the previous decade. In addition, businesses increasingly feared an alliance between the unions and New Left militants. In a special issue on the seventies, *Business Week* voiced fears of a challenge to "corporations and the middle- and upper-bracket income earners" from "the blacks, the labor unions, and the young."

American businesses responded to these threats by adopting a hard line against unionization, sometimes even in violation of labor law. They moved plants to right-to-work states and overseas. They created an extensive lobbying network in Washington— pro-business think tanks and policy groups as well as the newly established Business Roundtable of corporate CEOs—to promote tax cuts and the repeal or weakening of regulations. They lobbied for trade deals that not only removed tariff barriers to American exports, but eased overseas investment by protecting American firms from expropriation.

Business wasn't the main force behind the 1965 Immigration and Nationality Act, but it certainly took advantage of it. Through family reunification, the act led to a flood of new immigrants, including unskilled labor from Latin America and Asia. Agribusiness, food processing, meatpacking, construction, hotel, restaurant, and other service businesses used these workers, many of whom were undocumented or not eligible for citizenship, to push down wages and to resist or undermine unions. Businesses would later fight any attempts to penalize them for hiring undocumented workers.

70   One example is what happened with Midwestern meatpacking plants. According to a *New York Times* report in 2001, "Until 15 or 20 years ago, meatpacking plants in the United States were staffed by highly paid, unionized employees who earned about $18 an hour, adjusted for inflation. Today, the processing and packing plants are largely staffed by low-paid non-union workers from places like Mexico and Guatemala. Many of them start at $6 an hour." According to a Pew report, by 2005, between 20 and 25 percent of the workers in these plants were undocumented.

There wasn't widespread public support for these measures. The 1965 immigration bill was not popular, and by the late 1990s, states had begun passing referenda against illegal immigration that were also directed implicitly at legal immigrants. There was also public skepticism about trade deals, and opposition to American firms moving plants overseas. I remember once attending a convention of the Christian Coalition, a major organization of conservative evangelicals run by two pro-business Republicans, Pat Robertson and Ralph Reed. Robertson and Reed got the organization to endorse the North American Free Trade Agreement (NAFTA), but when I talked to the group's rank-and-file I found almost universal opposition to it. A November 1993 Gallup poll found opposition to NAFTA at 46 percent, with only 38 percent in favor. In January 1999, a Pew poll found 54 percent of the public opposed to granting China most-favored-nation trading status and 32 percent for.

In spite of public skepticism, business carried the day in the Republican Party—and eventually in the Democratic Party as well. Operatives crafted a majority coalition that was composed of the traditional Republican business class, small businesses and farmers, and white working-class voters who had begun fleeing the Democratic Party because of its support for racial integration and affirmative action, feminism, and the secular counterculture. There was an implicit arrangement by which the major business lobbies would acquiesce in Republican opposition to abortion, gun control, or

affirmative action in exchange for working-class support for reductions in regulations and taxes.

The one area in which Republican business and the new white
working-class Republicans could wholeheartedly agree was cutting
social spending. Businesses generally favored any spending cuts
that would lower pressure to raise taxes on them and their stock-
holders. The working and middle classes, with some justification,
believed they would have to pay the bulk of the taxes to support programs that they believed would primarily benefit minorities and
the poor and not themselves. This opposition to spending (and to
any tax increases thought to support it) was capsulized in a general
opposition to "Washington" and to "big government."

Many Democrats initially resisted the neoliberal agenda, but
attempts in the first two years of the Carter administration to
strengthen labor law, progressive tax reform, consumer regulation,
and campaign finance reform were beaten back by Republicans and
the business lobbies. In addition, Democratic policymakers found
themselves hamstrung by the combination of growing unemployment and inflation—the result in the latter case of rising energy and
food prices. This "stagflation" (stagnation + inflation) defied the
usual Keynesian demand-side remedies, and there was little support for going beyond those remedies to extensive price controls.
By the late 1970s, the Carter administration had acquiesced to
supply-side business tax cuts and to a monetarist strategy of using
high interest rates and rising unemployment to curb inflation.

Over the next 12 years, Democrats, led by the "new Democrats,"
would accept other key aspects of the neoliberal agenda, including
trade pacts like NAFTA that eased foreign investment, deregulation
of finance, and immigration measures to accommodate unskilled
and later highly skilled guest workers. Democrats would continue to
fight Republicans on some social spending measures and on income
and inheritance tax changes, but once the Republicans won control
of Congress in 1994, Democrats would be forced into uncomfortable

72   compromises. Attempts to revive labor legislation would simply fail. Election battles would almost invariably leave the heights of the neoliberal approach untouched, and focus instead on social policies such as abortion or gun control and on relatively marginal differences over social spending and taxes.

The key contention that sustained the neoliberal agenda was that the older New Deal liberalism, by focusing on raising consumer demand and reducing inequality, would stifle growth and reduce Americans' standard of living. By contrast, the neoliberal and supply-side agenda, while not directly confronting economic inequality, promised to spur economic growth, which would benefit all Americans. As Ronald Reagan, borrowing from John Kennedy, put it in the 1980 campaign, "a rising tide will lift all boats." Similar kinds of arguments would be made in Europe by the "Third Way" centrists, who were partially inspired by Tory prime minister Margaret Thatcher.

But even by the late 1980s, reality on the ground appeared to contradict these claims of widespread prosperity. In the 1980s, growth and employment lagged behind that of previous decades. The shape of the economy also began to change under Reagan. The Reagan and Bush administrations ignored calls for an industrial policy that would protect and help expand America's manufacturing sector. Instead, Reagan's reliance on high interest rates and an overvalued dollar helped accelerate the decline of America's manufacturing industries, fueling the growth of finance and financial services.

By the end of the '80s, large swaths of domestically based industries, including consumer electronics, machine tools, and textiles, had disappeared. The jobs in these industries were replaced by lower-wage service sector and higher-wage professional-level jobs—many either employing or employed by information technology—which created an indentation in the middle of the workforce and a rise in inequality. Economic historian Peter Temin argues that these neoliberal policies created a "dual economy"

composed of a high-wage FTE (finance, technology, and electronics)
sector and a low-wage one of semi-skilled and unskilled workers
that straddled a shrinking middle-income group of manufacturing
and white-collar jobs.

Along the same lines, economist Stephen Rose has shown that
the rising difference in income and wealth prevailed not just between
the 1 percent and the 99 percent, but between the top 30 percent—
including a growing upper middle class—and the bottom 70 percent. These trends, reinforced by further financial deregulation, an
overvalued dollar, and regressive tax policies, would continue up
through the onset of the Great Recession and fuel discontent among
the middle and lower-middle classes, many of whom felt cast aside
by the move toward a post-industrial economy heavily dependent
on finance and financial services. (As I will recount, something very
similar happened in Western Europe.)

The first visible crisis came in 1991, when the U.S. suffered from
a peculiar recession that seemed to drag on for four more years in
joblessness and wage stagnation. In addition, many Americans were
troubled by the continuing loss of manufacturing jobs to Japan and
Western Europe, and the rapid rise in illegal immigration in the
Southwest. Public opinion expert Daniel Yankelovich wrote, "Even
though they can't put their finger on it, [people] fear something is
fundamentally wrong with the U.S. economy."

When party leaders' promises—that free trade deals would
create far more jobs than they would threaten, that immigration
measures would stop the flood of immigrants entering the country
illegally, and that financial deregulation would have no ill effects—
proved false, it sparked a populist challenge to the prevailing consensus. That challenge came in the 1992 and 1996 elections from
Texas businessman Ross Perot, and from former Nixon and Reagan
aide Pat Buchanan. Perot represented a left and center-left populism, and Buchanan a challenge from the right, but like other American populists, they didn't fit the conventional conflict between
Democrats and Republicans or between liberals and conservatives.

74   Instead, they arose precisely because the leading Democrats and Republicans were ignoring popular concerns about American manufacturing, immigration, and lobbying in Washington.

Ross Perot

Perot grew up in Texarkana, a small farming town in East Texas that used to be a stopover for People's Party agitators. His father was a cotton broker who struggled to make a living during the Great Depression. Following two years at junior college, Perot talked a retiring senator from neighboring Arkansas into appointing him to the Naval Academy. After graduating, Perot spent two years at sea before obtaining an early discharge in order to go into business.

Perot began his career selling and servicing mainframe computers for IBM, but in 1962, he set up his own data processing company, Electronic Data Systems, which he turned into a multibillion-dollar enterprise. In 1985, he sold it to General Motors with the idea that he and EDS would have a leadership role within the faltering company, but when GM's management ignored him, he left and started Perot Systems. The experience helped turn him into an outspoken critic of corporate America and of the Republican and Democratic politicians who had coddled it.

Perot had been an active Republican. In 1968, he loaned members of EDS to the Nixon campaign. But he was a moderate. In Texas, he devoted himself to improving the state's school systems, and particularly those schools that primarily catered to minorities. He was pro-choice and in favor of gay rights and gun control. He was not viscerally opposed to government intervention in the economy like some hardline conservatives, and after his experience with GM, Perot became convinced that government had to take a stronger and more effective hand in steering the economy. That put him directly at odds with the Bush administration, which condemned "industrial policy." In the spring of 1992, Perot gave his consent to his followers putting his name on the ballot for an independent run for the presidency.

Perot portrayed himself as an unpaid servant of the people against a corrupt government and inept corporate hierarchy. America's CEOs like GM's Roger Smith, he argued, were too concerned with quarterly returns, and political leaders with poll findings. The White House and Congress, he charged, were under the grip of an army of lobbyists, including those representing foreign companies and governments, which had descended on Washington over the prior two decades. Perot promised to reverse the relationship between the people and their government. "We own this country," Perot told the National Press Club in March 1992:

> Government should come from us. It now comes at us with a propaganda machine in Washington that Hitler's propaganda chief, Goebbels, would have just envied. We've got to put the country back in the control of the owners. And in plain Texas talk, it's time to take out the trash and clean out the barn, or it's going to be too late.

Like a conventional pre-Reaganite Republican, Perot wanted to balance the budget. But he also wanted to prevent corporations from transferring their jobs overseas, and opposed NAFTA. "The White House is all excited about the new trade agreement with Mexico. This agreement will move the highest paid blue-collared jobs in the U.S. to Mexico. This is going to create serious damage to our tax base during this critical period. We have got to manufacture here and not there to keep our tax base intact," Perot told the Press Club. Perot promised that he would restore American manufacturing jobs and that consumers would once again see American products in stores. "We need jobs here, and we must manufacture here if we wish to remain a superpower. We must stop shipping manufacturing jobs overseas and once again make the words 'Made in the USA' the world's standard of excellence," he declared.

Perot had been skeptical of the Bush administration's decision to intervene militarily to oust Iraq from Kuwait. He thought the

76   United States had to stress burden sharing with its allies in Europe and Asia and to focus on rebuilding its economy. "Our highest foreign policy priority is to get our house in order and make America work again," he declared. To do that, he favored public investments that would target "industries of the future" after the manner of Japan's ministry of international trade and industry. He dismissed the objections of free market advocates. "Don't they realize that the biogenetics industry is the result of our federally funded research universities and the National Institutes of Health?" he declared.

To reclaim Washington for the people, Perot advocated tightening the restrictions on former officials becoming lobbyists, reforming campaign spending to limit contributions, shortening the campaign season, making voting more accessible ("Why do we have elections on Tuesday? Working fellows can't get there"), and using computers to create "electronic town halls" where the nation could learn about and debate issues. Perot promised to overcome the "gridlock" (a term he popularized) between Republicans and Democrats. He pledged that he would be the "servant" and that the people would be the "boss." But in Perot's contempt for Congress and the political parties and his proposal for electronic plebiscites, he was in effect putting himself in a position of a super-president who would have an unmediated relationship to the American people. Like Long, he was seen as "dictatorial," even by his own voters.

Perot quickly climbed to the top of the polls. In a CNN/*Time* poll in May, he had 33 percent to 28 percent for Bush and 24 percent for Clinton. But Perot was not prepared for the kind of intensive questioning that the press then subjected him to. Perot's own conspiratorial streak also undid him. He had trouble confirming a claim that the Black Panther Party, on contract with the Viet Cong, had once tried to break into his house. As he began to falter in the polls in July, and after his campaign manager resigned, Perot suddenly quit the race. But on October 1, Perot reentered the race. His eccentricities had already doomed his chance to win, but his exceptional performance in the debates—he memorably warned in the October 15

debate that NAFTA would create a "great sucking sound" on Amer-   77
ican jobs—kept him in the race until the end. He won 19 percent of
the vote overall and more than 25 percent in nine states. In an exit
poll, 40 percent of voters said that they would have voted for him if
they thought he had had a chance to win.

Perot took voters almost equally from the Democrats and the
Republicans. In focus groups he did for Perot, Frank Luntz found
that "not once did a Perot supporter identify either Perot or himself as liberal or conservative." In November exit polls, Perot did best
among voters who identified themselves as "moderates" and "independents." Pollster Stanley Greenberg characterized his voters as
representing "the radical middle—split evenly between conservatives and liberal/moderates." His highest numbers were among
voters who believed their financial situation was "worse now than
in 1988." Perot was more in the tradition of the original populists
and of Long, but his voters had something of the Wallace rightwing
populist outlook. In a post-election survey, Greenberg found that
a majority of Perot's voters thought that "business corporations"
did not "strike a fair balance between making profits and serving
the public," but they also strongly supported the idea that "it's the
middle class, *not* the poor, who really get a raw deal today." (It was
not surprising that Perot voters by two-to-one subsequently backed
Republicans in the 1994 congressional races, which the GOP swept.)

In his initial campaign speeches, Perot started off with an attack
on the deficit, but later in the campaign, he began by attacking
trade deals and runaway shops and K Street lobbyists. That resonated with his voters. According to the exit polls in November, when
voters were asked, "Overall, would you say U.S. trade with other
countries creates more jobs for the U.S., loses more jobs for the U.S.,
or has no effect on U.S. jobs?" Perot voters said by 49 to 35 percent
that trade loses more jobs. As Ruy Teixeira and Guy Molyneux noted
in their 1993 election study, "Some of Perot's biggest applause lines
in the televised debates—both as measured in the studio and among
viewers in the home—were those that bluntly asserted the need to

78   limit the influence of foreign lobbyists and take a tougher U.S. trade stance." He and his vote represented the first clear repudiation of the neoliberal agenda.

Pat Buchanan

The same year that Perot ran, former Nixon and Reagan speechwriter Pat Buchanan challenged George H. W. Bush for the Republican nomination. He ran against Bush primarily from the right, criticizing the president for reneging on his vow not to raise taxes. But Buchanan also criticized Bush for overextending America's commitments abroad and for neglecting America's economic challenge from Japan and Western Europe. "We can't just let foreign imports come in here and rob us of American jobs," Buchanan declared in a campaign speech. Buchanan got a surprising 38 percent in New Hampshire, a sure sign of Republican dissatisfaction with Bush, but because he was seen as a protest candidate, Buchanan failed to top that in any of the subsequent primaries.

Buchanan decided to run again in 1996. This time, he took aim more explicitly at the neoliberal agenda that Republicans and Democrats shared. On the eve of the campaign, Buchanan wrote, "As transnational corporations compete ever more ferociously, First World workers become expendable. . . . What has global competition done for the quality of life of Middle America? What, after all, is an economy for, if not for its people?" In another column, he warned, "The battle for the future will be as much a battle within the parties as it will be between the parties, a battle between the hired men of the Money Power who long abandoned the quaint but useless old ideas of nationhood—and populists, patriots and nationalists who want no part of [Secretary of the Treasury under Bill Clinton] Robert Rubin's world." During his campaign, he fired salvos at corporate America and Wall Street. "There will be no more GATT deals done for the benefit of Wall Street bankers," Buchanan promised during a campaign stop in Youngstown. And of NAFTA: "You don't force Americans making ten bucks an hour to compete with

Mexican workers who have to work for a dollar an hour." At the same   79
time as immigration was becoming a big issue in Europe, Buchanan
was also the first major presidential candidate to single out illegal
immigration. He promised, in fact, to stop immigration altogether.
"A country that loses control of its borders isn't really a country
anymore," he declared.

Buchanan, who famously described his campaign as rallying
"peasants with pitchforks" against the "establishment," astonished pundits in Washington as well as party leaders by winning the
Alaska and Louisiana caucuses, coming within two points of favored
Senator Bob Dole in Iowa, and then winning the New Hampshire
primary. But after New Hampshire, party leaders and pundits closed
ranks behind Dole, and Buchanan failed to win another primary. His
failure was partly due to voters seeing him as they did in 1992, as a
protest candidate. He had never, after all, held an elective office. He
was pugnacious, eloquent, funny, and at times nasty and at other
times generous, but he was not presidential.

The collapse of Buchanan's candidacy was also due to what happened to the American economy. Like Perot in 1992, Buchanan initially benefited from a flagging economy. Even by early 1996, the
United States had not fully recovered from what had been called a
"jobless recovery" and lagging wage growth. By the spring of 1996,
however, unemployment was dropping below 5 percent, and real
income had begun to rise. Clinton would cite the awakened economy
that year to defeat Dole in the November election, but even by the
late spring, it had undercut Buchanan's candidacy.

With the economy booming in the late 1990s, neoliberalism
seemed to be working. The gap between the very rich and everyone
else was growing, legal and illegal immigration was soaring, and
America's trade deficit was increasing, but neither Perot, who ran
again in 1996 as the Reform Party candidate, nor Buchanan, who ran
again in 2000 as the Reform Party candidate, could get any traction.
And what doubts the early dot-com recession of 2001 would have
sown about neoliberalism were overshadowed by the September 11

80   terrorist attack and the Iraq War. But Perot and Buchanan had none-
theless demonstrated the potential for a revolt against neoliberalism among the "middle American radicals." The complaints that
Perot and Buchanan voiced would be heard again after the financial
crash of 2008.

The Tea Party

Like the crash of 1929 that led to the Great Depression, the global
financial crisis of 2008 was rooted in long-term, systemic problems. Asian countries were sending back dollars acquired from
trade surpluses. With the high-tech boom exhausted, and manufacturing still generally plagued by global overcapacity, these dollars
were directly or indirectly fueling consumer debt, particularly in
housing. The housing boom was sustaining demand in an economy
that might have otherwise slowed. When the housing bubble burst
in 2007, millions lost their homes and financial institutions were
put at risk. A steep recession followed. But the crash was also precipitated by the politics of neoliberalism—by financial deregulation
under Carter, Reagan, and Clinton, and lax regulation under George
W. Bush; by trade and investment policies that led to unwieldy
dollar surpluses in the hands of China and other Asian nations; and
by tax policies and anti-union business practices that widened economic inequality and led to the need to prop up consumer demand
through the accumulation of debt.

The financial crisis became widely visible in September 2008
when the New York investment bank Lehman Brothers had to close
its doors. The crash helped elect Barack Obama and a Democratic
Congress. Obama's majority reflected the growth and increased
Democratic commitment of the peculiar coalition that had backed
McGovern in 1972. These included minorities, who were making
up a growing percentage of the electorate, single women, and professionals. It appeared at the time that by responding forcefully to
the crash, Obama might be able, like Roosevelt in 1933, to create
a new, enduring Democratic majority. But it was not to be. There

was a dramatic difference from the start: While Roosevelt had been
pushed by Long and the labor movement from the left, Obama
almost immediately felt pressure from a new populist movement on
the right.

Obama may have contributed to the public turning rightward.
While Roosevelt went after the "moneychangers" during his first
months in office, Obama's rhetoric and initiatives reflected a def-
erence toward Wall Street and the free market. In his inaugural
address, he cast blame equally on Wall Street and Main Street for the
crisis. "Our economy is badly weakened, a consequence of greed and
irresponsibility on the part of some, but also our collective failure to
make hard choices and prepare the nation for a new age," he declared.
Obama's Justice Department did not prosecute or even single out
any of the major players in the financial crisis. And on the advice
of his treasury secretary, Timothy Geithner, Obama delayed introducing specific financial reform measures during his first months
in office for fear they would shake business confidence. He also gave
bailing out the banks priority over aiding insolvent homeowners.
That approach would later spark a reaction from the left, but in the
first year of Obama's presidency, it left a political vacuum that was
filled by the angry right.

The right reacted in particular to initiatives that Obama undertook in his first year. First, he championed several measures to
combat the recession. These included a $787 billion stimulus bill
and a $75 billion bill to help homeowners threatened by foreclosure.
Second, he introduced his plan for national health insurance. To
win the support of insurance and drug companies, Obama cobbled
together a complex plan that would mandate individuals not covered by their employers to buy insurance from exchanges; the plan
would subsidize uninsured lower-income individuals who might
not be able to afford insurance on the exchanges. Typical of post–
New Deal Democratic social policy, it clearly addressed the needs
of lower-income groups, but didn't appear to offer as much to the
middle class or, in this case, to senior citizens, who were informed

82   that the plan would be financed by reductions in the growth of Medicare spending.

The reaction spawned the Tea Party movement, which attacked neoliberalism from the far right. The movement was sparked by CNBC commentator Rick Santelli's denunciation of Obama's mortgage plan. "This is America," Santelli, speaking from the floor of the Chicago Mercantile Exchange, exclaimed. "How many of you people want to pay for your neighbor's mortgage that has an extra bathroom and can't pay their bills?" Santelli called for a "Chicago Tea Party" to protest the administration's plan. Santelli's plea was answered by a group of bloggers, policy wonks, and Washington politicos who organized Tea Party protests in February in 30 cities and then more protests in April and September.

The Tea Party was never a single, unified organization. Instead, it consisted of myriad local groups that were independent of each other but united by social media. There were several national Tea Party groups that used their mailing lists to raise money and boost candidates, and two corporate-funded Washington groups, FreedomWorks and Americans for Prosperity, which exploited the movement to further their own lobbying agenda. Sociologists Theda Skocpol and Vanessa Williamson estimated that, in 2011, when the movement was probably at its height, Tea Party groups boasted 160,000 members. That doesn't include several million people who during Obama's first term took their cues from what they understood the Tea Party to be advocating. That helped nominate a score of "Tea Party candidates" for the House and Senate in 2010.

There was never a common platform for the Tea Party groups, but there was a certain argument that ran through many of the groups' positions. Santelli expressed it in his rant: the idea that America is divided into "makers" and "takers"—people who earn a living and pay taxes and people who live off of what other people earn. The Tea Party activists viewed Obama's stimulus package and mortgage relief through that prism. They saw themselves as having to pay higher taxes in order to cover for other people's mistakes in buying mortgages they couldn't afford. The Tea Party position was summed up in a bumper sticker that read, "You are not entitled to what I have earned."

The Tea Party also viewed the Affordable Care Act that Congress passed in 2010 as a program aimed at getting people who already had insurance to pay higher premiums and co-payments, so that those who didn't have insurance could afford it. Seniors on Medicare, who had paid for their insurance, would also see their benefits reduced in order to cover the cost of the Affordable Care Act. Emily Ekins, who did extensive interviews with Tea Party members, writes that the Tea Partiers "tended to view the ACA as a redistributive transfer program that they would be disproportionately responsible for funding." Tea Partiers viewed illegal immigration the same way. In their interviews, Skocpol and Williamson report, "the major concern was the illegitimate and costly use of government funds and services by illegal immigrants."

Many of the local Tea Party groups were part of the tradition of American populism and reflected opposition from the right to the neoliberal consensus. They objected to the residual elements of New Deal liberalism that neoliberalism had retained, even those popular among Republicans. If anything, they were a throwback to the Jacksonian proto-populists. The Tea Partiers' argument about "makers" and "takers" recalled the "producerism" of the Jacksonians and the People's Party, which was rooted in a distinction between productive and unproductive elements of society. Bankers, land speculators, and gamblers were typically numbered among the unproductive—as were, for the populists, recent immigrants who took jobs from native-born Americans.

The Tea Partiers initially singled out Obama for coddling the "takers," but after Republicans won the Congress in 2010 but failed to deliver on the Tea Party's nonnegotiable demands to repeal Obamacare, the Tea Party focused their ire on the Republican establishment. Tea Party candidates ran against both Senate Majority Leader Mitch McConnell and House Majority Leader Eric

84   Cantor—and in the latter case, won. McConnell and Cantor's sin lay in refusing to go all the way in repudiating even the bare rudiments of the neoliberal consensus between the parties and in failing to block even discussion of immigration reform.

Cantor's sin also lay in being too close to Wall Street and the Business Roundtable. In the primary, Tea Party candidate David Brat said, "All the investment banks in New York and D.C.—those guys should have gone to jail. Instead of going to jail, they went on Eric's Rolodex, and they are sending him big checks." This side of the Tea Party, which echoed the original People's Party, was largely ignored by political scientists and other commentators, even after Trump's presidential campaign brought it to the surface.

The right wing's success during Obama's first term was in marked contrast to its relative obscurity during Roosevelt's first term. In the 1930s, there was rightwing opposition to the New Deal led by the Liberty Lobby, but it amounted to a footnote compared to Long and the labor movement on the left. Part of the reason for this was the difference between the political economy of the Great Depression and the Great Recession. During the Great Depression, unemployment climbed as high as 25 percent, and threatened the middle as well as the lower classes. The middle-class voters who looked to Long feared "being plunged back into what they viewed as an abyss of powerlessness and dependence." They didn't scorn those below them, but identified with them.

During the Great Recession, most Americans enjoyed the protections created by the New Deal and Great Society. They didn't have to fear actual starvation, homelessness, and having their savings wiped out in a bank crash. The recession far less affected the older, white middle classes, who formed the base of the Tea Party movement, than it did the lower classes. During the Great Recession, the middle class, defined as the third quintile in income statistics, lost pre-tax income, but when post-tax and transfer payments are included, didn't lose income from 2007 through 2011. Unemployment rates were also far higher for those with only a high school

education or less than for those with some college or a bachelor's
degree. That created a situation in which what parts of the middle
class feared most was having to subsidize through higher taxes or
healthcare premiums those in the lower classes or illegal and recent
legal immigrants. It encouraged a rightwing rather than a leftwing
response to the Great Recession and to neoliberalism. A populist
response would eventually come from the left, but it would not
initially be as widespread or emanate from the same part of the
electorate.

Occupy Wall Street

By February 2011, Obama had come under attack from the left for
not moving aggressively against Wall Street. That month, a website,
AmpedStatus.com, published a report on the American economy
entitled, "The Economic Elite vs. the People of the United States."
Its author, David DeGraw, wrote, "It's time for 99 percent of Americans to mobilize and aggressively move on common sense political reforms. It has now become evident to a critical mass that the
Republican and Democratic parties . . . have been bought off by a
well-organized Economic Elite who are tactically destroying our
way of life." When the AmpedStatus site was mysteriously knocked
offline, the hacker group Anonymous helped create a new site, and it
joined with AmpedStatus to form a new effort called A99.

A99 called for an occupation of Zuccotti Park near Wall Street on
June 14. The demonstration fizzled, but the organizers got together
with another group, the New York City General Assembly, that had
been protesting city budget cuts and wanted to organize an occupation for the fall. A month later, a Canadian anti-capitalist publication, *Adbusters*, citing the success of the Egyptian demonstrations
in Tahrir Square, put out a call on its blog for an occupation on September 17 that would "set up tents, kitchens, peaceful barricades
and occupy Wall Street for a few months." While *Adbusters* billed
itself as anti-capitalist, it rejected defining the occupation's goal as
"the overthrow of capitalism" for fear that it "will quickly fizzle into

86   another inconsequential ultra-left spectacle soon forgotten." It suggested coming up with "a deceptively simple Trojan Horse demand ...that is impossible for President Obama to ignore."

The organizers failed to come up with a single demand—there seemed to be too many of them, most of which demanded an end to the reign of neoliberalism—but on a new Occupy Wall Street website, they came up with a simple slogan, borrowed from the original AmpedStatus post, "We are the 99 percent that will no longer tolerate the greed and corruption of the 1 percent." That slogan, which framed the protest in populist terms, defined the movement as an attack on growing political and economic inequality. On September 17, somewhere over a thousand demonstrators showed up and about 300 ended up camping out on Zuccotti Park. And over the next month—aided by police overreaction—the occupation and the demonstrations it spawned attracted thousands in New York. New Occupy movements sprung up in scores of American cities. Occupy Boston, Chicago, Oakland, Los Angeles, and Washington, D.C., to be sure, but also Occupy Tupelo, Wichita, Tampa, Nashville, Missoula, Birmingham, El Paso, and many other cities and towns. It drew primarily from the college-educated young (reducing or writing off student debts was a prominent demand), but also from veterans of past anti-globalization struggles, like the demonstrations in Seattle in 1999 against the World Trade Organization.

Part of the key to Occupy's initial success was that it struck a popular nerve that went well beyond the demonstrators. It exposed the fallacy of neoliberalism's claim to "lift all boats." In his book *Occupy Nation*, sociologist Todd Gitlin wrote, "Unlike any other movement on the American left in at least three-quarters of a century, this movement began with a majority base of support.... What it stood for—economic justice and curbs on the wealthy—was popular." But the movement's rejection of formal leadership, and as the months went on, the reversion to obnoxiously disruptive tactics that affected more than the movement's overt targets, finally undid it. When New York mayor Michael Bloomberg cleared Zuccotti Park

of occupiers on November 15, the movement dissipated and, except
for a few web pages, disappeared as an organized force.

But Occupy Wall Street's symbolic impact was huge. It brought the issue of political and economic inequality, an issue that lay at the heart of the challenge to neoliberalism, to the fore—not just in the United States, but in Europe, where populist parties in Greece and Spain were inspired by the movement's example. Micah White, the American senior editor of *Adbusters* who helped inspire the movement, called it a "constructive failure." In the 2012 election, Obama borrowed from Occupy Wall Street's rhetoric to pillory Republican Mitt Romney. And Occupy's radicalism would recur in more organized form—when a Vermont senator would decide to run for president in 2016.

The Silent Majority and the Political Revolution

Donald Trump and Bernie Sanders

In an interview with the *Washington Post* in July 2015, former Maryland governor Martin O'Malley dismissed Bernie Sanders as a "protest candidate." "I'm not running for protest candidate, I'm running for President of the United States," O'Malley declared. But after receiving 0.57 percent of the vote in the Iowa caucus on February 2, O'Malley dropped out, while Sanders, who tied Clinton in Iowa, moved on to New Hampshire, where he won the primary easily and established himself as a viable contender for the nomination.

Donald Trump's candidacy was also greeted with derision. Two weeks after O'Malley dismissed Sanders's candidacy, the Huffington Post's Washington editors announced that they wouldn't "report on Trump's campaign as part of the Huffington Post's political coverage. Instead, we will cover his campaign as part of our entertainment section. Our reason is simple: Trump's campaign is a sideshow." Six months later, with Trump leading the Republican pack in the polls, Huffington Post editor Ariana Huffington sheepishly announced they were moving their coverage of him back into their politics section.

Many political experts attributed the candidates' success to something other than what they were advocating. Trump's coalition, the

New York Times wrote, "is constructed around personality not substance." Sanders's success was attributed to his "authenticity." A column in Politico asked why Sanders's young supporters "are so obsessed with Sanders's authenticity?"

Part of the candidates' appeal did lie with their personal style. Sanders, the 74-year-old democratic socialist, exuded a passion and sincerity that appeared to be lacking in Hillary Clinton's campaigning. As a man of the turbulent '60s, when the young were unwilling to accept the status quo, he was able to establish an emotional bond with young voters. And Trump, a seasoned television performer, had the rare skill of saying virtually the same thing to one audience after another but appearing each time to be having a conversation with his audience. His performances were in marked contrast to the wooden style of his chief rival, former Florida governor Jeb Bush.

But over the decades, there has been no absence of candidates who appear authentic, but who haven't fared as well as Sanders. They include Iowa senator Tom Harkin and former Vermont governor Howard Dean on the Democratic side and former Pennsylvania senator Rick Santorum and former congressman Jack Kemp among the Republicans. Equally, there have been Republicans like Pat Robertson or Pat Buchanan and Democrats like Jesse Jackson who could entertain and enliven an audience as effectively as Trump, but who never got as far as Trump did.

What's missing from these explanations is the way Trump's and Sanders's political messages resonated with large parts of the electorate. From the right and left, respectively, Trump and Sanders were taking aim at the neoliberal consensus, to which many voters, without naming or identifying it as such, had become hostile, particularly in the wake of the Great Recession. Trump and Sanders were continuing what Perot and Buchanan had started, but with a success that suggested the political consensus had become increasingly vulnerable.

90   **Trump and Neoliberalism**

Trump was the son of a real estate developer from Queens who had made a small fortune building and renting out low- and middle-income apartments in the borough. Donald Trump aspired to more—he wanted the wealth and prestige from building and living in Manhattan. Thanks to his father's money and connections, Trump eventually developed a billion-dollar business out of hotels, apartment buildings, casinos, and other properties. He almost went under in the 1990s as the Atlantic City casinos he had bought or built went belly-up. He restored his reputation as a mogul and recouped some of his losses through starring in a television show, *The Apprentice*. He also gained the celebrity he sought. In 1981, when Trump was only 35, he was featured in *People* magazine. He joined exclusive clubs frequented by sports stars, gangsters, and other nouveaux riches.

Real estate developers like Trump need licenses and sometimes contracts from cities and states, and have to be perpetually wooing politicians. He courted and funded Democrats as well as Republicans, and for his first decades in business, kept his political opinions largely to himself. But under the tutelage of Republican operative Roger Stone, who after Roy Cohn's death in 1986, became Trump's *consigliere*, Trump began to dabble in national politics. In 1987, he ran a full-page ad in the *New York Times* and other major dailies titled "There's nothing wrong with America's foreign defense policy that a little backbone can't cure." In October that year at the invitation of a New Hampshire Republican who wanted to draft him for president, he aired his views on defense, trade, and business at a Rotary Club luncheon in Hampton, New Hampshire. Trump attracted a larger crowd than any of the announced Republican candidates, but he demurred from running.

In 1999, Trump actively sought the nomination of the Reform Party, which Ross Perot had created as a vehicle for his second presidential run in 1996. Stone formed an exploratory committee for him, but Trump backed out after several months and ceded the

nomination to Pat Buchanan. In 2011, he again hinted at interest in
the Republican nomination; after Mitt Romney's loss, Trump began
preparing for the 2016 race with appearances in Iowa the next year
and at the Conservative Political Action Conference in Washington.

Trump's views, as expressed over these two decades, defy easy
categorization. On the issues that Democrats and Republicans normally battle over, such as abortion, gay rights, and social spending,
Trump, like Stone, was a moderate Eastern Republican similar, say,
to former Republican senator Alfonse D'Amato or even Democrat Ed Koch. He supported abortion rights ("I'm very pro-choice,"
Trump declared in 1999), he wanted to protect Social Security and
Medicare from cuts, and he even backed some kind of universal
national health insurance. "I'm a conservative on most issues, but
a liberal on health," he wrote in his 2000 campaign manifesto, *The
America We Deserve*. As a real estate developer, he enthusiastically
favored infrastructure spending that many conservative Republi
cans disdained.

In the 2016 campaign, he abandoned his support for abortion
rights, a political necessity in Republican primaries. But he retained
his defense of Social Security and Medicare and even suggested—
without spelling out a plausible program—that he would replace
the Affordable Care Act with a program for universal health insurance. He also backed massive expenditures on highways, bridges,
and airports.

If he had based his campaign on this moderate Republicanism,
Trump probably would not have won a single delegate. He would
have suffered the same fate as Howard Baker, Lamar Alexander,
Jon Huntsman, and other centrist candidates. But he combined his
moderate Republicanism with a set of sentiments and convictions,
some of which went back two decades or more, that were very similar to those of Perot, Buchanan, and Wallace. They challenged the
prevailing Democratic and Republican views of foreign policy, trade
and investment, immigration, and race. They formed the substance
of his campaign.

Defense and national security: As the Cold War ended, leading Republicans and Democrats had sought to maintain the alliance system forged during the Cold War and to support American military intervention abroad to sustain the American-led system. In his first public statement of his views in 1987, Trump insisted that the United States get Japan, Saudi Arabia, and other allies to pay for the protection they were getting from the U.S. The United States, Trump wrote, "should stop paying to defend countries that can afford to defend themselves." Trump wanted the country free to devote its resources at home to "our farmers, our sick, our homeless." In the 2016 campaign, he would return to the same point. "You have countries in NATO that are getting a free ride," Trump complained on CNN. "It's very unfair. The United States cannot afford to be the policeman of the world anymore, folks. We have to rebuild our own country."

Like Perot and Buchanan, Trump went from insisting on "burden sharing" to questioning America's Cold War commitment to NATO and to other alliances. In his 2016 campaign, he criticized NATO as "obsolete" and "expensive." Trump also opposed American military intervention when there was not a direct threat posed to the United States. Perot and Buchanan had both rejected George H. W. Bush's intervention in Kuwait. Trump criticized George W. Bush's invasion of Iraq. Trump insisted that his skills as a dealmaker could improve American diplomacy. Unlike his opponents in 2016, he didn't promise to tear up the Obama administration's agreement with Iran. Instead, he said he would "police that deal." While he promised to destroy ISIS, he suggested that he could make a deal with Russian president Vladimir Putin, whom he admired, to end the Syrian conflict. Taken together, Trump's views, like those of Perot, represented a version of foreign policy realism that was contrary to both Republican neo-conservatism and Democratic liberal interventionism.

Free trade: Along with Buchanan and Perot, Trump opposed NAFTA and the pre-WTO most-favored-nation trading status for China.

He claimed these agreements cost American jobs by incurring trade 93 deficits. Other countries, he said in 1999, "can't believe how easy it is to deal with the U.S. We are known as a bunch of saps. We need our best people to negotiate against the Japanese and many other countries." Trump promised to get business leaders to negotiate these treaties.

In his 2016 campaign, Trump opposed the Trans-Pacific Partnership agreement that the Obama administration had signed, but Congress had not ratified. And Trump continued to rail against trade arrangements with China, Japan, and Mexico, with China drawing the most ire. "Our country is in serious trouble. We don't win anymore. We don't beat China in trade. We don't beat Japan, with their millions and millions of cars coming into this country, in trade. We can't beat Mexico, at the border or in trade," Trump declared in the first Republican debate in August 2015. To force China to revalue its currency to make its exports more expensive, and American exports to China cheaper, Trump proposed threatening them with a 45 percent tariff on their exports to the United States. And he reiterated his promise to have businessmen and not "political hacks" negotiate trade deals.

Outsourcing and offshoring: In 1999, Trump's principal case against trade treaties was that they allowed foreign countries to keep out American goods while sending their own goods to the United States. But beginning with his 2011 manifesto, *Time to Get Tough*, Trump, like Perot and Buchanan, began to criticize American corporations for taking advantage of trade treaties to outsource their production to Mexico, China, and Japan and to establish factories in these countries that would export goods back to the United States, in both cases depriving American workers of jobs. In *Time to Get Tough*, he proposed a 15 percent tariff on goods that were outsourced.

In the 2016 campaign, Trump singled out specific corporations for shipping or planning to ship factories and jobs either south of the border or overseas. In his announcement speech in July 2015,

94   he dwelled on the example of Ford saying it was going to build a $2.5 billion car and truck plant in Mexico. Trump said that if he were president, he would call the CEO of Ford and threaten him with a 35 percent tax on every car and truck that Ford shipped across the border. Trump also criticized Nabisco for planning to move its plant from Illinois. "They are moving their plant to Mexico. Why, how does it help us?" Trump asked during a speech in Dallas in September 2015. And in the Republican primary debate in February 2016, he went after Carrier for moving a plant and 1,400 jobs from Indianapolis to Mexico. "In the old days, they moved from New York to Texas," Trump said. "Now they go from this country to another country, finding lower labor and lower taxes, they have no real loyalty to the United States."

Like Perot, Trump wanted to restore American manufacturing—it was central to his promise to make America great again. Trump increasingly used the same language as Perot. Speaking in New York after his primary victory April 19, he said, "Our jobs are being sucked out of our state. They're being sucked out of our country, and we're not going to let that happen anymore." Liberal commentators and economists charged that Trump was deceiving the public by promising to bring back jobs that could never be restored. That was probably true. But Trump was taking aim at the skewed distribution of jobs and income that neoliberal economics had created over the prior decades.

Trump also denounced corporate plans—dubbed "tax inversions"—by which corporations moved their headquarters overseas in order to avoid paying American taxes. Trump made these criticisms of corporate offshoring and outsourcing and tax inversions in every speech of his that I heard. Together, these stands struck at the heart of the neoliberal agenda. And in June, after he sewed up the Republican nomination and turned his attention to the general election, he began reemphasizing these themes in his speeches. In a June 22 speech on "The Stakes of this Election," Trump asked "Bernie Sanders's voters to join our movement: so together we can fix the system for *all* Americans. Importantly, this includes fixing all of our many disastrous trade deals. Because it's not just the political system that's rigged. It's the whole economy. It's rigged by big donors who want to keep down wages. It's rigged by big businesses who want to leave our country, fire our workers, and sell their products back into the U.S. with absolutely no consequences for them. . . . It's rigged against you, the American people."

Immigration: When Trump was seeking the Reform Party nomination in 1999, he agreed with Buchanan, his rival for the nomination, on only two issues, trade and immigration. In his campaign book, he wrote:

> America is experiencing serious social and economic difficulty with illegal immigrants who are flooding across our borders. We simply can't absorb them. . . . The majority of legal immigrants can often make significant contributions to our society because they have special skills and because they add to our nation's cultural diversity. . . . But legal immigrants do not and should not enter easily. It's a long, costly, draining, and often frustrating experience—by design. . . . It comes down to this: We must take care of our own people first. Our policy to people born elsewhere should be clear: Enter by the law, or leave.

Trump did not waver from this stance over the next 16 years. In his 2011 book, he wrote, "Illegal immigration is a wrecking ball aimed at U.S. taxpayers. Washington needs to get tough and fight for 'We the People,' not for the special interests who want cheap labor and a minority voting bloc." In the 2016 campaign, he not only opposed illegal immigration, but favored deportation. His case against illegal immigration was partly economic—they drove down wages and raised social costs—but also sociocultural—they were a cause of crime. He proposed that Mexico finance a wall with its trade surplus from the United States to stop illegal immigration.

96   Trump's views on immigration displayed a special animus toward Mexican Americans. Trump described Mexico as sending to America people who bring "crime" and "drugs" and who are "rapists." He described a judge in a lawsuit brought against Trump University as a "Mexican," even though he was born in Indiana, and called for him to step down from the case. Trump's view recalled the nineteenth-century nativists of the Know-Nothing Party and the People's Party support for deporting Chinese laborers. But where the People's Party's racist or xenophobic views of the Chinese were secondary to the thrust of their populism, Trump's views of Mexicans—as well as of Muslim immigrants—became increasingly central to his appeal.

Race

As a real estate developer, Trump and his father had been sued in 1973 for discriminating against African Americans in renting their properties. But as a public personality, Trump did not have a reputation as a racist, and in its first years, Trump's show, *The Apprentice*, was extremely popular among African Americans. But in April 2011, as he was contemplating running for president, Trump challenged Obama to prove he had been born in the United States and not Kenya. Trump persisted even after Obama had produced his birth certificate, only finally acknowledging Obama's native birth in mid-September 2016. That sent a message to voters uncomfortable with America's first black president. Trump also sent a message to these voters when he refused to reject the endorsement of white supremacist David Duke, even claiming that he didn't know who Duke, whom he had condemned years before, was. He told journalist Jake Tapper, "Well, just so you understand, I don't know anything about David Duke. Okay? I don't know anything about what you're even talking about with white supremacy or white supremacists." But in contrast to his statements about Mexicans and Mexican immigrants, Trump's racial appeals were dog whistles to a limited group of voters rather than clear declarations. They were not as central to his 2016 campaign and to his populist appeal. Someone who voted for Wallace in 1968 could be assumed to have opposed racial integration; someone who voted for Trump in 2016 may not have held any animus against black people.

The Silent Majority

On the surface, Trump appeared to be an unlikely candidate for a populist campaign. He was, after all, a billionaire who flaunted his wealth. But Tom Watson had also been a wealthy landowner and Ross Perot was also a billionaire. What's important is that Trump, like the Texarkana-born Perot, wasn't a perfect fit for upper class America. He was still the boy from Queens who aspired to live on the Upper East Side, but ended up spending his time at demimonde hangouts like Studio 54 rather than the Harvard Club.

Trump's view of his social class was also influenced by Roger Stone. Stone had gotten his start in politics doing dirty tricks for Nixon's 1972 campaign. Like Trump, he was a moderate Republican on issues like abortion and social spending—he and his first wife founded Republicans for Choice—but he liked to frame campaigns in frankly populist terms of "we the people" vs. the special interests. Trump's biographer Michael D'Antonio writes of Stone:

> In general, Stone's attacks were intended to persuade voters that the GOP, which was traditionally the party of big business and the country-club set, was actually the anti-elite party of the working class.

Trump took this tack in his campaigns. In an op-ed in the *New York Times* in February 2000, Trump explained that he was abandoning his presidential bid because he no longer saw the Reform Party as a viable vehicle. But he said he regretted not being able to run "a race against Mr. Bush and Mr. Gore, two establishment politicians." "I felt confident," he wrote, "that my argument that America was being ripped off by our major trade partners and that it was

98 time for tougher trade negotiations would have resonance in a race against the two Ivy League contenders." (Trump failed to note that he had graduated from an Ivy League university.)

In 2016, he portrayed himself as the champion of the "silent majority"—a term borrowed from Nixon—against the "special interests" and the "establishment" of both parties. "The silent majority is back, and it's not silent. It's aggressive," Trump declared in Dallas. At rallies, the campaign gave out signs, "The silent majority stands with Trump." In January, right before the Iowa caucuses, Trump ran an ad titled "The Establishment." Seated behind a desk, he said, "The establishment, the media, the special interest, the lobbyists, the donors, they're all against me. I'm self-funding my campaign. I don't owe anybody anything. I only owe it to the American people to do a great job. They are really trying to stop me."

Some of Trump's demands reflected his own peculiar brand of salesmanship. In *The Art of the Deal*, Trump explained that a "little hyperbole" helped sell products. And in this sense, a proposal to ban *all* Muslims or to slap a 45 percent tariff on Chinese imports or to get Mexico to pay for a wall may have been deliberate attention-getting ploys, not to be taken seriously. But they were also typical of a populist approach. They were his equivalent of "free silver" or Long's confiscatory tax on the wealthy—incapable of being negotiated, even by the great dealmaker, but just for that reason dramatizing the difference between what the "silent majority" wanted and what the "establishment" would condone. Trump's supporters didn't necessarily believe that he could get Mexico to pay for a wall or that he could deport all immigrants who had entered the country illegally. What they heard in his demand was a point of demarcation between what "we" wanted and what "they"—Congress, the Mexican president—would accept.

Some of Trump's demands about trade and runaway shops and his tirades against lobbyists, big donors, and special interests recalled Perot, but Trump conducted himself much differently from Perot. Perot's manner was professorial and at worst

condescending—he was widely and unfairly criticized for referring to an NAACP audience as "you people"—but he was not
nasty toward those who disagreed with him and didn't scapegoat
out groups. Trump was highly personal in his attacks on rivals
and bigoted in his characterizations of nationalities and religions and demeaning in his attitude toward women. (When Hillary Clinton declared her candidacy, Trump tweeted, "If Hillary
Clinton can't satisfy her husband what makes her think she can
satisfy America?")

While Trump's views most clearly echoed the rightwing populism of Wallace and Buchanan, his manner was different from
those men as well. Wallace studiously avoided appearing bigoted
toward black people. He almost always couched his proposals in
terms of state's rights or some other abstract principle. And, unlike
Trump, Wallace was an experienced professional politician. He
enjoyed sparring with critics and protestors at his rallies. By contrast, Trump repeatedly displayed the thin skin of a businessman
who treasured his celebrity. At his rallies, he cheered supporters
who beat up protestors. And he tried to turn his supporters against
the press. Trump's actions reflected a bilious disposition, a mean-
ness borne out of bare-knuckle real estate and casino squabbles—
in 1993, Trump tried to repeal a law allowing destitute Indian tribes
to operate casinos—and a conviction, borne out of his financial success or, perhaps, arrested development, that he could say in public
whatever he thought in private about Mexicans or women without
suffering any consequences.

Stone himself formally left as the campaign's head in August 2015
after Trump excoriated Fox News commentator Megyn Kelly, although Stone remained a supporter and advisor. From Stone's stand-
point, Trump's nastiness detracted from his anti-establishment
message. But Trump continued to climb in the polls. His nastiness—
seen as defying standards of political correctness—combined with
his substantive appeals on trade, immigration, and runaway shops,
tapped into a vein of support among Republicans and independents.

100   Trump and the Republicans

Trump's success threatened the coalition that conservative Republicans had forged in the 1970s. That coalition included the party's business interests and white working- and middle-class voters who had begun fleeing the Democratic Party in the 1960s. Trump's candidacy drove a wedge into that coalition. Trump's stands against neoliberal economics and neo-conservative foreign policy deeply offended the party's upper crust of business leaders, think tankers, writers, editors, columnists, and television and radio hosts. These leaders waged a vigorous and unsuccessful multimillion-dollar campaign against his candidacy. Their real target was often Trump's positions on the economy and foreign policy. After Trump's tirade against multinationals and trade deals in his June speech on "the Stakes" of the election, top Republican donor Paul Singer warned that if Trump were elected, it would cause "a widespread global depression." But Trump's intemperance and bigotry allowed them to condemn him on other counts without emphasizing their substantive concerns with his foreign and domestic economic views.

Trump's political base was among the party's white working- and middle-class voters—precisely the voters who had originally flocked to Wallace and then to Nixon, who had been attracted by Perot and Buchanan, but who now felt that they had found a champion in Trump. He had become the voice of middle American radicalism and more broadly of the white Americans who felt left behind by globalization and the shift to a post-industrial economy. Two extensive polls of Republican voters, the first by the American National Election Studies (ANES) in January 2016 and the second by the Pew Research Center in March, reached the same conclusions about Trump's supporters.

Trump's supporters were older and disproportionately less educated—the surest sign of class standing—than those of the other candidates. In 1971, when Donald Warren surveyed Wallace voters, a working-class voter could be assumed to have no more than a high school education. By 2016, these voters might have gone to junior college or a trade school and have an associate's degree. By that standard, 70.1 percent of Trump voters in the ANES survey were not college graduates, compared to 45.1 of Republican establishment favorite John Kasich's voters. In income, half of Trump's voters made less than $50,000 a year, while only 35.3 percent of Kasich's voters made that little. These Trump voters can be characterized as the descendants of those white working-class voters who begin leaving the Democrats in the '60s. Already alienated from Washington and the changes they had seen around them in 1972, they had become even more so in 2016, as the Great Recession seemed like the final blow to their economic prospects in an economy that disproportionately favored the upper middle class and very rich.

Of all the Republican voters, Trump's appear to have been the most worried by the Great Recession, even if they themselves were not thrown out of work. They were the most pessimistic about the economy. According to the Pew poll, 48 percent of Trump voters thought economic conditions in the United States were poor compared to 31 percent of Cruz voters and 28 percent of Kasich voters.

There were also clear differences between Trump's and other Republicans' supporters over immigration and trade. According to the Pew poll, 69 percent of Trump voters thought immigrants did more to burden than to strengthen the country. For Kasich voters, this was 40 percent. According to ANES, 66.4 percent of Trump voters opposed birthright citizenship for immigrant children born in the United States. That was compared to 26 percent of Kasich voters. According to Pew, 67 percent of Trump supporters thought free trade agreements were bad for the United States compared to 46 percent of Kasich supporters and 40 percent of Cruz supporters. Trump voters were also the least likely to think that people should be more sensitive in what they say about people with different backgrounds. According to ANES, 75.7 percent of Trump voters, compared to 45.9 percent of Kasich voters, thought people were too easily offended.

102   Trump supporters in the Republican primaries fit the profile of middle American populism. They were skeptical about the powers below *and* above. According to the Pew poll, 61 percent of Trump voters thought that the U.S. economic system unfairly favored the powerful compared to 51 percent of Kasich voters and 45 percent of Cruz supporters. In interviews I conducted at rallies, Trump voters invariably praised his self-financing, which was seen as making him independent of special interests and lobbyists. It was an important part of his appeal, as it was of Perot's.

        Trump's voters, like Wallace's, also continued to favor the universal social programs that had originated with the New Deal, while opposing programs like the Affordable Care Act that they thought primarily benefited minorities and the poor. According to the Pew poll, 73 percent of Trump voters opposed any reduction in Social Security. Trump's voters were economic populists; they were not free market libertarians like many of the wealthy backers of groups like the Club for Growth or FreedomWorks; and they were also not hardline social conservatives who put a candidate's stand on prayer or abortion first and who were willing to go along with the Republican business agenda.

        Trump's appeal to middle American radicals held up during the fall election against Hillary Clinton. In the final tally, he won over many traditional business Republicans and evangelicals who simply preferred him to Clinton on issues like taxes, government spending priorities, abortion, guns, and judicial nominations. But in winning swing states like Ohio, Pennsylvania, Michigan, Wisconsin, and North Carolina, Trump depended on support from voters who combined the peculiar elements of economic progressivism and social conservatism that Donald Warren had discovered in analyzing Wallace's vote. These were all states whose manufacturing industry had been decimated in the early 2000s. North Carolina, for instance, lost 43 percent of its manufacturing jobs between 2000 and 2011; Michigan 47 percent; Pennsylvania 35 percent.

These job losses affected white workers without four-year college degrees, many of whom were working in and around manufacturing. These workers swung most decisively away from the Democrats and toward Trump in 2016. According to voting analysts Rob Griffin, Ruy Teixeira, and John Halpin, Clinton lost 8 percentage points among these voters in Michigan; in Ohio, she lost 17 points. Surveying extensive polling on the 2016 vote, analyst Emily Ekins described Trump's staunchest supporters as "trade skeptics" who "look more like Democrats on domestic economic issues, particularly on the nation's wealth distribution, concern over old-age entitlement programs, and animus toward Wall Street," but also as possessing "a strong sense of their own racial identity and . . . Christian identity," taking a "restrictionist approach to immigration" and feeling "the greatest amount of angst over race relations."

Sanders and the Billionaire Class

Sanders, like Trump, was raised in one of New York's outer boroughs, but the resemblance ends there. Sanders grew up in Brooklyn in humble circumstances. His father was a Jewish émigré from Poland who sold paint and his mother the daughter of émigrés. He went to the same high school that Ruth Bader Ginsburg and Chuck Schumer attended, and he spent a year at Brooklyn College before transferring to the University of Chicago, where he graduated in 1964. He lived on a Kibbutz in Israel for six months, returned to New York where he worked at odd jobs, and in 1968, he and his first wife moved to Vermont as part of the New Left's back-to-the-land movement.

The Brooklyn in which Sanders grew up was a hotbed of leftwing politics and culture, and Sanders, when he came to Chicago, joined the Young People's Socialist League, the youth wing of Norman Thomas's Socialist Party, and the Congress of Racial Equality (CORE), which at the time was a militant civil rights group. He read Marx and the history of American socialism, and got arrested in civil rights protests, but he never took the turn toward sectarian

104 violence the leaders of SDS (Students for a Democratic Society) took in the late '60s. Instead, Sanders combined a commitment to the socialism of Eugene Debs with various counterculture enthusiasms, including free love, Reichian therapy, ecology, home birth, and home schooling.

Living on odd jobs while raising a young child, Sanders ran for Senate twice and governor twice in the '70s on the ticket of the Liberty Union, a leftwing third party in Vermont. Disillusioned—he got no more than 6 percent of the vote—he quit the Liberty Union in 1977. Four years later, he ran for mayor of Burlington, and to the surprise of the town's leaders, won by 10 votes over the Democratic incumbent. Sanders was a successful mayor. He was reelected three times and helped turn the town of 45,000 into one of New England's most livable cities. In 1990, he won Vermont's seat in the House of Representatives, and in 2006, when Republican Jim Jeffords retired, Sanders won one of the Senate seats.

In his Liberty Union campaigns, Sanders advocated for socialism. In the diary he kept of his Senate campaign in 1972, he wrote of a campaign stop, "I even mentioned the horrible word 'socialism'—and nobody in the audience fainted." He would recommend Albert Einstein's essay "Why Socialism" to anyone interested. In that essay, Einstein wrote that the only way to remove the "evils" of capitalism was "through the establishment of a socialist economy. . . . In such an economy, the means of production are owned by society itself and are utilized in a planned fashion." As mayor, Sanders fretted that he couldn't bring socialism to Vermont. "If you ask me if the banks should be nationalized, I would say yes," Sanders told the *Baltimore Sun*. "But I don't have the power to nationalize the banks in Burlington."

During Sanders's second, successful run for Congress in 1990, his view of socialism softened and increasingly came to resemble social democracy. "To me socialism doesn't mean state ownership of everything by any means," he told the AP in November 1990. "It means creating a nation and a world, in which all human beings have a decent

standard of living." In his 1997 autobiography, *Outsider in the House*,
Sanders did write, "Bill Clinton is a moderate Democrat. I'm a democratic socialist." But in this book he most often describes himself as a
"progressive." By the time he was elected to the Senate, he explicitly
equated socialism with Scandinavian social democracy. "I'm a democratic socialist," he told the *Washington Post*. "In Norway, parents get a
paid year to care for infants. Finland and Sweden have national health
care, free college, affordable housing, and a higher standard of living."

What hadn't changed over the years was Sanders's indictment
of capitalism. He still saw yawning economic inequality. In his 1971
campaign, he had called for radical tax reform directed at the "two
percent of the people controlling one third of the country's wealth."
In his 1996 Senate reelection campaign, he attacked the influence
of the "one percent." In the House and Senate, he stood firm against
the party's embrace of neoliberalism. He opposed NAFTA and the
agreements with China, tax cuts on business, budgets that reduced
social spending, and financial deregulation. He continued to dissent in the Obama years. In December 2010—in a move echoing
Huey Long's rejection of Roosevelt's Government Economy Act in
1933—he staged a one-man filibuster against the budget and tax
agreement that Obama, chastened by congressional losses, had
worked out with the Republicans that prolonged the Bush tax cuts
for the wealthy.

Sanders first started thinking seriously about running for president in April 2013, when he called a meeting in Burlington with his
top friends and advisors to discuss whether he should do so. The
group speculated that Sanders's outrage over income inequality
might find a ready reception in 2016. They noted that the Occupy
Wall Street protests had dissipated, but that the issues they had
raised were now widely discussed. Sanders took another two years
to make a final decision, but in April 2015, he told his friends he
was running. In an interview with Rachel Maddow on MSNBC that
month, Sanders, noting "this strange moment in American history, when our middle class is disappearing, when we have so many

106   people living in poverty, when we have to deal with climate change, when we have to deal with the horrendous level of income and wealth inequality," asked,

> [H]ow do we address these issues in a way that takes on the billionaire class. Where they have significant control over the media, where they by and large determine the legislation that goes on in Congress, and as a result of *Citizens United* are prepared to buy the United States Congress."

As his campaign unfolded, Sanders unveiled a set of radical reforms that would, among other things, entail government reassuming control over the private market. He proposed Medicare for All (which would remove private insurance as a middleman and guarantee health insurance as a right), free tuition to public colleges financed by a transaction tax on Wall Street speculation, a carbon tax to reduce carbon emissions, the reinstatement of the Glass-Steagall Act separating commercial and investment banking, and public campaign financing.

Sanders's critics among Democrats argued that his proposals were impractical because they would never get through a Republican Congress. A column in *New York* magazine was entitled, "What Bernie Sanders Doesn't Understand About American Politics." Sanders responded that, to obtain any of these reforms, there would have to be a "political revolution" that pitted the power of the people against the billionaire class. "If we are going to transform America," Sanders said during a speech in North Las Vegas in November, "we need a political revolution. Millions of people have to stand up and get involved in the political process in a way we have not in many, many years."

In an editorial, the *New York Times* criticized Sanders's "facile calls for revolution," but what Sanders meant by "revolution" was greater active participation in politics rather than armed struggle to seize state power. Coupled with his demand for reform of campaign

finance, Sanders was actually making a much more arguable point   107
than the *New York Times* and other critics were willing to acknowledge: namely, that to achieve the kind of significant change in the
existing relationship between the government and economy that his
reforms would entail would require a major shift in political power
and allegiance in the country, such as had happened between, say,
1929 and 1935.

In an interview with Stephen Colbert, Sanders said that he
would prefer to describe his proposals as "progressive" rather than
as "socialist" or "liberal." That use of the term "progressive" made
sense, but historically speaking, American progressivism had arisen
as an alternative to populism and socialism. Where populism had
rested on a conflict between the people and the establishment, and
socialism on a conflict between the working class and the capitalist
class, progressivism sought to reconcile classes—to remove antag-
onisms. "'I am for labor,' or 'I am for capital,' substitutes something
else for the immutable laws of righteousness," Theodore Roosevelt
wrote in 1904. "The one and the other would let the class man in,
and letting him in is the one thing that will most quickly eat out the
heart of the republic."

Sanders's political approach and his demands fit more appro-
priately into the American populist tradition of the People's Party,
Long, Perot, and Occupy Wall Street. He aimed to rouse the people
against the "billionaire class." And his demands created a political
divide between the 99 percent and the 1 percent. They defined the
conflict rather than providing an opening to negotiations. There was
no way that the insurance and drug companies would permit "Medicare for All" without what Sanders called a political revolution, or
that the banks and other Wall Street firms would submit to further
regulation or pay transaction taxes so that Americans could go to
public college for free. In a manner recalling how the political elites
dealt with Long and Perot, Sanders's critics argued that his numbers didn't add up, as if the demands in a campaign needed to pass
muster at the Congressional Budget Office.

108   Sanders agreed with Trump about trade treaties and foreign investment. "My understanding, talking to many economists, is that NAFTA, PNTR [permanent normal trade relations] with China, other trade agreements have cost this country millions of jobs," Sanders told the *New York Daily News*. He added, "I don't think it is appropriate for trade policies to say that you can move to a country where wages are abysmal, where there are no environmental regulations, where workers can't form unions." But Sanders was a leftwing and not a rightwing populist. Unlike Trump and his supporters, he didn't blame unauthorized immigrants for the plight of American workers or seek to end terrorism by banning Muslims from coming into the country. He was entirely focused, as he explained to Maddow, on combating the "billionaire class."

The Bernie Voters

In the 2016 election, Sanders lost the battle for the nomination, but the support for Hillary Clinton may not have reflected the extent to which Democrats and Democratic-leaning independents were supportive of his approach. Much of the nominating contest hinged on the belief of African American and older voters that Clinton was more electable in a general election and more prepared, after her years at the highest levels of power, to assume the presidency than the 74-year-old democratic socialist who during the election showed very little interest in or knowledge of foreign policy. But something can still be learned from looking at Sanders's core supporters.

Sanders's support, like Trump's, showed how much the Great Recession had radicalized significant parts of the electorate. Of all voting groups, his voters were the most harshly critical of the American economic system. In the Pew poll, 91 percent of Sanders's voters thought that the "U.S. system unfairly favors the powerful." That's in comparison to 73 percent of Clinton voters and 61 percent of Trump voters. According to Pew, 82 percent of Sanders's voters also thought that corporations "make too much profit." In the ANES poll,

90.2 percent of Sanders's voters thought the differences in income
between the rich and poor were larger than they were 20 years ago.

Sanders's voters were also the most pessimistic about their own
and the country's economic future. That, too, shows the impact of
the Great Recession. In the Pew survey, 57 percent—far more than
any other Democratic or Republican voting bloc—thought that hard
work is no guarantee of success. In the ANES survey, 63.3 percent
of Sanders's supporters (compared to 43.2 percent of Clinton supporters) thought there was either no or little opportunity for the
average person to get ahead in America.

On average, Sanders got his greatest support among young
people. From my observations at rallies, many of these young voters
were either going to college or had recently graduated from college.
They were, in effect, the descendants of the McGovern generation
who began gravitating to the Democratic party over post-material
social and environmental concerns and over moral outrage at the
Vietnam War and later the American invasion of Iraq and, more
recently, in the wake of the Great Recession, what they saw as the
irresponsibility of Wall Street and the billionaire class.

But there was also a material dimension to their concern that
Sanders touched. They were worried about the opportunities that
awaited them, or that they had found, on the job market. They found
less autonomy in their work; they made less than they had expected.
In the wake of the Great Recession, these young voters became concerned whether *any* jobs would await them, and whether they would
ever be able to pay back the debts they had incurred to go to college.

They might, of course, be won over to neoliberal economics by a
reversal of these trends in the economy, but it's not likely to happen.
In the last decades of the twentieth century, economists talked about
a college graduate wage premium, but it shrunk after the boom of
the late 1990s. According to the Economic Policy Institute, the real
inflation-adjusted wages of young college graduates were 2.5 percent lower in 2015 than they were in 2000. At the same time, student
debts—a key issue in the Sanders campaign—skyrocketed, rising by

110 84 percent from 2008 to 2014. In addition, graduates of community and four-year colleges increasingly have to find roles within a labor force divided into specialized niches that are being continually reshaped by information technology. That has probably contributed to the rising levels of anxiety that psychologists have found among college students. If these trends continue, a large number of radicalized American voters will begin moving through the electorate.

Sanders's identification as a socialist would have certainly become a handicap in a general election, but there is some indication that it may have helped him among younger voters. In a January 2016 survey by the polling group YouGov, young adults 18 to 29 had a favorable view of socialism by 43 to 26 percent, with the remainder having no opinion. Democratic voters had a favorable view by 42 to 34 percent. These results—inconceivable 50 or even 25 years ago—are partly the result of the Cold War's end and the identification of socialism with European social democracy rather than with Soviet communism. Some Sanders supporters that I interviewed cited European social programs. But others, reminiscent of nineteenth-century Christian socialists, stressed the cooperative nature of socialism in contrast to capitalism. In either case, younger voters' attraction to socialism is the flip side of their growing disillusionment with capitalism in the wake of the Great Recession.

Younger voters were also not turned off by Sanders's age, nor by his ignorance of pop culture. There was an affinity between Sanders, who had come of age in the raucous sixties, when young people were determined to look beyond the status quo, and his young supporters. While older voters and liberal pundits evaluated Sanders's program by whether they could be included in the president's Fiscal Year 2018 budget, younger voters liked the visionary sweep of Medicare for All and Free Public College. They understood that adopting programs like these couldn't happen within the current "rigged system" and would require a political revolution. The contrast couldn't have

been sharper with Clinton's campaign that lacked any visionary
component and dwelt entirely on lists of incremental changes.

Sanders's impact (like Long's) will most likely be felt in the Democratic Party, where it has already accelerated the turn against neoliberal orthodoxy on finance, trade, and capital mobility, although not necessarily on unskilled immigration and guest workers. Young people are not a functional voting bloc except as students, but Sanders's campaign has revealed the extent to which the Great Recession radicalized the descendants of the McGovern generation. They could be a major force in American politics for years to come—and one that could eventually seal the doom of the neoliberal orthodoxy.

The Rise of European Populism

In the last decades of the nineteenth century, as the People's Party was erupting on the American scene, Europe was seeing the emergence of Social Democratic parties inspired by Karl Marx's theory of socialism. Over the next 70 years, Europe would see a few parties and movements that could be described as populist, such as Pierre Pojade's Defense Union of Shopkeepers and Artisans during the 1950s, but nothing on the scale of America's Populist Party until the 1970s. Europeans would call these parties, which only began to flourish in 1990s, by the American-derived name. It's "populiste" in French and "populist" in German.

Like the original American People's Party, the European parties operated within the electoral arena and championed the "people" against an "establishment" or "elite." France's National Front (later renamed the National Rally) represented the "little people" and the "forgotten members" against the "caste." Finland's Finns Party wanted "a democracy that rests on the consent of the people and does not emanate from elites or bureaucrats." Spain's Podemos championed the *gente* against the *casta*—the people against the establishment. Italy's Beppe Grillo railed against what he called the "three destroyers"—journalists, industrialists, and politicians. Geert

Wilders's Freedom Party represented "Henk and Ingrid" against "the political elite."

The first European parties were rightwing populist. They accused the elites of coddling communists, welfare recipients, or immigrants. As a result, the term "populist" in Europe became used pejoratively by leftwing and centrist politicians and academics. Political scientist Cas Mudde writes, "In the public debate populism is mostly used to denounce a form of politics that uses (a combination of) demagogy, charismatic leadership, or a *Stammtisch* (pub) discourse." A recent study of European populist parties by a reputable think tank was titled, "Exposing the Demagogues." In the last decade, however, leftwing populist parties arose in Spain, Greece, and Italy that directed their ire against the establishment in their country or against the European Union headquarters in Brussels.

The main difference between American and European populists is that while American parties and campaigns come and go quickly, some European populist parties have been around for decades. That's primarily because Europe has multi-party systems, and many of the countries have proportional representation that allows smaller parties to maintain a foothold even when they are polling less than 7 percent in elections. (In France, which has a majority system in presidential elections, the National Front [FN] has still been able to win not only local elections, but seats in the European Parliament, which are allotted proportionally.)

The European parties muddled along in the '70s and '80s, but they caught fire in the 1990s for some of the same reasons that American campaigns did. In Europe, in the wake of the downturn during the '70s, a neoliberal outlook replaced one heavily influenced by social democracy and Keynesian economics. The Socialist, Social Democratic, and Labour parties as well as the Christian Democratic, Conservative, and Liberal parties embraced this outlook, and when it failed to create buoyant prosperity, that left an opening for populists. So, too, did the leading parties' commitments to immigration

114   within the EU and asylum from countries in North Africa and the Middle East.

The End of the Boom

Populist politics were largely absent in Western Europe in the three decades after World War II. In those years, Socialist, Social Democratic, and Labour parties shared power relatively equitably with Christian Democrats, Tories, Gaullists, and other centrist and center-right parties. In France and Italy, even Communist parties had a subordinate role. The parties and their supporters in business, labor, and the middle classes, eager to avoid the clashes of the 1920s, cooperated to expand social programs. Countries established universal access to healthcare, generous unemployment benefits and family allowances, and free college education. The center and center-right parties held power more often than not, but a politics borne of reform-minded social democracy and Keynesian economics predominated in the same way that New Deal liberalism held sway in the United States even during Republican administrations.

What sustained this social democratic approach was the economic boom. Western Europe benefited from what economist Brad DeLong called a "virtuous circle":

> Trade expansion drove growth, growth drove expanded social insurance programs and real wage levels; expanded social insurance states and real wage levels made for social peace, social peace allowed inflation to stay low even as output expanded rapidly, rapidly expanding output led to high investment, which further increased growth and created the preconditions for further expansions of international trade.

During this period, unemployment rates were impossibly low. The rate was 0.6 percent in West Germany in 1970, 2.2 percent in the UK, and 2.5 percent in France. In France, this era was called *les trente glorieuses*, or 30 glorious years.

But Europe began to suffer a downturn in the early '70s. The principal cause, as in the United States, was a combination of a profit squeeze from a militant labor movement and the development of global overcapacity in key postwar industries like textiles and steel. But in Western Europe, the slowdown was aggravated by the abandonment of capital controls and America's abandonment of a fixed and overvalued currency that had given Europeans a price advantage. The energy price hike that began in 1973 also hit oil-dependent Europe particularly hard. Growth slowed and unemployment rose. Comparing the period 1950 to 1973 with the period from 1973 to 1995, France's average rate of growth fell from 5.1 to 2.7 percent; Germany's from 6.0 to 2.7 percent; and Sweden's from 4.1 to 1.5 percent. During the 1960s, unemployment in Western Europe averaged a lowly 1.6 percent. By the end of the 1970s, unemployment rose to more than 7 percent. In Italy, which had enjoyed 3.2 percent unemployment in 1971, unemployment among 14- to 29-year-olds rose to 17.2 percent by the decade's end.

As the economy slowed, government revenues declined, while social welfare expenditures rose sharply. In 1976, with deficits soaring and balances of payments in arrears, both Great Britain and Italy had to ask for loans from the International Monetary Fund. Throughout Western Europe, governments tried to limit wage increases in the face of inflationary pressures, but faced militant opposition from powerful labor unions. In Italy, a wave of strikes and student demonstrations from 1969 through 1973 forced concessions in wages and social benefits. In Britain, a miners' strike in early 1974 caused the Conservative government to declare a three-day workweek to conserve energy. During the boom, wage increases could be absorbed by higher productivity; but during the slowdown and inflation, they only increased pressure on prices, threatening the balance of trade.

All in all, the slowdown undermined social democratic and Keynesian policy. It turned a virtuous circle into a vicious one. Because of rising oil and food prices, deficits meant to stimulate the

116   economy and reduce unemployment could lead to inflation, which in turn could undermine investment and reduce employment. With heightened competition within a global free market, deficits could lead to more demand for imports and to a growing trade deficit, which threatened a country's currency. These pitfalls of the old approach became apparent first in Great Britain and France. The European version of neoliberalism arose out of the experience that these two countries faced.

In the winter of 1978–79, attempts by Labour prime minister James Callaghan to limit wage increases led to a wave of strikes, creating what was called the "winter of discontent." Callaghan's failure to halt Britain's combination of inflation and unemployment led to his defeat in 1979 by Tory Margaret Thatcher. Thatcher had broken with her own party's commitment to Keynesianism. She resorted to what came to be called a neoliberal strategy. She focused on increasing the "supply side"—corporate rates of profit—rather than the demand side. By curtailing the money supply, she raised interest rates, which created a deep recession, which in turn reduced the pressure on wages and prices and the demand for imports, forced obsolete firms out of business, and helped bolster profit rates in the firms that survived.

Thatcher also removed regulations on industry and finance, and lowered taxes on business and the wealthy. She privatized some government industries, and attempted to downsize others. When coal miners resisted massive layoffs in 1984, Thatcher held out successfully against them, as Ronald Reagan had done against the air traffic controllers. Over 250,000 jobs in national industries were lost, but as a result, the remaining industries became more efficient, and after 1984, the economy began to slowly pick up. Writes historian Tony Judt, "There is no doubt that Britain's economic performance *did* improve in the Thatcher years, after an initial decline from 1979–81."

But, as happened in the United States, the distance between the top earners and those in the middle and bottom widened, and the middle-income blue-collar worker was threatened with extinction. During Thatcher's years (when the top income tax rate dropped from 60 to 40 percent), the top fifth of all earners increased their share of the nation's income from 36 to 42 percent. Manufacturing, a source of many middle-income jobs, fell from 18 percent of GDP when she took office to 15 percent when she left in 1992. The trend toward inequality continued under Britain's subsequent Labour and Tory governments. By 2010, manufacturing accounted for 10 percent of GDP, and inequality had continued to rise.

In France, inflation had climbed to 14 percent by the 1981 presidential election, and 1.5 million were unemployed. That allowed François Mitterrand to be elected the first Socialist Party president of the Fifth Republic. Mitterrand tried to develop an alternative to Thatcher's neoliberalism. Elected in 1981 after a center-right government had failed to halt France's slide, Mitterrand and his advisors assumed that the downturn had exhausted itself and that global demand would soon be picking up. With a parliamentary majority, Mitterrand and the Socialists enacted a huge boost in social spending aimed at redistributing wealth and fueling consumer demand, and they undertook extensive nationalizations to assure that the profits businesses received were reinvested. If it wasn't socialism, it was a leftwing version of Charles de Gaulle's command economy.

Mitterrand's policies did boost economic growth. France's economy grew 2 percent in his first two years, while most of Europe's economies were in recession. But by the same token, with the rest of Europe and the United States in recession, the demand for France's exports lagged well behind French consumers' demands for imports. France's trade deficit almost doubled during Mitterrand's first year. That created a balance of payments crisis.

Ordinarily, a country running very large trade deficits can devalue its currency, which would make its imports more expensive and its exports cheaper. But France feared devaluation. Oil was priced in dollars, and if France were to devalue its currency, its oil bills would soar, negating any effect the devaluation would have on

118 its trade balance. In addition, France, concerned about its currency being destabilized by a floating dollar, had agreed in 1979 to join with West Germany and the four other members of the European Economic Community in creating a European Monetary System (EMS) that required maintaining its currency within a fixed range.

Mitterrand's minister of research of industry, Jean-Pierre Chevenement, advocated leaving the EMS and letting the Franc fall. But Mitterrand, who was also under the sway of the "Franc fort" (strong Franc) as a symbol of France's greatness, decided instead to go along a similar road as Thatcher. Beginning in 1982, he reduced demand for imports by reducing consumer demand through cuts in spending and tax increases and by freezing wages. Unemployment rose from 7.3 percent in 1981 to 10.5 percent in 1985, but inflation slowed and the trade balance improved, and after falling, growth began to inch up. It wasn't entirely clear at the time, but Callaghan's failure and Mitterrand's U-turn signaled the end of postwar consensus around social democracy and Keynesian economics.

Socialist Lionel Jospin, who was prime minister under Mitterrand's successor, Jacques Chirac, ended up privatizing more of the firms that Mitterrand had nationalized and reducing taxes on the wealthy. After being highly critical during the election of the EU's growth and stability pact limiting the size of deficits, Jospin adhered to it. After taking office in Germany in 1999, Social Democratic chancellor Gerhard Schröder oversaw an agreement between German unions and management to hold down wages. In 2003, Schröder championed the controversial Hartz laws that also put downward pressure on wages. In 2003, Schröder championed the controversial Hartz laws that made it easier for firms to hire and fire workers. Labour prime minister Tony Blair, who took office in 1997, continued Thatcher's policy of deregulating finance and business. Asked in 2002 what her greatest achievement was, Thatcher replied, "Tony Blair and New Labour. We forced our opponents to change their minds."

Some of the Socialist, Social Democratic, and Labour parties
succeeded in winning office and even reelection, as Blair did, but
in abandoning their support for an expanding public sector and for
viable manufacturing industries in favor of supporting free trade,
deregulated finance, and a globalized capitalism, they began to for-
feit the loyalty of their working-class constituents. That, along with
the disintegration of the Communist parties in France and Italy after
the fall of the Soviet Union, left an opening for a new appeal to the
working classes. And the opening, particularly for a rightwing populism, was enlarged by an additional factor—the rapid growth of a
non-European immigrant population at the same time job opportunities were no longer plentiful.

Immigrants and Islamists
During the boom years, Northern European countries, faced with
severe labor shortages, began actively recruiting guest workers. In
West Germany, there were 95,000 recruited workers in 1956; by
1966, there were 1.3 million. Two million migrant workers came
into France from 1946 to 1970, along with 690,000 dependents.
Belgium, the Netherlands, Great Britain, Denmark, and Switzerland had similar programs. And in these countries, employers began
recruiting workers independently without authorization. Some
countries like Sweden opened their borders to any immigrant who
wanted to work. And former colonial powers like France encouraged
their former subjects to emigrate. By the early 1970s, there were 4.1
million foreign-born workers in Germany; 1 million in Switzerland;
and 3.4 million in France.

During this time, there was little anti-immigrant sentiment
in Western Europe. The migrants didn't compete with the natives
for jobs, and they were seen as temporary residents who would
eventually return home. But the situation changed in the 1970s
when labor shortages transformed into labor surpluses. Western
Europe ended formal recruitment of foreign workers and even

120   offered workers financial incentives to return to their homelands, but that had unexpected consequences. Workers from other European countries tended to return home, while workers from Africa and the Middle East, where economic conditions were worse than those in recession-hammered Europe, stayed and took advantage of the legal opportunity to bring their families to live in Europe, where they reproduced at a higher rate than native Europeans. As a result, the numbers of immigrants continued to rise, and the proportion of those that came from non-European societies did as well. In France, the proportion of immigrants from the Maghreb region of western North Africa increased by 16 percentage points from 1968 to 1982.

In the '80s and '90s, a dramatic increase in asylum-seeking refugees from Africa and Asia further swelled the proportions of non-European immigrants—from 75,000 in 1983 to almost 320,000 in 1989. Since then, these numbers have continued to grow. In Denmark, the number of non-European immigrants increased by 268,902, or 520 percent, between 1980 and 2005, making up 90 percent of the total increase of immigrants to Denmark. Where the previous generation of immigrants had often worked in manufacturing, many now found themselves without jobs or taking menial jobs in hotels, restaurants, or in construction. They clustered in downscale communities inside or on the outskirts or Paris, Marseilles, Antwerp, Brussels, Rotterdam, or Copenhagen. Crime became rife in many of these communities, and some of them, largely populated by Muslims, became cut off culturally from native communities.

Fear and anger over the influx of immigrants from non-European countries began to show up in European polling in the early 1990s. In the Eurobarometer polls taken by the European Commission in 1991, 23 percent of respondents from the 12 nations of the European Economic Community thought that their countries should not accept immigrants from countries south of the Mediterranean. In France, it was 33 percent; in Denmark, 25 percent. In France, 56 percent of respondents thought their country had too many immigrants, and 24 percent thought that France should not accept people seeking asylum. There was a pronounced jump even from 1988. In the autumn 1988 survey, 18 percent of respondents in the EC countries had wanted the rights of immigrants restricted; by 1991, it was 33 percent.

According to the first European Social Survey, done in 2002, the main complaints about immigrants (in this order) were that they made crime worse, took out more social benefits than they paid for in taxes, and took jobs away from natives. Many European leaders ignored or denigrated these sentiments. The European Commission that studied attitudes toward immigrants was called "The Commission of Enquiry on Racism and Xenophobia in Europe." Initially, political parties, especially the Socialist and Social Democratic parties, urged acceptance of the immigrants, including immigrants who had entered the countries illegally. That left a political vacuum that the rightwing populist parties filled.

The Populist Right

Many of today's populist organizations in Western Europe can trace their ancestry from the anti-tax groups of the 1970s (which resemble the American anti-tax movement of those same years) and from nationalist organizations with questionable ties to former fascists and Nazis. Jean-Marie Le Pen, the founder of the National Front, got his start in French bookstore owner Pierre Poujade's anti-tax movement of the 1950s. The National Front, which Le Pen founded in 1972, combined remnants of Poujade's shopkeepers' movement with critics of France's decolonization, some of whom, like Le Pen, looked back favorably on Vichy France and downplayed the evils of Hitler's Germany. During the 1970s, the FN, which was militantly anti-communist and anti-tax, barely counted in the polls. The FN got 0.76 percent in the 1974 presidential election.

The Danish People's Party was a spin-off from the Progress Party, which tax lawyer Mogens Glistrup founded in 1973. Glistrup, who eventually went to jail for tax evasion, called for abolishing the income tax. The party did surprisingly well in the 1970s, but less

122 so in the 1980s when the Liberals and Conservatives coopted its anti-tax message. It was revived in 1995 when Pia Kjærsgaard split off and formed the People's Party. The Austrian Freedom Party grew out of the postwar League of Independents, which included former Nazis, and advocated the restoration of the German nation. In 1956, it was succeeded by the Freedom Party, which continued (but moderated) the League's German nationalism, and which functioned as a submissive junior partner to the reigning Social Democratic and Christian Democratic parties. Like the other parties, it initially combined nationalism with libertarian anti-tax economics.

Then, from roughly the late 1980s through the early 2000s, these and other older parties, as well as some new populist parties that formed, took off and became players in Western European politics. The National Front, which gravitated between 10 and 15 percent in national elections in the 1990s, got 16.8 percent for Le Pen as its presidential candidate in the first round in 2002, knocking Socialist prime minister Lionel Jospin out of the runoff. In its very first national election in 1998, the Danish People's Party got 7 percent. Then, in November 2001, it received 13 percent, putting it in third place. The Austrian Freedom Party went from 16.1 percent in 1990 to 26.9 percent in 1999. The Swiss People's Party went from 11.9 percent in 1991 to 22.5 percent in 1999. And the Norwegian Progress Party went from 3.5 percent in 1985 to 13 percent in 1989 to 15.3 percent in 1997, making it Norway's second largest party.

The most immediate factor in the parties' rise was the way they tied themselves to the growing popular disapproval of non-European immigrants and asylum seekers. During the last two decades of the twentieth century, the parties turned their attention from communism and taxes to immigration. In the fall of 1992, the Austrian Freedom Party announced an "Austria First" initiative that included a constitutional amendment declaring Austria a land of non-immigrants. The new Danish People's Party, formed out of the Progress Party in 1995, introduced a ten-point plan that called for repatriating asylum seekers and repealing Social Democratic

legislation that had allowed immigrants to vote in local elections   123
after three years. In Norway, the Progress Party, which had earlier
been divided over its attitude toward immigration, adopted a hardline stance in the 1997 elections, raising its national vote from 6.3
percent in 1993 to 15.3 percent.

In his study of the European politics of immigration, Christopher Caldwell described the Danish People's Party as "the most
immigrant-obsessed party in Europe." Unlike other Western European countries, Denmark largely escaped the downturn that came in
the 1970s. Of European countries, it has one of the most generous
welfare states, and the least economic inequality. What sparked
the backlash to immigration and asylum seeking were sociocultural rather than strictly economic concerns. Danes weren't worried
that immigrants would take their jobs, but that they wouldn't work
at all and would become free riders on Denmark's generous welfare
system. (Denmark, for instance, grants up to 90 percent of previous
salary for four years for workers who lose their jobs.) That concern
was partly economic, but more broadly it stemmed from the idea
that the Danish welfare state, financed by high taxes, was based on
mutual trust among Danish citizens who shared the same values of
work and family and who would not take advantage of the Danish
state's generosity. As more Muslim immigrants from the Middle
East and North Africa entered Denmark, the critics of immigration
also raised concerns about crime and religious practices.

Much of the inspiration for the People's Party stand on immigration came from a Lutheran pastor, Søren Krarup. "Between Glistrup and the founding of the People's Party is a gap," Mikael Jalving,
a columnist for *Jyllands-Posten* and the author of a book on Krarup,
explained. "The gap was taken up by Søren Krarup." Beginning in the
1980s, Krarup argued that Danes had a special culture informed by
Lutheranism to which Islam, which he saw as a political movement
and not simply a religion, was antithetical. Krarup's crusade against
Denmark's immigration policies was sparked by the Danish Parliament's passage in 1983 of an Alien Act welcoming refugees who had

124   begun pouring into Europe from the Iran-Iraq war, and who after the act began entering Denmark annually by the thousands rather than hundreds. Krarup denounced the act as "legal suicide" for allowing "the uncontrolled and unconstrained mass migration of Mohammedan and Oriental refugees [who] come through our borders." In 1997, Krarup was invited to address the newly formed People's Party's convention, and in 2001, he was elected to Parliament from the party and headed its immigration and naturalization committee.

The People's Party campaigns were incendiary. One campaign poster from 1999 showed a woman with a *burqa*. The text read: "Your Denmark: A multiethnic society with rapes, violence, insecurity, forced marriages, oppressed women, gang crimes." The leading Social Democratic and Liberal parties dismissed the party and its leader, Pia Kjærsgaard, who had been a home health aide. In a debate in Parliament that year, Social Democratic prime minister Poul Nyrup Rasmussen told her, "You are not house-trained," using a word, *stuerene*, that normally refers to animals who have not learned to urinate in litter boxes.

But Kjærsgaard had the last laugh on Rasmussen. After the September 11, 2001, al Qaeda attack in the United States, concern about Islamic immigrants rose in Europe. In that November's election, which was dominated by the issue of immigration, the People's Party's 13 percent of the vote helped deprive the Social Democrats of the largest number of seats in Parliament for the first time since the party's formation in 1924. A majority of blue-collar workers backed the People's Party and the Liberal Party.

In France, the issue of immigration had become interwoven with the issue of Islamic integration as early as the 1980s when a controversy broke out over Muslim girls wearing headscarves to school. In 1995, an Islamic group set off bombs in the Paris subway. In April 2002, French concern over Islamic immigration, reinforced by the September 11 attacks, played a role in Jean-Marie Le Pen's second place finish over Jospin, who had legalized 80,000 immigrants who had entered France illegally.

The same concerns also contributed to an astonishing election
in the Netherlands. In the Netherlands, the major party leadership
strongly supported immigration and the ideal of a multicultural
Holland. When Hans Janmaat, the leader of the dissident Center
Democrats, declared in 1997 that "Holland is not a country of immigrants" and "we will abolish the multicultural society as soon as we
get the chance and power," he was indicted and convicted for inciting
racial hatred. In 2002, in the wake of September 11, Pim Fortuyn,
a colorful public speaker and magazine columnist who had been
kicked out of another party because of his anti-Islamic views, established his own party, the Pim Fortuyn List, and campaigned against
Islam's influence in Holland. Fortuyn was assassinated nine days
before the election by a leftwing activist who objected to his attacks
on Islam, but in the election, Fortuyn's party still took 17 percent of
the vote, making it the second largest in Parliament. Without Fortuyn, the party eventually fell apart, but it was succeeded in 2006 by
Geert Wilders's highly successful Party for Freedom.

Populists and the Welfare State
As populist parties gained support for their stand against immigration, they widened their political base. The first populist parties, such as the National Front and the Freedom Party, had been
petit-bourgeoisie parties. Their members were drawn primarily from
small towns in the countryside, and were small business proprietors
and small farmers—many of the same groups that had launched populism in the United States and spearheaded the rightwing in Europe
between the world wars. But in the 1990s, Europe's populist parties grew largely by expanding their base into working-class constituencies that had formerly supported Social Democrats, Socialists,
Laborites, and Communists. In France, Le Pen's National Front began
winning support in blue-collar towns in the North. Voters who had
backed Socialist François Mitterrand in the 1988 presidential race
accounted for one-third of Le Pen's support in the 1995 presidential
contest. "We are the party of the working class," Le Pen boasted.

126   That wasn't just because these parties were critical of immigrants. It was also because these parties, which had once reflected the anti-tax, anti-government views of small business, began to embrace parts of the social democratic agenda on welfare and government. In France, Le Pen's National Front became a defender of the welfare state. It no longer called for the abolition of the income tax. Denmark's People's Party broke with its parent group's anti-tax focus. It became a defender of Denmark's generous public sector, with the proviso that its benefits be limited to Danes. Norway's Progress Party took a similar tack in the 1997 elections.

In Austria in the early 1990s, the Freedom Party, which had been steadfastly libertarian in its economics, took advantage of the dominant parties' embrace of neoliberalism. In order to prepare for EU membership, the Social Democratic Party and Austrian People's Party, working in a "grand coalition," had championed massive privatization of Austria's industries, which led to the loss of about 100,000 jobs. In response to the public clamor over the move, the Freedom Party became a defender of the welfare state and critic of the EU's economics and globalization. The strategy worked. In the 1986 elections, 10 percent of the party's voters were blue-collar workers; by 1999, 47 percent were. Rightwing populist parties got the same kind of results throughout Western Europe. Thanks to the reaction to immigration and neoliberalism, what had been petit-bourgeois parties had become workers' parties.

The Founding of the European Union
The final reason for the rise of the populist right was the operation of the European Union and of the Eurozone. After World War II, French and German leaders, eager to avoid another continental war, took the first steps in integrating their economies. In 1951, France and West Germany, along with the Netherlands, Luxembourg, Belgium, and Italy, established the European Coal and Steel Community on lands that the two world wars had been fought over. In 1957, the six nations established a free trade area, the European Economic

Community. Then in 1992, at Maastricht, the six, plus Greece, Spain, Portugal, the UK, Ireland, and Denmark, took the fateful step of setting up a European Union, within which goods and people could move freely. The countries, except for Denmark and the UK, also committed themselves to a common currency, the Euro, which would begin circulating in 1999.

France and Germany were always the main movers behind the EU; their principal motive was to integrate Germany into a European community. But economics also figured in the design of the EU. Once, after the United States abandoned Bretton Woods, Europe's currencies began floating in value, and smaller countries like the Netherlands that were dependent on exports wanted to provide some stability to their currencies. Former French finance minister Dominique Strauss-Kahn described the Euro as "a tool to help us . . . resist irrational shifts in the market." The French also thought (mistakenly) that by subordinating the Deutschmark to a European Central Bank, which would be in charge of the Euro, France would no longer be subordinate to Germany's economy. And lesser economies like those of Spain, Greece, or Italy wanted the lower interest rates and greater foreign investment that they expected would come from having the same currency as the Germans and French. But whether wittingly or not, the EU and Eurozone institutionalized the rule of neoliberalism.

To accept the subordination of their currency to the Euro, the Germans demanded and got agreement from the other countries to a Stability and Growth Pact that put the ECB in charge of limiting members' deficits to 3 percent of GDP and debt to 60 percent of GDP. The Eurozone members believed that by limiting deficits, they would limit domestic inflation and therefore would keep the relationship among their countries in balance. This proved to be mistaken, but together with the creation of the Euro itself, the Stability and Growth Pact did have the effect of ruling out Keynesian strategies for economic recovery. The Keynesian strategy had relied on running deficits. If the deficits threatened to upset the trade balance,

128   the country could use tariffs or a devaluation to protect its balance of payments. But devaluations were now impossible and tariffs forbidden. As a result, the dominant center-left or center-right parties found themselves hamstrung in the face of economic downturns and open to challenge from the populist right and left.

In its founding, the EU also adopted a principle of freedom of movement for people and businesses ("freedom of establishment") among its member nations. That reflected a desire to establish a common identity among the nations that had been at war with each other. But it also reflected business priorities. As the EU expanded eastward, European businesses in the West liked the idea of being able to import lower-wage labor from the East for restaurants, hotels, and construction without having to file papers. And businesses in the higher-wage West were now free to move their factories to the lower-wage East, as many began to do.

Labor unions grumbled at the freedom of establishment, while the rightwing populists took aim at the policy of open borders, which had the effect of undermining member countries' efforts to control immigration and asylum-seeking. Open borders meant, for instance, that legal or illegal immigrants or asylum seekers from North Africa could migrate from France or Italy to the Netherlands or Denmark. During the debate in Denmark in 1998 over the ratification of the Treaty of Amsterdam, which affirmed the EU's acceptance of open borders, the "no" vote ran a campaign headlined, "Welcome to 40 million Poles."

But the EU's administration was insulated from these protests. The EU's economic and immigration policies were chosen and reviewed by the member countries, but in such a way that the average citizen had little input into them. Of the EU's principal institutions, only one, the European Parliament, was elected directly—and it only had the power to approve or disapprove proposals and budgets submitted by the European Commission, whose members were appointed by the leaderships of the member states. The European Commission oversaw the daily operations of the EU, including its bureaucracy. The European Central Bank was controlled by a council of representatives from member banks. The European Court of Justice was appointed by member states. It was to issue rulings, but its deliberation and opinions were kept secret. In his prescient book about the European Union, Perry Anderson wrote, "What the core structures of the EU effectively do is to convert the open agenda of parliaments into the closed world of chancelleries."

Some leaders of the populist right were initially in favor of the EU. Jean-Marie Le Pen saw it as a vehicle for French dominance of the continent and a bulwark against Soviet communism. In the National Front's 1985 platform, he wrote, "The European Union will remain utopia as long as the Community doesn't have sufficient resources, a common currency and a political will, which is inseparable from the ability to defend itself." But after the fall of the Soviet Union and after it had become clear that the EU would have a will of its own, Le Pen soured on it, comparing Maastricht to the Treaty of Troyes, which in the fifteenth century ceded the throne of France to England.

Other populist parties joined in rejecting the EU's "democracy deficit." The Danish People's Party called for Denmark to leave the EU. The Swedish Democrats declared, "European cooperation is a good thing, but a new European superstate is not." The populist parties' unhappiness with the EU was shared by many European voters. In preparation for signing the treaty at Maastricht, France and Denmark held referenda. The French barely approved the treaty by 51.1 percent, and the Danes defeated it by a similar margin, narrowly approving it later after Denmark was allowed to opt out of several provisions. After the EU invited Norway to join, 52.2 percent of its voters turned membership down. Sweden's voters narrowly approved membership by 52.8 percent. In September 2000, 53.2 percent of Danes voted against joining the Eurozone; and three years later, 56.1 percent of Swedes rejected the Eurozone.

In response to widespread dissatisfaction with the EU's structure, the federation's leadership adopted a new constitution that

130   made minor adjustments. But in 2005, 54.9 percent of French voters and 61.5 percent of Dutch voters rejected the constitution. At that point, the EU withdrew the constitution, and relabeled it a treaty so that it would not have to be subject to popular ratification. That sparked cries of bureaucratic manipulation. Within the EU, opposition to the new constitution was led by the populist right parties, and as with their opposition to immigration, Islam, and neoliberal austerity, it boosted their support among the public. It also allowed those parties, which had been tainted by their links to European authoritarianism, to claim the mantle of democracy.

The Limits of Leftwing Populism

Syriza and Podemos

From 2003 through 2007, Europe seemed to be in passable shape. Growth in Europe averaged a low, but not disastrous 2.75 percent a year. The unemployment rate fell from 9.2 percent to 7.2 percent. The populist wave receded. But the financial crash that spread to Europe in late 2008 and the growth in refugees and Islamist terrorism that seemed to be tied to Western interventions and civil wars in the Middle East, South Asia, and North Africa sparked a populist revolt.

This populist reaction was different from the 1990s in one important respect. In the northern tier, where the Great Recession did not strike as forcefully, and where many of the asylum-seekers clustered, rightwing populism predominated. But in Southern Europe, where unemployment reached Great Depression levels, a new leftwing populism emerged in Spain, Greece, and Italy. When the major center-left and center-right parties, hobbled by their country's membership in the Eurozone, failed to revive their nation's economies, voters began looking to the new populist parties in these countries for answers.

The Eurocrisis

The financial crash, which surfaced in the United States in September 2008 with the collapse of Lehman Brothers, spread by the year's end to European banks, which had heavily invested in American derivatives. Credit dried up, borrowers defaulted, investment lagged, and unemployment rose. By 2009, the EU's average unemployment rate was 9.6 percent; in 2012, it would be 11.4 percent. And it would be far worse in Southern Europe—18 percent in Spain in 2009 and 25.1 percent in 2012. By 2012, the United States would begin pulling out of the Great Recession, but in Southern Europe it would endure, and would call into question the viability of the EU and the Euro.

In the United States, the immediate cause of the crash was financial deregulation and fraud. In Western Europe, the cause of the deepening recession was perverse financial regulation. The Eurozone, which went into effect in 1999, included 19 nations at varying degrees of economic development and with very different kinds of economies. Germany and the Netherlands, for instance, were export-driven high-tech economies. Under Gerhard Schröder, German unions had agreed to restrain their wage demands. As a result, German wages actually ran behind productivity in the 2000s, making German products extremely competitive within the EU and internationally, and resulting in soaring trade surpluses.

Spain and Greece, by contrast, had lower-tech economies that relied on construction, tourism, financial services, and agriculture. Until they joined the Eurozone, these economies had managed to keep their current accounts balanced at moments of crisis by devaluing their currency. (Spain had devalued its currency four times between 1992 and 1995.) But when they joined the Eurozone, they no longer had control of their exchange rates. What they lost in flexibility, however, they seemed initially to gain in attractiveness for foreign investors. In the past, foreign investors might have worried that they would lose money if one of these countries got in trouble and devalued its currency. But with the Euro, regulated

by the ECB, that wouldn't happen in Spain any more than it would
happen in Germany.

So, in the early 2000s, when Spain and Greece (as well as the other PIIGS, Portugal, Ireland, and Italy) ran large trade deficits, foreign investors, led by Germany, plowed their trade surpluses back into these deficit countries in the form of bank loans and bond purchases. In the 2000s, the demand-driven economies enjoyed a boom in office, home, and hotel construction; they were able to sell their government bonds; salaries and wages rose above productivity; and unemployment fell. Their membership in the Eurozone seemed to be an unmitigated blessing.

But when the financial crash hit, credit dried up internationally, home and office buyers began defaulting, and investors began pulling out of these countries. The Spanish and Greek banks that had funded the new hotels and housing developments and office buildings were suddenly stuck with billions in bad loans. (The area outside Madrid has remained dotted with large, unfinished housing developments.) With the banks threatening to go under, the Spanish and Greek governments attempted to bail them out, but that merely transferred the bad loans and the debts from private banks into the public sector, and created a "sovereign debt crisis."

These debts proved a mortal risk to these countries. As the debts mounted, the bond rating agencies lowered the countries' ratings, and interest rates on their payments rose, enlarging, in effect, the debts themselves. To repeat: Under normal circumstances, these countries could have begun to dig themselves out of a fiscal hole through devaluation, but that option was closed as long as they remained in the Eurozone. That left three options. First, they could convince the creditor countries, chiefly but not exclusively Germany, to forgive their debts. That proved impossible. The German electorate, along with the Finns and Dutch, loudly protested any bailout. Second, they could leave the Eurozone entirely and accept radical devaluation of their new currency. But voters in these countries didn't want to leave the Eurozone. They feared chaos and, particularly among

134   the elderly, the loss of savings and of fixed incomes. Or third, these countries could undertake a severe version of what Mitterrand had to do in 1982—curtail spending and raise taxes resulting in even higher unemployment, but also a reduced demand for imports, and eventually and hopefully, by lowering wage costs, more competitive exports.

Greece was one of the first countries unable to service its debts. When the center-right New Democracy Party, which controlled the government, asked for aid from the "Troika" of the European Commission, ECB, and IMF, the Troika demanded in exchange that Greece take harsh austerity measures to shrink the public sector, reduce wages, raise taxes, and privatize public assets. Facing protests, the New Democracy government balked and called new elections, which the Panhellenic Socialist Movement (PASOK) under George Papandreou won.

When economist Yanis Varoufakis, who was then advising PASOK, advocated defaulting on the debts, the leadership dismissed such an idea as "treasonous." Seemingly at a loss, the Socialist government signed a memorandum in May 2010 with the Troika that in exchange for 110 billion Euros in loans, which would be recycled back to the original creditors, Greece would undertake harsh austerity measures. These included massive budget cuts and a sharp increase in Greece's value added tax (VAT). These measures depressed demand and led to higher unemployment. Due to the closure of businesses, they also increased the budget deficit. "The sovereignty of Greece will be massively limited," Jean-Claude Juncker, the former president of the European Commission, boasted.

After settling with Greece, the Troika dealt with Spain, which was also being ruled in 2010 by socialists, the Spanish Socialist Workers' Party, or PSOE. In exchange for 50 billion Euros in loans, the Spanish government agreed to sharp budget cuts, including the end to a family allowance provision and the reduction of old-age insurance through extending the retirement age. After the Socialist government had been voted out of office in November 2011 and replaced by the center-right People's Party, the Spanish government agreed to even more draconian budget cuts, including a big increase in the VAT, and a labor law that would make it much easier for employers to fire workers.

Measures of austerity like this can work, as Thatcher's experience in the 1980s showed, but only when the country undergoing them already has viable export industries (which can include financial services) *and* is surrounded by countries with buoyant economies that are eager to buy imported goods and services and to invest in lower-wage industries. Greece did not benefit from either of these conditions—and Spain only benefited marginally. In Greece, the Troika's austerity measures merely made things even worse, and led to further bailout talks, and to additional measures of austerity. These measures also sparked a populist revolt directed against the EU's false promises of prosperity and against both the Socialist and center-right parties that had agreed to them.

Syriza's Ascent to Power

Greece only emerged from the shadow of dictatorship in 1974 when the ruling colonels were forced out by their own military sponsors after they provoked a war with Turkey in Cyprus. Constantine Karamanlis and New Democracy won elections the next year, but in 1981, the Socialists under Andreas Papandreou, the father of George, took office, and with occasional interruptions from New Democracy, remained in power for most of the next thirty years.

PASOK succeeded in creating a low-grade version of social democracy in Greece, with a system of pensions, a National Health Service, and a public sector at roughly the size—16 percent of GDP—of some other EU states. What PASOK failed to do was limit the high degree of tax evasion from the country's wealthy and from its large shadow economy, or reform the parties' practice of using the state sector as a bribe-taking patronage machine. Tax evasion deepened

136 the nation's deficits, and corruption by public officials bred distrust of both major parties, opening the way to a challenge to their rule from the left.

Greece's Communist Party had emerged from the dictatorship divided between an exterior wing that had remained out of the country and was totally subordinate to the Soviet Union and an interior "Eurocommunist" wing that sought to make Greece a democratic member of the European community. In 1989, with the Cold War waning, the two wings of the party came together to form Synaspismos, the Coalition of the Left and Progress. The remains of the pro-Soviet Communist Party eventually split off, but in 2004, what remained of Synaspismos joined with feminist and environmental groups to form Syriza, which stood for "coalition of the radical left." Syriza was initially a loose coalition that ran joint candidates, and its first efforts were decidedly mediocre. In the 2004 elections, it got only 3 percent of the vote, and even as late as October 2009, when the onset of the financial crash would sweep the Socialists back in power with 43.9 percent of the vote, Syriza only got 4.6 percent.

But the subservient response of the Socialists and the New Democrats to the EU's demand for austerity transformed Greek politics. Starting in May 2010, when the Socialist government agreed to the EU's demand for steep budget cuts, hundreds of thousands of demonstrators took to the streets in Athens and elsewhere. Many of the demonstrators were students and unemployed youth, but they were joined by striking workers. At the June 2012 elections, Syriza, headed by Alexis Tsipras, a civil engineer who had been a member of the communist youth organization and later the secretary of Synaspismo's youth organization, ran a campaign targeted at the Socialists' concessions to the EU. Syriza promised to rescind the memorandum with the EU, nationalize Greece's banks, raise taxes on the wealthy, and suspend debt repayment until Greece had recovered from the recession. This time, Syriza came in second to New Democracy with an astounding 26.9 percent of the vote. PASOK,

discredited by its embrace of austerity, came in a distant third with
only 12.3 percent. It has still not recovered from this vote.

In the 2012 elections, Syriza did best among young voters, the unemployed, and the urban employed in both public and private sectors. It did worst among housewives, senior citizens, and rural voters. While the party had its roots in the Eurocommunist left, Syriza shifted in 2012 to making a populist appeal. In 2009, Tsipras had barely referred to the "people," but in 2012, it became the constant referent in his speeches—occurring 51 times in his closing electoral address in June. In his speech, Tsipras declared about the coming vote, "Sunday is not just about a simple confrontation between Syriza and the political establishment of the Memorandum. . . . It is about an encounter of the people with their lives. An encounter of the people with their fate. . . . Between the Greece of the oligarchy and the Greece of Democracy."

After its success in the 2012 elections, Syriza ceased to be a coalition and became a united party under Tsipras's leadership. As it prepared for the January 2015 elections, it again focused its platform on rejecting agreements with the Troika—and this now included New Democracy's even more onerous agreement of 2012. "We will prevent our country from being turned into a debt colony," its platform declared. Varoufakis, who had left PASOK and would later become Syriza's finance minister, accused New Democracy's government of "acting like a model prisoner, obeying the Troika's instructions, while, on the side, pleading for a rationalization of the imposed policies, terms, and conditions." Some Syriza members wanted to abandon the Euro altogether, but the party's official position was that it wanted to remain in the Eurozone, but not under the conditions that the Troika had imposed. That set up a populist confrontation with New Democracy and with the Troika.

In the January elections, Greece's voters affirmed Syriza's stand and repudiated the New Democracy government. Syriza carried the legislature and the election with 36.3 percent of the vote to New

138   Democracy's 27.8 percent. (PASOK got a mere 4.7 percent.) Under Greek election law, the winner gets extra votes, so by gaining the support of the small Independent Greeks Party, Syriza took over the government. In February 2015, Tsipras and Varoufakis began negotiating with the Troika for a loan that would allow them to fend off the ECB and IMF, to whom Greece owed payments.

Both men came out fighting, Tsipras announcing that "the Troika is over." But as the negotiations proceeded, the IMF, the ECB, and the EU ministers, led by Germany, which had become the dominant power in the EU and its administration, held tough, demanding still more cuts in spending and tax increases as a condition for new loans, and rejecting the Greeks' plea to forgive part of their debt. Finally, in July, having defaulted on the loan payment to the IMF, Tsipras called for a referendum on whether to accept the Troika's deal. At Syriza's urging, 62 percent of Greeks voted to reject the Troika's offer. The stage seemed set for a final showdown between the Greek people and the Troika.

But Tsipras astonished Greek voters and many in his own party by returning to the talks and agreeing to terms that were even more onerous than the Troika had demanded earlier. More spending cuts, more tax increases, the evisceration of Greece's old-age pensions, new taxes on small and medium businesses that had been the heart blood of Greece's economy, and the sale of the state's remaining assets. Economist Paul Krugman termed the deal "madness." Wrote Krugman, "The European project—a project I have always praised and supported—has just been dealt a terrible, perhaps fatal blow. And whatever you think of Syriza, or Greece, it wasn't the Greeks who did it."

Unemployment in Greece remained at 25 percent and youth unemployment at double that. And Europe's economy remained stagnant. Economists Heiner Flassbeck and Costas Lapavitsas wrote, "The picture that emerges for Greece in view of these trends is simply appalling. The country appears trapped in low-growth equilibrium with exceptionally high unemployment and without command over

the instruments of economic policy that could alter its predicament.
The notion that low wages coupled with deregulation of markets
and privatization of public assets would lead to sustained growth is
entirely without theoretical and empirical foundation."

In the wake of the agreement, Tsipras called for new elections in
September as a vote of confidence. With turnout down, Syriza edged
the New Democracy again by 35.5 to 28.1 percent, but as Tsipras and
Syriza neared their second year of rule, their prospects darkened.
The Troika—now joined by a new institution, the European Stability Mechanism, making it a Quartet—continued to be in charge of
Greek economic policy, and continued to force further austerity in
exchange for bridge loans. Tsipras's government complained about
the terms but then, with a narrow 153–147 edge in the Greek Parliament, acceded to the Quartet's demand. In January and again in
May, huge protests greeted the new austerity measures, including a
three-day general strike. In polls in May 2016, Syriza already trailed
New Democracy.

PASOK had virtually disappeared, but in an odd way, Syriza
had replaced it as the center-left component of Greece's two-party
monopoly. Syriza no longer fought the establishment, but had in
effect become the center-left component of it, as PASOK was. It no
longer advanced demands that separated the people from an intransigent elite, but instead tried to nip away at the margins of the bad
deal forced upon it by the Troika-turned-Quartet. Economist James
Galbraith, who advised Syriza, argued it still had "a radical constituency that . . . would rally to any authentic opposition force if one
existed—which has proved for various reasons objectively impossible." But he acknowledged that it had come to operate "as the
unwilling agents of the Berlin finance ministry."

Political theorist Stathis Kouvelakis, who served on Syriza's
central committee, but quit over the July deal with the Troika, wrote
that the only way to put Greece back together is for it to leave the
Eurozone. "It's impossible to fight austerity or neoliberalism within
the framework of the existing monetary union, and, most likely, of

140   the EU as such. A rupture is indispensable," he wrote. But if such a rupture was ever possible in the days after the July referendum, the moment for it passed. As a populist party promising to fight against the forces trying to impose austerity upon the country, Syriza appeared to have failed, and it would pay at the price at the polls. In the July 2019 elections, Tsipras and Syriza were soundly defeated by New Democracy.

Podemos: Yes We Can
Spain, like Greece, never experienced the post—World War II flowering of social democracy that many of the countries in Northern Europe did. Until December 1975, Spain was ruled by dictator Francisco Franco. After Franco's death, his appointed heir, King Juan Carlos de Borbon, and Adolfo Suárez, one of Franco's top lieutenants, arranged for a parliamentary transition. They wanted to be part of Europe. Spanish philosopher Ortega y Gasset had written earlier, "Spain is the problem, and Europe is the solution." Suárez's Union of the Democratic Centre (UCD) won the first election in 1977, and the newly legalized Spanish Socialist Workers' Party (PSOE) came in second. Spain joined NATO in 1982—an important step in taming the Spanish military. But with a recession paralyzing Spain's economy, the UCD decisively lost the election that year to Felipe Gonzalez and the PSOE, which would rule Spain for the next fourteen years.

The PSOE (pronounced peh-soy) is Spain's oldest existing party, founded in 1879. It emerged from the Franco years as a Marxist, revolutionary party, but Gonzalez convinced its membership to remove any hint of Marxism from the party's platform and to fashion itself as a multi-class rather than simply a working-class party. In the 1982 campaign, Gonzalez still advocated nationalizing Spain's banks, creating almost a million new jobs through government spending, and leaving NATO, but he reneged on all these promises. Faced with 16.5 percent unemployment *and* 14.4 percent inflation, influenced by what had happened to Mitterrand in France,

and eager to join the European Economic Community, Gonzalez
adopted a Thatcherite strategy of reducing inflation through tight
money and high interest rates. While the unemployment rate soon
exceeded 20 percent, inflation began to go down.

Gonzalez initially won the grudging support of the labor movement for his economic strategy, but by 1986, Spain's unions were
up in arms, and staged two general strikes that frightened Gonzalez.
Gonzalez then increased government spending, laying the basis for
a rudimentary welfare state. But a steep recession began in 1992.
That, combined with growing charges of corruption—endemic to
Spain's patronage-based party system—contributed to PSOE losing
the 1996 election to the People's Party (PP), a right-center party that
had replaced the UCD as the principal opposition. Over the next two
decades, the PP and PSOE have exchanged rule in the same way as
Greece's PASOK and New Democracy once did.

In 2004, after eight years of PP rule, Spain elected PSOE's
José Luis Rodriguez Zapatero. Zapatero widened the scope of welfare payments and increased the minimum wage, but faced with
the global financial crisis, and pressure from ECB, Zapatero signed
a memorandum in 2010 to raise taxes and cut spending, and on
May 12 that year, announced large spending cuts. Zapatero was following the same path as Papandreou in Greece. A year later on May
15, young demonstrators gathered at Madrid's Puerta del Sol, where
they began a monthlong sit-in that spread throughout Spain.

The occupiers, dubbed the "Indignados" (outraged), were protesting Zapatero's spending cuts, bank evictions of people unable
to pay their mortgages, unemployment, and continuing corruption
in the two major parties. (One sign read, "Democracy is a two-party
dictatorship.") The leaders weren't affiliated with any political
party, and spurned identification with the organized left and the
labor movement. "We are neither right, nor left, we are coming from
the bottom and going for the top," a slogan proclaimed. The protests spread to 57 other cities, and at one point involved as many as
100,000 protesters in Madrid. The demonstrators held assemblies

142 and made proposals. Afterward, many of them continued to meet and demonstrate. In the November 2011 general election, PSOE suffered its worst defeat ever at the hands of the PP, and Mariano Rajoy became prime minister.

Pablo Iglesias, a young leftwing political scientist at Complutense University in Madrid, had begun a television debate show similar to William F. Buckley's *Firing Line*. The show became remarkably popular and the ponytailed Iglesias became a household name. In 2013, as unemployment rose to 26.3 percent in the wake of new spending cuts that Rajoy had imposed at the ECB's behest, Iglesias and other Complutense colleagues began discussing a political party that would capture the energy of the Indignados.

Iglesias had been a member of the youth wing of Spain's Communist Party, which after failing to build an electoral following in post-Franco Spain, had founded a coalition party called the United Left in 1986 that included peace groups and feminist groups. But Iglesias had drifted away from the Communists' hardline Marxism. When he approached them about joining forces, they dismissed him as having "the principles of Groucho Marx." In January 2014, Iglesias and other colleagues from Complutense University announced the formation of a new party, Podemos (We Can)—whose name echoed Obama's presidential campaign slogan.

The party's leadership consisted of political scientists and the leaders from some of the groupuscules that had been part of the May 15 movement. Most were in their thirties or younger. (Several leaders that I interviewed looked as if they would have been carded if they had tried to order a drink at a bar in the United States.) The new party wouldn't be organized like a conventional party. It would make ample use of television and social media to draw people together and to get its message across. It would also have a different political outlook from conventional leftwing groups.

Iglesias and his two closest associates, fellow political scientists Juan Carlos Monedero and Íñigo Errejón, were enthusiastic supporters of the "pink tide" that was sweeping Latin America. It

had begun with Hugo Chavez's election in Venezuela in 1999 and
continued with Evo Morales's victory in Bolivia in 2006. Chavez
and Morales had rejected the classic socialist strategy of championing the working class against the capitalist class and had instead
embraced a populist strategy of rallying their country's "bravo
pueblo" against the oligarchs. Iglesias and Monedero had become
advisors to Chavez, and Errejón had written his doctoral thesis at
Complutense on Morales's revolution. (It would later come out that
Monedero had been paid handsomely by Chavez.)

Monedero, who at 51 was the old man of the party and who had
been the director of the United Left, was a more orthodox leftist,
but Iglesias and Errejón combined the example of Latin American
populism with the work of "post-Marxist" political philosophers
like Ernesto Laclau, an Argentinian who taught at Essex University, and his wife, Belgian Chantal Mouffe. "A recent political initiative in our country would not have been possible," Errejón later
declared, "without the intellectual confirmation and learning from
the processes of change in Latin America" and without "an understanding of the role of speech, common sentiment, and hegemony
that is clearly indebted to the work of Laclau."

Laclau and Mouffe contended that the old leftwing categories of
"working class" and "socialism" were obsolete and had to be replaced
with a populist project pitting the people against elites and aimed
at creating "radical democracy." The goal of a populist party was to
knit diverse groups into a "people" united by a set of demands that
created an ideological "frontier" between the people and the elite.
Unlike other European intellectuals, Laclau and Mouffe defined
populism as a logic that could take either left- or rightwing form.
Errejón became an eager disciple—in 2015, he published a book
of conversations between him and Mouffe that became a bible for
Podemos cadres—and Iglesias in the first years of Podemos also
endorsed Laclau and Mouffe's view of populism.

Iglesias and Errejón called for a conflict between "la gente" and
"la casta"—the latter a Spanish word, but a concept borrowed from

144   the Italian and used by Beppe Grillo. The term referred to the major political and economic interests in Spain, or as Iglesias put it more colloquially in his book, *Politics in a Time of Crisis*, "the thieves who erect political frameworks for stealing democracy from the people." Iglesias and Errejón defined the conflict as being between the people and the elites rather than between "left" and "right." Influenced, perhaps, by the attitude of the Indignados, they saw Spain's left as stagnant and irrelevant—the United Left hadn't mounted a significant electoral challenge in almost two decades. The new party, Errejón explained in *Le Monde Diplomatique*, "would start a process or at least make possible a new political frontier which symbolically postulates the existence of a people not represented by the dominant political castes, and which is beyond left and right metaphors."

They also worried that the major parties would marginalize them by defining them as "the left." Iglesias warned that "when our adversaries dub us the 'radical left' and try, incessantly to identify us with its symbols, they push us onto a terrain where their victory is easier." In his dialogue with Mouffe, Errejón explained that "the elite were very comfortable with the left-right axis. They located themselves at the center-right/center-left, and placed the 'challengers'— those who defied them—at the margins."

Iglesias and Errejón were personally of the left (Podemos's bookstore in its Madrid café is filled with back copies of *New Left Review* and works by contemporary Marxists like David Harvey), but following Laclau and Mouffe, they didn't define Podemos's objective as socialism. "We openly acknowledge we are not opposing a strategy for a transition to socialism," Iglesias told *New Left Review*, "but we are being more modest and adopting a neo-Keynesian approach, like the European left, calling for higher investment, security, social rights, and redistribution." When I asked Segundo González Garcia, a top Podemos leader and a member of Parliament, whether they took any of the Latin American countries as models, he said, "We want our country to be closer to Northern Europe. Our model is closer to Sweden and Norway than Latin America. We want

a welfare state, a guaranteed income." (Spain's welfare state, even   145
before the spending cuts, was far less robust than those of the EU's
northern tier.)

Podemos, like Syriza, was an anti-austerity party contesting
the EU's rules and the Spanish government's capitulation to
them. Iglesias described Podemos's goal as "post-neoliberalism."
Its program that first year called for ending evictions, creating a
government-funded guaranteed annual income, auditing Spain's
debt with a view to not paying what was "illegitimate," making the
Stability and Growth Pact "flexible" and making it include "full
employment" in its objectives, democratization of Brussels and
rejection of the Lisbon Treaty, repeal of Spain's balanced budget law,
and a 35-hour workweek. Together, these demands established a
divide between it and the government and main political parties, as
well as between the Spanish people and Brussels.

By their own admission, Podemos's leaders thought that in
order to extricate Spain fully from the Eurocrisis, Spain would eventually have to abandon the Euro itself, but they were aware that
Spain's voters, who had earlier prospered under the Euro, were
unwilling to contemplate breaking with the EU. After decades of
isolation under Franco, Spanish voters wouldn't support a return to
Spain's own currency. Nacho Álvarez, a colleague of Iglesias at Complutense and Podemos's chief economist, told me, "No progressive
force dares to speak about exiting of the Euro, basically because the
southern populations do not even want to hear about that and this
is surely the only good solution, or at least 'final' solution to recover
democracy and sovereignty." So they limited themselves to threatening to repudiate Spain's debt and demanding a reformulation of
the Stability and Growth Pact.

As the European elections approached in May 2014, few Span-
iards had heard of Podemos. To publicize the party, the leaders put
the well-known Iglesias's photo on their literature. That, too, was
consistent with a populist strategy of using a leader as a unifying
symbol. To their amazement, the party won 8 percent—a significant

146 showing in a multi-party election—and five seats. Podemos's success in the European elections gave the party visibility, and as unemployment mounted, and charges of corruption began flying against the PP government, Podemos's poll numbers began to rise. From December 2014 through April 2015, polls for the forthcoming parliamentary elections in December 2015 actually showed Podemos leading both PP and PSOE.

Podemos's hopes had initially been buoyed by Syriza's success in Greece. In Athens in January 2015, Iglesias joined Tsipras onstage for a closing campaign event. They danced together to a Leonard Cohen song, "First we take Manhattan, then we take Berlin," but changed the lyrics to "First we take Athens, then we take Madrid." But as the furious battle between Syriza and the Troika raged that winter, and as rumors circulated that Greece was going to exit the Eurozone, Iglesias, mindful of Spanish voters' commitment to Europe and the Euro, began backing away from Podemos's identification with Syriza. Iglesias removed a photograph of him and Tsipras from his Twitter feed. "Spain is not Greece," he now declared. Iglesias made clear that Podemos favored reforming, but not leaving the EU and the Eurozone. In addition, Podemos dropped its demand for an audit of the federal debt, which might have justified selective defaults, and for a universal living wage. But after the spectacle of the Greeks rejecting and then Syriza accepting the Troika's demands, Podemos plunged in the polls to as low as 10 percent, falling behind a new center-right anti-corruption party, Ciudadanos, or Citizens.

The PP expected to win reelection. While unemployment was still 23.7 percent on the eve of the election, the economy had started growing, thanks in part to the ECB curiously ignoring a center-right government running deficits that exceeded the 3 percent limit. But Spain's political system was rife with bribes and kickbacks, and as the election approached, 40 PP officials were scheduled to stand trial for a kickback scheme. In the end, the PP got 28.7 percent—the

lowest percentage ever for a leading party—the PSOE 22 percent,
and Podemos got an impressive 20.7 percent.

Podemos's voting base had some similarity to Sanders's voters,
but was broader. Podemos won young voters and the voters in the
large metropolitan areas. Both Madrid and Barcelona elected mayors
affiliated with Podemos. By contrast, PP's base was middle and upper
class, older and rural or small-town, while the PSOE retained its traditional working-class as well as its middle-class support. But once
a two-party system, Spain has become a multi-party system. And as
the results for the December election bore out, neither the PP nor
PSOE had won enough seats for a ready-made majority. The incon-
clusive result led to five months of wrangling among the parties,
highlighted by PSOE's refusal to form a grand coalition with the PP
and Podemos's refusal to subordinate itself to PSOE in a center-left
coalition. The king finally called new elections for the end of June.

As the parties quarreled over the December results, a rift within
Podemos opened up between Iglesias and Errejón. With new elections likely, Iglesias decided that Podemos needed to get enough
votes and parliamentary seats to exceed PSOE. Podemos would then
be able either to be the dominant party in a governing coalition of
the left with PSOE, or if PSOE were to form a grand coalition with PP,
become the leading opposition party. He cast his eye on the United
Left, which had won 3.68 percent of the vote in December, and which
together with Podemos's vote, would have put them over PSOE's
total. In the face of Errejon's opposition to becoming a party of "the
left," Iglesias decided to negotiate a coalition with the United Left,
whose leadership had changed since 2013. He won their agreement
to run a combined slate, Unidos Podemos, in the election.

Iglesias and Podemos acquired the promise of the United Left's
votes without accepting its most radical measures, such as abolishing the monarchy and nationalizing banks. Eager to deflect any
charges of extremism, Podemos crafted a platform for Unidos
Podemos that was only a shade to the left of PSOE. Like PSOE, the

148 groups promised that Spain would adhere to the Eurozone's stability pact, but asked for a "new path of deficit reduction" that would be "more gradual than that raised by the European Commission." They insisted (implausibly) that Spain could meet this deficit target through public investment rather than cuts in social spending; and they asked for a boost in social spending primarily on education and healthcare, while dropping the demand for a guaranteed annual income or 35-hour week. And instead of calling explicitly for the cancellation or reduction of national debts, they called for a European conference to propose "the restructuring of the debt in the Eurozone area."

In the polls leading up to the June 26 election, Unidos Podemos was running well ahead of PSOE and within striking distance of the PP. PSOE and PP struck back by highlighting Podemos's ties to Latin America's authoritarian populism (and the collapse of Venezuela's oil-based economy) and the communist presence in Unidos Podemos. (The headline in the pro-PSOE *El Pais* on the formation of Unidos Podemos read, "Podemos seals deal with communist group to run together in new election.") To counter these charges, Unidos Podemos further attempted to soften its image. In the last weeks, it published its program in the form of a 192-page IKEA catalogue with photos of people using housewares accompanied by a list of 394 largely anodyne "demands," which included an Animal Welfare Act, emotional intelligence, care for forests, and citizen participation in government.

In the election—held on June 26, three days after the British had voted to leave the European Union—Unidos Podemos landed in third with an embarrassing thud. The combined list of Podemos and the United Left got the same number of seats—71 of 350—that the two parties had gotten in December, but they actually received 1.09 million fewer votes, due largely to abstentions in areas that had been Podemos's strongholds in December. PP improved its showing, but still did not have enough seats to form a majority. PSOE got fewer votes than it had in December, but was still far ahead of Unidos

Podemos. Its attempt to displace PSOE as the major party of the left
failed.

Monedero, who had left the party's formal leadership the year
before after the story of his Venezuelan funding broke, but who still
advised Iglesias, blamed Unidos Podemos's disappointing showing
partly on the "campaign of fear" conducted by the PP and PSOE, but
also on Unidos Podemos's failure to present a political alternative
to the PSOE. Monedero charged that the campaign, which was run
by Errejón, was "constantly filing down the rough edges" of its politics. It also relied, he charged, too much on conventional rallies and
on television and eschewed militant street protests with students,
social organizations, and unions. Monedero defended the alliance
with the United Left, contending that Podemos would have done
"even worse" without it. Errejón, in response, reiterated his opposition to having allied with the United Left. "Two plus two did not add
up to four," he said. Errejón said that Podemos had been "trapped" by
the alliance. "On the left-right axis, it is more difficult to build a new
majority," he said. "On that axis, fields remain immobile."

Could Monedero and Errejón have both been right—and wrong?
In the previous election, some voters had backed Podemos as a
populist protest party against the PSOE and PP. But with polls suggesting that Unidos Podemos might actually win, they had evaluated it and Podemos as a governing party and found it wanting. As
Errejón maintained, the alliance with the United Left had probably reinforced the "campaign of fear." So, too, did the British vote
to leave the EU, which caused the Spanish stock market to plunge on
the eve of the election, and may have led many voters to seek a safer
and known harbor in the PSOE and PP.

Monedero also had a point. By watering down their demands,
and failing to distinguish themselves from PSOE either in their
demands or actions, Podemos had abandoned its populist stance for
a center-left reformism and an appearance as just another political
party. Their demands no longer established a frontier between the
people and la casta. They were no longer clearly campaigning against

150   la casta. That may have accounted for many of the abstentions in their political strongholds. Voters were no longer inspired by their message or the way it was delivered.

In Greece, Syriza had abandoned its populist stance when it had come up against the power of the Troika. It had become another left-center party with incremental ambitions. But by the time Syriza abandoned its populism, it had already displaced PASOK. Podemos had no such luck. As Podemos became a party with incremental ambitions, Pedro Sanchez, after winning a leadership struggle in PSOE, moved the party to the left, threatening Podemos's survival. Unidas Podemos's vote declined in successive elections. In the November 2019 election, it came in fourth with 12.9 percent. It agreed to join PSOE's government as a junior partner. Like Syriza, its moment appeared to have passed.

Rightwing Populism on the March in Northern Europe

During the Eurocrisis, leftwing populist groups arose primarily in the South, while rightwing groups fared best in Northern and Central Europe. Much of this had to do with the rise in immigration there. In 2014, there were 280,000 migrants to Europe from the Middle East and North Africa; in 2015, the number grew to over a million. In 2000, 7.1 percent of Danes were first- or second-generation immigrants; in 2016, it was 12.3 percent. Sweden's immigrant population is 22.2 percent. In the United Kingdom, 630,000 immigrants arrived in 2015, which would have been equivalent to 3.2 million immigrants arriving in the U.S. that year.

The rise in immigration coincided with a rise in terrorist attacks, particularly in the North. From December 2010 to March 2016, there were nine major attacks in Europe. Four of the worst occurred in 2015 or 2016: In January 2015, the Charlie Hebdo massacre in Paris claimed 20; the November 2015 Paris attacks by ISIS killed 137; in Brussels in March 2016, three more ISIS suicide bombings left 35 dead; in July, a cargo truck drove into Bastille Day crowds in Nice, killing 85. In addition, there were sexual assaults involving refugees and immigrants from the Middle East and North Africa— the best known occurring in Cologne on New Year's Eve, 2015.

152   Together, the flood of immigrants, the terrorist acts, and sexual assaults lent credence to two decades of agitation by rightwing populist groups against immigrants and Islam.

Denmark and Austria: Populism Amid Prosperity

Leftwing populist groups flourished in the least prosperous European economies. Rightwing populism has found a home in some of the more and most prosperous countries. These are the countries where immigrants and asylum-seekers have aspired to live. Denmark has one of the world's most successful economies. It has the second highest per capita income in the European Union, trailing only Luxembourg. In 2016, it had only 4.6 percent unemployment. It was virtually untouched by the Great Recession. Its Social Democratic government might have been expected to win reelection easily in the June 2015 election; and the Social Democrats did win 26.3 percent, the highest percentage of any party in the election, while the vote for their traditional opposition, the Liberals, fell 7 percentage points, to 19.5 percent. But the Danish People's Party, campaigning on border controls, further restriction of immigration, and a critical approach to the EU, went from 12.3 in 2011 to 21.1 percent in the vote. They held the key to a ruling majority, and with their informal support the Liberals were able to displace the Social Democrats and form a government.

The People's Party didn't actually join the Liberal government, because they disagreed with the Liberal proposal to cut taxes for the rich. Explained Kenneth Kristensen Berth, who joined the party at its inception and is now a member of parliament and a party spokesman, "The problem was that the Liberal Alliance said to the Prime Minister that he should deliver tax relief for the most wealthy in this country. We wouldn't go into government on the basis of tax relief for the most wealthy." Like other rightwing populists, the People's Party are strongly supportive of the welfare state, as long as spending is confined to Danish citizens. In fact, on these issues, Berth acknowledged, they are closer to the Social Democrats. But they parted company with the Social Democrats and are aligned

with the Liberals on preventing asylum seekers from establishing
permanent residence in Denmark. "If we don't fix immigration,
there is no reason to fix the rest," Berth says.

In exchange for informal support from the People's Party, the
Liberals adopted the People's Party's agenda on immigrants, refugees, and Islam. They cut benefits to refugees and immigrants by
45 percent; they required pork in school and daycare menus (to defy
Islamic prohibitions on eating pork); they ordered the confiscation
of refugees' cash and valuables that exceeded $1,450—a move eerily
reminiscent of Nazi confiscation of Jewish valuables. These harsh
stances reflected significant popular opinion.

According to one newspaper poll in January 2016, 70 percent of
Danes thought refugees were the most important issue facing the
country, and 37 percent opposed giving any more resident permits
to refugees. In January 2016, Danish political experts, politicians,
and journalists, including those opposed to the People's Party, told
me they expected the People's Party to succeed politically. "I think
they are going to get the government soon," said Rene Offersen, a
prominent lawyer and Conservative Party member.

But that would not happen. In the wake of the People's Party
success, the Social Democrats adopted the People's Party stance
on repatriation. And the refugee crisis abated. In the 2019 election,
won by the Social Democrats, the People's Party got only 8.7 percent of the vote. It had suffered setbacks before and was likely to
revive, but not in the near future as part or at the head of Denmark's
government.

Austria, like Denmark, has enjoyed relative prosperity. Its unemployment rate from 2012 to 2016 hovered between 4.7 and 5.8 percent.
But its citizens have also been up in arms over refugees. It had 90,000
requests for asylum in 2015, the second most per capita in the EU.
While there were no terrorist attacks on its soil, it had murders and
rapes perpetrated by recent migrants.

Since 2013, Austria had been ruled by a "grand coalition" of the
Social Democrats and the center-right People's Party, with Social

154   Democrat Werner Faymann serving as chancellor. In 2015, Faymann joined German chancellor Angela Merkel in backing open borders for refugees, but when Faymann and his party saw polls showing the rightwing populist Freedom Party ahead in the forthcoming April presidential elections, Faymann changed course. In March, he capped the number of refugees. But it was too late.

In the April 2015 election, the Freedom Party candidate, Norbert Hofer, got 34 percent of the vote, compared to 11 percent each for the Social Democrat and People's Party candidates. In a runoff in May, the Green Party candidate, Alexander Van der Bellen, who had come in second in the first round, barely edged out Hofer by 50.3 to 49.7 percent. But because of improper counting of absentee ballots, Austrian courts ruled there would have to be a revote, which Van der Bellen won. The vote bore out the profile of many rightwing populist groups. Hofer captured nearly 90 percent of the vote among blue-collar workers and rural and small-town voters outside the main metropolises, while the Green Party candidate won white-collar voters and nine of ten cities.

UKIP: The Revolt of the Left-Behinds

Like Denmark and Austria, Great Britain, where the unemployment rate has been falling since September 2011 and was at 5.4 percent in 2016, has proven to be fertile ground for rightwing populism. Having led the successful fight to get Britain to vote itself out of the EU, the United Kingdom Independence Party (UKIP) has had the greatest impact on its country and on the EU of any populist party. That vote reshuffled politics and economics in the UK and cast doubt on the long-term future of the EU.

UKIP was founded in 1993, but remained a marginal single-issue party and pressure group for almost two decades. If it had an overall politics, it was anti-tax, economically libertarian, and socially conservative. Its primary base was in mid- to upscale shires that generally voted Conservative. It got 1 percent in the 1995 parliamentary elections, 2.2 percent in 2005, and 3.1 percent in 2010. Its success

began to come in elections for the European Parliament where it got   155
16.1 percent in 2004 and 16.5 percent in 2009, second only to the
Tories. That reflected the rise in opposition to the EU.

Popular opposition to the EU went back decades and was based
on the perception that, by joining the EU, the UK had abandoned its
own sovereignty. It drew on English or British nationalism. But by
2009, opposition to the EU had begun to spread from Tory towns
to the working-class areas in Northern and Eastern England that
regularly voted for Labour. And UKIP began to find voters there.
According to Robert Ford and Matthew Goodwin's extensive study
of UKIP and its supporters, the bulk of its support shifted to the
older, less-educated, and primarily male white working class. This
older working class had turned against the EU and was backing the
UKIP in some elections.

Many of these new UKIP voters were clustered in smaller towns
that had once been centers of manufacturing and mining, but that
in the wake of Thatcher and the 1980s had become industrial ghost
towns. Their inhabitants were the "left-behinds" of the UK's economic development. While London, as a center of finance and
financial and legal services, and the universities, as incubators of
high-tech development, had prospered, Britain's older industrial
areas had fallen into harder and harder times.

The growth in anti-EU sentiment among these voters was
fueled by the rise of immigration to Britain from Eastern Europe.
The biggest spike in immigration occurred after 2004. In that year,
eight countries from Eastern Europe, including Poland, Hungary,
and the Baltic states, joined the EU. In 2007, Romania and Bul-
garia joined. According to EU rules, the UK could have instituted
a seven-year transitional ban on emigration from these countries,
but Tony Blair, who was then prime minister, didn't do so. By 2015,
immigration had climbed to over 600,000 a year.

Londoners and residents of Great Britain's high-tech enclaves
welcomed the new immigrants, but many working-class voters
saw them as a further threat to their standard of living. During the

156 Brexit campaign, there was an intense debate over whether, and if so how, immigrants had actually affected native-born workers, but there was some agreement, expressed by Theresa May, who was then Cameron's Home Secretary, and who favored remaining in the EU, that the recent flood of immigrants had put "pressure on public services, on housing, on infrastructure . . . it can hold down wages and push British workers out of jobs." Studies from the government's Migration Advisory Committee had concluded, for instance, that immigration "lowers wages at the bottom of the wage distribution" and that during slow growth or a downturn, "working-age migrants are associated with a reduction in native employment rates."

The growing opposition to immigration was cultural as well as economic, particularly among senior citizens who had grown up in a Britain when, as late as 1964, 98 percent of the electorate was white. According to a 2013 British Social Attitudes survey, among those over age 65, 69 percent thought immigration should be reduced "a lot," 66 percent would mind "if a close relative married a Muslim," 61 percent thought being born in Britain was "very important" to being British, and 58 percent thought that having British ancestors was "very important" to being British. By contrast, only 13 percent of those under 35 thought having British ancestors was very important to being British.

But as late as 2010, opposition to immigration hadn't translated into large-scale support for *leaving* the EU. That happened largely out of the efforts of UKIP leader Nigel Farage, who after the party's poor showing in the 2010 general election, set about honing UKIP's message of opposition to the EU. Farage fused the incendiary issue of immigration with that of EU membership. UKIP adopted the position that the way to limit immigration was to get out of the EU. Farage also adapted UKIP's general political outlook to its new working-class voters, many of whom had once voted for Labour. He abandoned UKIP's commitment to laissez-faire economics. Farage proposed taking the funds that the UK contributed to the EU and using them to improve Britain's National Health Service.

Farage framed UKIP's anti-immigrant and anti-EU sentiment
in populist terms. UKIP claimed it was championing the people—
the left-behinds—against London's and Brussels's elites. Farage's
success showed up in the 2014 European Union election, when UKIP
came in first with 27.49 percent. That election was a clear indication that UKIP had put the issue of Britain's EU membership on the
country's political agenda.

Within the Conservative Party, Prime Minister David Cameron had to contend with a group of back-benchers who also
opposed Britain's membership in the EU, mainly British nationalists who represented the upscale areas where UKIP still had support.
To appease them, Cameron had promised in 2013 that if he were
reelected in the 2015 general election, he would hold a referendum
on EU membership. In the 2015 general election, Cameron was easily
reelected against a lackluster Labour opponent. UKIP got a respectable 13 percent, with some of its votes coming at Labour's expense.
After the election, Cameron set the referendum for June of 2016.

Cameron was confident that he could keep Britain within the
EU. He and his Chancellor of the Exchequer, George Osborne, joined
by Britain's top business leaders and major newspapers, warned
repeatedly that a decision to leave the EU could have dire economic
consequences. Labour Party leader Jeremy Corbyn waged a half-
hearted campaign for staying within the EU that probably failed to
sway potential supporters among the "left-behinds" while further
alienating what had once been Labour constituencies. UKIP led the
campaign against the referendum along with two prominent Tories,
former London mayor Boris Johnson and former cabinet member
and MP Michael Gove.

Farage conducted the referendum campaign in classic populist fashion, pitting the people against the establishment. On May
20, he told reporters, "It is the establishment, it is the wealthy, it
is the multi-nationals, it is the big banks, it is those whose lives
have really done rather well in the last few years who are supporting
remaining and against it is the people." Ten days later, he said, "This

158 is our chance as a people to get back at a political class that has given away everything this nation has ever stood for, everything our forebears ever fought for and everything we want to hand on to our children and grandchildren." Farage was not above using incendiary imagery to promote his cause. One UKIP poster, called "Breaking Point," showed streams of dark-skinned Middle Easterners pouring into Slovenia, presumably en route to the UK.

In the referendum, UKIP and the dissident Tories were able to build a majority for leaving the EU out of the working-class left-behinds and the middle-class British nationalists. Within England, Remain won heavily in London and in the bigger cities, except for Birmingham and Sheffield, and in university towns. Leave won in blue-collar towns and in the middle-class areas where Euroskepticism had been strong. The working class was key. Voters for Leave were concentrated among older and less educated voters and within towns where the median income was less than $45,000.

The decision to leave was a major victory for UKIP and a major defeat for the two establishment parties and the political worldview they promoted—one in which professional and managerial classes prospered, but the older working class succumbed to the global forces of mobile labor and capital. Tony Blair told Sky News afterward, "The center-left and the center-right have lost their political traction. The populist insurgent movements on the left and right are taking control right now."

As Blair suggested, UKIP's rise, and the decision to leave the EU, were tied to rejection of the broader neoliberal worldview. In March 2015, journalist David Goodhart, writing in the Labour magazine, *Prospect,* had made exactly this point in explaining UKIP's popularity:

> The modern social and economic liberalism, that dominates all the main political parties, has produced an economically abandoned bottom third of the population with no real chance of ever gaining a share in prosperity; and an even larger group who feel a vague sense of loss in today's atomized society in which the

stability of family and the identity of place and nation has been
eroded. UKIP voters are a compound of those ignored, abandoned,
and laughed at by the metropolitan liberals who, despite some
party differences, dominate our public and cultural life.

In the referendum, these voters had rejected not just the EU, but
its underlying economic and social philosophy.

After the victory of Leave, UKIP leaders talked of displacing
the Labour Party as Britain's second major party. Indeed, the referendum did show that there was a vacuum in British politics, particularly among what was once Labour's natural constituency. But
the referendum's results didn't necessarily put UKIP into a position of filling it. Populist parties can suffer when their demands
are peremptorily rejected, as Syriza's were by the Troika. Or they
can suffer when their central demands are met, as with the People's
Party in the United States. That was UKIP's fate.

Under Farage, UKIP had become more than a single-issue party,
but the call to leave the EU was nevertheless the single demand that
defined UKIP's defense of the people against the establishment.
After Brexit won, Farage quit as its leader, and the party began to
dissolve. When Theresa May, who replaced Cameron as Tory leader
and prime minister, failed to make good on Brexit, Farage formed a
new Brexit Party, which came in first in Britain's elections for the
European parliament in May 2019. The Tories replaced May with
Boris Johnson, who after negotiating terms of departure with the
EU, campaigned in December 2019 on a promise to leave the federation. Farage's party got only 2 percent and won no seats. It was finished as a force in British politics.

Marine Le Pen and the National Front
Of all the EU's nations, France has been most directly affected
by rising immigration and Islamist-inspired terrorist attacks. It
housed Europe's most important rightwing populist party, originally called the National Front. It rose from obscurity and from

160 roots in Nazi-occupied Vichy France to becoming France's second leading party. But to do so, it had to overcome its own past. That task fell to Marine Le Pen, the daughter of the party's founder Jean-Marie Le Pen.

Jean-Marie Le Pen, the FN's founder, was a verbal bomb-thrower who loved to *epater le bourgeois*—shock the bourgeoisie. He reinforced the image of the FN as a defender of Vichy France and as the voice of the French Pieds-Noirs who had angrily fled Algeria during its war of independence. Le Pen also famously declared the Holocaust a "detail" of World War II. And his top lieutenants were cut from similar cloth. Bruno Gollnisch, who was elected to the French National Assembly in 1986, was convicted in 2007 of Holocaust denial.

By reorienting the FN from opposing communists to opposing immigrants and Islam, and by supplementing the economic concerns of the shopkeeper with those of the unemployed steelworker, Le Pen added working-class voters in the North to the FN's Catholic, provincial base in the South. That led to Le Pen's astonishing second-place showing in the 2002 runoff against Socialist prime minister Lionel Jospin. But Le Pen's success was short-lived. Fearful of a Le Pen victory, Jospin and the Socialists advised their voters to support the unpopular incumbent, Jacques Chirac, the candidate of the center-right Rally for the Republic, in the next round. As a result, Chirac was able to rout Le Pen, 82 percent to 18 percent, in the final runoff.

Le Pen's failure in the second round suggested that there were strict limits to the FN's popularity. Too many voters identified the FN with the hated Vichy regime and thought of its leader as an anti-Semitic extremist. As his daughter Marine Le Pen put it, there was a "glass ceiling" that the FN could not break through. The 2007 election appeared to confirm that. Nicolas Sarkozy, who had been interior minister in Chirac's administration, and was running as the candidate of the center-right UMP, took a hard line against the immigrant youths who had rioted in 2005 and against immigrants in general. If they don't "love France," he declared, they should "leave it," and he proposed cutting immigration. By co-opting the

FN position, Sarkozy doomed Le Pen, who came in fourth in the first round with only 10.44 percent.

In the first round of the legislative elections that year, the FN did even worse, getting only 4.29 percent and winning no seats. That imperiled the party's state campaign funding, which depended on its winning seats. In January 2011, Jean Marie Le Pen, 82, decided to retire as the party chairman. That set up a leadership battle between Gollnisch and Marine Le Pen.

Marine Le Pen, who was born in 1968, was the youngest of Le Pen's three daughters. Her most vivid memory, recounted in her autobiography, *Against the Current*, was of someone blowing up their Paris home when she was eight in order to kill her father. No one was injured, but it was her introduction, she wrote, to a "world without pity." The next year, however, a wealthy patron without children left a fortune to Jean-Marie Le Pen, including a mansion in the Paris suburbs, where Marine and her sisters then grew up.

Marine Le Pen got a law degree and entered private practice, but in 1998, she took over the FN's legal department. She was elected a Regional Councilor from Nord-Pas-de-Calais, a beaten-down former mining region dominated by socialists and communists. Marine Le Pen is a tall, handsome bleached blonde with a commanding voice and quick wit. She has her father's toughness, and his willingness to withstand and then counter harsh criticism. She also shares her father's ardent French nationalism—she named her oldest daughter after Joan of Arc—as well as his opposition to immigrants who she believes challenge French values and culture. But she was of an entirely different political generation from her father and from many of the older FN followers.

Marine Le Pen is twice-divorced, pro-choice, and comfortable around gays. She did not inherit her father's anti-Semitism or his sympathy for Vichy or colonial France. In 2000, she became president of Generations Le Pen, a youth group whose mission in part was to alter the family's and the party's reputation. One of its groups was the National Circle of Jewish Frenchmen.

162   In her autobiography, she blamed leftwing human rights groups such as SOS Racisme for demonizing the FN, but she admitted that the party had also contributed to its reputation by continuing to "create polemics" that "reinforced the caricature" of the organization. She didn't single out her father, but his views were exactly what she had in mind. In 2008, she broke publicly with him when, in an interview with a French magazine, he once again described the Nazi gas chambers as a "detail." "I do not share on these events the same vision," Marine Le Pen told the magazine. She was also critical of Gollnisch's comments on gas chambers.

In the 2011 election to head the FN, she defeated Gollnisch by two-to-one among the membership—as much because of her name as her views. But once installed as president and as the party's projected presidential candidate for 2012, she set about de-demonizing (*dédiabolisation*) the FN and turning it from a rightwing sect into a "party like the others." She changed the party's outlook in three key respects:

Anti-Semitism and Pro-Vichy: Soon after becoming president of the FN, she condemned "what happened in the [concentration] camps as the height of barbarism" and made clear that anti-Semites and racists were not welcome in the party. She banned skinheads and anyone in combat-fatigues from the FN's first march. An FN circular said, "Marine Le Pen has warned that anything resembling a 'skinhead' in any shape or form will be excluded by all necessary means." She also began citing favorably Charles de Gaulle—who was despised by her father and his generation of Vichy loyalists. She repeatedly rebuked her father for his anti-Semitic outbursts, finally expelling him from the party in August 2015.

Immigrants and Islam: Le Pen was no less vehement than her father in denouncing attacks by Islamists and in tying them to what she claimed were France's lax immigration policies. After a French Muslim of Algerian descent, who had been radicalized in

Afghanistan, killed seven people in Toulouse in March 2012, Le Pen commented, "How many Mohammed Merahs arrive each day in France in boats or airplanes filled with immigrants? How many Mohammed Merahs are there among unassimilated children?" But Le Pen tried to create distinctions between what she was saying and past FN statements. She insisted she was not against Muslims or Muslim immigrants, but against those who violated French principles of *laïcité*—or secularism—by imposing their religion, either as politics or as cultural practices, on the public realm. "In France, we often say the U.S. is a multicultural society, but it's not. It's multi-ethnic, but one single culture. I don't say that nobody should enter our country. On the contrary, in the old days immigrants entered France and blended in. They adopted the French language and traditions. Whereas now entire communities set themselves up within France, governed by their own codes and traditions," she explained to an interviewer in 2011.

Economic Nationalism: Le Pen's biggest departure in policy was in her economics. She was influenced by having served as a regional councilor in an area devastated by deindustrialization whose working-class citizens felt abandoned by the major parties in Paris. Her views were also shaped by an advisor she hired to run her 2012 campaign. In 2009, she had met Florian Philippot, 30, a graduate of the super-elite École nationale d'administration. (Presidents Valéry Giscard d'Estaing, Jacques Chirac, and François Hollande were all graduates.) In 2002, Philippot had been an enthusiastic supporter of Jean-Pierre Chevenement, a founder of the French Socialist Party in 1969. Chevenement had resigned from Mitterrand's cabinet in 1983 over Mitterrand's U-turn and had also opposed Maastricht and the Euro. In 2002, he had run for president, with Philippot's support, as the candidate of a new leftwing nationalist party against Chirac and Hollande.

Philippot had gravitated from Chevenement's leftwing economic nationalism to the National Front by way of Jean-Yves Gallou,

164   a former FN member who had originally formulated its turn toward working-class economics. In 2011, Marine Le Pen hired Philippot to run her presidential campaign and to help develop its platform. Its platform on economics—minus the special preference in welfare and employment for the native French—could have been written by Chevenement. "Jean-Pierre Chevenement's project is carried forward by Marine Le Pen,"Philippot told *Le Monde* in 2012. As such, it was considerably to the left of many of the Social Democratic or Socialist parties on the continent and the Democratic Party in the United States.

The platform called for a "strategic plan for reindustrialization," tariffs and quotas to protect against "unfair competition," the separation of commercial from investment banking, a transactions tax on stock purchases, the nationalization of banks facing difficulties, a "cap" on credit card charges, opposition to cuts in social spending and to the privatization of public services, equal quality healthcare access regardless of income or location, and rejection of the European Union's attempts to impose austerity. The EU had led, the platform said, to "open borders inducing relocation, unemployment, market dictatorship, destruction of public services, insecurity, poverty, and mass immigration." The platform blamed Greece's debt crisis on "the elites who want to feed the new Minotaur to save the Euro." The FN demanded that France's relationship to the EU be "renegotiated" and a referendum held on the Euro.

The FN's new program on economic nationalism became as integral to its appeal as its opposition to mass immigration. Its entire program was now subsumed under the concept of defending French sovereignty—in an echo of Chevenement and earlier de Gaulle, *souveraniste* was the new watchword. In Le Pen's election brochure, its position on immigration, calling for a 95 percent reduction in annual entries, came on page seven after her position on consumer rights, the Euro, jobs, finance, pensions, and justice. Together, these demands established a divide between the FN's "little people" and the establishment, which Le Pen referred to derisively (combining the UMP and PS) as the "UMPS." Le Pen insisted her own party, the FN, was not a "right-wing" party. It was *ni gauche, ni droite*, as the campaign posters proclaimed—neither left nor right. That, again, fit the populist profile.

The first test of the FN's new politics and of Le Pen as a candidate came in the 2012 presidential election. Le Pen came in third with 17.9 percent of the vote, more than her father had ever gotten in the first round. The party did well above its typical performance among 18- to 24-year-olds (26 percent), office workers (23 percent), blue-collar workers (28.6 percent), and high school graduates (27 percent). It did worst among seniors, professionals, managers, people with advanced degrees, and Parisians. Le Pen's showing was, perhaps, helped by the public horror over the Toulouse shootings. In its next tests, however, it would benefit not only from new terrorist incidents, but from the growing unpopularity of François Hollande's government.

Decline of the Socialist Party

François Hollande, France's first Socialist president since Mitterrand, assumed office in May 2012 with unemployment at 9.7 percent. In his first campaign rally, he promised to get tough with bankers (finance is "my enemy," he proclaimed) and to bring down France's unemployment rate. Hollande also promised to end Sarkozy and Merkel's commitment to austerity economics—dubbed "Merkozy"—and epitomized by their crafting in 2010 an even more rigid version of the EU's Stability Pact. But outside of a surtax on millionaires, which Hollande rescinded after it failed to bring in significant revenue, he abandoned his promises to break with neoliberal orthodoxy.

As unemployment rose above 10 percent, and as Hollande was pressured by the ECB to reduce France's deficit to the 3 percent limit, he performed his own U-turn. He had already abandoned any effort to persuade Merkel to relax her support for EU-wide adherence to the stability pact. Now having announced that he had become a "social democrat" rather than a "socialist," he proposed to emulate Germany's earlier attempts to reduce its proportion of income

166   going to wages rather than profits by granting business generous tax concessions, while cutting social spending. Hollande called his new approach a *pacte de responsabilité*—a pact of responsibility—between the government and employers. Theoretically, in exchange for these tax concessions, business would hire more workers.

Hollande's measures alienated his own base among workers without visibly reducing unemployment. In the first major test, the municipal elections of 2014, the Socialists lost control of 113 cities and towns without winning any towns they didn't previously control. The FN did remarkably well. It got 8 percent of the total vote, even though it only ran candidates in a sixth of the municipalities. It won some important symbolic victories, including the mayor's office in Henin-Beaumont, a northern former mining town that Socialists had always controlled, and that was part of Marine Le Pen's Nord-pas-de-Calais region.

After the municipal election, Hollande replaced Prime Minister Jean-Marc Ayrault with Manuel Valls, who had strongly supported Hollande's U-turn. In May, however, Hollande and the PS suffered another setback. In the European parliamentary elections, Le Pen and the FN came in first with 24.85 percent, the UMP second with 20.8 percent, and Hollande's PS a distant third with 13.98 percent of the vote. The National Front did best in those blue-collar districts in the North that Socialists and Communists had once dominated. Under Hollande, the Socialists were losing what remained of their blue-collar base, but Hollande continued to meet the ECB's requirements and to emulate German labor policy.

In March 2015, Hollande unveiled new labor proposals that were reminiscent of the Hartz reforms that Schröder had introduced in Germany in 2003. They allowed employers to pay less for overtime, and to demand more hours of work from employees; they made it easier to fire employees and limited the damages firms would have to pay for unjustified dismissals; and they allowed firms to bargain with unions for a single company rather than for a sector—a big advantage for employers, as the experience of Federal Express in the United

States has shown. These proposals sparked huge demonstrations of
over a million people, and *nuit debout* (up all night) demonstrations
that mimicked those of the Indignados and Occupy Wall Street.

When Paris was hit with earthshaking terrorist attacks in January and November 2015, Hollande tried to take a tough line against
the perpetrators. He even advanced a proposal, opposed by many
in his party, that would have stripped dual citizens who committed
a terrorist act of their French citizenship. But the attacks clearly
boosted the FN. Wrote political scientist Pascal Perrineau, "Among
the French who are deeply concerned about their safety and who
also express concerns about immigration and Islam, the National
Front has now reached very high levels."

In December, France held regional elections—roughly equivalent to statehouse elections in the United States. And voters once
again repudiated Hollande and the PS. In the first round, Le Pen and
the FN came in first with 27.73 percent, the Republicans (the successor of the UMP) second with 26.65 percent, and the PS third
with 23.12 percent. In the second round, the Socialists and Republicans agreed to endorse whichever of their candidates stood the best
chance of defeating the FN candidate. The strategy worked. The FN
didn't win any regional presidencies, although it got almost 7 million
votes and won many lesser regional offices. The Socialist Party, which
had dominated regional governments, lost 15 regional presidencies.

Perrineau, using extensive polls taken immediately after ISIS
attacks in November, contended that the FN was expanding beyond
the small shopkeepers in the South and the blue-collar workers
in the North. By his estimates, the FN was backed by 35 percent of
the self-employed, 41 percent of office workers, and 46 percent of
blue-collar workers. In addition, the FN had broken through among
the public sector workers who had always been the bastion of
Socialist Party support. According to Perrineau, the FN was getting
30 percent of these workers, who, he explained, were reacting to "the
difficulties public servants confront with immigrant people in the
public hospitals and other public facilities."

Political scientist Laurent Bouvet attributed the FN's growing
support among the French middle class to that class's conviction that it has to pay for—literally and figuratively—the burden
migrants put on French social services. Bouvet said, "The middle
class is stuck in the middle, and they have to pay for the unemployed and the migrants. The public services, the social protections,
the hospitals, the universities, are falling apart. They are paying
more and are getting less. And they don't see those at the top of
the society making sacrifices. They can always put their children in
the best schools. The parties have nothing to offer, blood and tears,
more taxes, less social benefits, less jobs."

After the election, Hollande's approval rating stood at a historically low 15 percent. With the presidential elections looming
in the spring of 2017, Hollande and the French Socialists were in
disarray. Some Socialist Party members called for a general "primary of the left," which would include some of the smaller leftwing
parties, to choose an overall candidate. Frédéric Martel, a writer
advising a candidate on the Socialist left, said, "There is nothing
socialist in the Socialist Party anymore. Its base is mainly civil
servants with lifetime jobs, the new bourgeois of the left, people
attracted for something other than economic reasons such as gay
marriage."

Party loyalists blamed Hollande's ineptitude for the Socialists' decline, but the French Socialists were following the same
downward-sloping path as several other Socialist, Social Democratic, and Labour Parties in the EU, including PASOK in Greece and
Britain's Labour Party. All these parties have had difficulty dealing
with Europe's downturn and with the Great Recession. And in
France, a clear beneficiary was the National Front.

Calm France
As the 2017 presidential elections neared, Eric Zemmour, a conservative columnist for Figaro and the author of the best-selling Suicide Francais, said, "The French elite want to push the country to be

part of a European empire. The workers want to keep France national.
The elite want them to forget the old France. It is a war between the
elite and the people. Seventy percent of the French people want a
solution against Islam and foreigners, but seventy percent don't
want the National Front to come to power." When people think of
the FN, Zemmour explained, they have "a fear of civil war, fear of the
end of democracy, and fear of incompetence."

Marine Le Pen and her circle of advisors, headed by Philippot,
sought to shift the party's emphasis away from immigration and
Islam to economics and Euroskepticism. Le Pen applauded Britain's
vote on leaving the EU, and called for a similar referendum in France.

When I interviewed top Le Pen advisor Sebastien Chenu, he
said he was attracted by the party's Euroskepticism and by Le Pen's
refusal to oppose gay marriage. He didn't even mention immigration
or refugees until about halfway through the interview, and when I
asked him specifically about the party's stand, he lamented the party's demonization on the issue. "We are not going to throw away
people who are immigrants," he said. He also rejected any comparison between Marine Le Pen and Donald Trump. "We don't feel close
to him," he said. "Take out the T and R, and you have UMP."

But the party's active voters were still driven primarily by opposition to immigration and Islam. In February 2016, I attended a regional
convention of the FN in Henin-Beaumont and interviewed several
of the local FN leaders as well as some of the rank and file. When I
asked them why they had joined the FN, they invariably mentioned
immigration first. Municipal councilor Antoine Golliot said, "It was
the fight against immigration that was the main thing that attracted
me to the FN. That is where the danger comes from." When I asked
him whether the FN attracted former socialists and communists, he
said, "We draw some from the right and some from the left, but overall
from both sides. What draws people the most is immigration."

In the south, the party's base among small business and elderly
retained the FN's older libertarian anti-tax economics and was
skeptical of Philippot's leftwing nationalism. The party's Catholics

170   in the south, including Le Pen's niece Marion Marechal Le Pen, who was a member of parliament and the party's vice president, were uncomfortable with Marine Le Pen's cosmopolitan outlook on abortion and gay marriage. Several of her key advisors, including Philippot and Sebastien Chenu, were gay, which prompted her father to rail against his daughter's "gay lobby." Marion Marechal Le Pen and those close to her also rejected Philippot's emphasis on economic nationalism.

"Unemployment is in third place behind security and identity," she said. "A father is afraid of his daughter wearing a burqa. It doesn't matter whether she will buy it with francs or euros." After the Nice attack, Marine Le Pen singled out "Islamist fundamentalism," while her niece framed the issue as Christians versus Muslims. "Christians must stand up to resist Islam," she declared.

But even in the face of opposition from within, Le Pen and her advisors were determined to soften her image. In January, the FN unveiled a new campaign poster. It showed a wistful Le Pen looking out from a rural background. It was titled in large white block letters, La France Apaisee, meaning "Calm France" or "France Calmed Down." The poster recalls Mitterrand's 1981 poster, which read Force Tranquille, or a "calming force." Both posters were meant to reassure voters that the candidates were not extremists who would threaten democracy and public order.

For Le Pen, such an approach carried the risk of diluting the party's populist message and distancing herself too far from her party's base. Bouvet says, "This kind of slogan is that of a regular politician. If she starts to be the usual politician, she will lose what is interesting in her—her ability to break through to disrupt the system."

But Le Pen was determined, as the 2017 presidential election neared, that the FN be seen as a "party like any other."

Le Pen didn't succeed in winning the 2017 vote, but she elevated her party to second place in French politics. The Socialist Party suffered from Hollande's unpopularity. The Republicans nominated a candidate who was subsequently indicted for corruption. That left Le

Pen, controversial leftist Jean Luc-Melenchon's new party, La France
Insoumise, and former Socialist minister Emmanuel Macron's new
centrist party, en Marche. Le Pen came in a close second to Macron
in the first round. In the second round, beset by popular fears of its
extremism, Le Pen lost to Macron. But her 33.90 percent doubled
her percentage from 2012 and from her father's showing in 2002. In
the election's aftermath, Le Pen moved once again to alter the party's image. While retaining and re-emphasizing its stance against
immigrants and refugees, the party changed its name from National
Front to National Rally and ditched its Euroskepticism and opposition to the Euro. (Philippot resigned from the party in September
2017.) Whether that would allow her to overcome finally the public's
"fear of civil war, fear of the end of democracy, and fear of incompetence" remained to be seen.

The Past and Future of Populism

Populist candidates, movements, and parties have historically served as early warning signs that a prevailing political consensus is breaking down—that significant parts of the public have felt that the established political and economic leadership have not kept their promises and been responsive to their concerns. Angry and disillusioned, they have responded enthusiastically to populist appeals. With public support, populist politicians have knocked on the doors of power, but in most cases (but not all!) have not been let in, as the major parties have finally taken heed of the concerns they have raised.

In the last two decades of the nineteenth century, American populists voiced public anger at how unregulated finance and the trusts were wreaking havoc on the farm economy of the South and West; Huey Long's Share the Wealth dramatized the gaps between rich and poor; the European populists of the last decades took aim at the growing divergence between North and South in the European Union and (within the countries) between financial, high-tech metro areas and the older towns and cities devastated by the loss of mining and manufacturing jobs.

In the 2016 election, both Sanders and Trump sounded the   173
alarm against policies pursued by Democratic and Republican
leaders. Sanders addressed the growing inequality of wealth and
power reinforced by regressive tax legislation, the gaping holes in
the social safety net from government neglect, the culpability of
banks, businesses, and a compliant government for the Great Recession, the growing economic plight of the young, and the failure of
business and government to address climate change.

Trump dramatized the harm that Chinese mercantilism
and capital had inflicted on American towns and cities that had
depended on manufacturing for their prosperity. He drew attention
to the way that massive legal and illegal immigration of unskilled
workers threatened the wages and burdened the towns and cities of
unskilled American workers. He appealed to these Americans who
had been deprived of their older way of life and work and, for that
very reason, put special emphasis on God, family, and nation. He
pointed to the "carnage" in American inner cities.

Sanders's and Trump's demands were predictably dismissed by
the country's political leadership and by business and media elites.
In the Democratic Party, Clinton supporters argued that Sanders's
proposals for Medicare for All, a $15 minimum wage, or radical tax
reform were unrealistic. They had, *New York* magazine columnist
Jonathan Chait wrote, "zero chance of enactment." In *Politico*, Princeton sociologist Paul Starr charged that Sanders's "attacks on bil-
lionaires and Wall Street are a way of eliciting a roar of approval from
angry audiences without necessarily having good solutions for the
problems that caused that anger in the first place."

Republican and business groups rejected Trump's tirades about
"bad trade deals" and runaway shops and Chinese mercantilism.
The Peterson Institute for International Economics warned that
Trump's "trade proposals could sink the economy." In the UK, opponents of Brexit warned that a vote for leaving the EU would crash
the economy. It would "spark," British Chancellor of the Exchequer

174   George Osborne warned, "a year-long recession." And the *Washington Post* denounced Trump's pronouncements on immigration as "nativist and xenophobic nationalism."

These charges against Sanders and Trump were not without some basis. If Sanders had won the presidency, he would have had an impossible time getting Medicare for All or his myriad new taxes on the wealthy through the Congress. (In Colorado, in November 2016, voters would reject a Sanders-backed single-payer "Medicare for All" proposal for the state by a four-to-one margin.) Trump's proposals often sprung from the top of his head. If Trump had slapped 45 percent tariffs on imports, as he had threatened to do during the campaign, he might have imperiled the economy. And Trump's statements about race and immigration, as well as those by UKIP and France's National Front, were laced with bigotry and nativism.

Yet the leftwing and rightwing populist campaigns did speak to genuine failings of neoliberal policies. Obama's Affordable Care Act had bypassed many Americans. In 2016, 26.7 million Americans were still uninsured, and according to the Commonwealth Fund, about 25 percent of the insured were underinsured. In 2016, 11.6 percent of youth, a key Sanders constituency, were unemployed. And while a black middle class had emerged from the sixties, and lived now in suburbs like Washington's Prince George County, there were predominately African American neighborhoods in cities like Chicago and Baltimore that were heavily afflicted by crime and joblessness.

In addition, Chinese mercantilism and business and bipartisan support for trade deals and tax breaks had led to the precipitous decline of American towns and cities that had depended on manufacturing for their prosperity. According to David Autor, David Dorn, and Gordon H. Hanson, China's imports between 1999 and 2011 cost the United States 2.4 million jobs and particularly hurt workers in the bottom 40 percent of income distribution. During the 2000s, the Commerce Department reported, American

multinational corporations cut their American workforces by 2.9 175
million, while creating 2.4 million jobs overseas.

Trump's, as well as UKIP's and the National Front's, bigoted
attacks on unfettered immigration nevertheless pointed to the failure
of neoliberal policy to protect less educated workers and their towns
from pressures on their wages and social services created by the
influx of less educated legal and illegal immigrants. The *Wall Street
Journal*, the Cato Institute, and a host of liberal economists insisted
that immigration was a win-win for the American workforce, but
they ignored its effect on lower-income, less-educated Americans.
Wrote Cambridge University economist Ha-Joon Chang, "Wages
in rich countries are determined more by immigration control than
anything else, including any minimum wage legislation."

European populists attacked not only costs of unskilled immigrants in wages and budgets, but the clash of culture, which they
blamed for growing crime and terrorist attacks. They identified
the rise of terror and lawlessness with Islam as a religion, and proposed restrictions on ordinary religious practices and on the construction of mosques. That was bigoted, but the rightwing populists
were still pointing to an uncomfortable reality that the leading parties preferred to ignore, or had even been responsible for. The influx
of immigrants and refugees from conflicts in South Asia, the Middle
East, North Africa, and the Balkans had created urban underclasses
that nourished crime and Islamic radicalism that had led to riots and
terrorist attacks.

In Sweden, the Sweden Democrats, a rightwing populist party
founded in 1988, steadily climbed in popularity until it became, in
the 2018 election, the country's third largest party. It blamed the
huge number of Muslim immigrants and refugees, who had entered
Sweden under its permissive border laws, for rising crime rates. The
other parties initially dismissed any attempt to link crime or terror
to migrants as evidence of racism and xenophobia, and reminded
voters of the Sweden Democrats' neo-Nazi roots, but the party was
pointing to something real. In 2017, for instance, one study found,

58 percent of those apprehended for crimes were migrants. Migrants made up 73 percent of those arrested for murder or manslaughter.

More broadly, the rightwing populists in the Scandinavian countries were exposing the degree to which permissive immigration policies were undermining their advanced social democracies, which were based on a common culture and values and even, particularly in the case of Denmark, a common religion. Taxpayers who supported these countries' advanced welfare states had to be able to assume that their very high taxes were going to support other citizens who shared their own commitment to family, work, and civic order. The rightwing populist parties pointed out the degree to which permissive immigration and asylum policies were undermining that trust.

The European populists of the left and right were also prescient in warning of the threat that the European Union, and particularly the creation of the Eurozone, posed to their nations' well-being. The EU's prohibitions on the country's using "state aid" to rebuild failing industrial sectors reinforced the division within countries between prosperous cities and ailing small and mid-sized towns. Its budgetary strictures—tightened even more in 2012 by a new Stability Pact—impeded nations' recovery from the Great Recession. And the reign of the Euro favored Germany and the export-driven low countries over countries like Italy, Spain, and Greece who, faced with rising trade and budget imbalances, could no longer use devaluations to correct them. The case against the Euro was not new. It was stated clearly by economist Wynne Godley in the *London Review of Books* in 1992:

> What happens if a whole country—a potential "region" in a fully integrated community—suffers a structural setback? So long as it is a sovereign state, it can devalue its currency. It can then trade successfully at full employment provided its people accept the necessary cut in their real incomes. With an economic and monetary union, this recourse is obviously barred, and its prospect

is grave indeed unless federal budgeting arrangements are made   177
which fulfill a redistributive role.

If the EU were to move toward a centralized fiscal and monetary
policy, as Varoufakis and other leftwing economists have proposed,
then the threat of socioeconomic crisis hanging over the Eurozone
might be eased, but there was huge resistance to doing that, particularly in wealthier Northern European countries, including Germany,
Holland, and Finland. To their credit, populists in the UK, France,
Spain, Italy, and Greece pointed to these problems, but they were
initially ignored. The fate of the American and European polities
will rest on the ability of each country's national leadership to heed
the warnings, and to incorporate what is constructive, while casting
out the bigoted and irrational, of the populist parties, candidates,
and movements.

The Nationalist Revival

Part Two

Understanding Nationalism

The *New York Times* runs a video series called "The Interpreter" where its reporters explain controversial ideas. In February 2018, it put up a video, entitled "National Identity Is Made Up." The *Times* contended that, "National identity is the myth that built the modern world, but it also primes us for dictatorship, racism, genocide." What does it mean to say that one's national identity is "made up" or a "myth"? Something that is made up or a myth is not true. It's a story. By that understanding, a person could say, "I'm not really an American," the way someone who plays in a band on the weekends, but is an accountant during the week, could say, "I'm not really a musician."

And what does it mean to say that our made-up identity "primes us" for racism and genocide? Does it prime us for other things that are not so terrible? Could it also prime us, for instance, to vote in elections? Or maybe it could also prime us to be concerned about a school shooting in Florida even though we live in Maryland and have never been to the city of Parkland and don't know any of the children who were shot?

The argument of Part Two is that national identity is not just a product of where a person is born or immigrated to, but of deeply

182   held sentiments that are usually acquired during childhood. Nationalism is not simply a political ideology, or set of ideas, but a *social psychology*. Nationalist sentiment is an essential ingredient of a democracy, which is based on the assumption of a common identity, and of a welfare state, which is based on the acceptance by citizens of their financial responsibility for people whom they may not know at all, and who may have widely different backgrounds from theirs.

The psychology of nationalism is the basis for nationalist politics, which can take very different forms—on the left, center, or right. Demagogues can exploit the sentiments on which nationalism is based to promote a nativist or imperial agenda, but political leaders can also appeal to nationalism to rally a citizenry to resist foreign conquest or colonial domination. Abraham Lincoln and Benito Mussolini were ardent nationalists. The French revolutionaries of 1789 were nationalists; but so, too, was Spanish dictator Francisco Franco's Falange. Theodore Roosevelt and George Wallace both claimed the mantle of nationalism.

The political direction that nationalism takes has depended on how a politician or political movement draws upon existing nationalist sentiments. Politicians, parties, and policymakers who simply discount these sentiments, or who identify them solely with right-wing excesses—as many in the United States or Europe have done—are likely to encourage exactly the kind of nationalism they might have wanted to avoid. That is the lesson of the rise of the Alternative for Germany (AfD), the Sweden Democrats, and Donald Trump.

Our current one-sided understanding of nationalism as the stimulus for racism and genocide comes out of the experience of World War II. After World War II, the leaders of the victorious powers tried to prevent the revival of the toxic, aggressive nationalism that had arisen in Germany, Italy, and Japan, which combined a quest for world domination with vicious scapegoating that, in Germany's case, led to genocide. In Europe, and to some extent in the United States, the very term "nationalist" and its cognates acquired

a pejorative connotation. To call someone a "nationalist" insinuated   183
some underlying sympathy for Nazis or fascists.

To prevent an outbreak of this toxic nationalism, the victors
devised regional and international organizations that were intended to
tamp down the urge for world domination and prevent the outbreak of
ethnic or racial nationalism. These included the United Nations, the
World Bank, the International Monetary Fund, and the European
Economic Community. Even NATO and the Soviet Union's Warsaw
Pact and Comecon were intended partly to prevent an eruption of
aggressive nationalism. Together, these institutions helped prevent
the outbreak of a new world war; they contributed to three decades
of rapid economic growth and prosperity; and they squelched the
development of the older nationalism that had sparked World War II.

Emboldened by these successes, and by the end of the Cold
War, policymakers in the United States and Europe embraced in the
1990s and early 2000s the growth of new international organizations and the expansion of older ones. They encouraged global economic integration, dubbed globalization, and the subordination of
national sovereignty to international rule. American president Bill
Clinton urged Americans to "embrace the inexorable logic of globalization." British prime minister Tony Blair said, "I hear people say
we have to stop and debate globalization. You might as well debate
whether autumn should follow summer."

During a fifteen-year stretch, the European Economic Community became the European Union. Most of the EU's continental
members were united by a single currency; EU-wide rules restricted
budget deficits and allowed the free movement of workers. "Rarely if
ever has there been a greater voluntary concession of national sovereignty than Europe's Economic and Monetary Union," *Financial
Times* economist Martin Sandbu wrote in *Europe's Orphan*. The EU
encouraged the idea that a French or German citizen could be, above
all, a citizen of Europe.

The World Trade Organization began operation in 1995, pur-
porting to take the resolution of trade disputes out of the hands of

184   individual countries and set limits not only on quotas and tariffs, but on government intervention to boost industries and exports. In 2001, with strong American support, China was invited into the new organization. On the European continent, the EU incorporated states that had been behind the Iron Curtain, and NATO expanded up to Russia's borders. And a new generation of multinational corporations and banks, untethered to particular countries, spanned the globe. When ExxonMobil CEO Lee Raymond was asked whether he planned to build more American oil refineries, he responded, "I am not a U.S. company and I don't make decisions based on what is good for the U.S."

During this period, both the United States and Europe opened their borders wide to immigrants and refugees. George H. W. Bush and Bill Clinton increased the annual entrants and included new groups of "guest workers." The European Union created open borders within it and welcomed refugees from the Balkans and later from the Middle East and Africa. When ten new countries (including eight from Eastern Europe) were admitted to the EU in 2004, the British, Swedes, and Irish waived the seven-year transition period before migrants from these countries could freely come to theirs to work.

Prominent thinkers and policymakers in the United States and Europe began to espouse a version of cosmopolitan democracy that promoted the transcendence and even abandonment of national loyalties. Mary Kaldor, David Held, and Daniele Archibugi advanced the notion of "cosmopolitan democracy." Held argued that the sovereign nation-state "would, in due course, wither away." Columbia University political scientist Saskia Sassen heralded a new "post-national and denationalized citizenship." Canadian philosopher Charles Taylor promoted the idea of "world sovereignty."

But a series of events disrupted the growing consensus around these new international and regional organizations and cut short the musings about world sovereignty. Russia predictably took offense at NATO enlargement. China became a regional military power with ambitions in the South China Sea and a global economic power

capable of gaming the international trade and monetary system.
Millions of jobs in the United States and Europe were lost to Chinese
imports, some of which were from American, Japanese, and European companies that had relocated or outsourced their production
from there in search of cheap labor costs. Illegal and legal immigration exploded in the United States and Europe; always something of
an issue, it became fused in the public mind with Islamist terrorist
attacks. Wars broke out in the Middle East, South Asia, and North
Africa—the result in part of American and European attempts to
extend their sway over these regions—that brought millions of new
asylum-seekers to Europe and the United States. The Great Recession of 2008 gave the lie to the promise of prosperity in Europe and
the United States.

Together, these developments created new winners and losers
in the international economy, new challenges to world peace, and
new fears and resentments. They reawakened nationalist senti
ments and antipathies that had lain dormant for decades. New politicians and parties have emerged that appealed to these sentiments.
They included the Tea Party and the candidacy of Donald Trump in
the United States; the United Kingdom Independence Party (UKIP),
which led the vote for the UK to leave the European Union; populist parties in France, the Netherlands, Denmark, Sweden, Finland,
Norway, Italy, Austria, and even in Germany; nationalist parties in
Hungary and Poland that have defied the dictates of the European
Union on immigration and liberal democracy; and the resurgence of
Russian nationalism under Vladimir Putin.

Liberals in the United States and social and Christian democrats in Europe have condemned many of these nationalist parties
and politicians. They have portrayed them, as the *New York Times'*
Interpreter does, as echoes of fascism and Nazism, or, in the United
States, as the heir of Ku Klux Klan—style white supremacy. To be
sure, many of these parties and politicians are deeply reactionary.
They have exploited nationalist sentiments to cripple political
opponents and in the process undermine democratic institutions.

186   They have demonized outgroups like Europe's Muslims or America's Hispanic immigrants and have fomented conflict with other nations. But in simply condemning these nationalist politicians and parties, cosmopolitan critics have ignored, or even scorned, the underlying sentiments to which these politicians and parties have appealed, and have failed to address the circumstances that have provoked these sentiments. They have ignored the degree to which the rise of these groups signals the breakdown of an old order that cannot simply be reaffirmed, but needs to be reconstructed.

    Politics is driven by complementarity. The political right from Edmund Burke to Ronald Reagan, as political scientist Corey Robin has argued, arose in opposition to the historic egalitarianism of liberals and the left. Similarly, the rightwing nationalism of Donald Trump or Hungary's Viktor Orban or Germany's AfD is a backlash to the cosmopolitanism and globalism of American and European liberals. These politicians and parties did not, of course, come out of nowhere. The Tea Party preceded Trump, Pegida was a precursor of the AfD, and Orban is in many ways a throwback to the Communist Janos Kadar or even Miklos Horthy regimes. But their successes and (in the case of Trump and Orban) triumphs were in many respects a rejection of the excesses and failures of their liberal cosmopolitan rivals.

I intend this as a book of analysis, not advocacy. But I'll say a little about how I come to this subject of nationalism. I am of the same generation as Donald Trump. I grew up at a time when, if you went into a store to buy something, you looked for the label "Made in the USA"—not out of patriotism, but out of the conviction that America made the best shirts, cameras, and cars. Trump's father was in real estate in New York. Mine manufactured dresses in Elgin, Illinois, until he went out of business in the 1950s and became a salesman. It was a shock to me, and to many in my generation, when American products seemed to vanish from stores and showrooms, replaced by televisions from Japan or South Korea and shirts and suits from

Southeast Asia, and when the great cities of the Midwest declined as   187
manufacturing moved south or abroad.

I was not bothered that American companies no longer dominated the market for T-shirts or toys, but I did worry that Americans had to buy flat-panel displays from overseas or that American
auto companies seemed in an unseemly rush to move their plants to
Mexico. I became sympathetic in the 1980s to politicians like Dick
Gephardt or David Bonior, who railed against unfair trade practices
and runaway shops. In 1995, Michael Lind and I wrote a manifesto for
the *New Republic* entitled "For a New Nationalism," where we warned
against a politics increasingly shaped by private interests. Political scientist Ruy Teixeira and I organized a luncheon salon, which
we called the "new synthesis group," and which we hoped would lay
the basis for a new political tendency in the Democratic Party that
would embrace an economic nationalism rather than the free-trade
let-her-rip globalization that Clinton Democrats and Newt Gingrich Republicans espoused.

None of that came to pass as we had hoped. In 2002, Teixeira
and I published a book, *The Emerging Democratic Majority*, in which
we predicted that, by the decade's end, the Democrats would have
created a majority based on support from women, professionals, and
minorities, along with about 40 percent of the old pro–New Deal
white working class. We described the majority's politics as "progressive centrism," which we envisaged as an extension of Bill Clinton's New Democratic views. We were right about the Democrats'
centrist politics and about the composition of the majority that
would win Congress in 2006 and the White House in 2008. What
we didn't anticipate was what happened next: the massive migration of white middle- and working-class voters to the Republicans,
which underlay Republican congressional successes and Donald
Trump's victory in 2016.

I first encountered Trump at a rally in New Hampshire in August
2015, twenty years after Lind and I had published our manifesto.
Trump's pitch was a mix of incendiary nativism about Mexicans

188   and Muslims, tirades against Jeb Bush and Obama, and wacky foreign policy pronouncements ("We should have taken Iraq's oil!")
with a ringing critique of footloose corporations and of trade deals
that had screwed American workers. Economic nationalism had
suddenly reemerged, but as part of a rightwing populist appeal. And
Trump's views of trade and corporate America remained central
themes in his campaign and important to his success in Midwestern
and southern towns that had been decimated by the loss of manufacturing jobs. For me, Trump's victory bore out the old adage, "Be
careful what you wish for, you might get it."

    If Part Two has an underlying political agenda, it is to identify
and reclaim what is valid in nationalism—and of the liberal internationalism of the post–World War II generation—from both the cosmopolitan liberals who believe in a borderless world and from the
rightwing populists who have coupled a concern for their nation's
workers with nativist screeds against outgroups and immigrants.

Why Nationalism Matters

Here are three anecdotes in search of an analysis:

When I was on tour to promote my book on populism, a member of the audience reproached me: "I don't understand why you are criticizing free trade," she said. "It has raised the standard of living of many people around the world." Before I could measure my words, I replied: "I don't give a damn about people around the world."

Several years before that, a German friend began telling me how upset his mother had been to see people in Berlin hanging Turkish flags outside the windows of their apartments to show support for Turkey's team in the European football championships. Though a devoted internationalist like many Germans of his generation, he agreed with his mother, but didn't want to say so outright.

When I was in Tokyo, a prominent Japanese intellectual took me out for sushi. When I told him that I had a favorite sushi restaurant back home, he complained about how Koreans were opening up restaurants in the United States that claimed to serve Japanese food.

Many people today, whatever their considered convictions or political ideology, are nationalists in their hearts. It can come out when they are grouchy and tired, as I was on my book tour, or in

190   response to an innocuous sporting event or the ownership of a sushi bar. But it's there.

Nationalism provides a framework—often unacknowledged—for our politics, expressed most clearly in the question of whether a policy is in the national interest. And in special circumstances, it can rise to the level of an explicit political ideology, as it has today in the United States, Europe, and parts of Asia: "America First" for Trump, "France First" for the National Front, "Italians First" for Italy's League Party, and "Russia for [ethnic] Russians" for the anti-immigrant DNPI. To understand the deep attraction of these ideological challenges and to assess whether they are constructive or destructive, progressive or reactionary, you have to understand the sentiments on which they are based.

Origins of Nationalism

The German philosopher Johann Gottfried Herder is credited with introducing the term "nationalism" in a work published in 1774. It didn't become a staple of political vernacular until well into the nineteenth century. But the key ingredient of what came to be called nationalism appeared much earlier: loyalty to a group larger than oneself. It resembles the loyalty felt within a biological family. The terms by which nations are described (in English, "homeland," "fatherland," "motherland," of which there are cognates like the German "Heimat" and the French "patrie") suggest the nation is an extension of the family.

Of course, a nation is not literally a family, but nevertheless there is a strong emotional tie that asserts itself. Group solidarity was indeed initially based on the survival of kinship groups that displayed loyalty. Azar Gat, a political scientist at Tel Aviv University, and author of *Nations*, writes that, "As Darwin himself suggested, under conditions of intense competition, a group which was biologically endowed with greater solidarity and with individual willingness to sacrifice for the group would defeat less cohesive groups."

Gat sees a progression from these smaller kinship groups that can
take the form of clans or tribes to what he calls an "ethnos"—"a
population of shared kinship (real or perceived) and culture"—to a
"people" that share a common understanding of their "identity history and fate"—to a "nation" in which a people become politically
sovereign. He presumes that the features of loyalty, solidarity, and
reciprocity that originated earlier in history are preserved in this
progression and give cohesion to the larger group of the nation.

Moreover, to join, and be part of, a group is in effect to cede part
of oneself. That can bolster an individual's self-esteem. When the
group succeeds, so do its members. On a trivial level, one sees this
among sports fans (i.e., fanatics). When the team wins, the fans win.
Citizenship in a nation can have the same uplifting effect. Identification with a nation can deflect an abiding fear of mortality. Even if
the individual is mortal, the nation itself is not. In his *Addresses to
the German Nation,* one of the seminal texts of German nationalism,
Johann Gottlieb Fichte writes of the "noble-minded man":

> Life merely as such, the mere continuance of changing existence,
> has in any case never had any value for him; he has wished for it
> only as the source of what is permanent. But this permanence is
> promised to him only by the continuous and independent exis-
> tence of his nation. In order to save his nation he must be ready
> even to die that it may live, and that he may live in it the only life
> for which he has ever wished.

Almost two centuries later, British Labour leader Neil Kinnock
would express similar sentiment: "I would die for my country, but I
would never let my country die for me." In *The Worm at the Core,* psychologists Sheldon Solomon, Jeff Greenberg, and Tom Pyszczynski
write, "People also gain a sense of symbolic immortality from feeling
that they are part of a heroic cause or a nation that will endure
indefinitely." In *The Psychology of Nationalism,* psychologist Joshua

192 Searle-White sums up the appeal of nationalism: "Nationalism provides us with a way . . . to feel moral, right, and just. It gives us a way to join with others in a heroic struggle. It gives a sense of purpose and meaning to our lives, and even to our deaths."

Learning Nationalism
During childhood, people today acquire a fear of death and a desire for social approbation, but the question is how these become linked to nationalism. Threats from other peoples and countries can always be important—and lead to the historical development of nationalism—but in everyday life, a significant role, according to British psychologist Michael Billig, is played by what he calls "banal nationalism." National pride and loyalty are inculcated through the routine details of living and learning. These include learning of a country's history and heroes, filtered through a rosy prism, visiting its monuments, taking part in its celebrations and holidays, saluting its flag, singing its national anthem, and referring to the nation's inhabitants as "we" and "us." (The controversy in the United States over Confederate monuments and "taking a knee" before the Star Spangled Banner brought to the surface the symbolic importance of national statuary and anthems.)

For many people, the most important gateway to nationalist sentiment is through religious belief and observance. Nationalism's promise of transcending the self dovetails with the promise of many religions of evading the fear of death. Christianity, Islam, and other world religions address the hope of escaping personal mortality and powerlessness through identification with a larger group and a higher power. In some countries, like Iran and Israel, nationalism is inextricably bound up with a religion. In other countries, like Turkey and India, the ruling political parties have identified the national culture with a religion.

Even professedly secular nations continue to frame their objectives, and the substance of their nationalism, in terms borrowed from their countries' religious history. They have re-adapted

religious customs, holy days, martyrs, sacred texts, and monu- 193
ments. Americans say the Pledge of Allegiance at the beginning of
the school day, celebrate presidents' birthdays, and revere the Constitution. Fallen heroes like Joan of Arc and Martin Luther King, Jr.
are celebrated. America's Memorial Day and Australia's Remembrance Day signify the transcendence of the self by the nation, as do
monuments like France's Arc de Triomphe and London's Cenotaph.

Political scientist Anthony Smith describes the modern nation
as "a sacred communion of citizens." He writes, "Investing 'our'
homeland with special qualities, and regarding it with reverence and
awe, as the birthplace of the nation or the resting-place of its heroes
and ancestors, is to continue in secular form the pre-modern practice of hallowing historic places and marking off sacred ancestral
territories." Religion, Smith concludes, "far from being squeezed
out of the frame of a secularizing modernity, re-emerges within it in
new guises. Its legacies are not buried and forgotten, rather they are
transmuted in and by nationalism."

Modern Nationalism
There is a heated debate among the social scientists who study
nationalism about when nations and nationalism originated. Traditionalists like Azar Gat or Anthony Smith believe that you can find
nations and nationalism as far back as ancient Egypt, Judah, China's Song Dynasty, or in pre-capitalist Poland, Hungary, France,
and Japan. These were nations, according to the traditionalists,
that commanded the loyalty of their peoples, as best evidenced in
wars. The Dutch historian Johan Huizinga made a strong case for the
emergence of nationalism during the Middle Ages.

Modernists like Benedict Anderson, Eric Hobsbawm, or Ernest
Gellner usually date the first nations and instances of nationalism from the French Revolution. (Liah Greenfeld puts the beginnings in Tudor England.) Modernists see the development of print
literacy, capitalism, and popular sovereignty as necessary conditions of nationhood. The nation, Hobsbawm writes in *Nations and*

194   *Nationalism since 1780,* is a "novelty." Some of this debate is purely
semantic.* But if you strip away the nomenclature, there is a way of
reconciling much of what is true in both approaches.

While the traditionalists are right that there were nations and
nationalist sentiment before 1789, a significant change in the nature
of both takes place in the seventeenth and eighteenth centuries. The
result is the elevation in importance of nationalist sentiment and the
development of a comprehensive nationalist politics and ideology.

In highly stratified and dispersed feudal Europe or Japan, nationalism primarily emerged when a foreign enemy was at the gates. Early
Japanese nationalism was spurred by an abortive Mongol invasion,
Chinese incursions, and the appearance of Christian missionaries
and Western traders. Gat describes nationalism during these wars:

> In times of national emergency the elites did not hesitate to appeal
> to and arouse the masses' latent national sentiments, even if their
> socioeconomic interests differed and the nobles' token willing-
> ness to take up the peasants' cause scarcely survived the time of
> emergency.

Outside of national emergencies, national loyalty in these
countries lay dormant and was subordinated to that of family, kin,
village, parish, fief, or domain. That began to change, however, with

---

*Just as with other political and historical terms (e.g., populism, liberalism,
society, people), the terms "nation" and "nationalism" cannot be subject to
scientific standards of definition without artificially limiting the scope of
analysis and without coming up with conclusions that defy common sense and
ordinary usage. For instance, Walker Connor, a highly regarded political scientist
who specialized in the study of nationalism, defined a "nation" as "the largest
group that shares a sense of common ancestry." ("The Timelessness of Nations,"
Nations and Nationalism, 10, 2004.) By this definition, he acknowledged, there
was a Basque, Polish, and Welsh nation, but not a British, American, or Indian
nation. That will make the Basques happy, I'm sure, but will bewilder Americans.
My own approach is to use the terms as popularly understood, and on that basis
to look backward in history to find how the sentiments and beliefs associated
with what people call nations or nationalism originated. A degree of inexactitude
is unavoidable.

the spread of print literacy; the replacement of feudalism with cap-
italism; the political revolutions in England, the United States, and
France; the unification of Germany and Italy; and the challenge of
Western imperialism in East Asia.

Literacy created the possibility for a popular politics and a
broadly accepted ideology of nationalism. In Europe and the United
States, Protestantism challenged religious and social hierarchy.
Capitalism undermined feudal hierarchy, and it centralized production and people in towns and cities, where they could exert their
influence *en masse*. Political revolutions destroyed the power of
the monarchy and nobility. Popular sovereignty didn't necessarily
require democracy, only the possibility of citizens massing in protest against a national administration, as they did in Europe in 1830
and 1848. Gat writes, "Two complementary processes were at work
fueling the age of nationalism: mass society and popular sovereignty greatly enhanced national cohesion and the people's stake in
the nation; and by the same token they opened the door and enabled
the expression of long-held popular nationalistic sentiments."

Ernest Gellner argues that by destroying local institutions and
hierarchies, industrial capitalism created a singular, direct relationship between the individual and the nation. "There is very little in
the way of any effective, binding organization at any level between
the individual and the total community," Gellner writes. "The *nation*
is now supremely important, thanks to the erosion of subgroupings
and the vastly increased importance of a shared literary-dependent
culture." As a result, Gellner argues, nationalist sentiment assumed
an importance that it had lacked in pre-capitalist societies.

The diminishment of these institutions has continued well past
the heyday of industrial capitalism. Modern capitalism's divorce
of production from the family—as described in Eli Zaretsky's *Capitalism, the Family, and Personal Life*—and the challenge to the traditional family from new sexual norms weakened a key institution
that allowed individuals to transcend their isolation. Science's conflict with religion dealt another blow to an important source of group

196 identity. The emergence of globalization in the 1970s has undermined the labor union and the locally owned factory and business
and the community they sustained. Finding themselves at the mercy
of currency flows, footloose multinational corporations, and migrant
flows, and afflicted by anomie and a sense of powerlessness—the
individual has little recourse except the nation.

Nationalism as a Framework
Nationalism provides a framework within which citizens and their
governments deliberate about what to do—and justify what they
have done. Citizens debate whether a policy is in the "national
interest." Even debates over globalization or free trade will usually
be waged on this terrain. In January 2017, in response to attacks by
Trump and his aides on "globalists," *Forbes* ran a column entitled
"Globalization Has Done a Lot of Great Things for Americans."

This approach is not hardwired into people's brains, but
learned; it can also be rejected, and has been, particularly during the
1990s, the heyday of globalization. Philosopher Jürgen Habermas
advocated a "post-national constellation." Ulrich Beck urged "a politics of post-nationalism" in which "the cosmopolitan project con-
tradicts and replaces the nation-state project." Martha Nussbaum
urged Americans to pledge allegiance to a common humanity. "They
are, above all, citizens of a world of human beings, and that while
they happen to be situated in the United States, they have to share
this world with the citizens of other countries."

Indeed, some policymakers and governments have championed policies like the reduction of carbon dioxide emissions on the
grounds that doing so would help the planet avoid a climatological
catastrophe, but in these cases, government officials can also argue
that their nation would benefit. There are, however, some circumstances in which a government might adopt policies that would
affect their citizens somewhat adversely in order to aid another
country that is facing a natural disaster. And even when undertaking
policies that they deem in the national interest, policymakers will

take into account their effect on other countries, and try, especially   197
if they are friends or allies, to limit any adverse consequence.

But in the great majority of challenges a country faces, public
officials and citizens will look primarily to what they believe is in
their nation's best interests. Oxford political scientist David Miller
writes, "In acknowledging a national identity, I am also acknowl
edging that I owe special obligations to fellow members of my nation
that I do not owe to other human beings."

Some advocates of cosmopolitanism reject this outlook on ethical grounds. In criticizing Democratic presidential candidate Bernie
Sanders for rejecting a policy of "open borders," journalist Dylan Matthews argued that Sanders "is obligated to weigh the interests of a
poor potential Nigerian immigrant equally to those of a much richer
native-born American. I think if he saw an immigrant drowning in a
pond, he has just as much of a duty to rescue her as he would if she
were a native-born American." Should Americans display as much
concern about Bolivians or Uzbeks as they do about their own citizenry? Maybe they should do so in some ideal world, but they simply
don't. Questions about what a nation should or should not do are
inevitably grounded in an existing common framework of concern.

At a similar time of global reach in the late nineteenth century,
British moral philosopher Henry Sidgwick made exactly this point.
The "cosmopolitan ideal," Sidgwick wrote, is "the ideal of the future"
but it now "allows too little for the national and patriotic sentiments
which have in any case to be reckoned with as an actually powerful
political force, and which appears to be at present indispensable to
social well-being. We cannot yet hope to substitute for these sentiments in sufficient diffusion and intensity, the wider sentiment
connected with the conception of our common humanity."

Nationalism and the Modern State
In modern nations, the loyalty and solidarity expressed by the
pronoun "we" underpins key institutions and practices. Nationalist sentiment underlies the public commitment to upholding the

198   results of elections and to adhering to laws without coercion. Writes David Miller, "Where the citizens of a state are also compatriots, the mutual trust that this engenders makes it more likely that they will be able to solve collective action problems, to support redistributive principles of justice, and to practice deliberative forms of democracy." When there isn't such a common nationalist sentiment, either because of civil disorder or because of the existence of rival nationalisms, as in pre–Civil War America or Iraq, Syria, Nigeria, and Spain today, the country becomes difficult or impossible to govern.

Nationalist sentiment underlies the acceptance or rejection of the welfare state. The modern welfare state has been built upon shared nationalist sentiments. Governments had to secure citizens' commitment to pay taxes to help their fellow citizens when they became sick or disabled, too old to work, or lost their job and couldn't quickly find another one. Citizens had to be able to identify themselves with the fate—"it could happen to me"—of other citizens they did not know. (This is what Benedict Anderson meant by calling a nation an "imagined community.") This willingness to identify with others assumed that their fellow citizens who received this aid conformed to certain cultural norms: that, for instance, they were or had been willing to work; that, if they were immigrants, they had entered the country legally and were committed to staying and working and that, in extreme circumstances, they would fight to defend the nation. They had to believe that the others shared the same nationalist sentiments—that they could be included in the use of the plural pronoun "we."

When this trust and feeling of reciprocity has broken down, then support for the welfare state has dissipated, as it did in the United States, amidst suspicion of what Ronald Reagan called "welfare queens," and in Europe, as suspicion has arisen that immigrants or refugees are free riders or "welfare tourists." At its extreme, it can be the basis for social exclusion of groups like Jews, Muslims, or Roma that are not deemed to be a trusted part of the nation.

In other words, nationalist sentiments can be the basis of social generosity or of bigoted exclusion. Nationalism is an essential ingredient of political democracies; but it can also be the basis for fascist and authoritarian regimes. What direction these sentiments take depends very much on the interplay between historical circumstances and the appeals that a country's parties, politicians, and officials make. Take the most extreme example of Hitler's Germany. Nazism is often portrayed as an inevitable outgrowth of German nationalism, but it did not have to be that way.

German nationalism was composed of the following: German Pietism, which emphasized feeling over reason, and came to identify the nation as the embodiment of Christianity and of Christianity's promise of eternal life; German romanticism, which, in the works of G. W. F. Hegel or Friedrich Schlegel, saw the nation as an organic whole and the individual as a mere fragment who lived through it and through the state; and the Prussian quest for power through the unification of the principalities into a powerful state. These three strains came together in Prussian-led Wilhelmine Germany. They were reflected in the rise of German Social Democracy (which advocated a socialist state) *and* later in the rise of Nazism and still later in Germany's post–World War II solidaristic mix of Christian and Social Democracy.

There was no unbreakable chain that connected early German nationalism to Nazism. The triumph of Nazism in the 1930s required, among other things, German defeat in World War I, the punitive terms of the Versailles settlement after the war, the specter of Bolshevism and the split in the Second International, the incomprehension of American, British, and French finance officials during the 1920s, and the utter failure of an embattled Weimar democracy. In short, nationalist sentiments do not necessarily lead rightward or leftward. They can shape the kind of government, but their ultimate disposition depends on a host of historical circumstances.

200 Nationalism as an Explicit Ideology

Since World War II, politicians, parties, and public officials have relied on the framework of nationalist sentiment to justify their initiatives, but they usually haven't specifically invoked nationalism to distinguish themselves from other politicians or parties. They haven't suggested that they alone represent the national interest and that their political opponents' commitments to the nation are equivocal. They haven't run on an explicit doctrine or ideology of nationalism. A politics based on this kind of an explicit appeal usually emerges only during times of social disorder—in the United States on the eve of the Civil War or in Europe between the two world wars or in countries in the throes of revolution. But this kind of explicit nationalist politics has resurfaced in Europe and the United States during the last decade.

There are at least three different kinds of explicit nationalist appeals. The first is intended to unite the nation against a foreign foe or a colonial power. This can occur during war or during conflicts over trade and territory or even over perceived wrongs from the past. What distinguishes these kinds of appeals is that they seek to unite an entire nation. The second kind of appeal attempts to unite a prototypical nation (such as "real Americans" or "true Poles") against an internal foe that is seen to threaten the nation's cohesion and integrity. Such foes can range from a monarch or an elite (who are seen either to represent only themselves or even a foreign interest) to an underclass or an outgroup or a secessionist movement. The third kind of appeal, which is characteristic of secessionist movements, seeks to unite a part of a nation, defined usually by a common territory and culture, against what has been a host nation. The Catalan appeal for secession against Spain or the Scottish appeal for independence takes this form.

The first and second of these nationalist appeals often occur together. Trump railed against China and Mexico for their trade practices *and* against illegal immigrants and proposed to ban visitors and immigrants from Muslim countries. Poland's government

attacked Brussels (the headquarters of the EU) and has contrasted   201
"true Poles," who support its agenda, with "Poles of the worst kind."
The Hungarian government complains of intervention from Brussels but also from Hungarian native and American citizen George
Soros and his allies in Budapest.

This kind of implicit nationalism can appear on the political
right or the left. It is often associated with the extreme right of Germany's Hitler, Italy's Benito Mussolini, Spain's Francisco Franco,
the Southern Confederacy and the Ku Klux Klan. But nationalism
was also central to the French revolutionaries of 1789, the North in
the American Civil War, the national liberation movements of the
twentieth century, and to Britain's resistance to the Nazi onslaught
during its "finest hour." Sociologist Craig Calhoun writes in *Nations
Matter*:

> From the eighteenth century revolutions, to the nineteenth-century "Springtime of the Peoples," to mid-twentieth-century
> post-colonial independence movements, nationalism has often
> been closely linked to the pursuit of greater self-government.

Whether on the left or right, most explicit nationalist movements and parties, and most nations during war or revolution, can
display the strengths but also the significant weaknesses of group
solidarity. By ceding their individuality to a larger group that defines
itself as the nation, the members of a movement or party or of citizens in war relinquish their moral judgment and intelligence to
the group, and most often to the group's charismatic leader. They
become susceptible to suggestion and can come to believe things
that they would ordinarily reject. They become capable of great
courage and sacrifice on behalf of ends both noble and ignoble. They
can display exceptional generosity and kindness or wanton cruelty
and vindictiveness.

In the wake of World War I, Sigmund Freud, writing in *Group
Psychology and the Analysis of the Ego*, described the psychology of

202   groups ("Massenpsychologie" might be more accurately rendered
as the psychology of "masses" or "crowds" or even "mobs") in a way
that applies to some explicit nationalist movements:

> When individuals come together as a group all their individual
> inhibitions fall away and all the cruel, brutal, and destructive
> instincts, which lie dormant in individuals . . . are stirred up to find
> free gratification. But under the influence of suggestion, groups
> are also capable of high achievement in the shape of abnegation,
> unselfishness, and devotion to an ideal. While with isolated indi-
> viduals, personal interest is almost the only motive force, with
> groups it is very rarely prominent. . . . Whereas the intellectual
> capacity of a group is always far below that of an individual, its
> ethical conduct may rise as high above it as it may sink below it.

A critical intelligence is often the first casualty of war, revolution, and impassioned nationalist appeals. Rightwing nationalists
have often based their appeals on exaggerated threats (for instance,
of Mexican rapists) or wild conspiracy theories, but in wartime, the
center and left often exploit the credulity of their followers. During
the first Gulf War, fought to prevent a large country from absorbing
its small neighbor, many liberals as well as conservatives believed
that Iraqi soldiers were taking Kuwaiti babies out of incubators and
leaving them to die.

Nationalist movements on the right have often advocated violence against their domestic as well as foreign adversaries. They
have sought to constrict rather than expand democracy. But there is
also a disturbing trajectory on the left: a long history of parties and
movements—from France's Jacobins to Russia's Bolsheviks to the
national liberation movements after World War II—that have begun
with a promise of democracy only to embrace tyranny and even
terror. In other words, there is a danger endemic to explicit nationalist movements on the right or the left. Even those that promise

liberation often end up promoting oppression. It's not a historical aberration, but is rooted in the psychological nature of explicit
nationalist appeals.

Causes of the Nationalist Revival

The conditions that have made today's citizenry in the United
States and Europe susceptible to explicit nationalist appeals go back
to changes in Western capitalism and politics that began at least in
the 1970s and to the big push toward a globalized politics and economics that began in the 1990s. What made many citizens in the
United States and Europe receptive to nationalist appeals is a perception that they and by extension their nations were in decline.
More broadly, it is a perception that their—and by extension their
nations'—*way of life* was threatened. Many of these citizens were
victims of the uneven development of the post-industrial global
capitalism that had taken hold in the 1970s and reached a denoue-
ment during the Great Recession.

While metro areas populated by the highly educated have prospered, towns that had depended on manufacturing and mining have
gone into disrepair. Factory and related business closings created
what British political scientists Robert Ford and Matthew Goodwin
have called the "left-behinds" who see themselves falling behind in
comparison to their compatriots. They blame trade, immigration,
Brussels, and Washington for their fate. Some liberal political scientists have insisted there is no economic basis for rightwing nationalist or populist politics, but the key consideration is not whether a
particular area is well or poorly off in absolute terms, but whether it
has experienced decline and whether its inhabitants feel themselves
significantly less well off than people elsewhere in their countries.

There have been several studies of the Brexit vote in 2016. By
comparing voting patterns with economic figures, Yann Algan,
Pierre Cahuc, and Marc Sagnier found that "*increases* in unemployment during the crisis period 2007–2015 (rather than the level of

204 unemployment in 2015) are strong predictors of Brexit vote." Econ-omists Sascha O. Becker, Thiemo Fetzer, and Dennis Novy reached similar conclusions in analyzing the Brexit vote by voting district. They found the vote to leave the EU was strongly correlated with areas that had once had strong manufacturing employment, but now suffered from low pay, rising unemployment, and declining public services. In Germany, the heart of the AfD's support is in former East Germany. Saxony and Saxony-Anhalt, two states where the AfD is particularly strong, have only a little more than half the per capita income of Munich's Bavaria or Frankfurt's Hesse. Austria's Freedom Party, Hungary's Fidesz, and Poland's Law and Justice all have their strongest support outside the more prosperous metro centers of Vienna, Budapest, and Warsaw.

Economic decline is often accompanied by a decline in the social network of unions, bars, and social clubs. In *The New Minority: White Working Class Politics in the Age of Immigration and Inequality*, polit-ical scientist Justin Gest describes the politics of two East London boroughs, Dagenham and Barking, that used to house a huge Ford plant that had radically downsized from a peak of 40,000 to 2,000 employees, leaving many of the original inhabitants without work. The social fabric of these boroughs, based on unions and pubs, has deteriorated. Gest writes, "Pubs are endangered in Barking and Dagenham today. Their primary consumers, white working class men and women, have less and less disposable income. With the loss of basic warehouse and manufacturing work, they can no longer afford to spend precious pence on pints at the pub, let alone tickets to local football matches."

The perception of economic and social decline was often linked to a perception of moral decline. This was seen to result from chal-lenges to the family and church perceived to be caused by femi-nists and secularists, and by the jarring customs of immigrants. Gest quotes a letter that a member of the Barking-Dagenham tenant association wrote to British prime minister David Cameron in 2012:

We used to be a very close community but over the last 15+ years this has changed so much and certainly not for the better. It would seem that immigrants from all over the world are encouraged to come to our borough to live, thus driving out the indigenous community one by one until now we have the situation where we are in the minority in a place we have lived for most of our lives. . . . The recent arrivals are only interested in their own cultures and, to a large degree, this is being encouraged by all the services created especially for them at great financial cost, while we sit on the sidelines and watch all this; we watch our elderly being frightened to go out because if they get on a bus they are likely to be the only person speaking English.

These citizens, like those in North Carolina towns that until very recently were centers of furniture manufacturing, or in northern French towns decimated by the loss of manufacturing and mining jobs, have felt left behind by post-industrial capitalism and by the libertarian, secular, and cosmopolitan culture of New York, San Francisco, London, Copenhagen, and Paris. They became prime candidates for an explicit nationalist appeal that would reaffirm their social identity and combat their own feelings of social isolation and political powerlessness.

In the United States, what made that group immediately susceptible to nationalist appeals was anger over trade deals that seemed to favor foreigners over the United States, a massive influx of legal and illegal immigration that appeared to take away jobs and raise social costs, and the onset of Islamist terror attacks to which they believed porous borders had made them vulnerable. In Europe, there was a similar mix, but the economic resentment was more focused on austerity promoted by the European Union than on trade deals. In both the United States and Europe, the fear and resentment over immigration, fused with a fear of Islamist terrorism, loomed as the single greatest precipitant of the new nationalism. Today's

206   conservative nationalism is a complex of attitudes and sentiments about economic, social, and moral decline—a fear that one's way of life is under attack—that has been catalyzed into a nationalist politics by the economic, social, and moral issue of immigration.

After the UK voted to leave the European Union, a British polling group did a survey to determine what had motivated the vote to leave and constructed a "word cloud" to represent the prominence of the different responses they got. Immigration was clearly number one. In April 2018, YouGov asked citizens from 11 EU countries what issues were the most important to them. Immigration was number one in all except for Spain and Poland. Terrorism was number two in all except for Spain and Poland (it was number one in Poland). Trump's vote in 2016, the successes of Le Pen's National Front, Orban's Fidesz Party in Hungary, Germany's AfD, and the League in Italy were clearly attributable to social anxiety over immigration and terrorism underlain by a perception of economic and moral decline. They were the proximate cause of the rise of the nationalist right.

Nationalists and Cosmopolitans

There is a key political division in the United States and Europe that is not between left and right or Christian Democrats and Social Democrats, but between what British author David Goodhart, analyzing the Brexit vote, calls "somewheres" and "anywheres." Somewheres usually live in small or midsized towns that were once centers of manufacturing or mining. They have an identity rooted in home, family, and nation—in the United States, often in faith and religion as well. They used to have multiple identities in union, company, and community, and used to be optimistic about their future, but are no longer. And they see their nation's well-being, standing, and social integrity being threatened by foreign trade, unscrupulous financiers, and, above all, mass immigration. Goodhart notes, "For several years now more than half of British people have agreed with this statement (and similar ones): 'Britain has changed in recent times beyond recognition, it sometimes feels like a foreign country and this makes me feel uncomfortable.'" One would find similar sentiments among Americans outside the big metro areas.

I don't know whether "anywheres" is the best term for the opposing outlook. The people Goodhart identifies as "anywheres"— young college graduates, professionals, people who live in one of the great thriving metro centers or upper tier college towns—wouldn't necessarily live *anywhere*. They would be comfortable in any of the other great metro centers, including Paris, New York, London, and Berlin, but don't send them to Buffalo or Calais or Magdeburg. "Cosmopolitans" might be a better term for them.

They have multiple identities, including a profession (with membership in professional associations) and a firm, a practice, or a university (in whose future they have a stake). They welcome immigrants, who often serve as maids, nannies, landscapers, roofers, cabdrivers, orderlies, home care aides, and waiters. They are not bothered by factory closings, which they see as the price of progress. They are not anti-nationalist, or unpatriotic. They would go to war if the country was attacked. They are proud to be American or French or British (or English), but unlike the somewheres, they don't depend primarily or even significantly for their self-approbation and esteem on *that* identity. It's not necessarily their hedge against individual mortality or anomie.

Anywheres, Goodhart writes, "have portable 'achieved' identities, based on educational and career success which makes them generally comfortable and confident with new places and people. Somewheres are more rooted and usually have 'ascribed' identities—Scottish farmer, working class Geordie, Cornish housewife—based on group belonging and particular places, which is why they often find rapid change more unsettling." The United States and Europe are rife with division between these two groups. The somewheres—who coincide roughly with the "left-behinds" of post-industrial capitalism in the U.S. and Europe—have provided the base of the explicit nationalist movements and parties. They voted for Brexit

208   and Donald Trump and they cheer Victor Orban in Hungary or Marine Le Pen in France.

The somewheres generally regard the anywheres as part of a global elite that is oblivious to them or, worse still, is trying to undermine their communities through shutting down their factories and mines and championing the influx of alien cultures. The anywheres—typified by a Wall Street, Frankfurt, or the City financier, a tenured professor from Oxford, Columbia, or Sciences Po, or a computer executive from Silicon Valley with multiple "achieved" identities—regard the somewheres as racists or misogynists or authoritarians who hearken to the Hitlers of history. The question for the future of politics in the U.S. and Europe is whether some kind of accommodation can be reached between these two very different political communities and sensibilities so that the worst excesses that can accompany explicit nationalism—the demagoguery, the rampant conspiratorializing, the scapegoating—can be marginalized. But for that to happen, the anywheres or cosmopolitans will have to exhibit greater understanding of what is driving many of their compatriots to support people like Trump and Orban.

(Let's)
Make America
Great Again

American nationalism has a long lineage, going back even before the revolution of 1776, and draws together an understanding of home, family, religion, and work into the idea of an American way of life. Much of the country's success over the centuries has been due to the widespread acceptance of a common identity and way of life. That has accounted for the country's enduring political institutions and for its successes in two world wars.

But as befits a nation that originally welcomed African American slavery and that after the 1830s began receiving a massive influx of immigrants, many of whom did not share what was then the prevailing culture, religion, and ethnicity, America has had continued debates over the definition of an American. These debates erupted into heated political conflict by the 1840s and in the 1860s into a civil war where over 600,000 Americans perished.

Over the last decade, rumblings over nationality, which began in the 1980s, have ascended to a deafening roar. Donald Trump won this support in 2016 most visibly over his opposition to illegal immigration, "bad trade deals," and "political correctness." In doing so, Trump, and the Tea Party movement that preceded him, were appealing to American citizens who felt that their nation and their

210 common purpose had been put in jeopardy. Trump fanned these sentiments, which are deeply rooted in America's past, and which have contributed to the country's great successes as well as failures, into a conflagration that carried him to the presidency and allowed him to build an ardent following.

Early American Nationalism

There is an anodyne version of American nationalism, popularized six decades ago by philosopher Hans Kohn, that American nationalism consists merely of support for "an idea, the idea of liberty under law as expressed in the Constitution." By contrast, Eastern (by which Kohn meant Eastern or Central European) or ethnic nationalism was "cultural" and based on "traditional ties of kinship and status." To be sure, there are differences. It no longer makes sense to talk of an "ethnic American." But American nationalism, no less than German, was born out of a core ethnic and religious identity. Over the next 225 years, that identity has been called into question, modified, and expanded, but never entirely lost. It has framed the current struggle over what it means to be an American.

The creation of an American identity began even before the revolution. There was a sense of common ancestry and belief that underlay the difficult transition from colonial Britain to revolutionary America and to the "we the people" of the Constitution. In his plea for a United States, John Jay, in *Federalist Paper, No 2,* described this basis for the new nation:

> Providence has been pleased to give this one connected country to one united people—a people descended from the same ancestors, speaking the same language, professing the same religion, attached to the same principles of government, very similar in their manner and customs, and who, by their joint counsels, arms, and efforts, fighting side by side throughout a long and bloody war, have nobly established liberty and independence.

In 1790, when the first census occurred, about 90 percent of white American settlers were British in origin—82 percent were English. An even higher percentage of them were Protestants. Not all the settlers had sided with the revolutionaries against the British, but the revolutionary victory in 1783 had consolidated the understanding of the settlers as "Americans" as distinct from "Britons" or "English." While the framers of the Constitution would resist the term "nation"—they preferred "union"—what came into being after the revolution was, however fractured into states, a new American nation where most of the inhabitants felt a sense of kinship.

Even those who could not trace their lineage to England sought to create a semblance of kinship. Political scientist Eric Kaufmann writes, "Among Pennsylvania Germans, for example, Zimmermann became Carpenter and Rittinghuysen was changed to Rittenhouse, while, among the Huguenots, revolutionary Paul Revere's surname reflects a change from the French Rivoire." In other words, even if Anglo American Protestants were not omnipresent, they exercised a kind of social hegemony. They constituted the initial image of the American.

This idealized American, as set forth in eighteenth-century American nationalism, was an English-speaking Anglo American who adhered to the tenets of a dissenting Protestantism that had traversed the Atlantic Ocean in the early seventeenth century. This religious outlook had reached other colonies from New England during the Great Awakening of the 1740s, and had created a common moral or religious community. As Alexis de Tocqueville commented later, "The principles of New England spread at first to the neighboring states; they then passed successively to the more distant ones; and at length they imbued the whole Confederation. They now extend their influence beyond its limits over the whole American world."

This Protestantism was structured around a set of beliefs that would continue to define American nationalism well after Americans ceased to remember who Jonathan Edwards or George Whitefield were or practiced biblical Christianity or were predominately

212   descended from English yeomen. These features included the following:

- *American Exceptionalism.* Americans were a "chosen people" that had a mission to transform the world by creating a "shining city on the hill," a "new Israel," or a "new Canaan" on the American continent.
- *An Apocalyptic Adversary.* In achieving their mission, Americans faced an implacable foe that had to be overcome. For the early settlers, it was Catholicism and the "Papal anti-Christ."
- *The Good Book.* Americans sought guidance from sacred texts. For the first settlers, it was the Bible as the word of God, but later it was the Declaration of Independence and the Constitution. (The constitution that the Connecticut colony ratified in 1639 is described as the world's first written constitution.)
- *Equality Before God.* The early settlers believed they enjoyed an unmediated relationship with God without the intercession of monarchies or popes. That became inscribed in the Declaration's words that "all men are created equal."
- *The Protestant Ethic.* The settlers believed that success through hard work was a measure of whether one was saved and that idleness was a mark of damnation.
- *Family, Church, and Nation.* Family and church became the bulwarks of nation. "Such as families are, such at last the church and commonwealth must be," wrote James Fitch in 1683.

The chief polarity defining American nationalism was that between the nation's chosenness and its adversaries, but the sense of American identity was always broader than that and included notions about liberty, equality, work, family, church, and textual authority. This definition was as "cultural" as that of other nations. Where it differed from Poland or Japan was that American national identity expanded over the centuries well beyond the original Anglo American ethnicity.

The Triumph of the Euro American

The initial image of the Anglo American would be undermined by waves of immigration—Irish and Germans in the 1840s and 1850s and Southern and Eastern Europeans from the 1880s to 1921, until Congress began drastically curbing immigration. Many Anglo American Protestants objected to the new immigrants, and there were pitched battles over immigration before the Civil War and from the late nineteenth century until the 1920s. "Blackness" was the ultimate badge of outsiderdom, but in the early twntieth century, it was not just African Americans who would be branded "colored," but also Eastern and Southern Europeans. When a young Harry Truman visited New York City in 1918, he wrote to his cousin, "This town has 8,000,000 people. 7,500,000 of 'em are of Israelish extraction. (400,000 wops and the rest are white people.)"

The immigrants from the 1880s and their descendants were able to assimilate, partly because of the restrictions on immigration in the 1920s but also because of World War II where white Americans fought side by side. After the war, Americans increasingly adopted the ideal of what Michael Lind in *The Next American Nation* called the "Euro-American." This new ideal included Poles, Italians, and even Jews alongside Anglo-Saxon Protestants in what was portrayed as the "American melting pot." In 1960, an Irish Catholic was elected president. In 1965, President Lyndon Johnson evoked the dream of the melting pot. "Our beautiful America was built by a nation of strangers. From a hundred different places or more they have poured forth into an empty land, joining and blending in one mighty and irresistible tide."

As the image of the American changed, so did the political framework of American nationalism. This framework was forced to adapt to the transformation of American capitalism and of America's place in the world. Instead of seeing their country as biblically "chosen," Americans proclaimed their "manifest destiny" as they spread over the North American continent. Later, as America became a global power, Americans boasted of the American Century

214   and of America as the leader of the Free World and of America as
the "indispensable nation." This notion of America's exceptionalism was sustained by America rising to become a global power,
by victory in two world wars, by a rising standard of living, by the
success of American manufacturing, and by the superiority of
American-made consumer goods.

The New Immigrants

Over the last fifty years, this consensus around the Euro American
ideal and around what C. Wright Mills called the "great American
celebration" has disintegrated. In its place, the United States has
endured what have been called "culture wars." They are very similar
to the political wars that took place from the 1880s into the 1920s,
but more bitter, protracted, and polarized. The first phase of these
culture wars stretches from the late 1960s until September 11, 2001.
They were partly precipitated by a dramatic change in the composition of the American citizenry through new waves of immigration
and partly, too, by African Americans winning their civil and political rights.

Inspired by the civil rights movement, Democrats in Congress,
led by Massachusetts senator Ted Kennedy, passed a new Immigration and Nationality Act that erased the discriminatory quotas
erected in the 1920s. Immigration was limited to 170,000 a year, and
the bill's supporters did not expect it would dramatically increase
immigration. But the bill's sponsors didn't anticipate that many
people from Mexico, Central America, and the Caribbean, as well as
from Asian nations, would take advantage of the bill's provision for
family reunification, which allowed relatives of citizens to emigrate
without respect to quotas.

In the 1950s, 68 percent of legal immigrants came from Canada
or Europe, but from 1971 to 1991, about half the immigrants came
from Mexico, Central America, and the Caribbean and another
third from Asia. In addition, as the guest worker Bracero program
was shut down for seasonal farm workers, immigrants from Mexico

began flooding across the border illegally. Their numbers totaled   215
540,000 in 1969, 5 million in 1996, and 8.4 million in 2000.

Many of the new legal immigrants, and a large majority of the illegal immigrants, were unskilled with little education. They took some jobs—for instance, in agriculture—that Mexican émigrés had historically taken. But they also competed with native born Americans for jobs in the hotel, leisure, meatpacking, and construction industries. In the Midwest, white, unionized meatpacking workers were replaced by low-wage immigrants. In Los Angeles, lower-paid immigrants replaced African American janitors. Construction jobs, once eagerly sought after by native workers, became the province of low-wage immigrant workers. And towns and cities found themselves burdened with the costs of providing social services, including bilingual education in schools and emergency room healthcare.

American identity had always been bound up in the universal use of English. But many of the Latino and Asian immigrants, like the generations of European immigrants in the 1880s, clustered in communities where they spoke their own language. By the 1990s, there was a backlash against the waves of immigrants. According to a 1994 survey, 66 percent of Americans favored decreasing the level of immigration. Eighty-nine percent thought immigrants would "increase unemployment." And 73 percent feared that immigrants would "reduce unity." In the 1994 General Social Survey, 63 percent favored making English "the official language." Thirty-two states adopted laws making English the official language. In 1994, Californians passed Proposition 187, banning illegal immigrants from receiving state funds and attending state schools, by 59 to 41 percent. The head of the group that put the referendum on the ballot said, "We have to take direct and immediate action to preserve this culture and this nation we have spent two centuries building up."

Declining America
During this period, Americans began to suffer doubts not only about who they were, but about America's historic role among nations.

216   The American defeat in Vietnam raised questions not only about America's military prowess, but about its mission in the world. In 1971, facing renewed competition from Japan and Western Europe, the U.S. suffered its first trade deficit in the twentieth century. That was followed by the energy crisis, which revealed America's dependence on Middle Eastern oil despots.

In the 1980s, Americans worried about whether they were losing ground to Japan and West Germany. Americans who went to shop for a television could no longer find American brands except for those names like RCA purchased by the South Koreans or Japanese. Americans also witnessed the disappearance of American manufacturing jobs, which were concentrated in what came to be called the "Rust Belt." The loss of jobs stirred discontent about trade. In a 1985 survey, 75 percent of Americans thought the trade deficit was a "bad thing." In a 1988 survey, nearly nine in ten respondents were concerned about "a loss of jobs due to foreign competition," and 72 percent backed restricting imports.

Americans also fretted about social and moral decline. White Protestant evangelicals, based primarily in the South and Midwest, joined the Moral Majority, and later the Christian Coalition. These groups contended that the country was in a moral tailspin that had begun in the 1960s with the rise of the counterculture, feminism, and secular humanism and with Supreme Court rulings that barred school prayer and later permitted abortion. On September 17, 1986, televangelist Pat Robertson, who would go on to found the Christian Coalition, launched his bid for the Republican presidential nomination at Constitution Hall in Philadelphia on the 199th anniversary of the signing of the Constitution. "A vision was born on this date of a nation united—a nation whose official motto was *E Pluribus Unum*—out of many one," he declared.

Worries about America's moral and social decline dovetailed with concerns about the explosion of welfare spending and the rise of urban crime. Many Americans blamed the rise of welfare spending—which evened out in the later 1970s but then exploded again in the late

1980s—on new Hispanic immigrants and newly empowered African Americans using relaxed welfare laws to get a free ride. In a December 1994 CBS/*New York Times* poll, 57 percent of respondents believed that "most people who receive money from welfare could get along without it," and only 36 percent believed they "really needed help."

Urban violence also became a major issue in response to the riots of the 1960s. As political scientists Thomas Cronin, Tania Cronin, and Michael Milakovich argued in a 1981 book, "the public fears engendered by civil rights protests and the violent reactions these protests occasioned—fear of disorder, fear of riots, fear of blacks" later became entangled with "the public alarm over street crime." In 1977, the National Rifle Association, which had primarily been concerned with gun training for hunters, shifted its focus to advocating for the rights of homeowners to defend themselves. Gun rights became bound up with concerns about the sanctity of home and about American identity and the decline of the country.

In the last third of the twentieth century, a succession of presidential candidates evoked these fears of economic, social, and moral decline. In the 1980s, Ronald Reagan trumpeted the "new patriotism" and proposed, "Let's make America great again." In 1992, Texas billionaire Ross Perot promised to reverse America's economic decline at the hands of Japan; and Pat Buchanan sounded the tocsin for a "cultural war . . . for the soul of America." With the exception of Perot, who was on the center-left, these nationalist campaigns sought to take America back to the 1950s. They were conservative or even reactionary in nature. The high-tech boom of the late 1990s temporarily quieted fears of economic decline, and ended Perot's and Buchanan's political careers, but at the beginning of the twenty-first century, the whole panoply of issues, causes, and concerns wrapped up in Americans' identity would return with a vengeance.

Terror, China, and the Great Recession

There were three developments in the early twenty-first century that intensified nationalist sentiment and laid the basis for the

218   conservative nationalism of the Tea Party and Trump. The first
was the terrorist offensive by radical Islamists against the United
States, which climaxed on September 11, 2001, killing almost
3,000. Walmart sold 366,000 flags the next two days. Country
singer Charlie Daniels, whose career appeared to have been floundering, scored a hit with a song entitled "This Ain't No Rag. It's a
Flag." Religious observance also flourished. The American Bible
Society reported a 45 percent increase in Bible sales. A 1977 book
entitled *Where Is God When It Hurts* immediately sold 750,000
copies. According to a Gallup Poll, church and synagogue attendance
reached heights not seen since the 1950s.

When sociologists Bart Bonikowski and Paul DiMaggio ana-
lyzed changes in "American popular nationalism" in the extensive General Social Survey, they found a marked intensification in
explicit and exclusionary nationalist sentiment from 1996 to 2004.
In 1996, 48 percent of the respondents limited a "true American" to
someone who was born in America, was a Christian, spoke English,
felt American, and had lived most of their life in the United States;
in 2004, it had gone up to 60 percent who limited a true American
to English-speaking Christians who had lived in America most of
their lives. And, as one would expect, the rise in nationalist sentiment from terror attacks by foreigners fueled anti-immigrant sentiments. The sociologists found that those respondents believing
in the limited definition of "true Americans" also strongly believed
that immigrants increased crime rates, took away jobs, and consumed too much government spending. In 2002, a year after September 11, Gallup reported that the percentage of Americans that
favored a decrease in immigration had risen from 41 to 54 percent.

With many Americans, the connection between immigration and terror may have been implicit. But when I went to Arizona
in 2005 to write about the support for Proposition 200, aimed at
illegal immigration, I found people expressing fears that terrorists
were going to come across the border. Said one Arizonan, "We have
many apprehensions of Pakistanis and Iraqis on the border. They

are coming in disguised as Hispanics and blending in." When I covered the 2010 Republican Senate primary in Arizona, I found Ari-
zonans fearing that al-Qaeda operatives were sneaking across the
border. This fusion of anti-immigrant sentiment with fear of terror
persisted well after the number of illegal immigrants entering the
U.S. had peaked in 2007 and had begun to decline.

The second development that sparked the rise in nationalist
sentiment was the emergence of China as a global economic power.
In 1978, under Deng Xiaoping, China had begun introducing market
reforms into what had been a rigidly planned communist economy.
These reforms, which included an opening to foreign investment,
led to rapid industrialization. From 1978 to 2012, China averaged
9.4 percent a year in GDP growth. But trade with the United States
was held in check by the 1974 Jackson-Vanik act, which said that
if a present or former communist country denied its citizens the
right to emigrate, it could not enjoy normal trading relations with
the United States unless Congress annually passed a special waiver.

China had routinely enjoyed a waiver, but after the government massacred protestors in Tiananmen Square in 1989, opposition grew in Congress to continuing China's "most favored nation"
trading status. Bill Clinton had campaigned in 1992 against granting
China a waiver, but once in office, pressured by the CEOs of multinational corporations and Wall Street investment firms seeking
a foothold in potentially the world's largest market, he became a
champion of U.S.-China trade, arguing annually for a waiver and
then for allowing China to enter the World Trade Organization on
generous terms.

Clinton argued that granting China a waiver and championing
its entry into the WTO would democratize China and lead to "hundreds of thousands of American jobs." The opposite occurred. The
Chinese regime became more autocratic—in retrospect, the 1980s
were the heyday of Chinese proto-democracy—and after China
joined the WTO, its trade surplus with the United States soared at
the expense of American jobs. According to an estimate by Robert E.

220 Scott of the Economic Policy Institute, the growth in the U.S.-China trade cost the United States 3.4 million jobs. (For more on this, see chapter thirteen.)

About three-quarters of the lost jobs were in manufacturing. Many had been held by whites who had not graduated from college and who were once charter members of the American middle class. The loss of these jobs contributed to what economists have called the "hollowing out of the middle class." It created a large group of discontented Americans who saw liberal trade policies, including the earlier North American Free Trade Agreement (which had gone into effect in 1994) and rapacious Chinese trade strategies, as the source of their ills.

According to an Allstate/*National Journal* poll in 2010, 61 percent of white Americans who had not graduated from college thought international trade had been bad rather than good for the American economy. Only 34 percent thought it was beneficial. This loss of jobs also contributed to more general fears of American economic decline. In the Allstate/*National Journal* poll, 47 percent of all the respondents thought China had the strongest economy in the world, compared to 20 percent for the United States. Fifty-eight percent of respondents feared that "it is inevitable that Americans' incomes will grow more slowly" because of competition from low-wage economies like China's.

The third and final development that stoked a conservative nationalism was the Great Recession. During the Great Recession, unemployment peaked at 10 percent in October 2009. The economy lost 8.7 million jobs between 2007 and 2014, including 1.4 million manufacturing jobs. The Great Recession reinforced opposition to China's trade strategies, but it also sowed division internally. Instead of creating solidarity between the middle and bottom rungs of the economic ladder, as happened during the Great Depression, the Great Recession heightened the resentment that many in the Euro American core felt toward African Americans and toward Latino immigrants, whom they believed to be benefiting

from government programs without paying taxes to support them.
It particularly enflamed anger at illegal immigrants. Those sentiments helped to give rise to the Tea Party and later to Donald Trump's candidacy.

The Tea Party

The Tea Party at its height was comprised of hundreds of uncoordinated local groups, two corporate-run and corporate-financed lobbies that co-opted the name, and several staff-driven political action committees. What was of interest was the spontaneity of the movement. It dated from a protest against the Obama administration's attempt to limit the Great Recession's damage through an $832 billion stimulus program. On February 19, 2009, CNBC commentator Rick Santelli, speaking from the floor of the Chicago Mercantile Exchange, let loose against the administration's plan to help homeowners who could no longer pay their mortgages. "*This is America!*" Santelli exclaimed. "How many of you people want to pay for your neighbors' mortgage that has an extra bathroom and can't pay their bills?" Santelli called for a "Chicago Tea Party" to protest the administration's stimulus program.

After a series of demonstrations on April 15, tax day, movement groups began to form around the country until there were as many as 200,000 people actively involved. Reflecting its name, the Tea Party replicated the original framework of American nationalism to the point of parody. At demonstrations, they flew the "Don't Tread on Me" flag designed by Christopher Gadsden in 1775 for the colonial rebels. They sacralized the Constitution as a Bible to guide their work. In speeches, Tea Partiers cited articles and amendments from the Constitution the way that clerics cite biblical verses. They invoked the Protestant Ethic, demanding that Obama, in the words of one sign, "Stop Rewarding the Lazy and Taxing the Working."

Tea Partiers' concerns about family, home, guns, work, and illegal immigration were subsumed under a conservative nationalism that aimed to restore the America of old. They saw themselves

222 as defending a way of life. Many of them had also participated in gun rights and Christian right organizations and incorporated their demands about protecting the traditional family and blocking gun control legislation into the Tea Party's agenda.

The Tea Party's principal adversary was Obama, who was their equivalent to the papal antichrist. When sociologists Christopher Parker and Matt A. Barreto made a study of Tea Party blogs in 2010, they found 33 percent of the content was devoted to "topics such as whether or not Obama actually had a valid U.S. birth certificate, or whether he had a secret agenda to make America a socialist welfare state, or whether he secretly prayed from the Koran in the West Wing."

Parker and Barreto contended that the Tea Party's fixation on Obama was due to the president being a symbol of the nation. "We submit that the strength of the Tea Party opposition has something to do with, frankly, the threat associated with a nonwhite commander in chief and what he represents to supporters of the Tea Party: a threat to the cultural dominance of 'real Americans,'" they wrote in *Change They Can't Believe In: The Tea Party and Reactionary Politics in America*.

What was probably at work here was an implicit acceptance of the Euro American prototype. The acceptance of that prototype allowed some Americans to believe, even in the face of contrary evidence, that a black man whose views they detested was not really an American—that he was born in Africa, where his father resided. They didn't necessarily believe that no black American was qualified to be president, but the fact that Obama's father was an African made him vulnerable to speculation that he was not really an American. It is doubtful, for instance, that if Obama's father had been born in Poland that Tea Party activists would have thought he was really Polish. (There was an echo of the Republican Protestant contention in the 1928 election that if Catholic Democrat Al Smith became president, his policies would be dictated by the pope in Rome.)

What was also at work was a credulousness borne out of individuals ceding their intelligence to a large group, in this case a

nationalist movement based on an invidious comparison between
"us and them." The Tea Party was rife with conspiracy theories that
no dispassionate individual of average intelligence and curiosity
could believe. These included: Obama was seen as creating a "one
world government" that would dictate what color cars could be; the
United Nations was preparing to station a guard at each person's
home; global elites had sown the Ebola epidemic in order to kill 90
percent of the population.

Trump's Nationalism
Trump, who adopted Reagan's campaign slogan (minus "Let's") of
"Let's Make America Great Again," was heir to the nationalism of
Reagan, Perot, Buchanan, and the Tea Party. Trump lacked Reagan's skill as an administrator and negotiator, as well as his public
geniality, but like Reagan, he had a sixth sense about what a significant part of the electorate really wanted to hear. And what it wanted
to hear were the mystic chords of American nationalism.

Trump had evinced nationalist sentiments well before he
declared for the presidency. He had been complaining since the late
1980s about America losing out on trade to Japan and then China
and being taken advantage of by its allies in Europe. He had a sense,
common to people who came of age in the 1950s during the Great
American Celebration, that America had lost out. "When I was
young, we were always winning things in this country," he explained
after the election. "We'd win with trade. We'd win with wars." And
he had a salesman's ability to adopt and mimic whatever sentiments he had not shared earlier, but that his customers wanted to
hear him express.

When Trump was vying with Buchanan for the Reform Party's
presidential nomination for 2000, he had criticized Buchanan for
his "disgusting" views on Mexicans. That changed as he began contemplating running for president as a Republican. In his 2011 book,
Time to Get Tough, he charged that "illegal immigration is a wrecking
ball aimed at U.S. taxpayers." And he began his 2016 campaign by

224 branding Mexican illegal immigrants "rapists" and demanding that Mexico pay for a border wall.

Trump also adopted the Tea Party's skepticism about whether Obama had been born in the United States. "Why doesn't he show his birth certificate?" he asked an ABC interviewer in 2011. Trump probably didn't believe Obama had been born in Kenya, but was currying favor with the Tea Party by championing one of the key tenets of their conservative nationalism. Trump was also not religiously observant, and had favored abortion and gay rights before contemplating a run for the Republican nomination, but during his 2016 campaign he attempted to ingratiate himself with the religious right by embracing its religious nationalism. In his speech in January 2016 at the late Jerry Falwell's Liberty University, Trump called for Americans "to band together . . . around Christianity."

As he began to campaign, Trump also abandoned his earlier support for a ban on assault weapons and his criticism of Republicans who "walk the NRA line." By April 2015, he was declaring, "I love the NRA. I love the second amendment." And as he found himself denounced for taking these various stands, he blasted the "political correctness" of his Republican and Democratic foes.

In his speeches and tweets, Trump stressed his success at business and his superior intelligence. As president, he boasted of his achievements. ("I truly believe that the first 100 days of my administration has been just about the most successful in our country's history.") He marketed a daily diet of claims that were patently false. He claimed that three to five million votes by illegal immigrants had cost him the popular vote. He waged war on his critics, especially in the press (who, he charged, produced "fake news"). He frequently violated the norms of polite discourse, branding his political rivals as liars. His views on women ("Look at that face. Would anyone vote for that?") and foreign countries (as "shitholes") would not have been out of place on a barstool, but had rarely been heard in political campaigns or from a president. His outsized personality and his

indiscretions offended political opponents, but they also helped to
create an impassioned following.

Trump's Following

Trump's success in November 2016 rested primarily on winning
Pennsylvania and Midwestern states that had backed Obama in 2012
against Mitt Romney. These, as well as the southern states that
Trump won, tended to be those hardest hit by the decline in manu-
ufacturing jobs. Trump's win in these states came from increasing
the Republican margin among white workers without a college
education—what pollsters refer to as "white working class" voters,
even though they include a number of small businesspeople. Many
of these voters fit the profile of the "left-behinds." In Michigan,
Ohio, and Pennsylvania, for instance, Trump won these voters by an
almost two-to-one margin.

Following the election, Trump lost some support—particularly, one imagines, from people who voted against Clinton rather
than for him in 2016—but he retained an energized core of between
20 and 25 percent of the electorate who told pollsters they "strongly
approve" of Trump's presidency. Many of them attended his rallies
and continued to display yard signs from the election. If their support was boiled down to particular issues, they were probably most
concerned about immigration and its link to terrorism. CATO Institute polling director Emily Ekins found that in the Republican primaries, Trump's supporters were 20 to 30 points more likely than
the supporters of other Republicans to favor restricting immigration across the board, building a wall, deporting illegal immigrants,
and temporarily banning Muslim immigrants.

What drives voters, however, is often not a single issue, but a
complex web of issues and concerns that represent a threat to a way
of life. In the 2016 election, these could be grouped around the conservative nationalist views that Trump strongly espoused. Both
Ekins and John Sides of George Washington University published

226   studies based on the extensive (8,000 respondents) survey of 2016 voters by the Democracy Fund Voter Study Group. According to their analyses, the bulk of Trump's primary vote and a little over half of his general election vote were made up of people skeptical of legal and illegal immigration, who believed their Christian identity was important to them, and who supported a Muslim travel ban. When asked, "What does it take to be truly American?" most of them believed it was important to have "lived in the U.S. most of your life," "been born in America," and "be Christian." They also thought discrimination against white people was a serious problem. According to Ekins, one group of primary supporters, which she called the American Preservations, and who made up about 20 percent of the primary electorate, enthusiastically backed Trump's attacks on past trade deals and on corporations that move jobs out of the country. They supported Trump "with far greater intensity" than anyone else, Ekins wrote.[*]

The intersection of Christianity and nationalism was particularly common among Trump voters. According to Sides, nearly two-thirds of Trump voters thought "being a Christian" was part of being truly American. Three sociologists, Andrew L. Whitehead, Samuel L. Perry, and Joseph O. Baker, using the Baylor Religion Survey conducted after the election, found that Trump supporters in the general election thought that the "success of the United States is part of God's plan," and that "the federal government

---

[*] Some political scientists have used regression analyses to determine what single factor most motivated voters to back Trump, and they have suggested variously that it was racism, nativism, misogyny, and authoritarianism. I don't put any stock in these kinds of analyses, which strike me as being partisan attempts to discredit Trump and his supporters. As Emily Ekins notes, "These models inherently assume each Trump voter places equal weight on each policy issue measured." Regression analyses don't measure the intensity with which a voter views one issue over another. I don't think it's accurate to explain most elections by looking at a single issue or concern, but my contention is that of all the issues immigration/terrorism was the most important. That conclusion is based as much on interviews and the political history of the last three decades as on polling.

should declare the United States a Christian nation." Those findings   227
showed an affinity between Trump's following and the Protestant
roots of early American nationalism.

The Psychology of Trump's Support

Trump's rallies during the campaign and his presidency, punctuated
by chants of "USA! USA!" displayed the irrationality that explicit
nationalist movements can inspire. The gatherings resembled at
times high school pep rallies before a big game with a rival team and
at other times angry religious revivals. When Trump would mention
illegal immigrants, his followers would shout back in unison, "Build
the wall!" He would then ask questions as if he were conducting a
responsive reading in church: "Who is going to pay for it?" And they
would shout back, "Mexico!" Trump fans also followed his lead in
demonizing his opponents—from Jeb Bush to Hillary Clinton.

Trump supporters displayed a credulousness similar to the
Tea Party and characteristic of crowds or mobs. They appeared to
believe that Trump would get Mexico to pay for a wall and that he
would deport 11 million illegal immigrants. Clinton was thought to
have already been indicted and wearing an ankle bracelet, to be suffering from Parkinson's disease or even from AIDS, which she sup-
posedly caught from her promiscuous husband.

Trump's followers also venerated him in a way that is very characteristic of the leaders of nationalist movements. Instead of being
offended by Trump's self-centered boasting, they saw it as confirmation of his larger self. Freud writes of the masses and their leaders
in the wake of World War I, "Even today the members of a group
stand in need of the illusion that they are equally and justly loved
by their leader; but the leader himself need love no one else, he may
be of a masterful nature, absolutely narcissistic, self-confident, and
independent."

Some supporters simply denied as "fake news" reports of
Trump's sexual escapades; others focused on the reactions to them
as "political correctness." But most of his followers, including

228   religious conservatives, simply let these and other apparent moral failings pass them by. After the revelation of Trump's affair with porn star Stormy Daniels, Robert Jeffress, the pastor of the First Baptist Church in Dallas, told Fox News, "Evangelicals know they are not compromising their beliefs in order to support this great president." That is characteristic of the way supporters regard their heroes. Few Americans allow John Kennedy's sexual escapades to blot his image. Similarly, few people even know that Martin Luther King plagiarized his PhD thesis or take seriously the reports that he frequently cheated on his wife. Those details became irrelevant, just as Trump's affairs became irrelevant even to his most pious followers.

Trump Supporters in Ohio
This description of Trump and his followers jibed with my experience covering Trump's campaign and interviewing his supporters during the 2016 election. To see whether the analysis still held up a year into Trump's presidency, I had a discussion in the suburb of a struggling Ohio industrial town with six men who had voted for Trump. Several had not backed him in the primary, but since the election they had become enthusiastic supporters. They included two blue-collar workers and three office workers (one unemployed, another retired) and a small businessperson. I asked them why they voted for Trump, and what "Make America Great Again" and "America First" meant to them. They had different emphases, but very similar overall views.

Trade issues loomed large in Ohio, and they applauded Trump's attack on "bad trade deals." One of them had worked for a plant whose operations had been transferred to Mexico after NAFTA passed. Another said of NAFTA, "I supported it at the time and I remember Ross Perot warning against it, and he was right." They frequently mentioned China. They were worried about China's growing industrial might and liked Trump's targeting of their trade practices. "I think he is in favor of sticking it to China. He wants a fair deal with

China. We're losing jobs." "China is our only serious competitor," 229
another commented.

They were very supportive of his stance against illegal immigration. "The main reason I voted for him was his immigration policy. I thought that was the single most important issue in the country," the retired office worker said. Another explained, "I think we need to worry more about American citizens than illegal aliens. We have to worry more about American jobs than about taking jobs away from Mexico or China." Another said, "We need to hold [the Mexicans] accountable . . . so that they are not burdening us with a bunch of unaccountable people who are coming across our border who might just be looking for work but they are depressing the wages of Americans and a certain portion of them really are criminals." I asked about whether they thought America was still a melting pot or a multicultural society. "I don't run around saying you have to call me European American or German American. I am an American. We're getting so far apart," one of the Trump supporters lamented.

They believed that America was suffering a moral decline. "A lot of people will say, I don't believe in God, but let's face it, this country was founded by Christian men, and our Constitution was based on a lot of Christian beliefs. Judeo-Christian beliefs. And I feel we've had a lot of politicians and administrations that have actively tried to destroy that." Several of them also attributed moral decline to the absence of a work ethic among some Americans. "There are a lot of people who are taking the easy road, taking the government handouts and not even looking for work," one said. Several cited African Americans as a case in point. "Look at the black population. Seventy-six percent are out of wedlock," one remarked. Another added, "If you want to talk about the African American population here or however you want to look at it, we have said the government is going to take care of everything. You don't have to be responsible."

The Trump supporters disliked Hillary Clinton. "She felt she was entitled. She felt like she was our dictator," one person said. But I was shocked by how angry they still were at Obama. They

230 said Trump's presidency was a direct result of Obama's failure. The slogan "Make America Great Again," one explained, was "a reaction to a president who hated or was ashamed of his country." He added, "He was clearly not American. He clearly was not interested in taking care of America." When I asked for examples of how Obama hated America, they said, "Where to start? How many hours would you like to be here?" I don't think they really believed that Obama wasn't born in America. When someone started to mention that, he was hushed. But they thought that what Obama did and believed disqualified him as an American.

They scorned "political correctness" and applauded those instances when Trump had incurred the most criticism. When I asked them about Trump's response to the armed white supremacists who had protested the removal of a statue of Confederate general Robert E. Lee in Charlottesville, Virginia—one of the white supremacists had also killed a counter-demonstrator—they sided with those who wanted to keep the statue and applauded Trump's initial response in which he blamed the protestors and counter-demonstrators equally for the violence. "I agree with what Trump said, which is that there were bad people on both sides." They also thought Trump was being accurate when he described Haiti and African nations as "shithole countries."

Several people talked about preserving gun rights and combating gun control as important to making America great again. This was weeks before the horrific school shooting in Parkland, Florida in February 2018, where 17 people were killed. After the shootings, one of the people from Ohio sent me a statement he admired from a Facebook friend of his. She had written:

> I have really come to absolutely loathe liberals. The very same people who created the psychotic society we live in now are also the same ones screaming themselves blue in the face about taking everyone's guns away. . . . The very same people who try and tell us that there's a gazillion different genders. . . . The very same people

who destroyed the sanctity of life by avidly supporting the right
to murder babies. . . . The same people who have worked tirelessly
attacking religion and telling everybody that they can decide for
themselves what's right and what's wrong. The only "religion"
they DO support? Islam. . . . The very same people who've done
everything they can to make men the enemy and destroy the
family unit. The very same people doing everything they can to
destroy this country and replace it with a totalitarian regime. . . .
You want to take my guns. Kiss my ass libs. . . . It ain't ever going
to happen.

Her statement reflected the deep polarization between Trump
supporters and the people they call "liberals." It drew together the
different strands of today's conservative nationalism: the threat
to guns and family and nation from Muslim terrorists and from
liberals.

During the last year of Trump's presidency, with the pandemic raging, and the left taking to the streets to protest police brutality, the polarization deepened, culminating in Trump supporters
storming the Capitol on January 6 to demand that Congress reject
the Electoral College results. That morning, one of the Ohio group
had written on Facebook, "Unless President Trump takes extraordinary measures in the next two weeks, we're on our own. We won't
get the republic back for many years, and not without a lot of sacrifice." His view was that "scheming criminal pieces of shit" had not
only stolen the election, but the nation.

The Cosmopolitans
Who Trump supporters identified as liberals were really a distinct
segment of those voters who might identify themselves in that
manner. Some of the self-identified liberals who backed Bernie
Sanders or Clinton in 2016 might have actually agreed with Trump
voters on some economic issues. The relevant polarity was not
really between nationalists and liberals, but between nationalists

232   and cosmopolitans. When Trump supporters blamed America's ills on liberals, they were often generally talking about cosmopolitans.

Cosmopolitans made up, perhaps, 15 to 20 percent of the electorate. They were more likely to be Democrats or Independents than Republicans. They were concentrated in the large metro centers and in smaller college towns. They were among the 36 percent of Americans who owned a passport and the 15 to 20 percent of adults who graduated from selective colleges. Many of them work in the upper rungs of services in healthcare, education, and government and in what economist Peter Temin described as the FTE sector of finance, technology, and electronics. They had multiple identities, particularly from their prestigious colleges, their professions, their accomplishments, and their civic associations that provided self-approbation and a hope for immortality. Many were in the top 20 percent in income or, if recent college graduates, would soon be there.

Like David Goodhart's English "anywheres," they were not anti-nationalist or unpatriotic. They celebrated Thanksgiving, and if they followed sports, probably cheered the United States team in the Olympics. They wanted to see America succeed in the world economy and supported the effort to wipe out the Islamist terrorists that threatened the United States, but they did not fly an American flag on their front porch, and they weren't appalled (as were the Trump supporters I interviewed) by black athletes refusing to stand for the national anthem. They wanted strict gun control; they thought people who were upset about illegal immigration were racists or nativists. They liked to think of America as a multicultural society rather than as a melting pot. They thought free trade was good for America. They utterly despised Trump. Many believed he was a fascist. They thought Hillary Clinton was on target in branding Trump supporters as "deplorables" and thought that most of those who voted for him were racist. After the 2016 election, a Silicon Valley executive wrote on Facebook, "One thing middle America could do is to realize that no educated person wants to live in a shithole with stupid people. Especially violent, racist and/or misogynistic ones."

There are scores of studies by political scientists about the
motivations and views of Trump supporters, but very few about
anyone resembling cosmopolitans. One of the few was a poll of the
founders of internet startups in Silicon Valley conducted by journalist Greg Ferenstein. Ferenstein summarized the responses: "They
want more global alliances at the expense of sovereignty, few restrictions on immigration, and believe in state incentives to make people
healthier, more educated, and civically active." According to Ferenstein, far more of them were Democrats than Republicans. Sixty
percent wanted to increase immigration. Twenty percent favored
totally open borders. Seventy-three percent put "global trade" as a
priority over "American workers."

In her campaign in 2016, Hillary Clinton represented in some
respects a less extreme version of this outlook. Even though she
had disavowed her support for the Trans-Pacific Partnership, it
was widely known that she had enthusiastically supported NAFTA,
the entry of China into the WTO, and the U.S.-Korea Pact. She
gave short shrift to preventing illegal immigration and opposed
deporting illegal immigrants unless they had committed violent
felonies. During the primary, she ran a campaign ad attacking the
Republican candidates for opposing multiculturalism and the use
of English over Spanish. In a speech after the election, Clinton
affirmed the cosmopolitan view of the result. She characterized her
voters as having come from "the places that are optimistic, diverse,
dynamic, moving forward" and Trump's campaign and his followers
as "looking backward. You know, you didn't like black people getting
rights; you don't like women, you know, getting jobs." Clinton was in
her way as polarized in her outlook as Trump was. They represented
starkly different and incompatible visions of America.

Is there any prospect for reconciling the two visions of America?
Perhaps, but there are immense difficulties. The two visions are
rooted in different economic and social experiences, and in wide
geographical differences. "A growing part of inequality in America,"
economist Enrico Moretti writes, "reflects not just a class but a

234   geographical divide." I remember that when I moved to Washington, D.C., in 1982, from what was then a decaying industrial Chicago, it felt like leaving one country for another. Living in Washington, one somehow feels closer to Paris or London than to Racine or Wichita. If anything, the social and economic distance between the parts of America has sharply increased since then. And these social, economic, and geographical differences, along with the exaggerated views they produce, have contributed to America's failure to confront its underlying problems.

The nationalist backlash has been in response to real failures in the American economy and society. America's middle class has been hollowed out. Imports from China (some of which came from American firms that have outsourced their production) have decimated many smaller and midsized towns and cities outside the great metro areas. Enormous numbers of unskilled immigrants have competed for jobs with Americans who also lack higher education and have led to the downgrading of occupations that were once middle-class; many of these immigrants, resembling those that entered the United States before the 1920s, have congregated in closed communities that have slowed assimilation. But in responding to the challenge of mass immigration, Trump and the Tea Party, like their Anglo-Saxon forbears from the 1840s or 1890s, resorted to nativist screeds and to threats of deportation, while in responding to destruction of small town life in states like West Virginia and Kentucky, they nurtured fantasies about reviving bygone industries like coal mining.

Cosmopolitans and the larger group of liberals have dismissed concerns about immigration and trade. For instance, an analyst from a Democratic think tank, the Center for American Progress, wrote that "immigrants complement native-born workers and increase the standard of living for all Americans"—with the inclusion of the adjective "all," a statement as implausible on the surface as any put forward about climate change by Tea Party activists or Trump supporters. Aaron Ruper from Think Progress described Trump's criticism of American business leaders for not doing more about unfair

trade as "striking a fascistic note." In response to the Trump admin-   235
istration's abominable policy of separating the children of illegal
immigrants from their parents, liberals and Democratic politicians and congressional candidates have called for abolishing rather
than reforming the Immigration and Customs Enforcement division of the Department of Homeland Security, which is in charge of
enforcing immigration laws, preventing the illicit passage of guns
and drugs, and looking out for potential terrorist threats.

In response to Trump's complaints about China forcing American companies to transfer high technology in order to gain access
to China's market—which could imperil America's chance of competing in the world economy—former Clinton and Obama administration official Lawrence Summers wrote, "China's extraction of
intellectual property through joint-venture requirements is largely
a problem for companies outsourcing production from the United
States, and not for American workers." The Trump administration's
rejection of a Singapore business, with apparent ties to China, to
take over a key American technology company, Qualcomm, also met
with criticism from Wall Street and Silicon Valley.

The polarization, based in part on the difference between cosmopolitans and nationalists, and reinforced by partisan politics, has
been particularly damaging to reaching any constructive solution to
the conflict over immigration and national identity. One can devise
on paper a set of compromises that would over a decade or two quiet
the roaring fires of nativism by allowing the millions of immigrants
already here, and those who will come in the future, to assimilate
into American society. Two things are required. The first is blocking
illegal immigration through stiff employer penalties, while giving
a path to citizenship for the roughly 11 million illegal immigrants
already here. These immigrants cannot simply be deported, and if
they remain in the U.S. illegally, they will continue to constitute an
inassimilable underclass.

The second thing to do is to reduce the annual number of immigrants, and to narrow the conditions for family reunification, while

236   giving priority to skilled immigrants. That will reverse the growth of immigrant ghettos, which slow assimilation, and allow those immigrants already here to move up the economic and social ladder. That is what happened as a result of the restrictive legislation passed in 1921, 1924, and 1929. These bills were highly discriminatory, but the reduction in immigration was a key to the assimilation of the Southern and Eastern Europeans who had immigrated over the prior forty years. Such a proposal can be effective without discriminating against particular nationalities.

But, regardless of how these proposals are framed, they likely cannot get through a Congress that is divided into conservative nationalists and liberal cosmopolitans. Conservative nationalists in the House of Representatives blocked legislation that would give illegal immigrants a path to citizenship. Democratic liberals and cosmopolitans denounced a bill introduced by conservative Republican senators Tom Cotton and David Perdue that would have cut in half annual immigration from roughly a million to 500,000, give priority to skilled immigrants, and narrowed the criteria for family reunification, even though their bill was almost identical to a set of proposals put forward in 1997 by a commission chaired by a liberal Democratic icon, former congresswoman Barbara Jordan, and which Bill Clinton extolled at the time.

The polarization between Republicans and Democrats on immigration is also driven by narrow partisanship. The Republicans want to curb immigration, and to prevent the 11 million illegal immigrants from becoming citizens because they fear they will become Democrats, while the Democrats see in the waves of new immigrants the creation of a "majority-minority" country in which the minorities will vote, as they presently do, disproportionately for Democrats. I think these projections are foolish, but they are widely held on both sides and make unlikely the resolution of a conflict that has been central to the rise of conservative nationalism.

The Disunited States of Europe

In 1941, as war engulfed Europe, Altiero Spinelli and Ernesto Rossi, two political prisoners who were interned on the island of Ventotene, drafted "The Ventotene Manifesto." They argued that the historic quest to establish nation-states had inevitably led to war. "The absolute sovereignty of national States has led to the desire of each of them to dominate, since each feels threatened by the strength of the others.... This desire to dominate cannot be placated except by the hegemony of the strongest State over all the others."

Spinelli, a former communist, and Rossi, who had broken with Mussolini, called for "the definitive abolition of the division of Europe into national, sovereign States" and the establishment of a new "European Federation." "The multiple problems which poison international life on the continent have proved to be insoluble: tracing boundaries through areas inhabited by mixed populations, defence of alien minorities, seaports for landlocked countries, the Balkan Question, the Irish problem, and so on. All matters which would find easy solutions in the European Federation."

In 1943, French businessman Jean Monnet, a member of the French National Liberation Committee in Algiers, wrote a memo making a similar point. "There will be no peace in Europe if the states

238   are reconstituted on the basis of national sovereignty," he wrote. "Their prosperity and essential social developments are impossible, unless the States of Europe form themselves into a Federation or one 'European entity' understood as a common economic unit."

Spinelli and Monnet are generally regarded as the founding fathers of the European Union. The Parliament building in Brussels is named for Spinelli, and a European Commission building in Luxembourg for Monnet. Their argument boiled down to this: To avoid the recurrence of another world war, the European nations would have to cede their sovereignty to a supranational federation. Nationalism was inherently toxic.

Over the next 60 years, the leading countries on the continent followed their script. In 1951, France, Germany, Italy, Belgium, Luxembourg, and the Netherlands set up the European Steel and Coal Community, headed by Monnet, which pooled production in two industries that had been a major cause of conflict. In 1957, the six countries signed the Treaty of Rome to create the European Economic Community, which promised a borderless single market in goods, services, capital, and people. In 1973, the UK, Ireland, and Denmark joined; Greece in 1981; and Spain and Portugal in 1986. That year, the members negotiated the Single European Act, which established a single market with a parliament, council, and commission.

Finally, in 1992 at Maastricht, the members agreed on a common currency that would take effect in 2001, and created the European Central Bank and a new organization that would be called the European Union. The single currency, the Euro, was to be the glue that bound together the union. Jean-Claude Juncker, who was then the prime minister of Luxembourg and who later became president of the European Commission, predicted that when citizens began using the Euro in 2002, "a new we-feeling would develop: we Europeans."

The EU also sought to ensure that its members were liberal democracies. With new countries clamoring for membership, the EU clarified its membership criteria at a 1993 meeting in Copenhagen. The Copenhagen criteria stipulated that:

> Membership requires that candidate country has achieved sta-   239
> bility of institutions guaranteeing democracy, the rule of law,
> human rights, respect for and protection of minorities, the exis-
> tence of a functioning market economy, as well as the capacity
> to cope with competitive pressure and market forces within the
> Union.

In other words, the European community was not simply a
customs union but a supranational organization. It was not just
intended to integrate the continent's economies, but to further the
spread of free market democracies. In 1995, Austria, Finland, and
Sweden joined. In 2004, the EU began admitting former communist states, including Poland, Hungary, and the Czech Republic.
There were now 28 eight countries in the EU, and 19 (with the UK,
Denmark, and Sweden the major exceptions) use the Euro as their
currency. With the UK's departure in 2020, there were 27.

There were notable dissenters to the transition from the EEC
to the EU. French president Charles de Gaulle and British prime
minister Margaret Thatcher both preferred that the EEC remain a
tariff-less customs union. Thatcher objected to giving the EU the
power to pass labor, consumer, and environmental regulations. She
also opposed the establishment of a common currency. "To try to
suppress nationhood and concentrate power at the center of a European conglomerate, would be highly damaging," Thatcher said
in 1988. But Thatcher was displaced in 1990 by the pro-EU John
Major. Polling showed some skepticism among the European public
about integration, but with de Gaulle having died and Thatcher
out of power, Europe's leaders greeted the experiment with great
enthusiasm.

Intellectuals were also enthusiastic. Habermas envisaged the
EU as a transition to a "post-national constellation." Tony Judt, in
his magisterial history *Postwar*, concluded that "nationalism had
largely come and gone," and heralded "Europe's emergence in the
dawn of the twenty-first century as a paragon of the international

240 virtues: a community of values and a system of interstate relations held up by Europeans and non-Europeans alike as an exemplar for all to emulate." The creation of the Eurozone was seen as the culmination of Spinelli and Monnet's vision, and in the first decade after the Maastricht agreement, the European Commission declared, "The euro is a resounding success. The single currency has become a symbol of Europe, considered by Euro-area citizens to be among the most positive results of European integration."

These accolades seemed premature at the time, but they now seem hopelessly outdated. Nationalism, once thought to be on the verge of extinction, has revived. Populist parties have advocated the reestablishment of a national currency and national control over borders. Secessionist movements have gained support in Scotland and Catalonia. Governments in Poland and Hungary have defied the EU's promise of liberal democracy. And, of course, the UK voted in 2016 to leave the EU altogether, and withdrew in 2020.

Common Currency
The advocates of a European federation framed their objective as a "United States of Europe." In 1955, Monnet organized an "Action Committee for the United States of Europe." But America's and Europe's histories are very different. The United States expanded outward from a core cultural-ethnic identity. Americans killed or drove off the Native Americans, whose cultures were seen to be incompatible. As the United States has grown over the years, it has incorporated different ethnicities and nationalities without abandoning the rudiments of its original culture, including, most importantly, its language. The United States is undergoing another struggle over assimilation similar to that which took place from the 1880s to 1920s, but it has shown in the past the ability to succeed at doing this. Europe has not had this experience, and to date, does not appear to have the cultural basis for doing so.

There is no common ethnic-cultural identity that marks off Europeans. Different nations are separated by dramatically different languages and cultures, with a few exceptions. Economic integration might be the basis for supranational integration. But the economic integration of the United States proceeded under the prior existence of a national state and common culture. During the Civil War, the power of the national state won out over the existence of a competing regional culture and economic system. Politics carried the day. But in Europe, it was hoped that gradual economic integration would lay the basis for a powerful supranational state.

The proponents of a common currency did recognize that they were dealing with very different economies. Roughly speaking, the leading Northern economies, led by Germany and including the Netherlands, Austria, and Belgium, have depended on export surpluses to drive consumer and business demand for their products and keep their workers employed. To maintain export surpluses, these countries had to keep productivity up and costs, including labor costs, down. In Germany, for instance, labor unions agreed in the 2000s to limit wage demands in exchange for a guarantee of secure employment.

The Southern economies, including Portugal, Spain, Italy, and Greece, were more dependent on domestic consumption, driven by non-tradable services, public spending, and private debt. Their rates of productivity were lower than those of the Northern countries. Before the introduction of the Euro, they had to use currency devaluations (which raised the cost of imports and lowered those of exports) to keep their trade deficits from spiraling out of control. The Italian lira, for instance, was devalued 11 times between 1979 and 1992, and between 1979 and 1999 it lost 53 percent of its value against the Deutschmark. That created a huge amount of volatility, making business planning difficult.

The proponents of the Euro hoped that the currency would lead to a convergence between the two economies. The common currency would rule out devaluations as a means to limit trade deficits; in addition, a Growth and Stability Pact (demanded by the Germans), which limited budget deficits to 3 percent of GDP, would rule

242   out using deficit spending to boost demand. That would force the Southern countries to raise productivity and lower costs. They, too, would become export countries. Europe as a whole would become competitive and united. That was the plan put forward by French finance minister Jacques DeLors in 1989.

In the early 2000s, both the North and South appeared to benefit from the Euro. Industries in the North got relatively lower exchange rates because the Euro's value reflected the bloc as a whole and not their strong individual economies. That helped their sales internationally. And within the Eurozone, they no longer had to worry about being priced out by devaluations. The South, on the other hand, benefited from relatively lower interest rates because the zone's lending rates reflected overall confidence in the new German-led zone. That allowed them to borrow to finance their deficits and private investments. These borrowings came primarily from Germany, Austria, Belgium, France, and the Netherlands, whose banks were, in effect, recirculating the countries' trade surpluses back to the deficit countries. From 1999 to 2009, the Greek debt held by Northern European banks increased 491 percent; Spain's indebtedness to these banks increased 554 percent.

That arrangement worked well until Lehman Brothers went under in September 2008 and banks in the United States and Europe began calling in loans. A year later, Greece revealed that its budget deficits were twice as large as first reported. At that point, the entire arrangement that had propped up the Eurozone during its first seven years crumbled. Interest rates began to climb; countries in the South faced bankruptcy. Unemployment shot up. Instead of convergence, the Euro had produced even wider divergence between the countries. As German economic sociologist Wolfgang Streeck from the Max Planck Institute in Cologne later put it, "An integrated monetary regime for such disparate economies as Europe's supply-based North and demand-based South cannot work equally well for both. The consequence is that qualitative horizontal diversity is transformed into a quantitative vertical inequality." That vertical inequality fueled a rise in nationalism in the Eurozone. Instead of "we," the Euro had created "us" versus "them."

In Greece, Spain, and Italy, the collapse of their economies sparked protest against Brussels and the European Central Bank for insisting that in order to receive a bailout, the governments would have to eviscerate their welfare and pension systems and sell off state assets. The populist parties Syriza in Greece, Podemos in Spain, National Front in France, and Five Star Movement in Italy, as well as the secessionist Northern League, voiced doubts about the Euro and the EU. Much of the anger was directed at Germany, which the parties believed controlled the Eurozone finance. In Greece, Germany's leading role in setting draconian conditions for a bailout led to public demonstrations and demands that Germany pay Greece reparations for World War II. In tabloids, German finance minister Wolfgang Schauble was regularly depicted wearing a Nazi SS uniform.

On the other side, governments and the public in Europe's Northern tier protested against bailing out the improvident South. In Germany, the Alternativ fur Deutschland (AfD) originated in 2013 as an anti-bailout party calling for Germany to leave the Eurozone. The Finns and the Dutch also denounced the bailout. The Finns (formerly the True Finns), a populist party founded in 1995, opposed the bailout of Portugal in 2011. "Why should Finland bail anyone out? We won't allow Finnish cows to be milked by other hands," the party's leader, Timo Soini, explained. Four years later, Soini called for Greece to be expelled from the Eurozone. Dutch prime minister Mark Rutte ran successfully for election in 2012 on a promise of "not one more cent for Greece."

The furor over the Euro temporarily abated in Spain and Portugal as their economies have picked up. In Italy, the two Euroskeptic powers that formed a coalition government in 2018 backed off from their opposition to the Euro. Fear of what leaving the Euro would entail, especially among pensioners living on fixed incomes, has overshadowed disillusionment with the Euro and the ECB. But there is

244   continuing resentment toward the EU, the Growth and Stability Pact, and Germany's role in Eurozone finance. Once thought to be a boon, the Euro is at best thought in the South to be a bearable burden.

According to the polling analysts *EUVision*, only 39 percent of Italians think it's been beneficial to be in the EU. In a poll in Greece in 2017, 53 percent thought joining the Eurozone was the "wrong decision" and only 38 percent the "right decision."

As currently structured, the Euro and the Growth and Stability Pact will continue to cause a wide divergence between the North and the South. In the wake of the Great Recession, some politicians and economists proposed a gradual withdrawal, perhaps through demoting the Euro to a secondary reserve currency that would work like the IMF's Special Drawing Rights; others advocated strengthening the EU's fiscal power so that it could act to stem economic crises in the manner of the American government. French president Emmanuel Macron proposed creating a Eurozone budget and finance minister post, but Macron's proposal had to be dramatically weakened to overcome objections from center-right and rightwing populist parties in Northern Europe.

Dutch prime minister Mark Rutte's approach was for the Southern economies to undertake "structural reform" that would turn them into export-driven, industrial replicas of the German or Dutch economies. German Christian Democrats put forth similar proposals. Their effect would have been to create a version of what Keynes called the "paradox of thrift." As all the nations of the EU joined Germany in attempting to create trade surpluses by holding down domestic demand, they would inhibit consumer demand in what has been the most important market for their goods—their fellow EU countries.

In theory, as Martin Sandbu argued in *Europe's Orphan*, the Euro could be made to work. But in the real world, the economic, political, and cultural are inextricably intertwined, and those measures that could turn the Euro to the advantage of the South as well as the North are blocked by those countries that either benefit from

the existing structure—as the Germans or Dutch do—or find the
attempt to emulate the Germans or Dutch impossible within the
constraints of their politics and culture. In the absence of reform, it
appears likely that the Eurozone's horizontal diversity will continue
to produce vertical inequalities. These will exacerbate the political
division and national resentment that the EU was supposed to clim
inate. And as recent years show, when resentment toward the EU's
economic role is fused with opposition to its policies on immigration, borders, and Islam, a garden-variety nationalism can become
toxic and dangerous.

European Citizenship
Europe's postwar planners envisaged eliminating borders in the
European federation. They hoped that would prevent the reemergence of a dangerous nationalism. From the end of World War II
through the 1990s, the countries in the EU gradually ended restrictions on where residents of any EU country could travel to or work
in. They also adopted rules on asylum that allowed millions of refugees into Europe from the Middle East, South Asia, and Africa. But
this effort, like that of integrating Europe's economies, began to run
aground in the 2000s when cultural and economic concerns about
migration became fused with fear of Islamist terrorist attacks.

    Europe's earlier experience with immigration was very dif-
ferent from that of the United States. During much of the last three
centuries, Europe's was a history of emigration, not immigration.
Europe's nations didn't really have to develop policies on immigration until the economic boom that hit after World War II and that
attracted workers to the industries of Northern Europe. At that
time, Europe's policies were focused primarily on guest workers.
Governments in West Germany, Belgium, the Netherlands, and
Scandinavian countries made bilateral agreements with Turkey
and countries in Southern Europe to send workers who would be
expected to return to their homelands after a specified time. In 1968,
the EEC approved freedom of movement for workers (not persons)

246   within the community. In West Germany, there were 500,000 Italians, 535,000 Yugoslavs, and 605,000 Turks working in manufacturing and construction by 1973. France and the Netherlands also admitted migrants from their former colonies, and Great Britain did the same for those from its Commonwealth.

When the economies in Europe declined in the early 1970s, Northern European countries tried to induce guest workers to leave, but many stayed and took advantage of reunification laws to bring in family members. Britain passed laws that, in effect, restricted citizenship to European migrants, but high birth rates actually increased the number of people of South Asian, Caribbean, and African descent. Having signed the 1951 Geneva Convention pledging asylum for refugees from political, sexual, and racial persecution, Europe also began receiving migrants from wars in Africa and Asia beginning in the 1980s. Over the next decade, with the outbreak of the Balkan wars, this trickle became a raging stream. In 1992, European nations received 672,000 applications for asylum. Many of these new migrants, as well as many of the old, were Muslims. Many lacked the educational background or work habits to fit quickly into the European economies. In France, the UK, the Netherlands, Belgium, and Germany (and later, too, in the Scandinavian countries), many immigrants were clustered into highly segregated communities that had high crime rates and a high incidence of welfare dependence.

Europe's history simply did not prepare it to deal with the questions of assimilation raised by these decades of migration. France, due in part to the circumstances of its own birth as a nation that incorporated and assimilated other nationalities within its territory, had the most liberal citizenship laws on the continent. Citizenship was according to birth—the *jus soli*. If you were born in France, you were French. So the children of migrants became French citizens. But in the 1980s, the presence of large numbers of Muslims, most of whom came from former French colonies, sparked calls to revise the *jus soli*. Jean-Marie Le Pen, the head of the National Front,

declared, "You have to deserve to be French." Even mainstream politicians objected. French Socialist Gaston Defferre warned that "the
rules of Islam . . . are contrary to all the rules of French law on the
custody of children . . . and they are contrary to [French rules on] the
rights of women." Over the next 15 years, there would be repeated
attompts to roviso the citiocnohip law,

But during the 1990s, the EU's planners took further steps
toward eliminating Europe's borders and opening them to immigrants and asylum-seekers. The EU nations adopted the Dublin Regulation in 1990, which set out a procedure by which asylum-seekers
would be processed for their ultimate destination at the EU country
at which they first arrived.

In 1993, Maastricht took effect, which codified court rulings
that residents (and not just citizens) of any EU state could travel to
and work in any other. In 1995, the Schengen Agreement, which had
been reached a decade earlier, took effect. It removed border controls within the EU. Anyone in one EU country could enter another
without having to show a passport. That also meant that noncit-
izens, including illegal immigrants, could travel easily from one
country to another. In 1999, members of EU's European Council met
at Tampere, Finland, to propose common EU policies on asylum and
migration. It was proposed that those who won asylum in one state
could "seek and obtain entry to all EU states."

The first signs of a revolt at the polls appeared. Le Pen's National
Front won 15 percent of the vote in the 1995 presidential elections.
In Denmark, the People's Party, which originated in 1995 out of the
protests of two Lutheran pastors against the threat that Muslim
immigration posed to Denmark's cultural heritage, won 7.4 percent in the 1998 general election. In Austria, the Freedom Party,
whose original leadership had ties to the country's Nazi past and
which focused on opposition to immigration under a program called
"Austria First," won 27 percent of the vote in 1999, coming in second
and entering the government.

248   Terror and Culture

In the early 2000s, the revolt gave way to a political rebellion. The catalyst was the onset of large-scale Islamist terrorist attacks in the United States and Europe. From 2004 to 2017, there were 13 major terrorist attacks in the EU, as well as the political assassination of a Dutch filmmaker.

In the 2002 elections, Le Pen finished an astonishing second to the eventual winner, Jacques Chirac, ousting the Socialist candidate who had been favored to win. In Holland, Pim Fortuyn, who was opposed to Muslim immigration ("I see Islam as an extraordinary threat, as a hostile religion"), founded the Pim Fortuyn List in 2002. His party won control of Rotterdam's government, and then two weeks before the general election in May, he was assassinated by an animal rights protester. His party still won 17 percent and became part of the government. Throughout Scandinavia, new parties running against open borders and Islam made significant inroads. In 2001, the Danish People's Party won 12 percent of the vote and became the third largest party. In Italy, the Northern League, at the time only a regional party, won 8.3 percent nationally in 2008, promising to protect Italy's "Christian identity" against Muslim immigrants.

In 2004, the EU began expanding into Eastern Europe, producing new waves of immigrants to Western Europe. The EU adopted a seven-year transition period for workers in the former communist countries to be able to work in whatever other EU country they wanted, but Britain, Ireland, and Sweden, eager for cheap labor, waived the transition period. As workers from the East traveled westward in droves, and as the Great Recession took hold, the economic case against immigration, particularly among Europe's left-behinds, rose to the surface. These left-behinds included industrial workers who lost their jobs as factories and mines closed in northeast England, northern France, East Germany, and small towns in Austria or Hungary or Poland.

Dissatisfaction with the economic burdens of immigration began to register. In a 2014 Pew poll in the EU, majorities in Italy,

France, and the UK, and 44 percent in Germany, wanted fewer immigrants. Majorities in Italy and France believed immigrants were taking their jobs and social benefits. The opposition to immigration was concentrated among the same group adversely affected by the downturn: unskilled and semi-skilled workers and their families who generally lived and worked outside the metropolitan areas. In the Pew poll, only 37 percent of UK respondents believed immigrants were taking their jobs and benefits, but a majority of those without a college education believed so. Then came a new round of asylum-seekers and terrorist attacks.

In 2010, the number of refugees from wars in the Middle East and North Africa began to rise—from 259,000 in 2010 to 627,000 in 2014. Many of these headed for Greece or Italy. In 2015, in response to the war in Syria and the chaos in Libya, the number of asylum-seekers skyrocketed—to 1.32 million in 2015 and 1.26 million in 2016. At the same time, there was a massive uptick in Islamist terrorist attacks in Europe, some of which were credited to the ISIS group. From 2014 to 2017, there were 36 terrorist attacks with casualties. These included major attacks in Brussels, Paris (twice), Nice, Berlin, London, Stockholm, and Manchester. Some of the terrorist incidents involved refugees. That brought to a head the issues of terror and Islam on top of what were growing economic and cultural grievances against migrants.

A Pew poll in July 2016 found that large majorities in Hungary, Poland, Germany, Italy, the Netherlands, the UK, Sweden, and Greece thought that admitting refugees would "increase domestic terrorism." Majorities in Greece and Italy and pluralities in Hungary and Poland thought diversity was making their country "a worse place to live." A Gallup poll in 2017 asked whether people in 14 European countries thought "acts of terrorism" by migrants were "a serious problem." Huge majorities in France, Denmark, Belgium, Portugal, and the Netherlands thought they were; the median across the 14 countries was 66 percent. Respondents from the same countries thought that "current immigration levels" were a "serious problem."

The political repercussions were dramatic. In Britain, the single most important issue driving the vote to leave the EU was immigration, and the most effective publicity was a poster, produced by UKIP, that showed a huge stream of swarthy migrants (actually Syrian refugees heading toward Slovenia) with the caption "Breaking Point: the EU has failed us all" and "We must break free of the EU and take back control of our borders." In France, Marine Le Pen got 34 percent of the vote in the final round against Macron, twice the National Front's previous total. In Denmark, the People's Party got 21 percent of the vote in 2015, up from 12 percent in 2011. In the 2015 election, the Finns Party came in third and became part of the government. In Austria in 2017, the Freedom Party got 27 percent of the vote and joined the government. In Norway's 2017 election, the anti-immigrant Progress Party came in third and became part of the government.

In Italy, the combination of the Great Recession and the flood of asylum-seekers, for which Italy was the first and sometimes the last stop, boosted the fortunes of anti-immigrant parties. In 2016 alone, 171,000 fled by boat to Italy—equivalent proportionately to 919,000 refugees from the Caribbean or Central America arriving in the United States. There were about 600,000 immigrants in the country illegally. In 2018, the League, which dropped "North" to become a national party, and which ran on the slogan "Italians First," got 17.4 percent of the vote. Former prime minister Silvio Berlusconi's Forza Italia got 14 percent, the Brothers of Italy, which has fascist roots, 4.35 percent, and Beppe Grillo's Eurosceptic Five Star Movement 32.66 percent. More Europe, the explicitly pro-EU party, got 2.55 percent of the vote.

The protests were grounded in genuine grievances, but in the hands of nationalist politicians, they descended into vilification. Muslims were viciously stereotyped, as typified by UKIP's poster in the Brexit campaign. Distinctions resurfaced between who were the real nationals. The term *Francais de souche* ("ethnically French"), which Marine Le Pen had banned in the course of trying to rid

the party of its Vichy roots, made a comeback. There was also an   251
attempt to rehabilitate the dark forces that had plunged Europe into
world war. One survey prior to the Italian election found that 32 percent of Forza voters and 38 percent of League voters had a "positive
or very positive opinion" of fascist dictator Benito Mussolini. So did
21 percent of Five Star voters. In this respect, the most disturbing of
the popular new parties—probably because it was least expected—
was Germany's Alternativ für Deutschland (AfD).

The Return of the Repressed
After World War II, West Germany discouraged any display of
nationalist sentiment or patriotism as being an echo of the Nazi
past. The first two triumphalist stanzas of the German national
anthem were excised. Thomas Kleine-Brockhoff, a former advisor to
Germany's president who now heads the Berlin office of the German
Marshall Fund of the United States, said, "Personally, I grew up in
the Seventies, and it was deeply shameful to be a German and to be
representing Germany. I was on the under-eighteen German basketball team. We would have these long basketball socks, German
colors, red and gold. We would roll them down. You would cover the
eagle on your chest."

Yet the West Germans didn't banish every manifestation of the
older nationalist sentiment. Germany's immigration law retained
its nationalist roots. It remained based on descent. The new constitution after World War II granted citizenship to "the entire
German people," including those who were living in East Germany
or Poland. So a German living in Poland could easily gain citizenship, but the children of a Turkish guest worker, who had been raised
and schooled in Germany and may have never even visited Turkey,
were denied citizenship.

In 1999, however, Germany modified its immigration law to
allow citizenship by birth and also to permit residents who stayed
longer than eight years to apply for citizenship. It also became a
favored destination for asylum-seekers. By 2007, Germany was

252 housing 578,879 refugees, more than twice as many as the United States and almost four times as many as France. At the same time, the threat of terrorist attacks surfaced. In 2006, Germany narrowly escaped a Madrid-like bombing incident when two suitcases of bombs left on a train by Islamists failed to go off. In 2007, police foiled a plot to plant 1,500 pounds of explosive around American targets in Germany. Two of the conspirators were German converts to Islam, one was a Turkish immigrant, and another was the son of Turkish immigrants who had obtained German citizenship.

Ordinary Germans began to be concerned about terrorism and about Germany's Muslim population. In a 2006 survey by Pew Research, 82 percent of Germans were very or somewhat concerned about the rise of Islamic terrorism. A 10-year survey beginning in 2003 by the University of Bielefeld found that only 19 percent of Germans believed Islam was compatible with German culture, and 46 percent thought there were "too many Muslims" in Germany. Then, in 2010, Thilo Sarrazin, a banking official and member of the Social Democrats, published a book entitled *Germany Abolishes Itself*.

Sarrazin's book argued for restricting immigration by Muslim groups. He charged that Turks and other Muslim groups had failed to assimilate and were living off the state in ghettos like Berlin's Neukolin, where as many as two-thirds of the 80,000 immigrant residents were on welfare. He warned that if the government didn't limit their numbers, they would eventually overtake ethnic Germans. Sarrazin's book was immediately condemned by political leaders and Germany's major publications, and he was discharged from his position with the Bundesbank—but it shot to the top of the bestseller list, eventually selling 1.5 million copies. According to *Der Spiegel*, party leaders from the Social Democrats and Christian Democrats were chastised by their rank and file for attacking Sarrazin. The seeds of a nationalist backlash had been sown.

The Alternativ fur Deutschland was founded in Berlin in February 2013 by economist Bernard Lucke, lawyer Alexander Gauland, and journalist Konrad Adam. It was primarily a Euroskeptic party

that, in the wake of Germany's role in bailing out Greece, called   253
for Germany to leave the Eurozone. Dubbed the professor's party
because of its leadership and its base among the educated middle
class, it got a surprising 7.1 percent in elections in 2014 to the European Parliament, which are usually a low-turnout forum for protest
voters. But the next year, at the party congress in Essen, the AfD
changed course.

Frauke Petry, a chemist and single mother from Dresden, joined
with Gauland in ousting Lucke from the leadership. Petry and
Gauland wanted the party to focus on immigrants and the Islamic
threat. Lucke resigned from the party, charging that Petry wanted
to turn it into the "PEGIDA party," the name of a Dresden-based
anti-Islamic group (Patriotic Europeans Against the Islamiciza-
tion of the West) that staged weekly demonstrations. In national
polls, the party looked doomed, floundering at 3 percent. But
Petry and Gauland's takeover came just two months before Angela
Merkel decided to open Germany's border to over a million Muslim
refugees.

"We Can Manage This"

In the summer of 2015, with Iraq and Syria engulfed in war, refugees
begin pouring into Southern Europe through Turkey and Greece.
Thousands encamped in Hungary in August seeking to enter Germany. Hungary's prime minister Victor Orban, claimed he couldn't
process them and called on Merkel to take them, which she agreed
to do, declaring in August that Germany's borders were now open
to any refugees who wanted to come. "We can manage this," she
famously declared. Over that year and next, 1.2 million refugees
would arrive, roughly equivalent to five million refugees arriving in
the United States over a year.

That fall, Merkel's initiative was widely praised. She was *Time's*
Person of the Year. The German press focused on the raucous rightwing opposition from PEGIDA and dismissed Merkel's mainstream critics as racist. Wolfgang Streeck says, "People were morally

254 compelled to shut up. It resulted in people who did not agree seeing themselves in newspapers, and on television, as Nazis, Holocaust deniers. They were excluded from the political community." There was little debate about migration in the political parties, especially on the left. Explained sociologist Anke Hassel, a research fellow at the union-backed Hans-Böckler-Stiftung, "It was very hard for the left to even discuss these issues because it is considered racist or xenophobic to discuss it."

Then, on New Year's Eve in Cologne, groups of men, identified as being Arab or North African, went on a rampage in the city center assaulting and robbing women—at least 24 women were raped. According to the chief prosecutor, the "overwhelming majority" of the men were asylum-seekers and illegal immigrants. Similar incidents—an estimated 1,200 attacks—occurred in Stuttgart, Dusseldorf, Hamburg, Dortmund, and Bielefeld. That abruptly ended the public's enthusiasm for Merkel's policy of open borders and boosted the fortunes of the AfD.

In three state elections held in March 2016, the AfD, running in opposition to Merkel's open borders, got 24.2 percent of the vote—the second highest—in Saxony-Anhalt, a downscale state in the former East Germany. It also came in a respectable third in two wealthy states in the former West Germany where disillusionment with Merkel's alliance with the Social Democrats ran high. Merkel sought to contain the damage by working out an agreement with Turkey to house future migrants from Syria there. The flow abated after the spring of 2016, but the political damage was done. In the September 2017 national elections, the AfD would come in third with 12.6 percent—ahead of the Free Democrats but also the Greens, the leading champion of an open borders policy. When the CDU/CSU and SPD agreed the next spring to form a coalition government, the AfD became the official opposition party in Parliament and became entitled to chair the powerful budget committee.

The AfD has some similarities to other nationalist and populist parties on the continent, but it is nationalist in a way that no significant German party has been since 1945. It represents a repudiation of what Germany, France, and the other countries that formed the EEC attempted to do. The party's official platform condemns the Schengen and Maastricht treaties for violating German "national sovereignty." It declares that the AfD is committed to "German is the predominant culture" and rejects "the ideology of multiculturalism." It declares that "Islam does not belong to Germany." It says that "German citizenship is inseparably linked to our language and culture" and rejects dual citizenship and granting citizenship to children by the fact of their birth regardless of their parents' nationality.

The AfD, like some of the smaller openly pro-fascist groups in Italy or the dissenting wing of the National Front, appears to be symptomatic of what Freud called the return of the repressed. This occurs when instinctual impulses—or in this case very ordinary nationalist sentiments—are completely blocked from expression because of their association with aberrant, ugly desires, only to return in their most primitive, brutal form.

In their public statements, the party's leaders suggested that anyone who was not of German ethnic descent was not really German. In June 2016, Alexander Gauland, who was then deputy chairman of the AfD, described Jerome Boateng, a star on Germany's soccer team who was born in Berlin of a Ghanaian father and German mother, as "alien," and said that people would not want "someone like Boateng as a neighbor." AfD leaders also flouted the taboos about Germany's Nazi past. Bjorn Hocke, one of the party's leaders and an elected official in Thuringia, said at a rally in Dresden in January 2017 that Germany needs to make a "180 degree turn" in its attitude toward World War II. Referring to the Holocaust memorial, he complained that the Germans "were the only people in the world to plant a monument of shame in the heart of their capital." Nine months later at a meeting at a nineteenth-century German war memorial, Gauland called on Germans to take pride in their military and not identify it with the Nazi period. "These years don't concern our identity anymore," he said. "Which is why we have the right not only to take back our country, but also our past." The AfD's parliamentary delegation recruited some of its staff from groups identified as neo-Nazi, including the NPD and HFD, which the government banned in 2009 for trying to indoctrinate young people with Neo-Nazi ideology.

Many AfD voters are former East Germans whose standard of living is still well below that of former West Germans. Many of them have also retained a strictly ethnic view of German citizenship. East Germany had a small migrant population from Vietnam, Cuba, and Angola, but they were segregated, never given even permanent residency, and were encouraged to leave after reunification. Critics of the AfD questioned why, given how few refugees actually migrate to that part of Germany, the former East Germans should have been so up in arms over the refugee crisis. One of them explained, "We voted AfD so we don't get any refugees in the first place. Once you've got weeds, they are hard to get rid of. So you make sure they don't grow to start with." A similar logic would prevail among many citizens in Eastern Europe toward the prospect of refugees being relocated there.

Hungary and Victor Orban
The final segment of the EU's original project, embodied in the Copenhagen Criteria, was the attempt to extend democracy across the continent by absorbing eight former Warsaw Pact countries. By admitting them to the EU, the EU's planners hoped they would be kept on a liberal democratic path. In 2004, five years after admitting them, EU commissioner Olli Rehn declared the move an unquestioned success. "Enlargement has served as an anchor of stability and democracy and as a driver of personal freedom and economic dynamism in Europe," he said.

Less than a decade later, however, there were questions about whether, in expanding eastward, the EU had created an albatross rather than an anchor. Prime Minister Victor Orban and his

Fidesz Party, running on an aggressive nationalist program, won   257
two-thirds majorities in 2010, 2014, and 2018 and have been taking
steps to create a one-party state, prompting charges from the EU
that they are violating article two of the EU's treaty requiring all
members to respect democracy and the rule of law. In Poland, Jaroslaw Kaczynski and his Law and Justice Party, which took over the
government in 2015, followed Orban's lead and incurred the same
charges from the EU.

Their violation of the Copenhagen Criteria raises questions
about the EU's original ambitions. Should the EU have admitted
these countries in the first place? And if it should have, should it
also have recognized that Hungary's and Poland's histories, and
their experience with nationalism, were very different from those of
the countries in Western Europe?

Hungarians date their nation from the coronation of the
Magyar king Saint Stephen, who had converted to Catholicism, in
1000. But in the succeeding millennium, they were butchered by the
Mongols, who killed off about half the population, and subjugated
by the Ottomans and then the Hapsburgs. Dragooned by Austria
into backing the Central Powers in the First World War, the Hungarians were punished by the victorious Allies. At Trianon in 1920,
Hungary lost 60 percent of its population and two-thirds of its land,
which originally spanned part of Romania and the former Yugoslavia and Czechoslovakia, leaving 3.2 million native Hungarians in
neighboring countries. Hungarians hoped to get these lands back by
allying with the Nazis in World War II, but lost them again afterward
in the Soviet occupation.

In Hungary, nationalism never acquired the bad name it had in
Germany. Instead, it was seen as the basis for the country's survival
over the centuries. It was a source of pride and at the time nurtured a
continuing fear of foreign domination. Cultural scientist Magdalena
Marsovszky writes, "Trianon was the cause of a great deal of con-
sternation, and an irrational fear of the 'death of the nation' took on
immense proportions." Hungary also had little experience of liberal

258 democracy. During its brief period of independence from 1919 to 1944, it was ruled by Admiral Miklos Horthy.

After Hungary gained its independence from the Soviet Union in 1989, its first governments were led by classic liberals and former socialists who had turned from Marx to Milton Friedman and from Lenin to Tony Blair. They enthusiastically embraced the prospect of a European Hungary as a counter to a Soviet Hungary. Orban's Fidesz Party, which started out as student dissenters to Soviet rule, originally advocated classical liberalism, but after faring poorly in elections, turned to Christian nationalism. Invoking the wounds of Trianon, Orban advocated "a unified nation, extending beyond national borders, belonging together." He combined that with a social welfare agenda that echoed Hungary's communist past under Janos Kadar.

Orban's party won the leadership in 1998, but the coalition splintered and lost power four years later. However, in 2010, in response to the austerity promoted by a coalition of liberals and former socialists in the wake of the Great Recession, Orban and Fidesz won the two-thirds majority necessary to alter Hungary's constitution.

Orban lowered utility prices, adopted a family allowance plan to give subsidies to people having children, and defended Hungary's national health system against efforts to privatize it. He also put into effect a strongly nationalist agenda. He allowed ethnic Hungarians outside the country to hold Hungarian passports and to vote in elections. At the same time, Orban took steps to create a one-party state similar to that which had existed in communist Hungary. Orban and Fidesz rewrote the constitution, gutted the power of the independent Constitutional Court to review legislation, and gave the executive and the legislature the power to appoint the members of commissions that were created to oversee the media and elections.

Orban consolidated the state media and put it in the hands of a council that Fidesz controlled. He required other journalists and publications to register with the government. They were subject to fines if their coverage was not "balanced." Orban's personal friends,

many of whom got rich from government contracts, acquired nearly
all of the country's media outlets. Orban, who funds a pro-Fidesz
think tank, attempted to intimidate independent ones, and took
control of state museums and theaters.

When the EU's justice commissioner in 2014 harshly criticized
Orban's revision of the constitution and threatened to strip Hungary of its EU voting rights, Orban struck back with a campaign
against "Brussels" and its "left corner." The EU became, in effect, the
latest foreign invaders to violate Hungary's sovereignty. At a speech
at an ethnic Hungarian summer camp in Romania, Orban invoked
Hungarian nationalism in defense of his measures:

> The Hungarian nation is not simply a group of individuals but a
> community that must be organized, reinforced, and in fact constructed. And so in this sense the new state that we are constructing in Hungary is an illiberal state, a non-liberal state. It
> does not reject the fundamental principles of liberalism such as
> freedom, and I could list a few more, but it does not make this
> ideology the central element of state organization, but instead
> includes a different, special, national approach.

In 2015, after Orban had won reelection and another two-thirds
majority, he found a new kind of foreign invader to single out. Refugees from the Middle East began streaming across Hungary's
southern border. In the first six months, 50,000 migrants entered
Hungary looking for asylum in the EU. In June, Orban began building
a fence across Hungary's border to keep out the migrants, but they
kept coming. By September, they were in Budapest's rail station
and on its highways trying to move northward to Germany. When
the European Commission decided at Germany's behest to establish quotas of migrants for each nation and allotted Hungary 1,294,
Orban refused to accept them.

Orban's rejection of the refugees and of those who championed
and sponsored them crystalized his case for Hungarian nationalism.

260   "The crisis offers the chance for the national Christian ideology to retain supremacy not only in Hungary, but in the whole of Europe," he said. He warned that the refugees were "overrunning us and threatening our civilization." "We do not want to see in our midst any minorities whose cultural background differs from our own. We want to keep Hungary for the Hungarians." Orban and Fidesz's stance on refugees was very popular in Hungary. According to a 2016 Pew poll, 76 percent of Hungarians thought the influx of migrants increased "the likelihood of terrorism."

In this crusade he found an enemy in George Soros, a Hungarian Jew who had migrated to New York and made billions as a currency speculator. Soros's Open Society Foundation had funded educational and human rights campaigns in Hungary for decades. In 1989, Orban himself had gone to school in England on a Soros grant. In September 2015, Soros had written a column recommending that the EU "accept at least a million asylum-seekers annually for the foreseeable future."

Orban launched a campaign against Soros with the premise, resting on little evidence, that Soros was behind a plan to turn Hungary into a haven for the refugees at the expense of its inhabitants. He installed hundreds of billboards in Budapest and throughout the countryside; one showed a smiling Soros and was captioned, "Let's not let Soros have the last laugh." Another read, "Soros wants to transplant millions from Africa and the Middle East. Stop Soros." I found the billboards extremely disturbing, as did people I interviewed from Budapest's Jewish community. With the April 2018 election approaching, Orban stepped up his attacks against the press and against the organizations and the university that Soros funded.

In the wake of Orban's 2018 election victory, several hundred academics from Europe and the United States signed an open letter to Merkel calling on her to dissociate herself and her party from Orban. "The price that Europe will have to pay for the failure to stand up to Orban is also much higher than you seem to realize," the letter read. "The European Union is founded on values including

democracy, the rule of law, and respect for human rights. By allowing
the Hungarian government to destroy democratic institutions and
to demonize minorities with impunity, the EU risks turning into
little more than a regional trade bloc devoid of common values."

But the question posed by Orban's success in office is whether
the EU overreached itself in going beyond being a regional trade
bloc: whether it took sufficient account of Hungary's history, in
which autocrats like Horthy and Kadar are esteemed by Orban's
supporters, and of its vibrant, but also highly defensive, nationalism. It's the same question that needs to be asked about its stand
against Poland's government.

Budapest in Warsaw

For all of Hungary's historical woes, those of Poland easily exceed
them. While Hungary retained a geographical identity as well as a
local culture during the centuries, Poland was not so lucky. From
the eighteenth century until World War I—at a time when modern
nations were forming in Europe and across the Atlantic—Poland
did not exist as a geographical entity. It was partitioned among Germany, Russia, and Austria. The Germans and Russians also did what
they could to wipe out indigenous Polish culture, but as often happens, they didn't succeed.

As a result, Poland's idea of its nationhood was nurtured for centuries when the nation itself didn't physically exist. It lent the idea of
Polish nationhood a special ethnic purity that encouraged solidarity
in the face of foreign domination on the one hand, and intolerance of
anything seemingly foreign on the other hand. Polish political scientist Leszek Koczanowicz has written, "The nation emerged as a pro-
jection of hopes and anxieties—or, to use a psychoanalytical term, as
a phantasm that left a heavy imprint on the lives of multiple generations of Poles. At its heart lay a dream of absolute national unity and
the appended belief that it was almost tangible, within reach."

During the centuries of partition and during the Soviet era, the
main enduring Polish institution was the Catholic Church. Like

Hungary, Poland dates its own origin to a ruler who in 966 joined the Roman Catholic Church. But even more than in Hungary, religious observance and belief has been central to Poland's national identity. It's a line that runs from Mieszko I in the tenth century up through Solidarity and Pope John Paul II down to Jaroslaw Kaczynski and his ruling Law and Justice Party today. Jacek Kucharczyk, president of the Institute for Public Affairs in Warsaw, explained the connection between the Church and Polish nationalism this way: "To be a true Pole," he said, "you have to be a Catholic."

Like Hungary, Poland also has a strong sense of having been victimized over the centuries, but particularly in the last century. During World War II, Poland was initially partitioned between the Nazis and the Soviet Union, and was afterward entirely under German control. During that time, 6 million out of 30 million Poles perished, including 3 million Jews. In retreat, the Germans reduced Warsaw, Poznan, and Lubin to rubble. Slawomir Sierakowski, the director of the Institute for Advanced Study in Warsaw, describes Poles as having "more the identity of soldier than a citizen. You are a member of a nation that doesn't have a state and is enslaved, and you fight all the time for freedom. This kind of identity doesn't fit well with liberalism, proportional values, and compromises."

Poland's transition out of communism was similar to that of Hungary and other Eastern European countries. Under Solidarity hero Lech Walesa, and his successor, former communist official Aleksander Kwasniewski, Poland went from a planned to a hyper-free market economy.

By the 2005 elections, Kwasniewski had worn out his welcome. Unemployment was at 17.7 percent. Government corruption was rife. Polish participation in George W. Bush's Iraq war was unpopular. That left an opening for two new parties: a center-right group, Civic Platform, similar to Germany's Free Democrats, and a new populist party, Law and Justice, founded by twin brothers Jaroslaw and Lech Kaczynski. The Kaczynski brothers, who were born in

1949, had both gone to law school in Warsaw and had then attached themselves to Walesa and Solidarity. Both men had initially held positions in Walesa's administration, but had broken with him, primarily over Walesa's reluctance to purge Poland's government of former communists.

In 2005, the brothers focused their campaign on crime, corruption, communism, and growing inequality. They advocated outlawing the Democratic Left Alliance because of its connections with the "criminal underworld." Jaroslaw Kaczynski charged that 10,000 former members of the communist secret police had jobs in Poland's police force. The Kaczynskis advocated a "moral revolution." They framed the election as a choice between "returning post-communism" and "regaining Poland by Poles." Lech Kaczynski, who ran for president, edged out the Civic Platform candidate, but Law and Justice won a bare plurality in Parliament with 27 percent of the vote and had to create a coalition. After two years of infighting with its coalition partners, the brothers called for a new election, and lost their majority to Civic Platform.

In 2010, Lech Kaczynski, who had remained president, died in an airplane crash. In the 2011 parliamentary election, Law and Justice was again bested by Civic Platform. Jaroslaw Kaczynski said afterward, "Viktor Orban gave us an example of how we can win. The day will come when we will succeed, and we will have Budapest in Warsaw." In preparation for 2015, Kaczynski mimicked Orban's potent blend of nationalism, cultural conservatism, and leftwing economics. Kaczynski, who had gained a reputation for abrasiveness in his brief tenure as prime minister in 2006–2007, became the backroom strategist and ran Andrzej Duda for president and Beata Szydło for prime minister.

Kaczynski gave only one speech during the campaign. He attacked Civic Platform for agreeing to the EU's demand that it accept 7,000 refugees from Syria. "There are already signs of emergence of diseases that are highly dangerous and have not been seen in Europe for a long time," he warned. Law and Justice attacked Civic

264   Platform for raising the retirement age to 67 and promised a program dubbed 500 plus—families would get 500 zlotys a month (about $150) for each additional child above one that they were raising. The proposal was supposed to boost the Polish birth rate and provide the equivalent of a guaranteed annual income for downscale rural Poles with large families. "This program gained Law and Justice huge popularity," explained political scientist Marek Cichocki. "It was the first real program after the transformation [from communism] to redistribute income."

This time, Law and Justice won a majority of seats. Once in office, Law and Justice continued to follow Orban's playbook. They lowered the retirement age for men and women, provided free medication for people over 75, and raised the minimum wage. They rejected EU demands to accept refugees. They promulgated their own version of Christian nationalism. Piotr Buras of the European Council on Foreign Relations in Warsaw says, "The story is that we are a nation that had to defend itself for centuries against the powerful neighbors, we were constantly under pressure, sometimes we lost politically, we lost our sovereignty, but we were always morally on the right side, we are morally superior to the others."

Following Orban's example, Kaczynski also took aim at Poland's constitution. Law and Justice adopted new rules for the Supreme Court that would substantially curb its independence. They repealed Poland's civil service regulations that insulated top officials from political pressure. In response, the European Commission initiated proceedings against Poland for its assault on the rule of law. Kaczynski portrayed the EU pressure on Poland as an attempt to reestablish foreign control. "The program of deep changes in our country will not slow down. On the contrary, there cannot be any talk about reaching an agreement with powers that for years treated Poland as their own private loot," Kaczynski told a Polish daily.

Kaczynski and his administration have constantly reminded Poles of Germany's occupation. He has demanded that Germany pay "huge sums" in reparations for World War II. When I interviewed

several cabinet officials and asked them about Law and Justice's
nationalist appeal, they went back to the lessons of the German
invasion of Poland. Maciej Pisarski, the Deputy Director of the
Department of Foreign Policy Strategy, said, "September 1, 1939, is
still a defining moment. Nothing was the same again. Many arguments today boil down to 1939. Because we were abandoned by our
allies and left to our own defenses, and suffered a total apocalypse,
we have to be able to stand our ground no matter what."

In the wake of the refugee crisis, Kaczynski condemned Europe
for its willingness to sacrifice its cultural and ethnic identity to
admit Muslim refugees. "There is a very deep crisis in Europe,"
he said. "It is a serious crisis of European consciousness, a crisis
of identity, which is coupled with the collapse of values and basic
social institutions." Kaczynski's stand against admitting the refugees in defiance of the EU was very popular. Asked by one poll
whether Poland should refuse to accept Muslim refugees even if that
meant a cutoff of the EU funds that Poland depends on, 56.5 percent
said yes and only 40.4 percent no. More than half have been willing
to leave the EU entirely, even though Poles generally support membership in the EU as a repudiation of their past association with the
Soviet Union and the Warsaw Pact.

With Poland, as with Hungary, EU officials underestimated the
historical undertow that prevents countries from moving easily
and smoothly from authoritarian pasts in which their own nationhood was constantly in question, but also in which nationalism
was a weapon against cultural extinction—to a liberal democratic
present in which questions of ethnicity and religion are put aside.
History generally follows a pattern of two steps forward and—if we
are lucky—only one-and-a-half steps backward. Post-Soviet Russia
looked like it was headed toward Western democracy in the 1990s,
only to end up with a deeply flawed democracy that echoed the old
Soviet or even Czarist past. Poland and Hungary have not become
autocracies, but their governments increasingly echo their recent
Cold War and communist past—Hungary's in particular, albeit

266   without Soviet domination. And the EU's attempt to bring these countries into line strengthened national resentment of outside interference and control.

The EU could well survive. Even many of its critics recognize that in a world increasingly dominated by the United States and China, the nations of Europe need a way of exerting their influence. The EU provides that. There is also an economic utility to the EU as a customs union and a passport-free zone, as the British who backed Brexit and who never had to put up with the Euro may belatedly discover. In the face of the pandemic and deep recession that struck in 2020, the EU, after a heated debate pitting several of the export-led countries in the North against the countries in Southern Europe, finally agreed to a large aid package targeted at Italy, Spain, and the countries most affected by the virus. That concession, backed by Germany's Angela Merkel, may have mitigated hostility toward the EU. But in the absence of a crisis that would unite the countries, as the Cold War had, Monnet and Spinelli's dream of a United States of Europe is likely to remain unfulfilled. Over the last three decades, the attempt to realize it has not brought the nations closer together, but in some respects driven them apart by awakening the nationalist sentiments it was supposed to eradicate.

Trump and the New World Disorder

There is no doubt that the attempt by the United States and Western Europe after World War II to prevent the reemergence of toxic nationalism was a success up through at least the 1970s. The formation of the EEC put the relationship between France and Germany on a new footing. The IMF helped to prevent the clashes over currency that had contributed to the Great Depression and war. During the Cold War, the formation of NATO created a stable alliance that was able to pursue a strategy of containment against the Soviet Union and the Warsaw Pact. In the Far East, the United States brought a pacified Japan under its security umbrella. The Cold War's end was seen as vindicating this attempt and as justifying the expansion of the regional and supranational arrangements that the U.S. and Western Europe had created.

In the wake of the Cold War's end, the U.S. embraced a foreign policy aimed at replacing the ideological and economic division between capitalist West and communist East with an American-dominated world order of American-style free market democracies. "The successor to a doctrine of containment must be a strategy of enlargement—enlargement of the world's free community of market democracies," Bill Clinton's national security advisor Anthony Lake,

268 declared in September 1993. But in attempting to create this new world order, the U.S., and to differing degrees, its Western European allies, were oblivious to the nationalist sentiments in the countries they were trying to bring into this community.

That failure of understanding was evident in the decision by NATO to enlarge its membership to the borders of Russia; in the American and British attempt to remake the Middle East by invading Iraq; and in the assumptions that Americans brought to their dealings with China. The United States, which has been driven since its founding by a messianic vision to remake the world in its own image, repeatedly failed during this period to recognize the particular history and mission that drives other countries.

During his presidential campaign, Donald Trump displayed a dawning recognition that this effort at global conversion had failed in the Middle East and with Russia and China. In reaction, Trump's approach, capsulized in his slogan "America First," was to replace America's broader ideological ambition with a narrow nationalism aimed at asserting America's material interests against those of rival nations. Trump also appeared to recognize that some of the global and regional institutions created after World War II had lost their way; but instead of attempting to revive or reform them, he largely eschewed alliances and international organizations in favor of the singular exercise of power.

The Mideast Imbroglio

As often noted, the most serious failure of American foreign policy during the last five decades was the Bush administration's invasion of Iraq in 2003. The Americans who promoted the invasion assumed, in the words of Vice President Dick Cheney, that Americans would be "greeted as liberators." Instead, the invasion awakened suppressed nationalist sentiments as well as tribal and religious hostilities. It dynamited the fragile scaffolding that had held together the tribes and religious groups in the nations that Great Britain and France had created after World War I. The invasion would eventually

inspire the rise of ISIS in Iraq and would contribute to the spread of
Islamist terrorism in Europe and the United States and to the flood
of refugees that destabilized Europe in 2015.

George W. Bush and his war council made the decision to invade,
but the seeds of it were sown in the debate in the 1990s about American intervention first in Somalia and then in the former Yugoslavia.
This debate pitted post-Vietnam liberals and neo-conservatives
against realists. The liberals and neo-conservatives believed that in
order to spread free market democracy, the United States could and
should remake other nations. In intellectual circles, the stance was
embraced by the editorial policies of the liberal *New Republic* and
the newly minted neo-conservative *Weekly Standard*. The realists
warned that such efforts would run roughshod over native nationalism and would tax American resources. The Clinton administration and the neo-conservatives backed American intervention in
the Balkans; and its relative success reinforced their convictions.
Clinton signed the 1998 Iraq Liberation Act into law, which committed the United States to "regime change," but not necessarily to a
ground invasion of Iraq.

Barack Obama initially ran for president in opposition to the
invasion of Iraq, but once in office, he, too, became involved with
the British and French in his own version of nation-building in
North Africa. The Libyan intervention, like that in Iraq, sundered
the country along tribal lines, and unleashed another wave of refugees to Western Europe. Obama, overly enthused about the effects
of the Arab Spring, made a similar error in Syria, putting America's
word, influence, and special forces behind a call for Syria's president
to step down. All these efforts, which were based on a misapprehension of other nation's histories, and which sought to impose American political and economic ideals, ended in disaster.

Russia and Cold War II
In Russia, the Clinton administration rested its hopes of transforming the post-Soviet nation on Boris Yeltsin's government,

270   which it helped to win the election in 1996. Clinton and his top advisors hoped that Yeltsin's election would strengthen Russian democracy. They also hoped that Yeltsin's adoption of an American plan to subject the Russian economy to "shock therapy" by selling off its assets and removing government regulations would lead to a capitalist recovery. They thought that through aiding Yeltsin they were bringing Russia into the American-European orbit. They didn't believe that their own initiatives to expand NATO to Russia's borders would endanger American-Russian relations. They were wrong on every count.

Yeltsin's policies led to a massive Russian depression—the Russian economy contracted 40 percent between 1991, when Yeltsin took power, and 1998. Then, in 1998, Russia endured a financial crash that almost took down Western economies. Yeltsin's privatization of assets led to the creation of a new class of Russian oligarchs and to deepening corruption. Yeltsin appointed as his successor Vladimir Putin, who promised to restore Russia's economy and position in the world.

Putin viewed the collapse of the Soviet Union as a "disaster." In his 2005 State of the Union speech, Putin, articulating widely held Russian convictions, famously said:

> Above all, we should acknowledge that the collapse of the Soviet Union was a major geopolitical disaster of the century. As for the Russian nation, it became a genuine drama. Tens of millions of our co-citizens and co-patriots found themselves outside Russian territory. Moreover, the epidemic of disintegration infected Russia itself.

In attempting to revive Russia, Putin assiduously avoided Marxist-Leninist fantasies of resurrecting the Soviet empire. Instead, like Orban in Hungary, he reverted to ethnic nationalism, and restored an older authoritarian tradition of Russian state rule. In 2000, after taking office, Putin said:

It will not happen soon, if it ever happens at all, that Russia will   271
become the second edition of say, the U.S. or Britain in which liberal values have deep historic traditions. Our state and its institutions have always played an exceptionally important role in the
life of the country and its people. For Russians a strong state is not
an anomaly that should be gotten rid of. Quite the contrary, they
see it as a source and guarantor of order and the initiator and main
driving force of any change.

Over his almost two decades of rule, Putin has steadily chipped
away at the brittle democracy Russia had put in place with American support after the Soviet Union dissolved. And he has aggressively reasserted his country's power and influence on its periphery
in Georgia and Ukraine and in the Middle East in Syria. What Yeltsin
described in 1994 as a "cold peace" is reverting to another Cold War.

An aggressive Russian nationalism was always waiting in the
wings, but America and its European allies played an important role
in bringing it onstage by discounting its importance. That began
with the attempt by the United States and Germany in 1990 to win
Soviet acceptance of German unification in exchange for a promise
not to expand NATO.* George H. W. Bush's secretary of state, James
Baker, assured Soviet president Mikhail Gorbachev and Foreign
Minister Eduard Shevardnadze that "there would be no extension of

* Whether the United States and Germany actually promised not to expand NATO
in exchange for Soviet (and then Russian) acceptance of German unification is
immaterial. It's enough to establish that Mikhail Gorbachev and Boris Yeltsin
and subsequent Russian leaders thought they had received such a promise.
However, I am convinced by an essay, based on new archival research, by Joshua R.
Itzkowitz Shifrinson of the George Bush School of International Affairs at Texas
A&M University ("Deal or No Deal, The End of the Cold War and the U.S. Offer
to Limit NATO Expansion," International Security, Spring 2016), that the U.S.
and Germany did make and break such a promise. Shifrinson cites numerous
statements to that effect from Secretary of State James Baker, German chancellor
Helmut Kohl, and German foreign minister Hans Dietrich Genscher to Soviet
officials. Baker and the Germans have denied making a formal written promise,
but Shifrinson argues convincingly that it was sufficient that they repeatedly
made oral promises.

272 NATO's jurisdiction for forces of NATO one inch to the east." But even before Bush had left office, American officials were debating whether to expand NATO eastward to include the former Warsaw Pact nations.

Bill Clinton, backed domestically by a coalition of liberals and neo-conservatives, convinced NATO's European members to embrace expansion. Clinton publicly unveiled his plan after Yeltsin's election in 1996. In 1999, NATO formally extended offers to Hungary, Czechoslovakia, and Poland, and in 2004 to seven other nations, including three that had also been part of the Soviet Union. Gorbachev, Yeltsin, and Putin denounced the decision. It ignored long-standing Russian fears, which went back to Napoleon's invasion of Russia in 1812, of being encircled and then attacked from the West. And it ignored the challenge to Russian *amour propre*, which is not inconsequential in foreign affairs. Citizens' identification with their nation is based on identifying with its success in the world—whether in athletic competitions or war—and any leaders' perpetuity in office depends on defending their nations against slights and insults. In the case of Russia, this meant restoring the nation's pride after the disintegration of the Soviet Union and of its empire in Eastern Europe.

NATO expansion was vigorously opposed by a wide range of American government officials who warned that by defying Russian national interests, the administration could eventually create a new Cold War. In an open letter to Clinton in 1998, over 40 foreign policy experts, including two former ambassadors to the Soviet Union, warned that in Russia, expansion "will strengthen the non-democratic opposition, undercut those who favor reform and cooperation with the West, bring the Russians to question the entire post−Cold War settlement, and galvanize resistance in the Duma to the START II and III treaties." In an interview with columnist Thomas Friedman about NATO expansion, George Kennan, the father of the containment policy toward the Soviet Union, said that "it shows so little understanding of Russian history and Soviet history. Of course there is going to be a bad reaction from Russia, and then [the NATO expanders] will say that we always told you that is how the Russians are—but this is just wrong."

But Clinton and his successors and the leaders of the European Union doubled down on a strategy of moving the Western alliance eastward to Russia's borders. The United States and its Western European allies also began intervening in Georgia and Ukraine in the early 2000s. The Russians attributed the color revolutions of 2004 in those countries, which brought pro-Western governments to power, to American funding of opposition groups. In April 2008, George W. Bush, with the support of presidential candidates Obama and John McCain, proposed that Ukraine and Georgia be asked to join NATO. Putin, who in the first years of his presidency, had actually worked cooperatively in Afghanistan with the United States, warned that the American plan posed a "direct threat" to Russia.

In 2008, the EU began negotiating an Association Agreement with Ukraine that would subject it to the EU's political norms and economic rules and inhibit its economic relations with Russia. In conducting the negotiations, political scientist Samuel Charap and sociologist Timothy Colton wrote in *Everyone Loses,* "Brussels acted as if Russia did not exist." The decision in November 2013 by Ukrainian prime minister Viktor Yanukovych to suspend negotiations over the agreement prompted the protests in the western Ukraine that culminated in his ouster the next February.

The Obama administration initially tried to play a mediating role in what was then called the Maidan Revolution, but after Yanukovych was driven out of office, the administration enthusiastically backed the new pro-Western government. Putin, citing the ouster of an elected president and the new government's subordination of Ukraine's predominately ethnic Russian east and south, reclaimed Crimea and backed the pro-Russian rebels in eastern Ukraine. The issue, Putin said, "is how to ensure the legitimate rights and interests of ethnic Russians and Russian speakers in the south and east of Ukraine." In leveling sanctions against the Russians, Obama's

274   assistant secretary of state, Victoria Nuland, continued to discount Russian nationalism. "Unless Putin changes course," she warned, "at some point in the not-too-distant future, the current nationalistic fever will break in Russia."

Contrary to Nuland's prediction, Putin's actions in seizing Crimea and backing a rebellion in eastern Ukraine against Kiev have remained highly popular in Russia. That perhaps led Obama's ambassador to Russia, Michael McFaul, and political scientist Kathryn Stoner-Weiss to argue that Putin's actions had nothing to do with Western policies, but were "a result of Putin's response to new domestic political and economic challenges inside Russia." In other words, Putin intervened in order to enhance his domestic standing, which was under attack. But their analysis begs the question. The reason Putin's actions were popular was because there was a sense of national grievance to which he could appeal. That grievance was partly the result of the prior decades in which the United States and the EU systematically and repeatedly ignored Russia's historic fears of encirclement and the "trauma" and "loss of face," in Charap and Colton's words, that it had suffered from the collapse of the Soviet Union.

The Chinese Dream
In the 1990s, the Clinton administration and other policymakers in Washington held similar false expectations about China. They predicted that by welcoming China into the WTO, they would put it on a path to becoming a peace-loving free market democracy that, like Russia, would fall within the America-led world orbit. In a speech promoting China's accession to the WTO, Clinton declared that "membership in the WTO, of course, will not create a free society in China overnight or guarantee that China will play by global rules. But over time, I believe it will move China faster and further in the right direction."

Here, again, nothing that the Clinton administration predicted came to pass. Washington policymakers expected that China's state-run industries would be unable to compete on a global stage, forcing China to adopt a privatized free market system that would integrate it into the American-led global economy. But instead, China and its state-run firms blossomed under the WTO. China figured out how to game the system by subsidizing export industries, holding down their own labor costs, and using currency manipulation to keep the prices of exports down and imports up. China also demanded that firms that wanted to set up shop in China share ownership and technology. Some industries and governments complained of China's tactics, but by the time they had won their cases against China in the slow-moving WTO tribunal, the damage had been done.

During the 2000s, China boomed. By 2009, it had surpassed its bitterest rival, Japan, as the world's second-largest economy. In the United States, Chinese imports—and American firms' decision to relocate or outsource their components to China rather than attempt to increase their productivity at home—created a large swath of boarded-up main streets in American towns that had once depended on manufacturing plants.

China, which had begun to entertain some measure of free political speech in the 1980s, reversed course after the Tiananmen Square revolt in 1989. Open dissenters were jailed. Under Xi Jinping, who took power in 2013, it abandoned the informal two-term limit that Deng Xiaoping had installed. The government combed the internet for even hints of dissent. The government has set up a social credit system that tracks individuals and is able to reward or punish them for their behavior with high or low scores. Faced with protests against government interference, Beijing quashed dissent in Hong Kong under a new security law that violated the 1997 promise of autonomy. It erected concentration camps in Xinjiang province to suppress the Uighur Muslim minority.

Finally, contrary to the expectations of the Clinton administration and Washington experts, China's foreign policy became less accommodating and increasingly displayed an aggressive nationalism. This should have come as no surprise to students of China's

276 history. China's nationalist aspirations go back even further than Russia's. They go as far back as the Han Dynasty that took power in 206 BC. In *Everything Under the Heavens: How the Past Shapes China's Push for Global Power*, Howard W. French writes:

> Practically speaking, for the emperors of the Central Kingdom, this place we call China, the world could be roughly divided into two broad and simple categories, civilization and noncivilization, meaning the peoples who accepted the supremacy of its ruler, the Son of Heaven, and the principle of his celestial virtue, and those who didn't—those who were beyond the pale.

In the known world of Asia where China's civilization reigned supreme, China's emperors established a system by which states that wanted to trade with it had to pay tribute. China's emperors were periodically challenged by foreign invaders, most effectively in the century that began in the 1840s with the Opium Wars, in which Western imperialist powers, led by the British, established spheres of influence. This century of humiliation continued through the Chinese defeat in the first Sino-Japanese war and the brutal Japanese occupation of two-thirds of the country before and during World War II. Since then, China's national aims have been driven by the attempt to reestablish its dominance. In his book *Asia's Reckoning*, Richard McGregor summed up China's regional objectives:

> China is not so much trying to build a new Asian community as reinstating the old tributary system that prevailed in much of the region until about two hundred years ago, in which smaller, lesser countries acquiesced in Chinese dominance in return for the hegemon's goodwill.

Under Deng in the 1980s and much of the 1990s, China kept its foreign aims concealed. Deng wanted China "to hide its light and bide its time." But emboldened by its economic success and by the

West's political and economic woes during the Great Recession, the
regime became more open and bolder in its aspirations.

Over the last decade, China attempted to assert its ownership
of the waters of the East China and South China Seas that include
islands and water claimed by Japan, the Philippines, Malaysia, Brunei,
Vietnam, and Taiwan. China has battled the Japanese over the Senkaku Islands in the East China Sea and the Philippines and Vietnam
over the Spratly Islands and the Scarborough Shoal in the South
China Sea. In May 2009, China declared to the United Nations,
"China has indisputable sovereignty over the islands in the South
China Sea and the adjacent waters, and enjoys sovereign rights and
jurisdiction over the relevant waters, as well as the seabed and sub-
soil thereof." When a UN tribunal rejected China's claims on these
islands and adjacent waters, China rejected its findings.

China's motives in these territorial disputes were partly
economic—there is undersea oil linked to both the Senkakus and
Spratlys—and partly military. The islands, while largely uninhab-
itable, constitute a ring that could potentially block China's naval
access to the Pacific Ocean. But more broadly, the claims were
intended to reaffirm China's supremacy within the region not only
over the smaller Asian countries, but also over Japan, which China
holds primarily responsible for its century of humiliation. Says historian Wang Gungwu, "If you mention Japan, that is what nationalism is all about. You don't find Chinese who are anti-British, but
they were the people who actually started it."

China's claims have put it in conflict with the United States. The
island disputes threaten two of America's key allies in the region,
Japan and the Philippines, and more broadly American naval hegemony in the Pacific. China's economic strategy also pitted it against
the United States. Its first step was to demand technology transfer
from American and other multinational corporations that wanted
to build plants in China. (What China couldn't acquire through
transfer it sometimes acquired through espionage or cybertheft.)
Then, in 2015, the Chinese party adopted a "Made in China 2025"

278 plan. The plan's ostensible aim is to make China self-sufficient in key high-tech industries, with 70 percent of components eventually being made by China. These include industries such as pharmaceuticals and aerospace that the United States has dominated.

China also used its growing economic clout to create alternatives to the American-dominated World Bank and American- and Japanese-led Asia Development Bank. In 2013, Xi unveiled plans for an Asian Infrastructure Bank that would be linked to China's "Belt and Road" Initiative to fund roads, ports, and bridges from Asia to Central and Eastern Europe. In a speech at the Communist Party Congress in 2017, Xi Jinping described a "Chinese dream" of making China a "global leader in terms of comprehensive national strength and international influence." Translated into the language of international competition, Xi wanted China to rival or displace the United States as the global leader in economics, reclaim military dominance in Asia, and become America's equal or better globally in power and influence.

Xi's reaffirmation of China's imperial aspirations was tied to an explicitly nationalist political appeal. The Chinese continue to embrace Marxism's idea of progress and Marx's skepticism about conventional capitalism, but Xi and the Chinese Communist Party have replaced Marxism-Leninism-Mao Zedong Thought as their popular ideology with a homegrown nationalism that promises the fulfillment of the "Chinese dream," the reincorporation of Taiwan into China, and warns against the threat of "Japanese militarism."

After Deng welcomed Japanese aid and investment in the 1980s, China under Jiang Zemin in the 1990s began to demand that Japan apologize for its brutal wartime occupation. Hostility toward Japan was widespread, but by evoking it, the party also filled a vacuum created by the abandonment of Marxism-Leninism. Ma Licheng, a former editorial writer for the *People's Daily*, and later a prime target of government critics, told Richard McGregor, "Nineteen eighty-nine was the turning point. We were moving into

nationalism. Sino-Japanese relations have nothing to do with Japan.
It is all about internal politics in China."

Japan apologized several times for its "war of aggression," but
the apologies were not accepted. When China continued to demand
apologies, these demands provoked a nationalist backlash in Japan,
which led to visits by Japanese high officials to the Yasukuni Shrine,
where (among others) convicted Japanese war criminals from World
War II had been enshrined. That set off a new series of rhetorical
rebukes and sharp territorial clashes between the countries over the
Senkaku Islands.

The Communist Party and the leading Chinese media reinforced
and strengthened what was already widespread public resentment
of the Japanese: Chinese textbooks stressed the evils of the Japanese; the resistance to Japanese occupation was dramatized on
television and in movies. In 2012, Howard French notes, over 200
anti-Japanese films were produced, and 70 percent of Chinese TV
dramas involved Japan and World War II.

Most recently, the Chinese leadership has put a positive spin on
China's nationalism, emphasizing not only economic achievement
but also leadership abroad. This spin has penetrated popular culture. In the summer of 2017, Chinese studios produced a movie, *Wolf
Warrior II*, that depicted Chinese special forces in Africa defeating
rebels backed by Western mercenaries. The movie set all-time box
office records.

In China today, an ambitious foreign policy, which seeks to fulfill Xi's "Chinese Dream," is linked to explicitly nationalist politics that connects the survival of the regime itself to its success in
attaining its regional and global ambitions. That sets it on a course
that could even lead to war. A direct clash with the United States is,
of course, possible, but what is more likely is that America would be
called upon to defend Japan, the Philippines, or even Taiwan. At the
least, there is the looming danger of a new Cold War, not only with
Russia but with China—one that is increasingly focused on China's

attempt to displace the United States at the apex of world power, putting both countries' deepest nationalist aspirations in conflict.

The Pivot to Asia

Barack Obama recognized the threat that China posed to the American economy and to American hegemony in the Pacific, and sought what he called a "pivot to Asia" in American foreign policy. But Obama's efforts to restrain China and challenge Chinese nationalism largely came to naught. In the end, Obama's pivot amounted, according to China expert James Mann, more to a "formulation than a policy."

Obama's main initiative was the negotiation of the Trans-Pacific Partnership, a trade agreement among 12 Pacific countries, including the U.S., Japan, Australia, Malaysia, and Singapore, but not including China. The TPP established a free trade zone among the signatories, with the usual perks for American multinationals and a tribunal to resolve investor disputes that nullified national sovereignty. But its main purpose was to firm up America's economic dominance in Asia and to isolate China as a rule-breaker. Obama explained candidly in a White House message, "We have to make sure the United States—and not countries like China—is the one writing this century's rules for the world's economy."

But Obama failed to sell the treaty to his own party. Liberal Democrats saw the treaty primarily as another invitation for American corporations to flee American wages and regulation and to avoid domestic accountability. Instead of countering this view by repeatedly stressing the treaty's geopolitical aims, Obama and the treaty's business supporters claimed it would net many thousands of new jobs, a position that TPP's critics, armed with continuing doubts about NAFTA's accomplishments, were easily able to counter. Hillary Clinton, who as secretary of state had championed the treaty, disowned it when she ran for president. Trump campaigned against the treaty, echoing liberal Democratic arguments that it would send American jobs to Southeast Asia; when he took office, one of his

first acts was to withdraw from the agreement. That spelled the end
of Obama's pivot to Asia. And it defined what would be Trump's
approach to foreign policy.

The False Song of Globalism

Trump was not a foreign policy thinker. His views were based
on visceral reactions to current events and on his experience in
business, and they were only slightly above the level of the-man-
in-the-street. But perhaps for that very reason, they diverged
from those of the Washington foreign policy establishment,
which was dominated by cosmopolitan liberals on one side and
neo-conservatives on the other. Trump's key experiences were
America's loss of absolute economic supremacy, evidenced in the
growing trade deficit to Japan and Germany and later China, which
he blamed on American trade deals and wily foreigners; and the
failure in Iraq, which he blamed on neo-conservative efforts at
nation-building. He viewed the Cold War's end not as an opportunity to create a new world order, but as a chance to withdraw from
expensive and increasingly ill-defined alliances and overseas commitments that had drained the American treasury and led to the
neglect of problems at home.

The Cold War view of the world had been a bipolar one of competing ideologies, economies, and militaries. In the wake of the
Cold War's end, Clinton, Bush, and Obama viewed global politics through a Lockean prism. They aspired to a world order dominated by the United States but held together by a social contract
among like-minded nations. Trump's view was more Hobbesian.
He viewed the world as independent-minded nations in conflict, and America's role as advancing its own interests against
those of its rivals. Unlike his predecessors, he clearly recognized
national differences and didn't aspire to transform other countries into American-style market democracies. He had no interest
in invoking human rights violations claims against China, Russia,
Turkey, Egypt, or North Korea. Based on his experience in business,

he admired what he thought of as strong leaders regardless of their commitment to democracy.

In competing within this Hobbesian world, Trump rejected what he called "globalism." Globalists either acted on behalf of the world's citizens rather than on behalf of their own nation, or at a minimum mistakenly believed that in acting for the globe's citizens they were acting for their own nation's. They made trade deals or worked in the United Nations or NATO in this spirit. That allowed other countries, like Mexico, China, or Japan, which were acting solely in their own interests, to take advantage of the United States. In a speech in Washington in April 2016, Trump said:

> No country has ever prospered that failed to put its own interests first. Both our friends and our enemies put their countries above ours and we, while being fair to them, must start doing the same. We will no longer surrender this country or its people to the false song of globalism. The nation-state remains the true foundation for happiness and harmony. I am skeptical of international unions that tie us up and bring America down and will never enter America into any agreement that reduces our ability to control our own affairs.

To put "America first," Trump disdained multilateral treaties and alliances. He disliked the WTO (potentially crippling it by holding up appointments to its appellate body). Instead, he wanted to sign bilateral agreements with countries. On his third day in office, he withdrew from the TPP. In his first meeting with Merkel, he proposed signing a bilateral trade deal with Germany. Merkel had to remind him that, as a member of the EU, Germany could not do so. He insisted on renegotiating NAFTA. He pulled out of the Paris Climate Accord and the six-party Iran nuclear agreement. In his first speech at NATO headquarters in May 2017, he revealed his lack of commitment to the organization by failing to endorse common

defense—a commitment that had been forged during the Cold War   283
when members feared a Soviet invasion of the West.

Trump also made light of the Group of Seven, which had been
created in 1976 in the wake of the Arab oil embargo to bring together
the world's leading economic powers—but which did not currently
include China and India, now the second- and seventh-largest economics, and had expelled Russia in 2014 because it had reclaimed
Crimea. On the eve of a summit in Canada in June 2018, Trump
urged the members to invite the Russians back. He then arrived late
and left early to meet in Singapore with North Korean dictator Kim
Jong Un. Trump's bilateral negotiations with Kim sidestepped the
six-party negotiations with North Korea that had included Japan,
China, South Korea, and Russia.*

Trade Deficits
The hallmark of Trump's foreign policy was his aggressive agenda
on trade, which, like his skepticism about NATO or the G-7, represented an instinctive recognition that American policy had become
obsolete. After World War II, the United States, which accounted
for about half of the world's gross domestic product, had sought
to restore the war-torn economies of Western Europe and Japan in
order to provide markets for its own goods, as well as to ward off the

* The one exception to Trump's dislike of alliances has been in the Middle East,
where Trump linked the United States with Israel, Saudi Arabia, and the United
Arab Emirates in an attempt to cripple the Iranian government. As recounted
by Adam Entous in the *New Yorker* ("The Enemy of My Enemy," June 18, 2018),
Trump had initially during his presidential campaign envisaged himself as an
honest broker and offshore balancer in the Middle East, but he was moved by
his son-in-law, Jared Kushner, and by Sheldon Adelson, the gambling mogul
and Trump's chief political donor, to ally himself with Israeli prime minister
Benjamin Netanyahu, who sought to draw the United States into an alliance
with the Gulf states against Iran. In describing the administration's objectives
in rejecting the Iran nuclear deal, Secretary of State Michael Pompeo suggested
that the administration is looking to undermine the regime itself—an indication
that the Trump administration may have made the same mistake about Iranian
nationalism that George W. Bush made about Iraqi nationalism.

284   rise of communist parties. It sent aid, and it tolerated tariffs and other kinds of trade preferences on the assumption that these countries needed them to rebuild their industries. By the 1970s, however, Western Europe and Japan were competing effectively with the United States.

Over the next decades, the United States pressured its economic competitors to remove trade barriers and to revalue their currencies, but often only after American industries had been decimated, either by foreign imports or by firms moving overseas in search of lower labor costs and less regulation. Some labor-intensive, low-wage apparel industries were hurt, but so, too, were basic industries like steel and aluminum, and newer industries like consumer electronics. During these years, the American economy and America's relationship with its competitors changed in a fundamental way. America began running huge trade and budget deficits that were financed by asset and bond purchases with dollars that competitors like Japan and later China were accumulating from their large trade surpluses with the United States. Metropolitan areas that depended on financial firms and on new digital or biotech industries (where the United States continued to enjoy superiority) prospered, but regions dependent on older heavy industry suffered, as trade deficits in manufactured goods grew.

The global cycle of deficits, surpluses, dollars, yen, and renminbi, first described in Taggart Murphy's *The Weight of the Yen*, created financial instability that led to the Great Recession. The dollars shipped back to the United States from foreign trade surpluses were usually not invested in productive enterprises or in infrastructure, but in stocks, bonds, and real estate. They contributed to the bubbles that precipitated the financial crash that led to the Great Recession.

Trump's trade policies were designed to reduce the trade deficit by imposing or threatening to impose tariffs on countries that, according to the administration, had acquired surpluses through limits on American imports or subsidies on their exports. China was the

chief, but by no means only, target. Trump also attacked German   285
car exports, which benefited from Germany's undervalued currency
(the result of its being averaged in with the weaker Eurozone currencies) and EU tariffs on American car exports. Trump tried to induce
American companies to stay home (or return home) by lowering
corporate tax rates and removing regulations; he tried to protect or
encourage industries like steel and semiconductors that the administration thought were vital to the nation's long-term military and economic security. Trump imposed tariffs on washing machines, solar
panels, steel, and aluminum and strengthened the hand of the Committee on Foreign Investment in the United States (CFIUS), which
blocked the acquisition of Qualcomm, a major American high-tech
firm, by a Singapore company suspected of being linked to China.

There were obvious drawbacks to Trump's trade strategy. It
was partly based on a simpleminded economics spelled out in a
September 2016 campaign document by Peter Navarro, who would
become a White House advisor, and Wilbur Ross, who would become
the secretary of commerce. From the Keynesian formula "Gross
Domestic Product = Consumption + Investment + Government
Spending + Net Exports," Navarro and Ross contended that a deficit
in net exports (exports minus imports) was detracting from growth,
and that by reducing or removing the trade deficit, the U.S. would
increase GDP. But as several economists pointed out, the other
three factors are not independent of net exports. A trade surplus,
for instance, can lead to a dramatic decline in consumption, and an
overall reduction in GDP. There was nothing magic, in other words,
about reducing the trade deficit. Moreover, in the post–Bretton
Woods economy, global trade depends to some extent on the U.S.
running trade deficits, which sustain the dollar as an international
currency, which benefits the United States.

Focusing on the reduction of the trade deficit, as spelled out
by Ross and Navarro, as its "primary" objective led the administration to impose tariffs on countries that are not blocking American
imports, and to get into political squabbles over special exemptions

286   like Canada's tariff on dairy imports—which are the equivalent of American tariffs on sugar imports. But there was another side to Trump's trade strategy that recalled proposals from the 1980s for an American industrial policy that would protect America's presence in key basic and high-tech industries. Steel and aluminum are essential to American domestic and defense manufacturing. Qualcomm is at the forefront of wireless technology and the next generation of 5G wireless transmission. However clumsy and ill-devised, Trump's trade strategy addressed the imbalances that grew up in the world economy after Bretton Woods, particularly in the American economic relationship with Japan and then China, and the uneven development of industry and finance within the United States that has left important industries in peril.

The Next Stage

In his foreign policy, Trump rejected tactics and strategies, institutions and alliances that had grown out of the global excesses and misbegotten optimism of the 1990s and early 2000s. In his own brutal way, Trump asked some of the right questions. Are Americans really committed to going to war over Estonia, as NATO's Article Five would require? Have countries like Germany taken advantage of the United States by failing to meet their defense obligations, allowing them to spend their savings on social needs, while the United States has had to spend its tax dollars on arms and armies? Has the WTO restrained, or acted as a cover for, China's mercantile trade policies? Was America's growing clash with Putin and Russia simply the result of Putin's neo-imperial, authoritarian inclinations, or had American derogation of Russian nationalism played a role? How much had America benefited from its capital being able to go where it wanted and from the massive influx of unskilled workers? Should America revel in its success as a service economy and cede its basic manufacturing capabilities to Asia and Europe?

Trump's own answers to these questions were often partially or even entirely unsatisfactory. He elevated the elimination of the trade deficit to a be-all and end-all. He attempted to keep American companies at home with huge tax breaks to them that they used to buy back their own stock. And the tax breaks retained incentives for companies to produce abroad rather than at home. In shedding American alliances, he may eventually inspire new alliances *against* the United States, even uniting old enemies like China and Japan. In his toxic rhetoric, he reinforced the worst tendencies in European and Asian politics.

The problem can be framed with a concept from Hegel's philosophy of history. Hegel used the term "Aufhebung" to refer to a process of historical transcendence by which a new stage of development is reached. Reaching that stage required negating what was obsolete or counterproductive while preserving what remained useful and constructive in order to create a new synthesis that transcended the old policies or ways of life. As a new stage of history, for instance, capitalism incorporated many institutions from feudalism, including the family and the town, but also negated the relationship between serf and lord and replaced it with a new relationship between wage-laborer and capitalist. It produced a synthesis of old and new.

Trump clearly rejected the excesses of the post–Cold War period, but he also cast aside what was positive and constructive in liberal internationalism—the attempt to create international obstacles to the outbreak of war and economic depression and to curb climate change. His approach negated the present excesses without recognizing what was still useful in the longer history of which they were an episode. The question about Trump is this: Will his successor, Joe Biden, be able to build upon his negation of what is obsolete in our current global arrangements to create a new order that will make depressions and wars unlikely? Or was Trump engaged in an act of destruction that will leave the country and the world in an even more parlous state than it is?

Nationalism, Internationalism, and Globalization

There are, of course, a myriad of meanings for the term "globalization." It was sometimes used to refer to the reach of the worldwide web. In *The Lexus and the Olive Tree*, Thomas Friedman, the tribune of globalization, marveled at the ability of his seventy-nine-year-old mother to play bridge over the internet with three Frenchmen. But as used by Bill Clinton and Tony Blair in their optimistic projections about the world's future, it can be boiled down to the following:

- *Capital mobility*: the ability of businesses and banks to invest in whatever country and currency they want without infringing on capital controls or having to fear nationalization or other kinds of government interference with their profitmaking and supply chains.
- *Free trade*: the elimination of tariffs and other informal barriers to trade, including government industrial and export subsidies, and the prohibitions on dumping excess capacity in other countries.
- *Floating exchange rates:* the elimination of the kind of fixed exchange rates that existed under the Bretton Woods agreement until 1973.

- *Immigration*: the reduction of barriers on immigration, particularly from less- to more-developed capitalist countries.

In its full-blown version—resembling Adam Smith's vision of
a national economy writ large—globalization has never fully been
realized, although the IMF and WTO have certainly tried. Some
Asian countries, led by China, have retained their control over currency transactions and foreign investment and have also heavily
subsidized their own industries to help them gain an advantage
in the world market. In Europe, Germany has enjoyed a currency
advantage in international trade due to its participation in the Eurozone. One result of this kind of partial globalization has been that
Germany, China, and other Asian countries have been able to rack
up large trade surpluses with countries like the United States that
have eliminated capital controls. These surpluses—when combined
with the free movement of capital and currency and widely fluctu-
ating exchange rates—have also contributed to a rash of financial
crises culminating in the Great Recession. (By my count, there were
zero from 1945 to 1973 and 13 from the Latin America Debt crisis of
1982 until the Great Recession.)

Another result of globalization has been a rise in inequality
and uneven economic development in the United States and other
countries that have followed the global deregulatory playbook
described as the "Washington consensus." In a prescient short
book, *Has Globalization Gone Too Far*, Harvard economist Dani
Rodrik warned in 1997 that the ability of corporations to move (or
threaten to move) wherever they wanted would give them inordi-
nate power over their domestic workers, who could not easily pick
up from Detroit and move to El Bajio. Capital mobility would exert
downward pressure on wages and contribute to the destruction
of the labor movement. It would also create a race to the bottom
over corporate tax rates—evidenced recently in the 2017 Republican tax bill—that would undermine the ability of governments to

290   finance generous safety nets for the workers who were displaced by globalization.

In the United States and Western Europe, the threat that capital mobility posed to workers' standards of living was reinforced by the massive influx of unskilled workers whom employers could use to transform mid-wage into low-wage occupations and to cripple the ability of unions to organize. The combination of capital mobility and unskilled immigration also deterred companies from lowering their costs through increasing productivity and is probably a factor in the slowdown in productivity over the last decade. And the combination helped transform politics by curbing the ability of Democrats in the United States and Social Democratic and Labour Parties in Europe to deliver the goods to their working-class voters, while enhancing the appeal of rightwing populist parties, who could combine economic attacks against globalization with cultural and nativist screeds.

Not everyone has suffered from the embrace of globalization. In the United States or the UK, workers and managers in finance and high-technology have benefited. As economist Stephen Rose has documented, the new capitalism has created a large, affluent upper-middle class. But it has also fueled rising discontent among workers and small businesspeople who feel left behind by global capitalism. They have formed the shock troops for the rightwing nationalism that has swept the United States and Europe. They are the products of the failure of globalization as a politics and political economy.

Globalism vs. Internationalism

What is the alternative? For Trump, it was a Hobbesian vision of world politics in which each nation pursues its own special interests in a zero-sum battle for power and prosperity. Trump and the rightwing populists were not entirely wrong about the need to assert national sovereignty. Without national control over multinational corporations and banks, and without control of borders and immigration, it

is very hard to imagine the United States becoming a more egalitarian
society with a generous safety net for those unable to work. In this
respect, the revival of nationalism was essential to moving the United
States and Europe away from the illusions and excesses of globalization. Globalization is incompatible with social democracy in Europe
or with New Deal liberalism in the United States.

But a Hobbesian nationalism has its limits. There are a host of
problems that can best be dealt with through regional or international bodies in which nations work cooperatively. These problems
include reducing carbon emissions to combat global warming, preventing nuclear proliferation, regulating international trade and
finance to guard against ruinous trade wars and contagious financial crises, and as we have learned, monitoring world health to prevent the spread of deadly epidemics. Regional and international
alliances and organizations are also essential to aiding the development of countries in Africa and Latin America, where famine, rampant corruption, gang violence, and tribal wars have created waves of
asylum-seekers in Europe and the United States.

There is a distinction to be made between *globalism*, which sub-
ordinates nations and national governments to market forces or to
the priorities of multinational corporations, and *internationalism*,
in which nations cede part of their sovereignty to international
or regional bodies to address problems they could not adequately
address on their own. The older forms of international organization
that grew out of World War II recognized this. The Bretton Woods
Agreement, which established the IMF, was a pact among nations,
and the nations retained their power to manage their trade and control capital inflows and outflows. The European Community was a
customs union without a common currency. It was not the "United
States of Europe."

Is this kind of internationalism now possible? In the wake of the
Cold War's end and the rise of China, there may be an even greater
need for cooperation than in the past, but it may also become more
difficult than ever to achieve. International cooperation has worked

292   best when it has been championed and overseen by a single great power that boasted superior economic and military might. In the nineteenth century, British naval and financial supremacy helped prevent the outbreak of major wars and crippling depressions. The subsequent outbreak of two world wars was partly the result of the breakdown in older alliances and in international finance caused by the rise of the United States and Germany as competitors to Great Britain. Economist Charles Kindleberger, who helped design the Marshall Plan after World War II, argued that global economic stability depended on a single hegemonic power.

The post–World War II international alliances and organizations were anchored by American economic superiority and military force. The Bretton Woods Agreement depended upon the dollar maintaining a fixed rate, to which other currencies could adjust. American economic aid provided Europe and Japan with dollars to reconstruct and to buy American goods. The American military didn't enjoy complete superiority, but the existence of NATO and the Warsaw Pact, and the threat of a nuclear holocaust, created a stalemate between the two great military powers that led to proxy wars but not to another world war.

The American military is still superior and the dollar remains the international currency, but under increasingly parlous circumstances. The growing proliferation of weapons and sharp regional rivalries in the Middle East, South Asia, and the Chinese and Russian periphery makes smaller conflicts possible; these could include lesser nuclear powers like Pakistan, Israel, or North Korea. The UN seems to be even more hampered by rivalry than in the past. The Great Recession stemmed in part from the growing economic imbalance between China and the United States, and in Europe between the countries in the North and South. These imbalances could result in new financial and political crises and make any kind of international economic cooperation difficult.

There are solutions on paper to these problems. To rebalance the global economy, Michael Pettis and other economists have urged the revival of Keynes's proposal during the negotiations at Bretton Woods in 1944 and 1945 to create an international currency union that would penalize countries running large trade deficits or surpluses. But Keynes's plan was rejected in favor of an American dollar–based plan, which worked as long as the American dollar could maintain a fixed exchange rate with gold. In the EU, Greek economist and former minister of finance Yanis Varoufakis has founded a group that advocates the political and economic unification of Europe. But these economic proposals depend for their enactment on the degree of cooperation they are supposed to create. They could come to the fore during a severe crisis, as the older proposals did in the wake of two world wars and the Great Depression, but who would wish a recurrence of these kinds of crises upon the world today?

The historic evolution of the nation took humankind many thousands of years. Human beings went from cooperative foragers to kinship groups to clans and tribes to nations. This evolution was initially dictated by a brute struggle for survival. People today may not face the threat of extinction, except from nuclear war, but they face severe challenges that will call for a learning process, compressed from thousands of years into decades, that will lead the world's nations, and the great powers in particular, to learn to live together peacefully and cooperate to meet natural, environmental, and economic challenges. Such an evolution would have to defy in some respects the logic of nationalism that leads to contests for national supremacy. In the wake of globalization's failure, can a new international order be created that acknowledges and doesn't sidestep or discount historic nationalist sentiments? That is the challenge that will determine the future over the remainder of this century.

The Socialist
Awakening

Part Three

Socialism
Old and New

The philosopher Fredric Jameson once wrote, "It is easier to imagine the end of the world than to imagine the end of capitalism." Jameson, hardly known as a staunch defender of capitalism (he's perhaps the world's foremost Marxist literary critic), didn't write this generations ago, but in 2003. In March 2020, as the novel coronavirus outbreak was putting millions of Americans under stay-at-home orders, and as Congress and the Federal Reserve had begun pouring trillions of dollars into the economy to soften the blow of a coming recession, Vox editor Dylan Matthews quipped: "The end of the world is making it easier to imagine the end of capitalism."

The coronavirus pandemic came barely five years after the United States and Western Europe were finally recovering from the Great Recession of 2008. It has not, and will not, spell the end of the world or of capitalism, but it has put the final nail in the coffin of the laissez-faire, globalized capitalism that prevailed since the days of Margaret Thatcher and Ronald Reagan and that was perpetuated, wittingly or not, by their successors. The era of big government, which Bill Clinton claimed was over under his watch, is back with a vengeance; and so is the attention of politicians, if only for the time being, to the welfare of the many, not just the few.

298   The politics and political economy in the United States and Europe (not to mention elsewhere) are entering a new era, just as it happened in the early 1930s, after World War II, and then again in the early 1980s. In the early 1930s, faced with the breakdown of the gold-based international monetary system and of untamed capitalism at home, the countries of the West went in very different directions. The United States went toward Franklin Roosevelt's New Deal; Central and Southern Europe went toward Nazism and fascism. Both alternatives, as socialist theorist Karl Polanyi described them in *The Great Transformation,* were attempts to use the power of government to protect the populace against the vicissitudes of the market.

The failure of market capitalism has been heightened by the threat posed by the novel coronavirus. All the weaknesses of the previous era—from the over-reliance on global supply chains to underfunded social services; from tax avoidance by the wealthy and large corporations to the immiseration of what are known as "essential workers"—have been laid bare. And after the threat of the virus recedes, the countries of the world will still face steep unemployment and a daunting task of economic reconstruction, along with the growing threat of climate change, that will require major public initiatives. These failures and weaknesses can be, as they were in the United States in the 1930s, the basis for a traditional leftwing alliance of the bottom and the middle of society against the very top. Or they can feed rightwing attempts to divide the middle and bottom through scapegoating.

Even before the current pandemic and recession, the breakdown in the older economic consensus had resulted in new and sometimes unforeseen political eruptions. Many of these occurred on the right, through the rise of a toxic "us vs. them" nationalist politics in the United States and Europe, and the move toward authoritarianism in Eastern Europe, Turkey, and India and toward a new cyber-totalitarianism in China. There have also, however, been

unexpected flare-ups on the political left and center-left. These
include a leftwing populism in Southern Europe, the rise of the
Greens on the European continent, the attempt by Britain's Labour
Party to revive its commitment to socialism, and the awakening in
the United States, the bastion of Cold War anti-communism, of a
new socialist politics.

The principal subject of Part Three is the rise of a socialist politics in the United States and the failed attempt to elect a socialist in
Great Britain. Like Part One and Part Two on populism and nationalism, I will try to describe and explain these political phenomena.
But as a longtime leftist who labored unsuccessfully decades ago
trying to create a socialist movement in the United States, and
whose hopes for a socialist politics have been rekindled by the
Bernie Sanders campaigns, I have definite views on what socialists
should and should not do to build a viable movement.

In the United States, the revival of interest in socialism has
been due to Sanders, who, when he began running for president
in 2015, was little known except in Vermont and on the left, and
was disdained by some of his colleagues in Congress. Running as
a "democratic socialist," he almost won the Democratic nomination against prohibitive favorite Hillary Clinton. Four years later,
Sanders again came in second, consistently winning the greatest
share of voters under age 45—voters who hadn't grown up in the
shadow of the Cold War and with the identification of socialism
with Soviet communism. In an October 2019 YouGov poll, 70 percent of millennials (ages 23–38) said they were "extremely" or
"somewhat likely" to vote for a socialist.

Sanders's failure to win the nomination was predictable, as there
are still too many older Americans who associate socialism with the
Soviet Union. But Sanders's campaigns had a dramatic influence on
the Democratic Party's agenda. A host of Democrats embraced his
plan for a single-payer healthcare system and his proposal to raise
the minimum wage to $15 an hour. Senate Minority Leader Chuck

300   Schumer, not known as a democratic socialist, embraced Sanders's plan to put workers on corporate boards. And Joe Biden, who bested Sanders for the nomination, gave key Sanders supporters prominent places on his policy task forces and crafted a campaign platform that reflected Sanders's influence.

The Democratic Socialists of America (DSA) has grown rapidly. In 2015, DSA had 6,000 members. A year after Sanders's campaign, DSA's membership had quintupled. After DSA member Alexandria Ocasio-Cortez's election to Congress in 2018, it rose to 56,000, making it the largest democratic socialist organization since the pre–World War I Socialist Party. In the wake of the pandemic and recession, it has grown to 70,000. DSA also boasts over a hundred officeholders, including four members of Congress. If the United States had a multi-party system with proportional voting, a democratic socialist party might in the next decade command a very respectable 15 to 20 percent of the vote.

The young people who have taken a positive view of socialism don't necessarily have a worked-out theory of socialism or socialist politics. In the United States, they often identify socialism with Scandinavian countries, and with public control of healthcare, education, and energy. They condemn the growing inequality of wealth and power and want a society based on cooperation rather than on cutthroat competition and on sexual and racial equality. They don't envisage the government owning Apple or Microsoft. Sanders's own explanation of democratic socialism runs along these same lines.

Some commentators have insisted that neither Sanders nor his young supporters are really socialists. To be a socialist, columnist Eric Levitz wrote in *New York*, is to advocate "the abolition of profit or worker ownership of the means of production." Paul Krugman defined socialists as people who want to "nationalize our major industries and replace markets with central planning." But that is not what the rising popular sympathy for democratic socialism

is about. Socialism is coming back in a form that is different not
only from the Soviet Union's or Cuba's communism, but from what
socialists who consider themselves to be "Marxists" have envisaged.
And it could play an important role in shaping voters' reaction to
what has been the greatest threat to Americans' well-being since the
Great Depression and World War II.

The Varieties of Socialist Experience

Just as there is no exclusive definition of populism, liberalism, or
conservatism, there is no singular definition of socialism. According
to Marxist theorist Raymond Williams's *Keywords: A Vocabulary of
Culture and Society,* the term "socialism" first appeared in English
in the 1820s and its French counterpart, "socialisme," in the 1830s.
Some thinkers were described as "socialists" who merely concerned
themselves with social matters, similar to what a sociologist would
do today. But in its critical use, it referred to thinkers who rejected
the competitive individualism of industrial capitalism. Socialism
was paired against individualism; cooperation against competition;
altruism against selfishness. It was initially inspired by the spirit
of the American Revolution ("all men are created equal") and the
French Revolution ("Liberty, equality, fraternity") and by the ethics
of the Sermon on the Mount. Over the subsequent centuries, it has
taken at least five different forms, only one of which comes directly
out of the work of Karl Marx.

Utopian Socialism: In the first half of the nineteenth century, Charles
Fourier, Robert Owen, Pierre Joseph-Proudhon, and Henri de
Saint-Simon were all described as socialists primarily on the basis
of their rejection of competitive individualism. In his *New Christianity,* Saint-Simon advocated a spirit of association and obligation toward the poor. Owen, a Welsh textile manufacturer, sought
to replace the prevailing factory system with a communal system,
which he called "villages of cooperation," where workers would live

302   and be fed and have their children educated. Fourier advocated communes called "phalansteries." Proudhon backed workers' cooperatives and a philosophy he called "mutualism." Fourier, Owen, and
Saint-Simon hoped to spread socialism by example. Industrialists
and workers would see that cooperative production was not only
morally superior, but more efficient.

Christian or Ethical Socialism: The Utopian Socialists like Saint-
Simon were influenced by Christian ideals, but there were a host
of Christian socialists in the mid-nineteenth century who traced
their views directly to the gospel. They included Philippe Buchez,
who was a member of the Saint-Simon Society, and Anglo-Indian
lawyer John Malcolm Ludlow, who founded a Christian Socialist
movement in England in the late 1840s that advocated giving "the
kingdom of Christ . . . the true authority over the realms of industry
and trade" and "for socialism its true character as the great Christian revolution." In the United States, Walter Rauschenbusch and
a young Reinhold Niebuhr played prominent roles in promoting
Christian socialism. Like Marxist socialism, it had an apocalyptic,
millennial element, expressed in the idea of creating the Kingdom
of God on Earth.

Orthodox Marxism: From the 1890s, when Marx's and Engels's theories became the official doctrine of Europe's leading socialist party,
the German Social Democratic Party (SPD), Marxism became the
touchstone for many socialists in the West. If you were a serious
and not merely a nominal socialist, you were a Marxist. Marx's and
Engels's own theories changed over their lifetimes, but there was a
core orthodox doctrine that became the starting point for many discussions of socialism. It was most clearly articulated by SPD leader
Karl Kautsky in *The Class Struggle*.

    According to orthodox Marxism, history was divided into dis-
tinct stages defined by relations of production (classes) and forces of

production (technology) and punctuated by revolutionary upheavals. Capitalism had succeeded feudalism, and socialism would succeed capitalism. It would be characterized by social ownership and control of the means of production; the disappearance of a capitalist class, markets, and money; and social and economic equality.

The revolution would be led by a homogeneous blue-collar working class, which as a result of industrialization, would encompass the majority of workers and would be conscious of itself as an oppressed class. Organized into unions and parties, it would respond to growing economic crises and to its own immiseration by overthrowing capitalism and establishing socialism. The revolution would be international ("Workers of the world, unite!") and would eventually result in the dissolution of national borders.

Marx and Engels drew a distinction between "utopian" and "scientific" socialism. "Utopian" socialism was based on wishful thinking and the power of example. By contrast, "scientific" socialism was rooted in inexorable historical trends that would make the fall of capitalism inevitable. But Marx's and Engels's scenario for the transition from capitalism to socialism never came to pass. Capitalism has not succumbed to collapse and socialist revolution. There is much to learn from their analysis of capitalism and of the transition from feudalism to capitalism, but Marx and Engels's view of socialism and of socialist politics proved to be as "utopian" as Owen's, Fourier's, and Saint-Simon's.

In retrospect, it appears that Marxist socialism was heavily influenced by Judeo-Christian eschatology. In *Meaning in History*, German philosopher Karl Lowith contended that in *The Communist Manifesto*, Marx was unconsciously mimicking the Judeo-Christian portrayal of the end times—Armageddon leading to the Millennium—in his account of a revolutionary class struggle that would culminate in pure communism and the withering away of the state. Marx and Engels were, of course, atheists, but that doesn't preclude their having unconsciously framed their theory

304   of history and politics in biblical terms.* Indeed, many socialist or communist organizations have unconsciously mimicked the behavior of Protestant sects.

Marxism-Leninism: Soviet dictator Josef Stalin promoted a distinct doctrine he called "Marxism-Leninism" after he seized power in 1928. Stalin foresaw a prolonged period of transition between capitalism and socialism characterized by "the dictatorship of the proletariat." Marx had used the term ironically—his model was the democratically elected Paris Commune of 1871—but Stalin used it to justify the dictatorial control of the state by the Communist Party, which could use its control in order to extirpate the enemies of socialism. Marxism-Leninism also came to be associated with Lenin's idea of the party as a disciplined elite (the "cadre") that knew the interests of the working class better than the working class itself did.

Against the orthodox Marxist view that socialism could only develop in advanced economies, or in tandem with other advanced economies, Stalin argued that socialism and the transition to communism could occur within an individual, less developed nation. China's and Vietnam's parties continue to use Marxism-Leninism to justify their dominance. And versions of Marxism-Leninism have popped up to justify regimes in Cuba and Venezuela.

During the sixties, some new left groups adopted independent versions of Marxist-Leninism that incorporated what they believed

* Lowith writes: "It is therefore not by chance that the 'last' antagonism between the two hostile camps of bourgeoisie and proletariat corresponds to the Jewish-Christian belief in a final fight between Christ and Antichrist in the last epoch of history, that the task of the proletariat corresponds to the world-historical mission of the chosen people, that the redemptive and universal function of the most degraded class is conceived on the religious pattern of Cross and Resurrection, that the ultimate transformation of the realm of necessity into a realm of freedom corresponds to the transformation of the civitas Terrena [city of man] into civitas Dei [city of God], and that the whole process of history as outlined in the Communist Manifesto corresponds to the general scheme of the Jewish-Christian interpretation of history as a providential advance toward a final goal which is meaningful."

to be Mao Zedong Thought. In the United States, the Black Panther Party anointed Stalin's *Foundations of Leninism* as its guide to
revolutionary organization. These groups quickly disappeared, the
product of FBI repression, the end of the Vietnam War, and their
own ideological folly. European and American Communist parties
that described their doctrine as "Marxist-Leninist" dissolved after
the collapse of the Soviet Union in 1991.

Social Democracy: In 1896, Eduard Bernstein, a top leader of the
SPD, took issue with his party's commitment to orthodox Marxism,
rejecting the Marxist insistence that a revolutionary rupture, led
by an immiserated blue-collar majority, would create socialism.
Instead, Bernstein argued that the white-collar and small-propertied
middle classes would continue to grow along with the working class,
and that both classes would thrive rather than suffer under a capitalist system that had learned to avoid crises. Socialism would
eventually arrive through the ballot and legislature—through an
accretion of reforms and through the gradual acceptance by capitalists themselves of socialist ethical ideals. Bernstein continued to
embrace Marx's goal of socialism, but he declared, "This goal, whatever it may be, is nothing to me, the movement is everything."

Bernstein's great contribution was to attempt to ground socialist
politics in the realities of capitalism—to recognize that the development of capitalism was not leading inexorably to a class struggle
between a blue-collar proletariat and a white-collar bourgeoisie
that would usher in an entirely new society and economy. But Bernstein was also wrong about capitalism having surmounted crises
and about capitalists' eventual acceptance of socialism.

During his lifetime, Bernstein's comrades denounced him as a
revisionist. But after World War II, the general thrust of his politics—
with an addition of the economics of John Maynard Keynes—became
the prevailing outlook of socialist parties, including the SPD. Even
when party leaders have abjured any allegiance to socialism, the parties have remained nominally committed to democratic socialism,

306 and factions within the parties have kept the flame alive. In Great Britain, for instance, Tony Blair's revision to the pro-socialist Clause IV of the Labour Party's constitution began nevertheless with the words, "The Labour Party is a democratic socialist party." But Bernstein's assignment of socialism to a distant, imperceptible future led some of these parties to accept the logic of market capitalism and to acquiesce in policies that eliminated significant differences between them and the parties of the center-right.

Post-Marxist Socialism

The leading socialist politicians in the United States and the UK and the great majority of people who voted for them do not endorse orthodox Marxism. And there is a group of socialist theorists— many of them former orthodox Marxists—who have tried to spell out the underlying assumptions of a new socialism and socialist politics. They include economist Thomas Piketty, philosophers Nancy Fraser and Axel Honneth, the late historian Martin J. Sklar, the late sociologist Erik Wright, historian James Livingston, political scientists Albena Azmanova, John D. Stephens, and Sheri Berman, and sociologists Lane Kenworthy, Fred Block, Margaret Somers, and Stephanie Mudge. One can find sharp disagreements among them, even about the use of the word "socialism," but on the basis of their work, one can see the beginnings of a new post-Marxist, post– Cold War, post-industrial socialist politics that comports with, and draws out the assumptions of, what today's socialist politicians and their voters are saying and thinking. These are its key features:

Socialism within Capitalism: The new socialists reject Marx's theory of punctuated stages of history as well as the social-democratic view of socialism as the end point on an infinite line. Instead, they see socialism as developing *within* capitalism, the way capitalism developed within feudalism. Socialism creates institutions and laws that fulfill the ethical ideals of liberty, equality, justice, democracy, and social solidarity.

Socialist economic institutions and programs can be developed   307
within capitalism that shift economic and social power from capital
("the rich and powerful") toward labor ("working people"). Examples can include a stiff wealth tax that can be used to fund public
programs or redistribute capital, "co-determination" laws that grant
workers' representatives equal power on corporate boards, the creation of regulatory agencies to police corporate behavior, and public
ownership and control of essential services or industries (such as
healthcare, education, transportation, and energy production). In
Capital and Ideology, Piketty describes a "participatory socialism"
in which workers would serve on corporate boards and in which "a
progressive tax on private wealth" would "diffuse wealth at the base
while limiting concentration at the summit," such that the capitalist
class would cease to be an inheritable caste.

In an essay, "The Capitalism-Socialism Mix," Martin J. Sklar
contended that the competitive capitalism of Marx's day had been
transformed into "a mix of public and private sectors as seats of
authority and initiative in shaping, planning, regulating, and con-
taining development, or, to put it in baldly ideological terms, the
mix of socialism and capitalism." Sklar described twentieth-century
American history as a symbiosis, and clash, between socialist and
capitalist relations of production. In *The Idea of Socialism,* German
philosopher Axel Honneth described "the social legislation of the
early twentieth century (e.g., the law of co-determination in West
Germany, minimum wages in various countries, etc.) not merely
as contingent measures, but as the first steps of progress along the
long and difficult path to the socialization of the labor market." Erik
Wright wrote of socialist reforms and institutions, including cooperatives, worker-owned business, and nonprofit businesses developing within the niches of capitalism and progressively expanding
their reach:

Alternative, noncapitalist economic activities, embodying democratic and egalitarian relations, emerge in the niches where possible

within an economy dominated by capitalism.... Struggles involving the state take place, sometimes to protect these spaces, other times to facilitate new possibilities. ... Eventually, the cumulative effect of this interplay between changes from above and initiatives from below may reach a point where the socialist relations created within the economic ecosystem become sufficiently prominent in the lives of individuals and communities that capitalism can no longer be said to be dominant.

In other words, the mix of capitalism and socialism would change in favor of socialism. Sociologist Fred Block, citing Polanyi's view of socialism as "the subordination of markets to democratic politics," contends that "there is no single moment of transition from a profit-oriented economy to a socialist economy; it is rather an evolutionary process through which there is an ever greater and deeper extension of democracy into economic decisionmaking."

Socialism as a Just System: Marx and many orthodox Marxists and Marxist-Leninists have tended to play down the ethical appeal of socialism. While Marx thundered against capitalist injustice in his political writings, he didn't believe moral considerations, but only economic exploitation, would drive the transition to socialism. The German philosopher Karl Volander recalled in 1904, "The moment anyone started to talk to Marx about morality, he would roar with laughter." But the new socialists, echoing the concerns of Christian and ethical socialists, place a high importance on the ideals of justice as integral to socialism.

The philosopher G.A. Cohen, whose initial work parroted orthodox Marxism, argued for the ethical appeal of community and equality in his last book, *Why Not Socialism?* Cohen describes a camping trip, where, typically, everyone is expected to do their share of the work, and where the goods are held in common and shared. "It is commonly true on camping trips," he writes, "that people cooperate within a common concern that, so far as is possible, everybody

has a roughly similar opportunity to flourish." Cohen envisaged
socialism as the attempt to extend the camping trip's "socialist way
with collective property and mutual giving" to parts of capitalism,
such as healthcare.

The new socialists also don't limit their effort to obtain justice
to the workplace. In the wake of the feminist and civil rights movements, they want, in Nancy Fraser's words, to "overcome domination across the board, in society as well as the economy." They don't
believe that ending economic exploitation will have a cascading
effect on all other forms of domination, but believe that socialist
reforms and institutions have to be measured by a broader yardstick
that includes racial and sexual equality.

The Primacy of Politics: The new socialists reject Marx's historical determinism—his view that growing crises would lead inexorably to socialism—as well as Bernstein's optimistic view that
growing prosperity would convince citizens from all classes of the
desirability of the socialist ideal. Many of them, including Piketty,
Berman, Fraser, Block, and Somers, were heavily influenced by
Polanyi's masterwork, *The Great Transformation*, which appeared in
1944. Polanyi described a "double movement" at the center of capitalism—an oscillating struggle that has pitted a dystopian ideal of
laissez-faire capitalism—in which workers, deprived of social protection, are at the mercy of the private labor market—against the
attempt by the working and allied classes to erect fortifications
against their isolation and exploitation.

New socialists see continual clashes between those who favor
one or the other side of Polanyi's double movement. In American
and European history, capitalism has gone through different eras
that have been defined by which of these forces reigned supreme.
In the United States, for instance, the period from 1932 to 1972 saw
the erection of extensive social protections against corporate capitalism and, after World War II, internationally against the rigidity
of the gold standard. In 1980, after a decade of turbulence caused

310   by economic downturns, an energy crisis, and rising international competition, the U.S. and Great Britain both entered a period where what Block and Somers call "market fundamentalism" held sway domestically and internationally.

During this recent period, socialist institutions within capitalism were dismantled or gutted. In the United States, for instance, government agencies meant to encourage unionization, regulate finance, and protect consumers and the environment were captured by those businesses they were mandated to regulate. In the wake of the Great Recession and the recession caused by the global coronavirus pandemic, the U.S. and Europe appear to be entering a new period in which it is likely that forces favoring social protection will hold sway. But it's not clear what political form that protection will take. It is by no means certain that it will be socialist.

In the 1930s, as Polanyi noted in *The Great Transformation*, both Roosevelt's New Deal (which he saw as a kind of proto-socialism) and Hitler's Nazism were reactions to economic collapse. Both offered extensive social protections. But in Hitler's case, he did so by eliminating democracy and scapegoating and murdering Jews and others deemed undesirable. Similarly, today, the breakdown of the economy during the Great Recession and the coronavirus pandemic could lead to authoritarian and even neo-fascist governments as well as democratic socialist ones. As Sheri Berman argues in *The Primacy of Politics,* what happens will depend on politics, not on inexorable historical laws.

Explicit and Implicit Socialism: To understand that socialism can develop within capitalism is to concede that socialist reforms and institutions have not necessarily been and will not necessarily be introduced in the name of socialism. Some notable institutions, such as Britain's National Health Service or Germany's co-determination law, were spurred by socialist parties. So was Francois Mitterrand's ill-fated enactment of the Common Program in 1981 or the Swedish Social Democrats' Meidner Plan, which

would have given stock in corporations to workers. But in the United
States, the New Deal and the reforms enacted during the Johnson administration, which shifted the balance of power from capital to labor, were not seen as "socialist"—except, perhaps, by conservative opponents.

There are two kinds of circumstances where this can take place. The first is when the word "socialism" has become so stigmatized that proponents of a reform hesitate to use it. That has certainly been the case in the United States during the Cold War era and remains so for many Americans born before 1980. In the 2020 Democratic primaries, Massachusetts senator Elizabeth Warren championed institutional reforms that were identical to those proposed by Sanders—for instance, putting workers on corporate boards and giving them stock. But she insisted she was a "capitalist to the bone."

The second, and more peculiar, circumstance is when a socialist reform is championed by politicians and parties that in other respects are overtly hostile to socialism and friendly to free-market capitalism. Many of America's most powerful regulatory agencies, including the Environmental Protection Agency and the Occupational Safety and Health Administration, were signed into law during the first term of the Republican Nixon administration. These reforms came from pressure from below, but they were supported by the administration. Currently in Europe, the Greens, which have often been friendly to free-market capitalism, have begun to support programs that would enhance public control of energy production.

In his last book, *How to Be an Anti-Capitalist in the 21st Century*, posthumously published in 2019, Erik Olin Wright warned that "perhaps the word 'socialism' itself should be dropped. Words accumulate meaning through historical contexts, and maybe socialism has been so compromised by its association with twentieth-century repressive regimes that it can no longer serve well as the umbrella term for emancipatory alternatives to capitalism." But he added that "in the first decade of the twenty-first century, the idea of socialism has regained some of its positive moral standing."

312

Populist Politics: The new socialists also reject the political scenario advanced by orthodox Marxists. They do not regard the industrial working class as the vanguard of a socialist revolution. In the 1985 book *Hegemony and Socialist Strategy*, which became the ur-text of post-Marxism, political theorists Ernesto Laclau and Chantal Mouffe wrote:

> What is now in crisis is a whole conception of socialism which rests upon the ontological centrality of the working class, upon the role of Revolution with a capital "r," as the founding moment in the transition of one type of society to another, and upon the illusory prospect of a perfectly unitary and homogeneous collective will that will render pointless the moment of politics.

Bernstein foresaw that the industrial working class would stop growing as a percentage of the labor force. But he mistakenly believed that it would be crowded out by the growth of a property-owning middle class. Instead, what has evolved is a waged and salaried labor force that is diverse (white and blue collar) and highly stratified in income, status, and authority, as well as often divided politically by race, nationality, and culture. It ranges from day-laborers to unionized college professors. It does not own the means of production, but it does not inherently see itself as a single exploited class, either. Indeed, segments of it are often at odds politically. If it is to be united, it will have to be through the medium of politics and not simply through metronomic appeals to "the working class."

In their book, Laclau and Mouffe recommend Italian revolutionary Antonio Gramsci's idea of a "historic bloc," but while that term has some explanatory power, it is unwieldy as a public rallying cry. ("Members of the historic bloc, unite!") Laclau and Mouffe would later embrace the populist use of the term "people," and in the last decades, socialists in the United States, Britain, Spain, Greece, and France have framed their appeals through political logic

of populism, pitting "the people," "the working people," or "working 313
families" against an "establishment" or "elite." Sanders sometimes will talk of the working class, but when he does, he invariably
includes people like teachers and nurses who would not have qualified under orthodox Marxist criteria.

The Socialist Appeal
Most of the new socialists were writing in the 1990s and early
2000s, when market fundamentalism still prevailed in the U.S.
and Europe. They were more advocating rather than describing a
socialist politics. The economies of the United States and Europe
were in decent shape, so their appeal was almost entirely moral. In
1994, the British philosopher G. A. Cohen, acknowledging that a
homogeneous working class could no longer be counted on to lead
the revolution, appealed to socialist values as the means to unite a
majority. "The moral force of those values never depended on the
social force supporting them that is now disappearing," he wrote. In
his last book, *Justice as Fairness: A Restatement,* published in 2001,
the moral philosopher John Rawls embraced a version of democratic
socialism as best satisfying his criteria for a just society.

A moral appeal, based on the Sermon on the Mount and the
egalitarian ideals of the American and French revolutions, was central to the rise of socialism. It was compromised by revolutions in
the Soviet Union, China, and the "Third World" that in the name of
socialism rejected liberty and democracy, but has revived since the
collapse of the Soviet Union. It informs socialists' rejection of economic inequality and of racial, sexual, and ethnic discrimination.
During the last decade, these appeals have been highlighted by the
anger at the power of a "billionaire class," of which Trump is a glaring
example, and by the protests against police brutality toward African
Americans, which have spread well beyond the black community.

But the Great Recession and the looming danger of climate
change, followed by the pandemic recession, have provided a set of
material grievances about capitalism and an interest in socialism.

314   Like the Great Depression of the 1930s, the pandemic recession
        could potentially unite the middle and bottom of society against the
        heights of power and wealth in a quest for economic security and
        justice. The principal obstacle, as in the past, will be a politics that
        uses sociocultural appeals to break up the left's historic constitu-
        ency. This tactic is traditionally employed by the political right, but
        it can also be introduced unwittingly by liberals and the left when
        they subordinate potentially unifying economic concerns to radical
        strictures over race, nationality, and gender that go beyond demo-
        cratic rights.

        The key figure in matching the ideals of socialism with the
        material grievances of the present has been Sanders. He more than
        anyone gave voice and prominence to democratic socialism. His
        own political career is testimony to the transition from orthodox
        Marxism to a new political philosophy that sees socialism devel-
        oping within capitalism and that adopts the political logic of pop-
        ulism rather than of traditional Marxist socialism. Inevitably, even
        Sanders will fade from the scene (his counterpart in Britain, Jeremy
        Corbyn, already has), but they helped inspire young people in the
        United States and Great Britain to embrace a new socialist politics.

        Whether a socialist politics becomes a significant alternative to
        an accommodating liberalism or conservatism depends on whether
        new generations of politicians and political organizations can mar-
        shal the growing dissatisfaction with capitalism into a viable pol-
        itics. That in turn depends on at least two things. First, they must
        avoid eschatological fantasies in favor of a vision of socialism
        that appears to be viable and feasible. Second, they should seek a
        common ground in economic grievance and democratic aspiration
        and avoid potentially divisive extreme sociocultural appeals that go
        beyond the ideas that informed socialism. These would include, for
        instance, contemporary opposition not simply to discrimination
        based on adopted genders, but any distinctions based upon gender,
        or support not simply for comprehensive immigration reform, but
        for no limits at all on immigration.

That socialists can avoid these pitfalls is by no means certain. In the UK, Corbyn and the young socialists in Momentum succeeded to some extent in formulating a viable socialism, but failed to unite Labour's traditional downscale constituencies with its growing support among young people in London and in university towns. In the United States, which lacks the equivalent of an even nominally socialist or social-democratic party, socialist politics is at a more rudimentary level, but the anti-capitalist sentiment and public sympathy for socialism is growing from one generation to the next. The question is whether this sentiment can become the basis for a formidable political movement. Besides Sanders and Ocasio-Cortez, there are no national politicians right now that can shape a post-Marxist socialist politics. DSA, while growing, is still a relatively small group that lacks a national presence. While the organization as a whole reflects the influence of Sanders's politics, the group's activist core also contains zealous orthodox Marxists and adherents of identity politics that could condemn it to irrelevance. Like Momentum, its politics often reflects the parochial sociocultural preoccupations of the big post-industrial cities and university towns.

More promising, perhaps, is the development of politicians and political organizations that, while not explicitly socialist, have adopted programs and policies that would achieve some measure of socialism within capitalism. That was certainly the case with Warren in the Democratic presidential race, and there are scores now of senators and House members who share her and Sanders's views on the need to change the balance of power and wealth in America. There are also many leftwing organizations that have adopted at least part of a socialist agenda, but they, too, shy away from the language of socialism. In a decade, these politicians and organizations and their successors may come to believe that an appeal to democratic socialism best captures the need to dramatically reform capitalism. Or, perhaps, socialism will appear, as Erik Wright suggests, under an assumed name.

American Socialism from Debs to Sanders

The two great figures in the history of American socialism are Eugene V. Debs and Bernie Sanders. Debs led the American Socialist Party during the early part of the twentieth century when it had some influence—enough certainly to strike fear in the hearts of American business leaders who were deathly afraid of what was called "class politics." Sanders has been responsible more than anyone for bringing a discussion of democratic socialism back into American politics.

Sanders traces his politics back to Debs. In 1979, he wrote and acted in a half-hour documentary celebrating Debs as "the greatest leader in the history of the American working class." With his thick Brooklyn accent, Sanders, who could not afford to hire a professional actor, recited Debs's injunction to "vote for the Socialist Party because it is the only party unequivocally committed to the abolition of the wage system." Sanders has a plaque of Debs in his Senate office and continues to carry Debs's key chain in his pocket as a political talisman.

Journalists and historians today also draw the connection between the two men. In *USA Today*, Jonathan Turley described Sanders as Debs's "obvious political successor." In the *New Yorker*, historian Jill Lepore describes Sanders carrying Debs's socialism "into the twenty-first century." And there certainly are respects in which Sanders has patterned himself after Debs. Like Debs, Sanders has refused to embrace what Debs called the "Democratic or Republican machine of capitalism." And like Debs, Sanders has thundered against what Debs called the "privileged class." But in understanding today's politics, the differences between the two men are more important than the similarities.

If you look at Debs's career, and the evolution of his political beliefs, he went from heading a business-friendly craft union to being an exponent of orthodox Marxist socialism, with some American variations. Sanders, on the other hand, went from being an orthodox Marxist to a congressman, senator, and presidential candidate who espouses something like the new socialism of Wright, Block, or Piketty. The two men's political journeys almost go in reverse.

From Owen to Debs

The first wave of socialist advocacy in the United States came during the first half of the nineteenth century and was inspired by the beginning of a factory system, which threatened the Jeffersonian promise of a classless democracy. There were hundreds of utopian communities established, including Robert Owen's New Harmony in Indiana and the Transcendentalists' Brook Farm outside of Boston. Most of these failed to survive the Civil War. Owen's attempt in 1825 to create a "community of equality" lasted only two years. The second wave came with the rapid industrialization that took place in the last three decades of the nineteenth century, which was accompanied by financial panics, economic downturns, the rise of the Populists, and the growth of a labor movement.

Like the utopians, the socialists of the late nineteenth century were intellectuals who condemned industrialization as a violation of America's founding principles and Christian ethics. George Herron, a Congregationalist minister, castigated capitalist competition as "the mark of Cain." "The day is coming," said Herron, "in

318   which a truly Christian social order would exist on earth, the fulfillment in the here and now of God's Kingdom of Heaven." In 1888,
Edward Bellamy, the son of a minister, published *Looking Backward*,
which became an international bestseller. It foresaw an America of
2000 in which industry was nationalized, incomes were equal, and
workers retired at age 45. Bellamy inspired 127 Nationalist Clubs to
be established, but they disbanded after Bellamy decided to back the
People's Party in 1892. One small and irrelevant Marxist socialist
group, the Socialist Labor Party, was founded in 1876. Composed
primarily of recent immigrants from Central Europe, it initially conducted its meetings in German.

What finally spurred the formation of a socialist movement
and party was labor unrest, which was heightened by the depression
of the 1890s, when unemployment rose to over 12 percent, wages
were cut, and many families, lacking the later benefits of a welfare state, found themselves in desperate straits. When the steel-
workers, rail workers, and miners went out on strike, the states and
federal government helped put down the strikes with force. In 1894,
34 American Railway Union strikers were killed. Debs, the leader
of the American Railway Union, who had earlier condemned strikes
and called for a harmonious relationship between workers and
employers, was radicalized by the experience.

Eugene Victor Debs was born in 1855 in Terre Haute, Indiana,
which had been a center of the Methodist Second Great Awakening. Debs was not observant, but his understanding of politics
and socialism was shaped by the prevalent social gospel. "What is
socialism? Merely Christianity in action. It recognizes the equality
in men," he wrote in 1898, the year he declared himself a socialist.
Debs had worked as a locomotive fireman as a teenager and had
become an official of the Brotherhood of Locomotive Firemen,
which functioned as a benevolent society. The young Debs was by
no means a socialist. "My view of capital and labor is that a community should exist between the capitalist and the laborer, instead of

antagonistic feelings," he declared. Debs opposed the great railroad
strike of 1877.

But a succession of strikes provoked by wage cuts during downturns, and paralyzing jurisdictional disputes during the strikes between railway unions, where the conductors refused to support the firemen and engineers, convinced Debs in 1893 to create a single railway union. The American Railway Union won its first strike but was destroyed during the Pullman strike the next year. Debs and other strike leaders were sent to prison. Jailed in a house in Woodstock, Illinois, Debs read Bellamy, Laurence Gronlund (the author of *The Cooperative Commonwealth*, a popularization of Marx), Marx's *Capital*, George Herron, and Kautsky. Debs recalled being most influenced by Kautsky's *The Class Struggle*, which had become the standard exposition of orthodox Marxism. The book, Debs wrote later, had helped him "out of darkness into light."

Debs did not immediately embrace Marxist socialism. In 1897, he tried to set up utopian colonies where laborers could "work out their own salvation, their redemption, and independence." But in June of the next year, he and Victor Berger, a Milwaukee socialist who was acting at that point as Debs's mentor in socialist politics, established the Social Democratic Party, and Debs ran for president as the party's nominee in 1900. A year later, the party was rechristened the Socialist Party. Debs would run again for president in 1904, 1908, 1912, and in 1920 when he was imprisoned in Atlanta for "sedition" because of his opposition to American entry into World War I.

There were elements of the Socialist Party and of Debs's socialism that were peculiar to America of the early twentieth century. The party had some support among trade unionists in the East and Midwest, but a third of its members came from west of the Mississippi, and many of these socialists were former Populists who were part of the region's farm economy. Many were driven by a simple hatred of Wall Street and big business. In these areas and in the Midwest,

320 the Protestant social gospel informed the party's socialist appeal. Its meetings, held in campgrounds and sometimes in buildings that also served as churches, were like revivals. After visiting socialists in Oklahoma, journalist Oscar Ameringer remarked, "They took their socialism like a new religion."

Debs, a stem-winding, thundering orator who spoke to crowds before there were microphones, framed his own appeal for socialism in Christian terms. "The workers are the saviors of society; the redeemers of the race," Debs declared. Jesus was the "master prole-tarian revolutionist and sower of the social whirlwind," Debs wrote. But his Christianity reinforced, and colored, an orthodox Marxism that he had learned from Kautsky. Socialism ("when the bells peal forth the joyous tidings") was a new stage of history that would inevi-tably be ushered in by a revolution that would occur when the working class, suffering from immiseration, overthrew the capitalists.

In his acceptance speech in 1912 for the presidential nomina-tion, Debs described a society "divided into two classes—capitalists and workers, exploiters and producers." Even though the American economy had grown about 4 percent a year since the end of the 1890s depression, Debs invoked the dialectic of immiseration. "So long as the nation's resources and productive and distributive machinery are the private property of a privileged class, the masses will be at their mercy, poverty will be their lot, and life will be shorn of all that raises it above the brute level."

The Socialist Party, Debs insisted, would not cooperate to pursue immediate reforms with the two capitalist parties (three in 1912, with Theodore Roosevelt's Progressive Party) or with Samuel Gompers's American Federation of Labor, which opposed Debs's socialism. "It is vain to hope for material relief upon the prevailing system of capitalism," he declared. "All the reforms that are proposed by the three capitalist parties, even if carried out in good faith, would still leave the working class in industrial slavery." Workers' only alternative was to vote for "emancipation" by supporting socialism and the Socialist Party.

Under Debs's leadership, the Socialist Party grew. In 1901, it had 10,000 members; by 1912, it had 118,000. It elected 1,200 public officials and published over 300 periodicals. Its main publication, the Kansas-based *Appeal to Reason*, had a circulation of almost a million. In the 1912 election, Debs garnered 901,551 votes, or 6 percent of the total. Party leaders looked forward to the Socialists doubling their membership by the next election, but the 1912 election was to prove the party's high-water mark.

In 1919, the party split over its response to the Russian Revolution of 1917, and over the call by the Soviets to engage in armed revolution. A new Communist Party attracted many of the party's foreign-language federations, which by the decade's end had made up half of its membership. By 1929, the party had shrunk to 6,000 registered members, and few were active. It revived briefly under ex-minister Norman Thomas's leadership, but never came close to regaining even the very modest influence it had enjoyed early in the century.

Why did the Socialist Party fail to gain a foothold in American politics? There is a century-long debate that began with Werner Sombart's 1906 treatise, *Why Is There No Socialism in the United States?* But there are really two different questions involved, although the answers are related. First, why did the Socialist Party fail? Second, why did socialism fail to win adherents?

The first question is easy to answer. In a two-party system, a third party can only break through if it stands for something that the other two parties are against or are indifferent toward, *and* if what it stands for has a significant public appeal—enough, for instance, to win states in the electoral college. The Republican Party that was founded in 1854 opposed the extension of slavery in the West that the Democrats and Whigs wouldn't halt; in 1968, George Wallace and his American Independent Party opposed racial desegregation that both major parties favored. The Socialist Party espoused a cause—socialism—that neither the Republicans nor the Democrats

322 supported, but socialism did not command a huge following in America. And by 1912, progressive Republicans or liberal Democrats were addressing issues like unemployment compensation that immediately concerned the workers the Socialists wanted to attract.

The second question of why socialism never attracted a large following is more difficult. Sombart himself cited the American workers' rising standard of living. That was certainly a factor, although not in the Great Depression. Also important was Americans' default suspicion of "big government," which goes back to the revolution of 1776, and made Americans suspicious of a politics that seemed to promise an overweening government. And then, of course, was the popular identification of socialism with Soviet communism, which during the Cold War subverted discussions even of democratic socialism. (The American Communist Party never had a significant public following. In 1932, its presidential candidate received 0.26 percent of the vote. It had its greatest success during the Popular Front period from 1935 to 1945 when its operatives concealed their ultimate objectives and often their membership in the party.)

Perhaps the most important reason of all, as sociologist Daniel Bell argued in *Marxian Socialism in the United States,* is that Debs's and the Socialist Party's conception of socialism was otherworldly. Echoing Lowith's analysis of Marxism, Bell noted the "religious chiliastic origin of modern socialism." "Socialism is an eschatological movement; it is sure of its destiny because 'history' leads to its goal," Bell wrote. Socialism was the second coming, the establishment of the Kingdom of God on Earth.

Debs's Socialist Party was not a religious movement as such, but it had significant elements of one. Religious movements seek converts, not voters. The lure of a religious movement is precisely its otherworldliness—its promise of redemption and salvation beyond the woes of present life. Politics, on the other hand, seeks majorities that will allow politicians to address present hopes and grievances, such as (in Debs's era) the prevalence of child labor, the absence of a minimum wage, the lack of unemployment compensation, the

frequency of farm foreclosures, and the use of the courts and of state
or federal troops against strikers. Debs's and the Socialists' popularity was based initially on some voters' belief that neither of the
major parties were addressing these immediate issues and that they
could only be addressed as a result of socialist revolution, which
would totally transform society. Politics and religion were fused, as
they were for Christian socialists like George Herron. But as soon
as the major parties did begin to address those immediate issues,
voters abandoned socialism's otherworldly appeal

If apocalyptical socialism's lack of appeal wasn't obvious in
Debs's time, it became obvious in 1932 when ordained minister
Norman Thomas ran for president against Franklin Roosevelt on
a platform claiming that only socialism could cure America's ills.
Despite being an effective orator who could appeal to moral and
religious stirrings, Thomas received 2 percent of the vote. Many of
the labor activists and officials who had remained in the Socialist
Party quit afterward, and the party itself became a playground for
followers of the exiled Leon Trotsky. These followers of Trotsky,
believing that Russia's Bolsheviks had succeeded because of their
"correct line" rather than their numbers, repeatedly divided themselves when faced with current political questions into further
factions and parties, each of which claimed to be more correct than
the others.

Victor Berger and Socialism in Our Time

Victor Berger and the Milwaukee Socialists are the exception that
proved the rule—that it was Debs's conception of socialism and
socialist politics that doomed the party. Debs was a centrist figure
within the party, while Berger was squarely on the right. Berger, who
immigrated to the United States from Austria at age 18, had been an
orthodox Marxist, but in 1901, he read and was deeply impressed by
Bernstein's *Evolutionary Socialism*.

Berger, who was editing German- and English-language newspapers, built the Milwaukee branch of the Socialist Party around

324 the idea that by winning immediate improvements for the city's working and middle class, such as the creation of a municipal water system or a minimum wage, the party would be creating the rudiments of socialism within capitalism. "In that way," he wrote, "we can have a great deal of 'Socialism in our Time' even though we cannot have the full-fledged Cooperative Commonwealth." Berger's socialism would also not exclude private property and ownership. "Everything the individual can own and manage best, the individual is to own and manage," he wrote. Berger did believe in the end goal of socialism, but cautioned that it would take "another century or two" and occur through a peaceful transition.

Berger was not Debs's match as a moral exemplar. He was a racist who supported the American Federation of Labor's exclusion of black people. But he created an effective political machine in Milwaukee that held power in the city with few interruptions from 1910 to 1960, and he was elected to the House four times. As one of only two Socialists in Congress, Berger worked, when appropriate, with progressive Democrats and Republicans on legislation. In Milwaukee, the Socialists stood for good government against a corrupt Democratic Party and a weak Republican Party. The Milwaukee Socialist Party's creation of a water and sanitation system earned it the sobriquet "sewer socialism" and "showcialists" from leftwing critics contemptuous of reforms that merely "patched up" capitalism without creating bell-ringing socialism.

Berger's achievement in Milwaukee could not necessarily have been replicated nationally—certainly not in the 1930s, when Roosevelt and the New Deal advanced the same kinds of reforms within capitalism that Berger had advocated. And from 1917 to 1989, the Soviet claim to socialism cast a shadow in America over any attempt to win support for any policy openly tied to "socialism." But if Sanders is linked to the past, it is not to Debs but to Berger. Berger's "Socialism in our Time" is the bridge to Sanders and the socialist awakening of the 2010s.

Sanders and the New Left

Sanders, who was born in Brooklyn in 1941 to working-class immigrants, was a participant in the beginnings of what C. Wright Mills in 1960 called the "new left." The new left, unlike the left of the 1890s or 1930s, was not primarily inspired by economic privation—the sixties were a boom time for the country—but by the rise of the civil rights movement, the movement for nuclear disarmament, and, after 1964, the movement against the Vietnam War. In 1961, Sanders transferred from Brooklyn College to the University of Chicago, which was an incubator of the new left.

At the University of Chicago, Sanders became a member of CORE, the civil rights group that was trying to desegregate the housing that the university owned. He also joined the Young People's Socialist League (YPSL), the youth branch of what remained of the Socialist Party. The national party was dominated by the writer Michael Harrington and his proponents, who were in favor of working within the Democratic Party to realign it. (Harrington would go on to found the Democratic Socialists of America in 1982.) But the Chicago chapter included Joel Geier and Mike Parker, who wanted to create a new labor party.

After graduation, Sanders spent six months on a Kibbutz in Israel, then relocated to New York City, and finally, in 1970, he moved permanently to Vermont. In moving to Vermont, Sanders embraced a very different strain of the new left—the counterculture. The "beatniks" of the 1950s had been an avant-garde artistic movement; the "hippies" of the 1960s counterculture were a social movement that embraced sex, drugs, and rock 'n' roll. The counterculture also had its political prophets who espoused a version of utopian socialism. One of these was Bronx-born Vermonter Murray Bookchin, an anarchist who despised the Marxist-Leninist groupuscules that arose out of the new left in the late 1960s and advocated instead the spread of "libertarian municipalities." In 1981, when Sanders first became a U.S. congressman in 1991, Bookchin's daughter Debbie would become his first press secretary.

By 1970, Vermont had become a center for back-to-the-land hippies. It was dotted with communes. One writer estimated in 1970 that there were 35,800 hippies in Vermont, comprising one-third of the state's residents between the ages of 18 and 34. Sanders's shack in Stannard was near Earth Peoples' Park, Quarry Hill, and New Hamburger Commune. Sanders was of a slightly earlier genera-tion—he was not big on drugs or rock 'n' roll—but he integrated his opposition to the Vietnam War and his vision of socialism with the preoccupations of the counterculture. In the *Freeman*, an alternative newspaper, Sanders attacked the American intervention in Vietnam and "a United States Congress composed of millionaires and state legislatures controlled by lobbyists." But Sanders, the newly minted utopian socialist, also assured his readers:

> The Revolution is coming, and it is a very beautiful revolution. . . . What is most important in this revolution will require no guns, no commandants, no screaming "leaders," and no vicious publica-tions accusing everyone else of being counterrevolutionary. The revolution comes when two strangers smile at each other, when a father refuses to send his child to school because schools destroy children, when a commune is started and people begin to trust each other, when a young man refuses to go to war, and when a girl pushes aside all that her mother has "taught" her and accepts her boyfriend's love.

Sanders first ran for office in a 1972 special election as the Senate candidate of the newly formed Liberty Union, a third party dedicated to ending "the war in Vietnam, the militarization of society, the prob-lems of the poor, and destruction of the environment." But in this election, and during his run for governor in November, Sanders also called for the abolition of "all laws dealing with abortion, drugs, sexual behavior (homosexuality, adultery etc.)," widening highway on-ramps to interstate highways to enable hitchhiking, and ending "compulsory education." And Sanders campaigned as a socialist. "I even mentioned

the horrible word 'socialism'—and nobody in the audience fainted," 327
Sanders wrote in a campaign diary of his gubernatorial race.

Over the next four years, Sanders would run once more for the
Senate and once more for governor. As the economic boom of the
1960s ended with a sharp recession and an energy crisis, Sanders
became focused more on economic issues. Sanders claimed he found
support for nationalizing banks. "We talked to working people and
we got through to working people," he said. "If you say that we have
to take over the banks and have a substantial number of people vote
for that position, that idea suddenly becomes acceptable reality."

Sanders had received only 2 percent of the vote in his first election, and 1 percent in his second, but in his 1976 gubernatorial run
he picked up 6.1 percent, enough to qualify the Liberty Union for an
ongoing spot on the ballot. The next year, however, Sanders quit the
Liberty Union, complaining that the party had become "dormant."

In 1981, at the urging of Richard Sugarman, a philosophy professor and friend, Sanders decided to run for mayor of Burlington, but
Sugarman warned Sanders not to make the election about his socialist
ideology. "No one gives a damn about your ideology," Sugarman
recalls telling Sanders. Sanders ran on a platform of opposing condo-
miniums on Burlington's waterfront and a property tax increase and
promising to recruit a minor league baseball team and to open a hill
for sledding during the winter. He rarely used the word "socialist." He
won by 10 votes against a Democratic incumbent.

Sanders's tenure as mayor recalled that of the Milwaukee
Socialists. Speaking to the *Burlington Free Press* the next year, he
described "one of his major priorities" was "to take the city from
what was a very inefficient government and to make it into a modern
corporation." And he succeeded in eliminating cronyism and bal-
ancing the city's books. Over the next eight years, he created affordable housing, initiated rent controls, established a land trust to
fund housing purchases by low-income Vermonters, turned Burlington's unsightly waterfront into a park, and revitalized the city's
downtown. He even got the Cincinnati Reds to start a farm team in

328   Burlington. In 1987, *U.S. News and World Report* chose him as one of America's top 20 mayors.

During that time, Sanders didn't conceal that he was a socialist. A Debs election poster hung in the mayor's office. He described himself to writer Russell Banks as a "Eugene V. Debs type of socialist." *Rolling Stone* called him "the red mayor in the green mountains."

But Sanders didn't draw a direct connection between being a socialist and what he did as mayor. He told a reporter from the *Baltimore Sun*, "We acknowledge very frankly our limitations. If you ask me if the banks should be nationalized, I would say yes. But I don't have the power to nationalize the banks in Burlington." He organized a Progressive (not a socialist) Coalition in Burlington that backed his policies and ran candidates for city council.

When he ran for Vermont's one congressional seat in 1988, he did run as a Debs socialist. When asked by the *Rutland Daily Herald* about socialism, he said, "I'm not afraid of government control in economics. And I'm not afraid of government control in major enterprises if need be." Attacked as a potential spoiler by Democrats, he countered that a victory for him would lay the groundwork for a leftwing third party in the country. Sanders lost by 8,911 votes to Republican Peter Smith.

In June 1989, after he had left his job as mayor, Sanders sounded the tocsin for a socialist third party. Speaking before the National Committee for Independent Political Action in New York, Sanders declared that "it is absolutely imperative that we build an independent, democratic socialist left which has the guts to raise the issues that all of us know to be true, but which are rarely even *discussed* within establishment politics." He was still following Debs's lead. A year later, however, he no longer was.

Swedish-Style Socialist

In his 1990 rematch with Smith, Sanders ran as an independent but no longer proposed building a new socialist party. Instead, he promised, if elected, to caucus with the Democrats. In response,

the Democrats ran only a token opponent against him and Smith. 329
Sanders also abandoned his orthodox Marxist view of socialism.
Instead, he styled himself a "Swedish-style socialist." As the *Burlington Free Press* reported, "Sanders says he supports democratic socialism as it exists in countries such as Sweden, where national healthcare and free college education are available."

Asked to define his kind of socialism, Sanders told the *Rutland Daily Herald*, "When I talk about democratic socialism, what I am talking about is a style of government which has existed on and off in Scandinavia, Austria, England, West Germany, and Canada." After Sanders was elected, he told the Associated Press, "All that socialism means to me is democracy with a small 'd.' To me, socialism doesn't mean state ownership of everything, by any means. It means creating a nation and a world in which all human beings have a decent standard of living."

What had happened? Sanders clearly became convinced that he could not be elected in Vermont or function in Congress as the candidate of a Debsian socialist party. But there were two other factors that swayed him, both of which were affirmed by someone who has worked in Sanders's office and his campaigns. First, Sanders's model of socialism had combined democracy with nationalization and a planned economy. When Sanders visited the Soviet Union in June 1988, he told reporters that Soviet officials hoped that through *perestroika* and *glasnost,* "democracy and socialism can exist in a compatible way." That seems to have been Sanders's hope as well, but the idea of socialism as a command economy of nationalized firms was dashed by the collapse of the Soviet Union.

Secondly, as a viable congressional candidate, Sanders had to confront the limits of what was possible at a time when the reforms of the New Deal, the Great Society, and even the Nixon years were under assault. He realized, the former aide said, that "there is only so much you can do in Congress."

By then, the Democratic Socialists of America, or the DSA, had been in existence for almost a decade. At a conference in 1991, Sanders

330   was asked by a small group of DSA members whether he believed that a capitalist society needed to be replaced with a socialist society. After declaring that he was a democratic socialist, Sanders responded, "At this point in American history, I would be very delighted if we could move in a conservative manner in the direction of a country like Sweden, which has a national healthcare system which guarantees free healthcare, which has free education for all its kids."

Sanders had traveled within a year from Debs's orthodox Marxism to a politics very similar to that of the Milwaukee Socialists. Socialist politics were no longer an all-or-nothing matter where you favored certain immediate reforms, but what really counted was replacing capitalism *in toto*. Socialist politics consisted of seeking reforms that freed Americans from capitalist market constraints in obtaining healthcare or a college education, or that enhanced the power of workers in their workplace or business. Sanders told the DSA, "I think what you are ultimately moving toward is partnerships. You are talking about democratic control of the economy, you are talking about a partnership between the private sector, the unions, the government, the working people." That's *not* public ownership and control of the means of production; but it would mean a significant increase in the power of workers to control their destiny. For Sanders, that represented a momentous shift in his outlook and it opened the way for a reappraisal in American politics of what socialism meant.

Socialism and the New Deal

As a member of the House starting in 1990 and then Senate from 2006, Sanders repeatedly put forth bills and amendments and took votes that reflected his democratic socialism. In a different era, perhaps, Sanders might have had considerable success with his initiatives. But at a time when Republicans were committed to market fundamentalism and the Democratic leadership was trying to envision a "third way"—that is, between New Deal liberalism and the

Republican priorities—many of Sanders's positions put him at   331
odds even with members of the Democratic Caucus. Sanders got few
bills or amendments passed and became known as a gadfly and an
outsider.

Sanders opposed a succession of "free trade" treaties, including
the North American Free Trade Agreement and the granting of
"most-favored-nation" trading status to China, on the grounds
that they would threaten American jobs by encouraging corporations to move out of the country or allow low-wage foreign competitors to put American firms out of business. He proposed a
Workplace Democracy Act that would make it easier for workers to
form unions, repeal right-to-work laws, and widen the definition
of employee protections under the National Labor Relations Board.
He convinced only two other House members to sponsor the bill.
Sanders began proposing a single-payer healthcare plan in 1993, in
contrast to the Clinton plan for "managed care." In 2007, he unveiled
a plan to encourage employee ownership and cooperatives. In 2010,
he staged an eight-and-a-half-hour filibuster against a bill negotiated by the Obama administration with Republicans that perpetuated Bush-era tax cuts for the wealthy.

Many of Sanders's legislative initiatives—including his version
of single-payer health insurance, dubbed Medicare for All, and a $15
minimum wage—became central to his presidential campaigns in
2016 and 2020. In October 2019, Sanders introduced a Corporate
Accountability and Democracy Plan that would guarantee workers'
representatives 45 percent of the members on corporate boards and
gradually increase workers' stock ownership until it reached 20 percent of the company. Sanders's plan would, he claimed, "fundamentally shift the wealth of the economy back into the hands of the
workers who create it," and "give workers an ownership stake in the
companies they work for." These proposals went beyond what was
then seen as garden-variety "liberalism" or "progressivism." They
reflected an attempt to establish socialism within capitalism.

332   Sanders was criticized by prominent Democrats like Congressman Barney Frank because he "never got anything done," but Sanders attributed his failure to a Washington politics controlled by large donors and corporate lobbyists. In 2014, as he pondered whether to run for president, he told Vox, "The major political, strategic difference I have with [President Barack] Obama is it's too late to do anything inside the Beltway. You gotta take your case to the American people, mobilize them, and organize them at the grassroots level in a way that we have never done before." That became the basis of his populist call for a "political revolution where millions of people get involved in the political process and reclaim our democracy by having the courage to take on the powerful corporate interests whose greed is destroying the social and economic fabric of our country."

Whenever he was asked about socialism during his first years in the Senate, Sanders would refer to what Scandinavian countries had accomplished. When the topic came up again in an October 2015 debate with presidential primary opponent Hillary Clinton, Sanders pointed out what "countries like Denmark, like Sweden and Norway . . . have accomplished for their working people." Clinton responded, "We are not Denmark."

Days later, historian Eric Foner penned an open letter to Sanders in the *Nation* suggesting that he look toward American history and not abroad in explaining democratic socialism. "Your response inadvertently reinforces the idea that socialism is a foreign import. Instead, talk about our radical forebears here in the United States." Foner described a history of radicalism that began with Tom Paine and continued through Frederick Douglass, Lincoln, the Populists, the Progressive Party, and Roosevelt's Second New Deal. "Your antecedents include not just FDR's New Deal but also his Second Bill of Rights of 1944, inspired by the era's labor movement, which called for the government to guarantee to all Americans the rights to employment, education, medical care, a decent home, and other entitlements that are out of reach for too many today." Foner

explained that socialism "today refers not to a blueprint for a future 333
society but to the need to rein in the excesses of capitalism, evident all around us, to empower ordinary people in a political system verging on plutocracy, and to develop policies that make opportunity real for the millions of Americans for whom it is not." Foner was situating the struggle for socialism within capitalism.

Foner did not talk to Sanders, but *Nation* editor Katrina Vanden Heuvel, who was a friend of Sanders's, sent him Foner's article. Another friend of Sanders's, historian Harvey Kaye, the author of a book on Roosevelt, was making the same case to the senator. Sanders responded. In a speech at Georgetown University the next month, he invoked Roosevelt and the Second Bill of Rights. Socialism, he explained, "builds on what Franklin Delano Roosevelt said when he fought for guaranteed economic rights for all Americans." In June 2019, at George Washington University, Sanders took the same tack. "In 1944, FDR proposed an economic bill of rights but died a year later and was never able to fulfill that vision. Our job, seventy-five years later, is to complete what Roosevelt started."

Critics of Sanders, including former Obama administration budget official and law professor Cass Sunstein, asserted that "Roosevelt was no socialist." But it is hard to deny that in Roosevelt's Second New Deal of 1935–36 (which established, among other things, a steeply progressive income tax, social security, and the National Labor Relations Board) and in his proposals for a Second Bill of Rights, Roosevelt was attempting, whether wittingly or not, to "rein in" capitalism. Roosevelt was enhancing the power and wealth of labor at the expense of capital. By citing Roosevelt's Second Bill of Rights, Sanders was making an argument for democratic socialism that began with Berger (with an assist from Bernstein), and went through Roosevelt and the Democrats of the New Deal. It was an important bid to give voice to millions of young people who, unbeknownst to most of their Cold War generation elders, had become deeply disillusioned with capitalism and, in looking for a political alternative, were receptive to a politics that called itself "democratic socialist."

334   Sanders combined an appeal to economic democracy with a moral appeal to community that evoked his earlier years in Vermont as well as the ideals of Christian and utopian socialists. Citing Martin Luther King, Sanders said, "I believe that the goal of human life, that you are richer emotionally as a human being, when we have a community, when we care about each other, when we love each other, when we are compassionate—not when we are stepping on other people." At a rally in Queens, Sanders asked his audience, "Are you willing to fight for that person who you don't even know as much as you're willing to fight for yourself?"

In the fall of 2015 and again in the fall of 2019, I asked participants at Sanders's rallies in New Hampshire, Virginia, and Nevada what they thought about socialism. Many were young people, but there were also a scattering of grandparents who had been around in the sixties. What I heard was dissatisfaction with capitalism and support for Scandinavian-style socialism. I also heard echoes of a Christian socialist commitment to cooperation rather than competition and to the community rather than to the individual:

"We care for each other. That's socialism."

"Bernie is a democratic socialist. That doesn't scare me. It inspires me. Because Bernie has recognized for a long time that our democratic political system is corrupt and leaving people behind. We need a government that is for the people. We aren't going to be rid of this label. It means making sure our economic and political system works for everybody."

"I'm a public-school teacher. I'm a socialist." (This was stated as if being a public-school teacher *entailed* her being a socialist.)

"It means social services."

"I've thought of myself as a socialist for years. I think of community, of looking out for everybody, not just for yourself."

"I think socialism is scary for a lot of people. But I think capitalism
is scarier. We need social programs, childcare, Medicare for All,
we need all these things to make society better. In Sweden they
don't say this will destroy the country. They have higher taxes,
but they don't have these concerns about losing your homes."

Not a single person told me that socialism meant anything like
"public ownership and control of the means of production." Sanders
had shaped how his supporters thought of socialism, but he was also
responding to their own inclinations about what was wrong with
capitalism and what needed to be done about it.

Perhaps the clearest sign that Sanders's concept had taken hold
was the rise of Congresswoman Alexandria Ocasio-Cortez. In 2016,
Ocasio-Cortez, who was working as a bartender and had not been
active in electoral politics before, was inspired to ring doorbells for
Sanders's campaign during the New York primary. Two years later,
recruited by some former Sanders staffers, she ran for Congress, and
to her own surprise, she defeated powerful ten-term incumbent Joe
Crowley, the fourth-highest-ranking Democrat in the House. Members of DSA had walked the streets for her, and halfway through her
campaign, she joined DSA and identified herself as a "democratic
socialist."

When she went to Congress in 2019 and was asked what it
meant to be a democratic socialist, she echoed Sanders's view.
When "millennials talk about concepts like democratic socialism,"
she explained to *Business Insider*, "we're talking about countries and
systems that already exist that have already been proven to be successful in the modern world. We're talking about single-payer health
care that has already been successful in many different models, from
Finland to Canada to the UK."

Sanders's Last Campaign

Sanders was denied the presidential nomination in 2020 for the second and likely the last time—he will be 83 on Election Day 2024. Various political analysts attributed his loss to a host of tactical errors, but the real problem was a familiar one in American politics. The American two-party system makes electability a factor in choosing a presidential nominee. When the opposing nominee is someone who is seen to be formidable and very dangerous, as Democrats saw Trump in 2020, then electability becomes the principal concern. Whether voters actually supported Sanders or not, many saw him, because of his leftwing stands and reputation as an outsider, as less electable than former vice president Joe Biden.

Sanders's chances also suffered because many voters over 45 were unwilling to support a candidate who identified himself as a "democratic socialist." Still others objected to programs like Medicare for All, which wouldn't benefit them if they already had private insurance or were on Medicare, and might significantly raise their taxes. In the end, Sanders could not overcome these reservations.

But even after the Democratic primary was essentially decided, Sanders continued to attract younger voters. He won a plurality of young voters even in states he lost decisively to Biden. And while Sanders's stand on Medicare for All probably hurt him during the primaries, the onset of COVID-19 and the massive loss of private health insurance by laid-off workers lent his plan an added plausibility. Arguments about spending too much for jobs and education that were used against Sanders also looked hollow in the wake of Congress's spending on the pandemic recession. To some extent, Sanders won the Democratic debate in 2020, but after he had already lost the nomination.

Sanders's political success was signaled by Biden's willingness to involve Sanders and his supporters in a set of task forces that were mandated to shape the Democratic platform and, if Biden were to win the presidency, his transition to office. Each task force was co-chaired by a Sanders ally and a Biden supporter. These included

two of Sanders's surrogates during the campaign, Ocasio-Cortez
and Rep. Pramila Jayapal, co-chairing the climate task force and the
healthcare task force, respectively. Biden also displayed a recognition that, in the face of the pandemic recession, he would have to
opt for the kind of "structural" change that Sanders and Warren had
advocated in the campaign.

Socialism After Sanders

If a new political tendency wants to gain influence in Germany or Spain, it will aspire to establish its own party. That was the path taken by the rightwing Alternativ fur Deutschland in Germany and the leftwing Podemos (now Unidas Podemos) in Spain. But in the United States, it is virtually impossible to start a new major party. That last happened in 1854.

Instead, new political tendencies have to gain influence by establishing dense networks of politicians, organizations, think tanks, publications, donors, dedicated supporters, and voters that can eventually dominate one of the major parties. That is how the conservative movement, which dates back to the 1950s, came to dominate the Republican Party in the last two decades of the twentieth century. With Sanders out of the presidential race, what are the prospects of a socialist tendency establishing this kind of network and gaining influence in American politics?

Heather Gautney, who was a senior aide to Sanders, wrote me after Sanders had dropped out of the race, "Sadly, I think that Bernie's exit means the 'socialist turn' will disappear from the mainstream of American politics unless he creates a new political

organization to carry the torch." Insofar as it is doubtful that the
79-year-old Sanders will create a new organization, Gautney's prediction about the future of American socialism might turn out to
be true.

But the future for socialism actually looks far less bleak. Growing
support for socialism, particularly among the young, predated Sand
ers's 2016 campaign. In May 2015, as Sanders's presidential campaign was just beginning, and as most voters didn't know who he
was, YouGov found in a poll that 36 percent of Americans between
ages 18 and 29 had a "favorable view" of socialism. In all, 26 percent
of Americans had a favorable view. And 43 percent of Democrats had
a favorable view of socialism. The conditions that led to this support
for socialism and skepticism about capitalism have, if anything, been
reinforced by the pandemic and economic recession.

Where it may look bleak is in the socialists' lack of an effective
political infrastructure that can mobilize and expand the universe
of Sanders's supporters. There are only a handful of socialist politicians in Washington. There is one significant socialist organization,
the DSA. There are a score of socialist publications and podcasts,
but no think tanks and no policy groups. DSA itself has helped elect
promising local officials, and its overall membership accords with
Sanders's democratic socialism, but orthodox Marxists have great
influence over the group's activist core and national leadership as
well as over America's main socialist publication, *Jacobin*.

What may redeem the promise of American socialism over
a decade or so is the existence of a dense network, comparable to
the conservative network of the 1970s, of "progressive" or "liberal"
national politicians, organizations (including labor unions), think
tanks, and policy groups that endorse much of the Sanders program, but are still unwilling to identify themselves and their platform as "socialist." They and their successors, more than today's
self-identified socialists, may hold the future of socialist politics in
their hands. They could eventually prove Gautney wrong.

340 **Socialism's Popular Base**

Over the last decade, there has been growing sympathy for socialism among Democrats, and particularly among the young, aged roughly from 18 to 40, including millennials (born between 1981 and 1996) and Generation Z (born after 1996). This sympathy showed up in Sanders's support in 2016 and 2020, and even to some extent in Warren's, and in the popularity of Ocasio-Cortez. In an NBC/*Wall Street Journal* poll in January 2020, 60 percent of Sanders's voters had a positive view of socialism, and only 4 percent held a negative view. (The rest declined to state.) Only 12 percent had a positive view of capitalism.

Sanders's support was concentrated among the young. In the 2016 presidential primaries, Sanders got more votes from 18- to 29-year-olds than Hillary Clinton and Donald Trump combined. In the Pew poll in January 2020 of Democratic candidates, Sanders and Warren supporters together accounted for 40 and 17 percent, respectively, of Democrats 18 to 29 years old. In the 2020 primaries where exit polls were taken, Sanders regularly won the 18- to 29-year-old vote, and only lost the 30- to 44-year-old vote in two southern states. In Michigan, after Warren had dropped out and he was paired against Biden alone, Sanders lost the primary but won 74 percent of the 18- to 29-year-old vote and 52 percent of those aged 30 to 44. He enjoyed similar margins in Texas, California, and Minnesota.

In a YouGov poll done for Data for Progress in December 2019, 21 percent of *all* voters preferred socialism to capitalism, 55 percent preferred capitalism, and 24 percent were not sure. That 21 percent conforms to the percentage of the electorate that a Sanders–Ocasio-Cortez party might sometime fetch in a multi-party system like Germany's. Among Democrats, 38 percent preferred socialism, 27 percent preferred capitalism, and 35 percent were not sure. Among 18- to 29-year-old Democrats, 47 percent preferred socialism, 18 percent capitalism, and 35 percent were not sure. Among 30- to 44-year-olds, 47 percent preferred socialism, 28 percent capitalism, and 25 percent were not sure.

YouGov also asked Democrats to choose a label from among "liberal," "progressive," "moderate," "socialist," and "none of these." The poll found that 18 percent identified themselves as "socialists." That's a step beyond saying one preferred socialism over capitalism. About a third of the Democrats from ages 18 to 44 identified as socialists, but the percentages fell precipitously for those 45 and older. Identification as a socialist actually increased as millennials entered their 30s, suggesting these voters won't follow the venerable maxim that, "If you're not a socialist before you're 25, you have no heart; if you are a socialist after 25, you have no head."

Almost a third of Democrats who had graduated from a four-year college but not pursued an advanced degree identified as socialists; only about a sixth of those who had not graduated or who had an advanced degree identified as socialists. In other words, those who identified as socialists were probably from the lower stratum of the college-educated. And those who thought of themselves as socialists were very likely to live in a city or suburb rather than in a town or in the country. The socialists were generally under 45, had graduated from college, and lived in big metro centers. But there were still significant numbers of socialists who had not graduated from a four-year college. They probably lived in metro areas. In analyzing voter returns from 1988 to 2000, Ruy Teixeira and I found that in the big metro centers, voters with some college but not four-year degrees voted for Democrats in roughly the same proportion as college-educated voters.

Education and Socialism
What is the highest level of education you have completed? By percentage of Democrats who identify as a "socialist."

No HS 3
High school graduate 16
Some college 17

2-year 17
4-year 31
Post-grad 16

Age Percentage of Democrats Who Identify as Socialists

18–29	26	55–64	12
30–44	32	65+	12
45–54	17		

If you look at Sanders's donors, who contributed an average of $18 to the campaign, there is a tilt toward professionals, but also a significant group of lower-paid service workers. The largest groups of contributors were software engineers, teachers, and nurses, but the biggest employers of donors were Walmart, Amazon (most of whose workers are not software engineers), Target, and the U.S. Postal Service. At Sanders's rallies, I found many of the supporters who were attending or had graduated from four-year colleges had gone to modest schools like Granite State in New Hampshire or George Mason in Virginia, and not to Dartmouth or the University of Virginia.

There is very little polling on what Americans think that socialism is, but what there is suggests that Sanders's democratic socialism reflected the prevailing sentiment. In September 2018, a Gallup Poll asked respondents what was "their understanding of 'socialism.'" Overall, 57 percent of Democrats and Democratic-leaning independents had a positive view of socialism, compared to 16 percent of Republicans. Among Democrats and those who leaned Democratic, a majority considered "socialism" to mean greater equality and enhanced social services, including "medicine for all." The rest of the alternatives were a grab bag that included being sociable and offering a "cooperative plan." Only 13 percent of Democrats saw "government ownership or control . . . of business" as socialism. In other words, Democrats who had a positive view of socialism were likely to see it along the lines of Sanders's democratic socialism and not along the lines of orthodox Marxism or Marxism-Leninism.

Disillusionment with Capitalism

What accounts for the rising support for socialism and opposition to capitalism, particularly among the young? Besides the Sanders presidential campaigns, there are three large events or developments and one underlying trend. The most important event is the Great Recession that began in 2008. It reinforced anxieties about capitalism and about economic security that had been building since the beginning of the twenty-first century. While the reaction to the recession spawned the Tea Party among many older Americans outside big metro areas, it provoked a spate of movements critical of capitalism among the young, beginning with Occupy Wall Street in 2011 and culminating in the Sanders and Warren campaigns.

The second is the specter of climate change. Many of the young harbor the same fears of the effects of climate change that earlier generations felt toward the possibility of nuclear war. According to a 2018 Gallup Poll, 70 percent of those age 18 to 34 worry a great deal or fair amount about global warming. Over half think it will pose a "serious threat" in their lifetimes. They blame climate change on the excesses of the fossil fuel industry and more generally on a capitalism run amok, and seek the arrest of it in a Green New Deal that would require massive government intervention in the private sector.

The third is Trump's election in 2016 and presidency. It has highlighted the irresponsibility of the "billionaire class" spawned by contemporary capitalism. It has also provoked a vigorous reassertion of a moral commitment to racial and sexual equality. The Black Lives Matter movement predates Trump's presidency, but the movements and the protests over police brutality that it helped lead were energized by Trump's casual bigotry and threats of repression. The protests have inspired doubts about what participants call "the system," a term that has a broader reach than simply the way local police departments are organized, and a call for equality that can extend to capitalism itself.

344   In addition, there has been a longer-term shift in the place of the college-educated young in the economy that has fueled doubts about the benefits of capitalism. College graduates went from about 5 percent of the labor force after World War II to about 35 percent in 2018. These young Americans hoped to find higher wages and what the '60s generation called "meaningful" work as salaried workers in industry and as professionals and managers. And they initially did. From 1991, for instance, to 2001, the gap in income between a male high school graduate and a male college graduate increased from $30,792 to $45,444 (in 2017 dollars). And there was a growing celebration of individual initiative, epitomized by the rise of the Silicon Valley startup.

But the standard of living of college-educated workers stopped rising around the time that the dot-com bubble burst in 2001. According to economist Elise Gould of the Economic Policy Institute, the average wage of college-educated workers was 2.4 percent lower in 2018 than it was in 2000. The decline in the college wage premium coincided with a stratospheric rise in the costs of higher education. The costs of obtaining a degree have risen 213 percent at public colleges and 129 percent at private universities from 1988 to 2018. That has in turn fed the astronomical increase in student debt—$1.6 trillion by 2019. Average student debt for the young rose from $17,297 in 2000 to $29,597 in 2015. The Great Recession accentuated the economic insecurity that the young experience. In 2010, the unemployment rate for 18- to 29-year-olds was 14.2 percent.

Just as factory workers at auto plants lost their assurance of lifetime employment at the end of the twentieth century, so, too, in the early twenty-first century did college graduates. Some millennials have found themselves "job-hopping." Some have taken jobs in the new gig economy without benefits, or they have worked for Starbucks as the so-called "barista with the BA." One survey of 40 Uber drivers in Washington, D.C., found that 29 had graduated from college, and 13 of them also had graduate degrees. If young people want to have children, buy a house, and settle down, the costs of housing have become prohibitive. According to a study by the real estate firm

Unison, millennials in Los Angeles with the median income would have to wait until they were 73 years old before they could afford to buy a house. The lack of secure employment fed fears about the costs of healthcare and insurance.

There were also growing doubts, especially among those without advanced degrees, about finding "meaningful work." According to a McKinsey Study in 2013, 48 percent of college graduates were in jobs like those at Starbucks or with Uber that did not require college degrees.

Software developers who wanted to write "cool" code ended up working for huge companies that dictated what they did. Teachers who wanted to help their students learn were increasingly forced to teach carefully prescribed curricula in order to prepare their students for standardized tests and were subject to the whims of highly politicized local and state boards. In other words, young college graduates increasingly found their expectations for secure, remunerative, and meaningful work dashed; and they increasingly blamed capitalism.

The onset of the pandemic and economic recession reinforced all these doubts and fears. Trump's ineptitude and self-dealing highlighted the importance of government acting in the social interest. Elizabeth Warren captured the new mood among many Americans in a quip: "Ronald Reagan famously said that the most terrifying words in the English language are 'I'm from the government and I'm here to help.' In this crisis, we've seen that the most terrifying words are actually 'We're in a crisis and the government doesn't have a plan to get us out.'"

The news site Axios summed up the effects of the new crisis on Generation Z's view of government. "They or their parents could lose employer-provided health insurance in the middle of a pandemic. That could fuel their already strong support for progressive, social safety net policies such as universal basic income and Medicare for All. They'll have experienced the impacts of the biggest government bailout in history—and [according to a January Pew poll]

346   70 percent already think government should do more to solve problems." In the first three months of the pandemic, more than a quarter of Americans under 25 lost their jobs. The conditions that have led to doubts about capitalism and support for democratic socialism over the last two decades can be expected to endure for the time being and even increase in intensity.

The Socialist Network

Can this growing disillusionment be mobilized in a socialist movement that would have an impact on American politics comparable to that which the conservative movement has had? That requires national political leadership and a broad network of organizations and publications. From 2015 to 2020, Sanders and Ocasio-Cortez were the lodestars of this new socialism. Their success not only fueled interest in socialism, but also gave it political direction. But at age 79, Sanders, having lost the nomination, is unlikely to provide leadership for a movement. Ocasio-Cortez has not been an outspoken proponent of socialism, only of socialist initiatives. She joined the DSA belatedly and is not known to be active in the organization. In the absence of new national leaders emerging, the task of championing socialist ideas and politics will pass for the time being to publications and organizations.

There are a host of publications that explicitly champion socialism. The most important of these is *Jacobin,* founded by Bhaskar Sunkara, the son of immigrants from Trinidad, in his dorm room at George Washington University in 2010. By 2014, it had 4,000 subscribers, which is respectable for a socialist journal. By 2020, it had 50,000 and was getting over two million unique visitors a month on its website. Nathan Robinson, a graduate student at Harvard, was inspired by Sunkara to start *Current Affairs.* Historian Michael Kazin and several young socialist intellectuals revived *Dissent.* There are also socialist podcasts, including the *Chapo Trap House, Season of the Bitch,* and the *Trillbilly Workers Party.*

Though there are several socialist organizations in America, most of them resemble small religious sects. The only significant one is the Democratic Socialists of America. DSA was a product of a merger in 1982 between the Democratic Socialist Organizing Committee (DSOC) and the New American Movement (NAM), to which I had belonged. DSOC grew out of a split in the old Socialist Party in the early 1970s between supporters and opponents of the Vietnam War. DSOC, led by Michael Harrington, drew together socialists who had been leery of the new left, but who opposed the Vietnam War and supported antiwar candidate George McGovern in the 1972 election. NAM was an attempt to create a socialist organization that rejected the new left's descent into Marxist-Leninism and echoed its earlier commitment to participatory democracy. DSOC was primarily based on the East Coast, NAM in the Midwest and West Coast. DSOC sought to realign the Democratic Party; NAM devoted itself primarily to local organizing. Together, the groups had several thousand active members.

When the merger occurred in 1982, the country was mired in a deep recession, and the Reagan White House and the Republicans were on the defensive. Conditions seemed ripe for a revival of the left. But within a year, the economy had begun to recover, and in 1984, Reagan was easily reelected. The new organization began to hemorrhage members and chapters. In 1987, its political director decided he was no longer a socialist and went off to graduate school. When Bhaskar Sunkara went to his first DSA meeting in 2007, he found it composed of "relics" who reminisced about the battles between socialists and communists.

Sanders's campaign was a turning point for the DSA. In 2015, Sunkara and another young socialist, Dustin Guastella, launched a petition drive to convince Sanders to run for president. They became instrumental in getting DSA behind Sanders's candidacy that year. By the summer of 2016, the DSA's membership had grown to 8,500. Trump's election then brought about another spurt. On the day of Trump's victory, 1,000 people joined the DSA. Between then and July 1, 2017, DSA gained 13,000 new members. In 2014, the Austin, Texas, DSA chapter had 14 members; by the end of 2016, it had 700; by 2019, it had 1,300.

DSA's composition also changed dramatically. In 2013, the average age of a DSA member was 68. By 2017, when DSA conducted a survey of its membership, the average age was 33. Almost every respondent was college-educated. Six of 10 had a masters, Ph.D., or professional degree. Only 3 percent had blue-collar jobs. But 13 percent were unemployed—a clear indication of the plight of the college-educated millennials. Jonah Furman, who worked as a labor liaison in the 2020 Sanders campaign, described DSA as an organization for "downwardly mobile millennials." DSA has chapters in 49 states and the District of Columbia. The biggest chapters are in Los Angeles, the East Bay Area, Chicago, New York, and the Washington, D.C., metro area. About 10 percent of the membership live in New York City.

The pandemic and recession have brought a spurt in membership. About 15,000 new members joined from March to June 2020. Chicago's chapter gained 600 new members.

Most of the DSA's chapter activity is locally driven. Chapters have backed rent control initiatives; they have been active in unions and tried to organize new ones; they have promoted the Green New Deal, and worked with immigrant organizations on a campaign to abolish the U.S. Immigration and Customs Enforcement. Their most notable activity, however, has been in running candidates. Over a hundred DSA members hold political office. These include six Chicago city council members. In November 2018, DSA members won city council races in Colorado (Aurora and Boulder), Connecticut (Middletown and Wallingford), Indiana (West Lafayette), Massachusetts (Medford and Cambridge), and Michigan (Lansing). In 2020, DSA showed their clout in New York City races, contributing to three wins by new candidates in state assembly races and helping DSA member Jamaal Bowman upset incumbent congressman Eliot Engel in the Democratic

primary. With Bowman and newly elected St. Louis congresswoman 349
Cori Bush, DSA now totaled four members of Congress. (At its peak,
the old Socialist Party boasted two House members, Berger and a distant relation of mine, New Yorker Meyer London.)

With Sanders's presidential campaign over, however, the DSA
faces a new challenge. As long as Sanders was running for president,
he defined what it meant to be a socialist—not for every reader of
Jacobin, but for the 10 million or so Democrats who voted for him
and for most of the people who told opinion polls that they prefer
socialism to capitalism and identify as a "socialist." By backing
Sanders, the DSA implicitly embraced a post-Marxist democratic
socialism. That potentially gave it contact with a base of millions of
voters, many of whom agreed with all or part of Sanders's program,
but not necessarily with the label of "socialist." DSA's challenge is
precisely to bring this electorate around.

Berniecrats and Trotskyists
If you look at the DSA's membership of approximately 70,000,
there are probably 1,500 to 2,000 dedicated activists who live and
breathe the organization. Beyond that, there are about 15,000 members who go to at least several meetings a year and can be called on
to work on campaigns. (These numbers account for the 24 percent
of the organization that voted in the 2019 referendum on whether
to endorse Sanders.) The other members pay annual dues the way
that they would annually contribute to the Sierra Club or Planned
Parenthood.

Many of the paper members and some of the semi-activists are
what Sunkara has called "Berniecrats"—they were inspired to join
the DSA by his campaign and share his view of socialism as Scandinavian social democracy and as the fulfillment of Roosevelt's
Second Bill of Rights and an opposition to racial and sexual discrimination. Some of the activists and political officials among
DSA's leaders have broken with orthodox Marxism. David Duhalde
joined DSA's youth group in 2003 when he was at Bowdoin. After

350 graduation, he was an organizer for the Young Democratic Socialists. He became DSA's deputy director in 2015, at a time when the
membership exploded. After the 2016 election, he became the political director of Sanders's Our Revolution, and is now the vice-chair
of DSA's Fund, which gives grants to organizations and publications. "I view socialism emerging through social democracy," says
Duhalde. "I see a lot of striving for a social democracy in a [Eduard]
Bernstein fashion that will one day become a socialist society. . . .
I'm more concerned with building social democracy day to day than
with what socialism looks like when we get there."

Khalid Kamau helped organize a Black Lives Matter chapter in
Atlanta in 2015. In 2016, he joined DSA and worked on the Sanders
campaign, becoming a convention delegate. That experience, he says,
inspired him to run for city council in 2017 in South Fulton, southwest of Atlanta; he won with 67 percent of the vote. With the council
merely being a part-time job, Kamau moonlights as a Lyft driver.

Kamau described himself as a "Christian, vegan-eating socialist."
"At my church," he explains, "we had a young lady. She wasn't going
to be able to go back to school because she couldn't pay her bills. We
raised a thousand dollars to pay her bills. That's socialism." When
a DSA caucus proposed that the organization only back candidates
who were declared socialists, he disagreed. "When we are involved in
a campaign," Kamau, who was the chairman of Metro Atlanta DSA,
said, "it helps if they are socialist. But if they are half-decent, that's
fine. Socialism is about people being more important than profits."
Kamau added, "To me the journey is more important than the destination." When I told him that he was echoing Bernstein, he said he
didn't know about "evolutionary socialism."

Vaughn Stewart, 31, is a state legislator from Montgomery
County, Maryland. Originally from Anniston, Alabama, he and his
wife moved to Maryland after he finished law school. He worked
briefly with a downtown D.C. law firm, but decided to go into a politics. A member of the Metro D.C. DSA chapter, he credits his election in 2018 to DSA members knocking on doors for him. "For me,"

he says, "democratic socialism means more democracy in the work- 351
place, more representation on corporate boards, or more utilities
that are nationalized, with the hope that we can have permanent
prosperity for all. My generation feels we were wronged and the vil-
lain is capitalism, and the alternative is socialism."

But DSA also includes its share of orthodox Marxists. Some
joined DSA out of two Trotskyist organizations that originated from
the group that Joel Geier and Mike Parker, who had been part of the
YPSL chapter at the University of Chicago when Sanders was there,
formed with Marxist theorist Hal Draper. This group, the International Socialists, later split into two small, disciplined sects:
Solidarity, which still exists, and the International Socialist Organization (ISO), which disbanded in March 2019. Members of both
groups have played a significant role in political debates in the DSA.
David Duhalde calls them the "neo-Draperites."

Dan La Botz is the elder statesman of these groups. He remains
in Solidarity, along with about a hundred other DSA members. La
Botz believes that socialism is a separate stage of history that can
only be achieved through a revolution. "You don't get any of these
things except through a violent upheaval that transforms the constitution and the country. I don't see incremental changes." He
rejects the idea of achieving change through the Democratic Party.
"I think it is a capitalist party. I don't think anyone can take it over,"
he explained. He supported Sanders, but he does not think he is a
socialist. "I don't think Bernie was a social democrat. I think he was
a New Deal liberal."

Some young DSA members became convinced by reading and
discussion that orthodox Marxist socialism made sense. Ari-
elle Sallai is a recent college graduate who lives in Los Angeles and
has worked in the entertainment industry and at nonprofits. She
is the chair of housing programs for the large Los Angeles chapter.
"To me," she explained, "being a socialist means understanding the
class project. It is the belief that workers should seize the means of
production. Workers should control the means of production. For

352   example, it is the abolition of private property." I asked her whether, under socialism, people could own their homes. "We should live collectively," she insisted.

These orthodox Marxists make up a large part of DSA's most active core. Many of them function through organized caucuses that take positions and run slates for national leadership. Bread & Roses has attracted these orthodox Marxists. It describes itself as a "caucus of Marxist organizers" and stresses the "centrality of class struggle." At the 2019 convention, it advocated a strategy of "class-struggle elections" that would have limited DSA to endorsing socialist candidates. It declares that "the Democratic Party is not and never will be a party of and for the working class" and seeks, when the time is right, to break off and form "a mass working-class party." This is the same position that Geier and Parker, who later formed the International Socialists, were taking in 1962. It's worth noting that none of the groups that grew out of that original Trotskyist organization have had any luck organizing "a mass working-class party."

The conflict between the post-Marxists and the Marxists emerged clearly at the 2019 convention and had repercussions on how DSA responded to Biden's winning the nomination from Sanders. At the convention, the delegates narrowly defeated the Bread & Roses proposal to limit endorsements to socialists, but they backed a related proposal from a onetime member of Solidarity that the organization should not endorse any candidate in the 2020 election except Sanders. "DSA should make it clear that we will not endorse corporate politicians," Andrew Sernatinger declared.

At the time, the vote appeared to be aimed at Elizabeth Warren, whose platform was very similar to Sanders's, but it put the organization on record not supporting any challenger to Trump but Sanders. *American Prospect* editor Harold Meyerson, who came to DSA through DSOC, commented afterward, "It's a good thing that organizations don't have children or grandchildren. If they did, you could envision little tykes (well, little infant prodigies) fifty years from now asking their grandparent—the Democratic Socialists

of America—'What did you do in the war against the neofascist   353
Donald Trump?' only to be met by an awkward pause."

By early April, when Sanders conceded and endorsed Biden, the
nation was in the throes of the pandemic and recession; to many
Americans, the threat posed by Trump's potential reelection loomed
larger than ever. Some DSA members favored reconsidering the convention decision, but the National Political Committee rejected
the idea. "We are not endorsing Joe Biden," it tweeted, without any
explanation. Meagan Day, a member of Bread & Roses and *Jacobin's* campaign correspondent, applauded the decision. "There's
no way we would have caved to pressure and endorsed Biden," she
wrote. *Jacobin* editor Sunkara, one of DSA's leading intellectuals,
announced he would be voting for Howie Hawkins, a member of
Solidarity running as the Green Party candidate.

David Duhalde acknowledged that if the referendum were held,
"the broader membership would probably be okay if we endorsed
Biden." Nathan Newman, a professor at CUNY, wrote, "That this
decision was made without a vote of the membership is why I'm not
renewing my DSA membership. I would bet if a full vote of the membership was done, members would endorse Biden to defeat Trump."
But a month later, DSA's National Political Committee doubled
down on its decision, voting 13 to 4 not to "ask members in swing
states to consider voting for Biden." The political committee added,
"We believe Biden's anti-Chinese xenophobic messaging & the
allegations of sexual assault against him exemplify how corporate
Democrats allow the advance of far-right politics, white supremacy,
misogyny, and capitalism."

The DSA leadership, driven by orthodox Marxists and latter-day
Trotskyists, downplayed the gravity of the choice facing the American electorate in 2020, with Biden as the only alternative to the man
Sanders called "the most dangerous president in the modern history of this country." Instead, they sought to make a statement about
the capitalist nature of both parties. By doing so, DSA cut itself off
not only from its own Berniecrats like Newman and from the several

354   million Americans who had come to question capitalism, but also from the broader political universe of progressives, left-liberals, and leftists who may not call themselves socialist, but support socialist initiatives.

Longtime DSA member Leo Casey, the director of the American Federation of Teachers' Albert Shanker Institute, commented, "The November election is seen as absolutely pivotal and decisive in the mass popular left—unions—and in organizations of color, civil rights, feminist, environmental, immigrant rights, LGBTQ folk. If the response of the DSA is, 'Sorry, there is no socialist running so we are going to ignore it, and throw our energies into the battle for state representative,' it will be irreparable to the DSA." But the group's leadership was in the clutches of Marxist antediluvians who were willing to risk isolation from the people whose support they needed to build a popular socialist movement.

The Culture War

The historic task of socialists and the broader left has been to unite the bottom and middle of society around an agenda that shifts power and wealth from capital to labor. To do that, socialists have to find common ground around economic grievances and democratic aspirations. In the United States, that has always been made difficult by regional economic disparities (which fuel cultural differences) and racial and ethnic divisions.

In the U.S. today, one of the deepest divisions has been between the politics of post-industrial metro centers like New York, Chicago, or the Bay Area and the small and mid-sized towns in the Midwest and South that have been decimated over the last 40 years by the loss of industrial jobs and stable communities. The former, along with most college towns, have been home to Democrats and liberals; the latter to the downscale whites who voted for Trump in 2016. There are significant numbers of metro Democrats and middle-American whites who agree on issues like Medicare and minimum wage. As political scientist Lee Drutman found in his survey of the 2016

election, the most dramatic difference between the voters from 355
these two regions is over sociocultural issues—gender, family, race,
nation, religion, guns, and immigration—not economics.

Just as socialists isolate themselves from the broader electorate
by taking orthodox Marxist stands on economics and politics, they
cut themselves off by taking extreme positions on cultural issues
that go beyond a commitment to democracy and equality. That
holds even for winning the support of those who consider themselves "progressive" or "liberal." The larger liberal electorate is fully
supportive of gay marriage and opposes job discrimination against
transgender people, but is wary of transgender activists who advocate the abolition of gender. They support affirmative action and
oppose any form of discrimination against African Americans, but
they are not ready to endorse reparations. They decry racial injustice in policing and in the courts, but they are not ready to abolish
prisons and defund the police. They favor comprehensive immigration reform, but they oppose open borders.

On each of these social issues, DSA takes the most radical stand.
DSA has gone on record in favor of "open borders." At its Atlanta
convention in 2019, it backed a proposal for the "uninhibited transnational free movement of people"—a proposal that, if carried
out, would undermine popular support for generous welfare programs, including Medicare for All. At the convention, DSA adopted
a resolution for a "police and prison abolition" working group.
During the protests against police brutality toward African Americans that began in the spring of 2020, DSA echoed the demand
for "defunding" rather than "reforming" the police—a demand
that, without footnotes of explanation, a majority of Americans
opposed—presumably because they saw it as threatening their own
safety. But DSA's national leadership went even further, advocating
"abolition as the path forward."

DSA could certainly grow in size and influence in years to
come—the combination of the coronavirus and recession and
the specter of climate change will create greater skepticism about

356 capitalism. Its elected officials, who have to deal with actual voters, and who are realistic about what the organization can and should accomplish, could lead the way. But for DSA to accomplish its objectives, it will need to wean itself away from orthodox Marxism and from extreme positions on cultural issues that reflect its own narrow social base rather than the aspirations of most Americans.

The Shadow Socialists

The heavy lifting of creating a "historic bloc" for democratic socialism may be done by politicians, publications, think tanks, and organizations that are not overtly identified as socialist. They form a shadow socialist network that is at least as powerful as the conservative network of the 1970s. Minus the label, their view of capitalism is similar to that of Sanders and to the young Americans who identify themselves as "democratic socialists," and they are promoting many of the same policies as Sanders and Ocasio-Cortez, including the Green New Deal and Medicare for All, but they don't want to suffer the stigma of being identified as "socialist."

Many intellectuals of this kind describe themselves as "social democrats"—a label that has no currency in American politics. They include Robert Kuttner, a founder of the *American Prospect*, *New York Times* columnist Jamelle Bouie, and political scientist Sheri Berman. Kuttner, Berman, economist Joseph Stiglitz, and political scientist Dani Rodrik share Karl Polanyi's view of capitalism. "There is almost a Polanyi secret handshake," Kuttner says.

Stiglitz, who wrote the foreword to a new edition of *The Great Transformation*, calls himself a "progressive capitalist," and warned Democrats in 2019 of the political perils of nominating someone identified as a "socialist," but his prescriptions are consistent with the idea of establishing socialism within capitalism. Indeed, Stiglitz admits that the "new breed of American democratic socialists—or call them what you will—is simply advocating a model that embraces government's important role in social protection and inclusion, environmental protection, and public investment in infrastructure, technology, and education. They recognize the public's regulatory role in preventing corporations from exploiting customers or workers in a multitude of ways."

Key think tanks include the Economic Policy Institute in Washington and the Roosevelt Institute in New York. The Roosevelt Institute's "New Rules for the Twenty-First Century" is a blueprint for subordinating markets to social needs and changing the balance of wealth and power. It proposes to

> rethink the markets-first approach in favor of a pragmatic assessment [and] to deploy the power of government to directly provide goods and services and tackle the challenges our nation faces; restructure the economy by writing new rules that strike at the heart of today's concentrations of wealth and power; and reform our political institutions, so we can make both the private sector and the government work for all of us again.

Key publications, most of whom employ socialists as editors and staff writers, include the *Nation*, the *New Republic*, the *American Prospect*, *N+1*, *In These Times*, *Mother Jones*, and the *Intercept*. Similarly, there are scores of organizations that include socialists. After Biden secured the Democratic nomination, eight of these organizations, Alliance for Youth Action, Justice Democrats, IfNotNow Movement, March for Our Lives Action Fund, NextGen America, Student Action, the Sunrise Movement, and United We Dream Action called on Biden to endorse Sanders's agenda, including Medicare for All, a wealth tax, and a Green New Deal. Other prominent leftwing groups include the Working Families Party and People's Action. Much of the labor movement has always been congenial to socialist economic reforms. Meyerson, who has covered labor, estimated that "at least half the union staffers under thirty in D.C., no matter the union, think of themselves as socialists."

Many elected Democrats are socialists in all but name. Since 1932, the Democratic Party has never been, strictly speaking, a

358 "capitalist party" or a "corporate party," as the orthodox Marxists in DSA assert. It has always been mixed in its loyalties to labor and capital, and has included politicians whose primary loyalty is to the former rather than the latter. These politicians, often backed by organized labor, have proposed measures that would introduce elements of socialism within capitalism. In the House of Representatives, the Progressive Caucus, which Sanders and Congressman Ron Dellums, a member of DSA, founded in 1991, has 95 members. Its two co-chairs both endorsed Sanders for president. Its key agenda items are Medicare for All, a Green New Deal, and a wealth tax.

In the Senate, about one-fourth to one-third of the Democrats regularly champion bills that would shift power to labor. Sanders has now gotten 16 sponsors for the Workplace Democracy Act and 14 for Medicare for All. Senator Edward Markey got 14 sponsors for his and Ocasio-Cortez's proposal for a Green New Deal. Regulars on Sanders's bills include Warren, Sherrod Brown from Ohio, Tammy Baldwin from Wisconsin, and Jeff Merkley from Oregon.

During the Democratic primary, *Jacobin* drew sharp contrasts between Warren and Sanders, but their platforms were virtually identical. Warren emphasized the need for a wealth tax far more than Sanders did. She also stood on picket lines and proposed putting workers on corporate boards, as well as federal chartering of corporations, which would allow the government to regulate corporate behavior. Earlier, she was responsible for the creation of the Consumer Finance Protection Board. In Barack Obama's first term, she was the principal critic of the administration's coddling of the financial industry.

Her foes on Wall Street discounted her claim to be "capitalist to the bone." "She says she's a capitalist, but she's not a capitalist. She's really a democratic socialist in some ways. She wants to fundamentally change how an American company is governed," financier Steven Rattner declared. Many of her supporters also saw through her protestations. "I'm for Warren," John Turner, a young debate coach at Dartmouth, told me. "What is important is the issue

of equality. She has gone from being conservative Republican to a   359
democratic socialist." When I reminded him that Warren described
herself as a "capitalist," he said, "She has to say that. We don't have
a vocabulary for democratic socialism, so it is hard. But the wealth
tax fits that."

Sherrod Brown, who briefly contemplated a run for the presidency, is from Mansfield, Ohio, a town that has suffered from corporations shutting down or moving out. He has worked closely with
Sanders in the past. They opposed trade deals that they believed
would hurt American workers. Brown has proposed legislation that
would reward companies for investing in American jobs and that pay
a living wage. His bill would charge corporations a "freeloader fee"
when they pay their employees so little that they have to go on food
stamps and Medicaid. Like Warren, he steers clear of being identified as a socialist. When one writer suggested that he sounded like
Debs, he said, "Jeez, don't put that down."

In July 2020, Biden's task forces issued their reports. They
called for a large-scale industrial policy that would aid, but also
direct, American economic development; energy policies to achieve
a carbon-free economy by 2050; the creation of a "public option"
for national health insurance that could be the opening wedge for
a single-payer system; proposals to strengthen labor unions by
strengthening the enforcement of existing laws and removing legal
impediments to organizing that states have erected; and a redistributive tax increase on corporations and the wealthy to fund the new
programs and investments. These proposals represented a distinct
leftward shift from the conciliatory liberalism of the Clinton and
Obama presidencies to initiatives that would change the balance of
power between labor and capital.

The fate of these socialist initiatives, whether put forward by
socialists in name or not, will depend finally on whether there is sufficient pressure from below that can overcome predictable opposition from the "wealthy and powerful" both within the Republican
and Democratic parties. New Deal liberalism was sustained for

360 decades by the existence of a powerful labor movement and its allies in mainline churches, including, notably, the Catholic Church. These groups, too, had prominent national leaders. Is there something similar that could sustain a shift leftward in American politics, that could lead to the enactment of reforms that would create socialist institutions within capitalism?

The labor movement, which once represented a third of non-farm powers, and was a large political presence in the states and in Washington, is down to 10 percent (and only 6 percent in private industry). Its national leadership is weak and divided. It will be difficult to mount a challenge to conservative business predominant in American politics without a revival of the labor movement, which certainly could be aided by the enactment of the labor law reforms that Biden's workshops proposed. Many of the popular movements, like Black Lives Matter, also lack national leadership, which allowed the protests against police brutality to descend in some cities into mayhem. The coming years will test whether the growing sympathy for socialist reform among political intelligentsia and among the young can be buttressed by organized power and by effective leadership.

British Socialism and Nationalism

There are striking resemblances between the recent development of socialist politics in Britain and the United States. The revival is concentrated among young people in large metro areas and college towns; the leading issues have included climate change, growing inequality, student debt, deteriorating public services, support for immigration and minority rights, gender identity, and job security. Both movements were led by septuagenarian veterans of the new left—Jeremy Corbyn and Bernie Sanders.

But the difference is that in the case of Great Britain, there has been a public discussion of socialism (not confined to the academy and small journals) for over a century, and a major political party, Labour, that since 1918 has at least been nominally committed to socialism. Labour, with a powerful union movement underpinning it, actually has also had a chance to put its very non-Marxist socialist politics into practice.

There may be a lesson for American socialism in Corbyn and Labour's abysmal failure in the December 2019 elections. This was due in large part to Corbyn and the Labour Party's response to Brexit. That may seem peculiar to Britain, but it reflected a rejection of a nationalist outlook that had been key to Labour's success

362 after World War II. Labour's rout may also have been due to the kind of sociocultural factors that have shaped the outlook of American socialists and have made it difficult to conceive of socialism as a majority politics.

The Origins of British Socialism
The British Labour Party was always the least Marxist of European socialist parties. It didn't even commit itself to socialism until 1918, 18 years after it was founded. British socialism began with Robert Owen's communal enterprises. In the late nineteenth century, as socialists began to organize politically, the two most prominent groups were the Christian Socialists and the Fabians. And to this day, both groups play important roles in British politics.

The British Christian Socialists, like their American counterparts, were primarily drawn from low church (Quaker, Methodist) Protestant denominations. Influenced by the theory of evolution, they conceived of God working his will in the world to create the Kingdom of God on Earth. They stressed the brotherhood or fellowship of man as the overriding ethical concern; they rejected class conflict as a means toward socialism. One of their early leaders was Ramsay Mac-Donald, who later became the first Labour prime minister.

The Fabian Society originated in 1884 as a spin-off from the Christian Fellowship of New Life. The Fabians were primarily Christian Socialists who wanted to work for immediate economic reforms. The society was named in honor of Roman general Quintus Fabius Maximus Verrucosus who sought a slow step-by-step victory, rather than a single climactic victory against the superior Carthaginian army. Many of the famous British socialist intellectuals and politicians belonged at one point to the Fabian Society, including (atheist) George Bernard Shaw, Sidney and Beatrice Webb, H. G. Wells, Clement Attlee, Anthony Crosland, Harold Wilson, Tony Benn, and Tony Blair.

Its guiding philosophy was reform, not revolution. Eduard Bernstein, who lived in London from 1887 to 1901, had been inspired

by the Fabians. There were political differences among the Fabians,
but they became known for their support for ameliorative social
reform, including national health insurance, and for the nationalization of industry. They were statists; they were not enamored of actual
working-class ownership and control. Shaw quipped that "an army of
light is no more to be gathered from the human product of nineteenth
century civilization than grapes are to be gathered from thistles."

British Marxism was initially an import from Germany. It only
played a significant role during the Great Depression when, convinced that capitalism would collapse of its own accord and preparing
the way for socialism, Harold Laski and other Labour Party Marxists
argued against Keynes's proposals for bringing the economy out of
its slump. During Labour's brief time in power from 1929 to 1931, the
debate over policy, Keynes wrote, was polarized between "the pessimism of the revolutionaries who think that things are so bad that
nothing can save us but violent change, and the pessimism of the
reactionaries who consider the balance of our economic and social
life so precarious that we must risk no experiments."

Socialist Nationalism

British socialism really came into its own in July 1945, when the
Labour Party, led by an Oxford-educated lawyer, Clement Attlee,
took office with a majority on a promise to establish "the socialist
commonwealth of Great Britain." With Britain, once the proud leader
of world capitalism, heavily in debt and its empire dissolving, Attlee
abandoned the dreams of imperial Britain and focused instead on
reviving the British nation. His was a combination of socialism and
nationalism.

The Labour government established a National Health Service that employed doctors and owned hospitals and provided free
healthcare to British citizens. The government nationalized about
20 percent of the economy, including gas and electricity, mining,
radio, civil airlines, railroads, and trucking. It did so by creating
public corporations that were run independently by boards of

364   directors appointed by the relevant government minister. Labour's postwar nationalizations made no provision for including worker or union representation. It was government through experts as the Fabians had advocated.

In 1952, Aneurin Bevan, who as health minister had overseen the creation of the National Health Service and who was seen as the leader of the party's left wing, defended the Labour government's approach to socialism:

> A mixed economy is what most people of the West would prefer: The victory of Socialism need not be universal to be decisive. . . . It is neither prudent, nor does it accord with our conception of the future, that all forms of private property should live under perpetual threat.

According to Bevan, a full-blown socialism would consist of "public property" being the dominant, but not the only, type of property ownership. It would not entail direct worker control and ownership of the means of production. The working class would be represented through the state. The Attlee government also broke from Marxist orthodoxy by promoting economic nationalism. Historian David Edgerton recounts in *The Rise and Fall of the British Nation* that, in its 1945 manifesto, the party's election year platform, the term "socialism" appeared once, and "socialist" twice, but "nation" and "national" nearly 50 times.

For Labour, putting Britain first meant abandoning the economic liberalism and globalism of free trade and the gold standard. "Leaving behind economic liberalism meant creating not just an economic border but increasingly a culture of national self-supply," Edgerton wrote. The Attlee government used tariffs and subsidies to boost British industry and agriculture, and kept in place wartime capital controls to discourage the export of capital. And the strategy worked. Britain, which had relied on food imports since the repeal of the Corn Laws in 1846, became self-sufficient in agriculture. By 1950, a reviving British economy was leading the world in car exports and had the world's highest proportion of workers engaged in manufacturing. Stalin and the Nazis robbed the term "national socialism" of any except the most heinous connotations, but what the Attlee government did combined a commitment to democratic socialism with one to economic nationalism.

In 1951, Labour lost its parliamentary majority to the Conservatives, even though it won a higher percentage of the popular vote. Labour did not return to power until 1964 under economist Harold Wilson. Wilson had little interest in expanding public ownership beyond renationalizing steel. Instead, Wilson stressed what he called "democratic" and "socialist" planning. He established a new Ministry of Technology and Department of Economic Affairs to promote economic growth. He increased funding for universities and established polytechnics. But in 1970, with the economy having slowed down, and the government forced to devalue the pound, Wilson lost a close election to the Tories.

Out of power, Labour moved left under the leadership of Tony Benn, who became chairman of Labour's National Executive Committee. Benn, the son of a former Labour MP and of a feminist theologian, was a Fabian and Christian Socialist who wrote that his socialism "owes much more to the teachings of Jesus . . . than to the writings of Marx, whose analysis seems to lack an understanding of the deeper needs of humanity."

As Wilson's Minister of Technology, Benn had embraced the prime minister's emphasis on economic growth rather than public ownership. A number of things influenced Benn's move leftward. Benn was impressed by a "work-in" at the Clyde Shipyards, where the workers, in defiance of a government plan to shut down the yards, kept on the job until the Tory government gave in and submitted a plan for maintaining the shipyards. Benn also fell under the sway of new leftists from the Trotskyist International Marxist

366   Group who established an Institute for Workers' Control. In 1971, Benn outlined a plan for "industrial democracy" to entrust "individual firms to the people who work in them."

In 1973, the Labour Party, urged on by Benn, issued a program drafted by socialist Stuart Holland that combined a call for industrial democracy with extensive nationalization and planning. A National Investment Bank would purchase controlling shares in the 25 largest corporations; and the government would assert its power to oversee the investments of a hundred other corporations. Wilson, who had remained party leader, was unenthusiastic. When Labour regained Downing Street the next year, Wilson installed Benn as the Secretary of State for Industry, a position that would presumably put him in charge of implementing the manifesto. But industry pressure and opposition from civil servants led to Wilson ignoring the plan.

Benn had opposed Britain's entry in 1973 into the European Economic Community (EEC), the precursor of the European Union, under the Conservatives, and in 1975 Labour held a referendum on whether Britain should remain in it. Wilson allowed his ministers to vote their conscience, and Benn led the opposition to the EEC, charging that it was a "capitalist club" that would restrict Britain's ability to protect its industries. But with Labour divided and the Tories united in favor of remaining in the EEC, the referendum passed easily with 67.2 percent of the vote. Benn had been repudiated and was subsequently demoted from Secretary of State for Industry to Secretary of State for Energy. The affirmation of Britain's entry into the EEC and demotion of Benn spelled the end of British socialist nationalism.

Rolling Back Socialist Nationalism

Margaret Thatcher, who held office from 1979 to 1990, was a classical proponent of the free market. She believed in the employers' side of what Polanyi termed the double movement of capitalism. She set out to destroy what the Labour Party had wrought since 1945. That included nationalizations, union advances, and local control

of taxes and public investments. To the extent that Labour had created countervailing institutions—the hallmark of socialism within
capitalism—she wanted to destroy them. "We have done more to
roll back the frontiers of socialism than any previous Conservative
government," Thatcher boasted in 1982 at the Conservative Party
conference.

In six successive acts from 1980 to 1990, Thatcher made it
increasingly difficult for labor unions to organize and to strike.
Due in good part to these acts, labor union membership fell from
11,498,000 in 1979 to 9,585,000 in 1991—from over 50 percent to
less than 35 percent of workers. That reduced the power of unions to
determine wage and working conditions within industries as well as
weakening the Labour Party, which depended on organized labor for
votes, money, and electioneering.

Thatcher sold off the industries that the Labour Party had
nationalized, including British Aerospace, British Telecom, British
Gas, British Steel, British Shipbuilders, and electric and gas utilities. She even sold off government research institutes, such as the
Plant Breeding Institute. She slashed spending on education and
housing, skewed the tax code toward the wealthy, and transferred
the power of local governments, which were often in Labour Party
hands, to the national government.

Thatcher repudiated the Labour Party's economic nationalist
agenda, which to a great extent prior Conservative governments had
shared. She removed capital controls on currency convertibility and
on foreign investment and allowed foreign investors to buy British
assets, including banks, at their pleasure. Her "big bang" deregulated London's banking industry. According to a BBC report 30 years
later, the big bang produced "a free-for-all as brokers, jobbers, and
the City's traditional merchant banks merged. Some were bought by
UK clearing banks but many more were snapped up by much bigger
U.S., European, and Japanese banks."

Disadvantaged by an overvalued pound caused by high interest
rates and by government neglect, British manufacturing sharply

declined. Britain became a net importer of manufactured goods and of foodstuffs. London, buoyed by the growth in financial services, became wealthier, while the towns and cities, particularly in the North, that had been devoted to manufacturing and mining went into arrears. Thatcher was forced out of office by her own party in 1990—ironically—over her refusal to join the European Exchange Rate Mechanism, the precursor of the Euro. There were limits to Thatcher's abandonment of the national economy. She was replaced by John Major, who, racked by a succession of scandals, was defeated for reelection in 1997 by Labour candidate Tony Blair.

Tony Blair and the Third Way

Tony Blair and his Chancellor of the Exchequer, Gordon Brown, temporarily resurrected the Labour Party's electoral fortunes—Blair and then Brown would hold office from 1997 to 2010—and they also shored up some parts of the British welfare state. Blair introduced a minimum wage that aided the poor and put money back into education. But with respect to British socialism and its national agenda, they represented a continuation of Thatcher's policies. When asked what her greatest achievement was, Thatcher responded, "Tony Blair and New Labour. We forced our opponents to change their minds."

Blair and Brown let Thatcher's financial deregulation stand. Brown went a step further. He took the Bank of England, which had charge of monetary policy, and the Financial Services Authority, which oversaw the banks, out of Treasury and made them independent agencies, removing them from direct public accountability. Instead of funding infrastructure improvements with public money through taxes, Blair slashed corporate taxes and used Private Finance Initiatives (PFIs) to finance school, hospital, road, and other myriad repairs. Businesses provided the capital in the form of long-term loans with generous interest that taxpayers would have to pay back over 20 or 30 years. The PFIs, as the New Left Review's Robin Blackburn wrote, "brought a deterioration in public-sector service standards and democratic accountability."

With a large majority, Blair could have repealed the employment   369
laws that Thatcher had passed to hamstring labor unions, and real-
tered the balance of power between capital and labor, but he never
attempted to do so. Convinced that Thatcher's defeat of the miners'
strike in 1984–85 had cemented her popularity, he distanced the
party and prime ministership from labor unions by ignoring the
party institutions like the National Executive Committee where
unions had influence and by soliciting business political funding to
reduce the party's reliance on union money. He didn't re-nationalize
the firms that Thatcher had sold off.

Blair had promised "a new Britain" and "a nation with pride in
itself," but ended up binding Britain's economy closer to that of a
German-led Europe and its foreign policy to an American-led imperium. Blair followed Major's, but not Thatcher's, lead by locking
Britain into the EU, including its immigration and asylum policies. Blair actually hastened the influx of unskilled or semi-skilled
Eastern Europeans into Britain, which helped precipitate the crisis
over Brexit.

Blair and American president Bill Clinton advocated a "third
way"—in Blair's case, between socialism and Thatcher's laissez-
faire capitalism. They endorsed spurring growth through outsourcing
and financial deregulation—an approach to finance that helped pave
the way for the Great Recession. As prime minister, Blair joined
Clinton in proselytizing for globalization—an approach that was
antithetical to the socialist nationalism that the Labour Party had
embraced after World War II. "I hear people say we have to stop and
debate globalization," he said in a 2005 speech. "You might as well
debate whether autumn should follow summer."

In 2007, Brown succeeded Blair, who had worn out his welcome by gulling the public about the threat of Iraqi "weapons of
mass destruction" and committing British forces to the ill-fated
American invasion of Iraq. If Brown had called an election that year,
he might have won, but he waited until 2010, during the throes of
the Great Recession. Blamed in part for Britain's financial crash,

370   Brown lost to Tory David Cameron. Cameron, following the lead of
        Thatcher during the deep 1979 recession, cut spending and raised
        taxes. As a result, Britain didn't really escape negative growth until
        2013. While Cameron's policies had made things worse, much of the
        public still blamed New Labour for the recession, and in 2015, with
        the economy finally picking up, Cameron easily defeated Labour
        candidate Ed Miliband. Miliband resigned as party leader after
        the defeat, and he was succeeded, to the astonishment of Labour's
        members of Parliament, by Jeremy Corbyn.

The Rise of Jeremy Corbyn

In 2013, Miliband had accepted the recommendation of a commission that the party should choose its leader by an overall vote of the
membership rather than the current method of giving members a
third of the vote and apportioning unions and Labour members of
Parliament a third each of the vote. Blair and New Labour favored the
change because they thought it would help distance the party from
union control. In addition, Miliband recommended giving those
who pledged support for the party's principles and paid a modest fee
a chance to vote in the leadership election.

None of the initial candidates to succeed Miliband came
from the MPs who had opposed New Labour. At a meeting, leftwing Labour MPs, having failed to recruit more prominent candidates, chose Corbyn, a crusty, little-known, rebellious backbencher,
to represent them. In his campaign for the leadership, Corbyn
denounced the Tory austerity and repudiated his own party's participation in the Iraq war. He appealed for a type of society where
"we each care for all, everybody, caring for everybody else; I think it's
called socialism."

Britain's mainstream papers, including the *Guardian* and *Financial Times*, adamantly opposed his candidacy. Blair warned that the
Labour Party was in "mortal danger." But Corbyn was able to sidestep the major papers and the Labour Party's established leadership.

He and John McDonnell, who managed his campaign, and his campaign staffers recruited 16,000 volunteers. They waged a campaign over social media. And two of the major unions hoping to "break the grip of the Blairites" backed him.

Inspired by Corbyn and his attack against Cameron's austerity, 183,658 joined the party from May to September, and another 110,827 purchased voting rights as supporters. Corbyn won 59.5 percent of the vote. One post-mortem described Corbyn's recruits as "a coalition of idealistic youngsters, anti-austerity union activists, and grizzled left-wingers returning to the party they quit in disgust under Blair." Vernon Coaker, who ran one of the rival campaigns, attributed Corbyn's success to his appealing to a "moral sense of purpose rooted in Methodism, rooted in Christian socialism, rooted in the Levelers. . . . Jeremy's got that at the same time as other Labour people have lost it."

In the wake of Corbyn's victory, McDonnell and Jon Lansman, who got his start as a 24-year-old working on Benn's 1981 campaign for deputy leader, decided to establish a new organization that would mobilize the young volunteers from the campaign. In October 2015, Lansman, together with James Schneider, a recent Oxford graduate, and two schoolteachers, Emma Rees and Adam Klug, created Momentum. Initially an independent organization, it would eventually become a formal part of the Labour Party in order to fend off Trotskyist groups that wanted to use it as a recruiting ground. Over the next six months, it would attract about 4,000 members through online petitions and would begin to build a rudimentary grassroots organization. Then came Brexit and the attempt to unseat Corbyn.

A Sixties-Style Anti-imperialist
Corbyn was known as a protégé of Tony Benn, but it was not so much of Benn the economic nationalist, but of Benn who, after he lost the race for the party's second-in-command in 1981, increasingly turned his attention to foreign affairs. Corbyn, born in 1949, first

372 became involved in politics through the Campaign for Nuclear Disarmament, where much of the British new left of the sixties cut their
teeth. When he graduated from high school, he joined the British
equivalent of the Peace Corps, the Voluntary Service Overseas, and
was sent to Jamaica to teach school. He later toured Latin America,
where he became enamored of the Latin American left. (His second
and third wives both came out of the Latin American left.)

He returned to England and settled in North London, where
in 1983 he was first elected to Parliament. His main focus was foreign affairs, where he espoused a sixties-style anti-imperialism
directed at the U.S. and his own country. He backed Fidel Castro
in Cuba, Daniel Ortega in Nicaragua, Hugo Chavez in Venezuela,
Nelson Mandela in South Africa (Corbyn was arrested several
times in anti-Apartheid demonstrations), and the Palestinian
opposition to the Israeli occupation. In 1984, he and Benn got
in trouble with Labour leadership for inviting Sinn Fein leader
Gerry Adams to Parliament during the Irish Republican Army's
war against the British in Northern Ireland. He opposed Blair's
and Clinton's bombing of Iraq in 1998, and was a founder of the
Stop the War Coalition against the British and American invasion
of Iraq. In 2015, before he was recruited to run for leader, he was
hoping that the new party leader would appoint him to the Foreign
Affairs Select Committee.

Over the years, he deferred on domestic questions to his friend
and ally John McDonnell. McDonnell, the son of a Liverpool dock-
worker, went to a night school college and later got a master's degree
in politics, and became a policy advisor in the early 1980s to the radical Greater London Council before Thatcher shut it down. In 1997,
he was elected to Parliament. When asked in 2006 what were his
greatest influences, he cited, "Marx, Lenin, and Trotsky." He would
often describe himself as a "Marxist," but as his influence on Corbyn's economics would reveal, his positions were more in line with
Benn's socialism of the early 1970s than with the *Communist Manifesto* or Lenin's *State and Revolution*.

Corbyn Accepts Brexit

In the 2015 election, Cameron had promised Eurosceptic Tories and supporters of the United Kingdom Independence Party (UKIP) that he would hold a referendum the next year on the United Kingdom's membership in the EU. Cameron expected the referendum to fail easily, but to his surprise, it passed, 52 to 48 percent in June. The vote cut across party lines with Tory middle-class voters teaming up with Labour voters in towns devastated by deindustrialization to pass the referendum. Tory and Labour critics of the result blamed it on white racism and imperial nostalgia. But as Edgerton convincingly demonstrates in his account of post–World War II Britain, British nostalgia about the past wasn't for the days of Queen Victoria, but for the postwar period after the empire was dissolved when Britain enjoyed national self-sufficiency under governments that urged people to "buy British."

There was a small group of Labour members, founded in 2010 and dubbed Blue Labour, whose founder, Maurice Glasman, campaigned for Brexit, but the majority of Labour's MPs had been in favor of remaining. Corbyn, who had earlier joined Benn in calling for Britain to leave the "capitalist club," backed "remain," but on the eve of the vote, he told a television interviewer that he was "seven or seven and a half" out of ten in favor of remaining in the EU. The MPs blamed Corbyn's lukewarm support for the referendum passing and also for Labour setbacks in local elections earlier that year. That June, 75 percent of Labour MPs voted "no confidence" in Corbyn, precipitating a recall election. Corbyn was again believed to be doomed, but with Momentum, whose membership had doubled almost overnight after the announcement of the recall, taking to the streets and online, Corbyn got 61 percent of the vote against the recall.

As the debate over Brexit proceeded, Corbyn faced a difficult choice. While many of Labour's new voters, drawn from young college-educated cosmopolitans, had backed "remain," Labour's older blue-collar pro-"leave" rank-and-file provided the decisive

374   margin in two-thirds of Labour constituencies. If Labour were to oppose Brexit even after the referendum had won, it would risk these constituencies and any hope of a majority. With some unintended assistance from Tory prime minister Theresa May, who had replaced a chastened Cameron after Brexit had passed, Corbyn finessed the conflict within his political base.

In January of 2017, Corbyn upset the Remainers by declaring his support for leaving the European Union and eliminating free movement among the EU nations. He favored a "soft Brexit" that would preserve Britain's role in the single trading market, but allow the British to use "state aid," which had been forbidden by EU regulations, to rebuild its industry. In April, Theresa May, wanting a clear mandate to negotiate, called an election for June. At the time, Corbyn trailed May by as many as 24 points in opinion polls. But Corbyn had two advantages over May. First, by being for Brexit, Corbyn won the support of blue-collar Brexit voters in Labour's traditional strongholds. And by favoring a "soft Brexit," Corbyn won the support of the young Remainers in London or Oxbridge who saw his plan as preferable to May's hardline proposals for Brexit.

Secondly, Corbyn won the battle of the manifestos. Labour's manifesto was in the Fabian tradition of Attlee's 1945 and Wilson's 1974 manifestos. It promised to re-nationalize rail, energy, water, and mail services, all of which had fared poorly in the private sector. It proposed to restore higher tax rates on the wealthy and business to fund free childcare and elder care and to prevent planned cuts in welfare and social security and to end fees on university enrollment. At the same time, the manifesto acknowledged the complaints about open borders voiced by "leave" voters. It promised to "protect those already working here" by ending "the exploitation of migrant labour undercutting workers' pay and conditions."

The Tory manifesto, on the other hand, ignored years of growing resentment toward Cameron's austerity policies. It stipulated that before receiving home healthcare, the elderly would have to exhaust the value of their savings, including the value of their homes. It also

set new limits on social security payments for pensioners. These   375
provisions provoked an outcry. May tried to revise them, but the
damage was already done, and she and the Tories sank in the polls.
May barely edged out Corbyn by 42 to 40 percent. If the election
had taken place several weeks later, Corbyn would have replaced her
as prime minister. If that had happened, the election would have
seen a new kind of majority coalition for Labour. Corbyn had solid-
ified his control of Labour, but as it happened, the election was the
high-water mark for his leadership.

Labour's Millennial Supporters

The 2017 election showed how Labour's political base was changing.
Labour dramatically increased its margin among the young, the
college-educated, the urban, and the black and minority voters.
Labour got 31 percent of the 18- to 24-year-old vote in 2010; 43 percent in 2015; and 62 percent in 2017. In other words, over seven years,
Labour doubled its percentage among the youngest voters. Labour
got 30 percent of the 25- to 34-year-old vote in 2010 (less than the
Conservatives); 36 percent in 2015; and 56 percent in 2017. If the
vote had been held among 18- to 34-year-olds, Corbyn would have
won in a landslide. The resemblance to Sanders's base is striking.

Labour also dramatically increased its vote among the college-
educated. It went from losing this vote by a point in 2015 to winning
it by 17 points in 2017, 49 to 32 percent. It also increased its vote in
greater London from nine points in 2015 to 32 points in 2017; and
among Blacks and other minorities, among whom it took 73 percent of
the vote. The reasons that drove young people to Corbyn and Labour
were probably very similar to those that drove young people in the
United States to Bernie Sanders. Their expectations of a future way
of life had not been met. Their lives had proven less secure and stable
than they expected. They were not confident their situations would
improve. Wrote the late Mark Fisher, a hero to many of the activists in
Momentum, "It is not an exaggeration to say that being a teenager in
late capitalist Britain is now close to being reclassified as a sickness."

After the election, Momentum grew to 40,000 members and about 200 local groups, primarily based in England. In September 2018, a slate endorsed by Momentum won all nine open seats on Labour's National Executive Committee. At the annual Labour Party conferences, Momentum started a parallel festival of ideas, called "The World Transformed." By 2019, when I attended the September conference in Brighton, TWT, headquartered in a big park and two gigantic tents, and attended by thousands of Labour delegates and visitors, looked like something between a county fair and a campground revival meeting.

During Corbyn's time as leader, his followers tried to forge what he called a "twenty-first century socialism" for Britain. Labour think tanks, some old and some new—including the New Economics Foundation and the Center for Labour and Social Studies (CLASS)—issued reports and analyses and recommendations for Labour's manifesto. Organizations like Extinction Rebellion and Reclaim the Power sprung up to promote climate change and a Green New Deal. *New Left Review* remained the flagship of British socialism, but it was joined by webzines like *Red Pepper, Open Democracy, Canary,* and *Evolve Politics.*

If there was an idea that united the different groups, it was combating climate change through a Green New Deal—an idea that had originated with Ocasio-Cortez and Senator Ed Markey's plan in the United States. The Green New Deal was seen as a way of addressing a major challenge to the planet with an "ecosocialist" program that would require public ownership and lead to full employment. Grace Blakeley, a fellow from the pro-Labour Institute for Public Policy Research, framed the choice as being between "extinction and utopia." Some of the groups like Extinction Rebellion demanded a carbon-free Britain by 2025; others settled on 2030.

There were also interesting attempts to resume the attempt in the early 1970s to go beyond the Fabian program for nationalization. A group called "We Own It" devised complicated schemes for democratic ownership and control ("This isn't about nationalizing") of public transport, water, energy, and the Royal Mail. The Green New

Deal embraced democratic planning of resource use. But as I found
at the DSA convention in the United States, the proposals coming
out of Britain's new left also reflected the age and social and economic circumstances of the people making them and were not really
designed with the idea of creating popular majorities that would
unite different parts of the population. They were based on faith
rather than political calculation.

A prime example is the much-touted London-based Extinction Rebellion, which first made the news when it blocked bridges
over the Thames in November 2018 to protest government inaction.
Its demand for a carbon-free Britain in 2025 would have entailed
replacing millions of automobiles and 90 percent of home heating
devices, suspending air travel, and radically altering people's diet
and work lives. Most scientists would regard 2030 as a radical and
probably unattainable target without massive disruption and 2050
as a reasonable one.

There was no support at The World Transformed for Brexit.
The young British left was squarely in the "remain" camp befitting
above all their post-industrial metropolitan location at the center
of globalized finance. Their analysis betrayed a contempt for British
nationalism. It attributed support for Brexit to imperial nostalgia
or anti-immigrant racism. There was no support for restrictions
on immigration to protect workers from low-wage competition. On
the last day of the Brighton conference, when the MPs had to leave
for the opening of Parliament, the activists who remained passed a
resolution on immigration to "maintain and extend free movement
rights"—a direct repudiation of Labour's 2017 manifesto, which had
said "freedom of movement will end."

The Socialist Manifesto

In June 2019, Theresa May resigned, having failed to win Parliament's agreement to a Brexit deal she had negotiated with the EU.
The Conservative MPs elected Boris Johnson, a former journalist,
mayor of London, and May's former foreign minister, to replace

her. After several false starts, Johnson finally got a majority in Parliament to agree to the outline of a new Brexit agreement he had negotiated with the EU, and to call for a new election in December. Almost 20 points ahead in the polls, Johnson wanted to use the election to give himself an unassailable majority to finalize a deal with the EU.

Over the six weeks of the campaign, Johnson and the Tories remained well ahead except during the week that Labour issued its manifesto. During that week, Johnson's campaign staff told the *Financial Times*, Corbyn and Labour pulled within four percentage points of the Tories. That suggested that whatever the electorate's opinion of Corbyn and of Labour's position on Brexit, it supported the most radical manifesto that Labour had ever issued. The manifesto backed widespread nationalization of the energy and transportation sectors and worker stock ownership in their businesses. It proposed a new Ministry for Employment Rights charged with "shifting the balance of power back towards workers."

But when the novelty of Labour's manifesto wore off, the Tories were able to reestablish their earlier lead. Conservatives routed Labour, winning 43.6 percent of the vote and 365 seats, to 32.2 percent and 202 seats for Labour. It was Labour's worst showing since 1935. Labour once again won the young—those 18 to 24—by 38 points over the Tories, and those 25 to 34 by 32 points. It also won those with a college degree or more. But it lost the working class decisively. Labour won London and the constituencies with a high percentage of professionals, but was blown away in small and mid-sized towns, even ones that had been Labour strongholds for almost a century. Labour lost most of what had once been its working-class base and relied for its support primarily on the younger urban voters who had come into the party in the last decade. It ceased to be a "workers' party" and became a party of college-educated cosmopolitans.

Reasons for Defeat

Labour might have lost in any case, but it lost decisively because it abandoned the commitment to nationalism that had been at the heart of the Labour Party's socialism since 1945. That was evident in its failure to develop a coherent position on Brexit. Under pressure from his cosmopolitan base, which favored holding a second referendum on Brexit, Corbyn capitulated. During the election, he promised to renegotiate in three months a Brexit agreement and then hold a binding referendum on it—in effect, to accomplish in three months what it had taken the Tories three years to do. Corbyn wouldn't take a position on how he would vote on the referendum, but his second-in-command, McDonnell, made it clear that, whatever the results of Corbyn's negotiation, he would vote for "remain." It was an utterly incoherent position, and also lacked any credibility.

In the election, Labour lost "remain" votes to the Liberal Democrats who promised to tear up Brexit and remain in the EU and they lost Labour supporters of "leave" to the Tories and their slogan of "Get Brexit Done." Corbyn's approach, it became clear, was not capable of winning a plurality, let alone a majority, of British voters.

Labour also lost because of Corbyn's personal unpopularity, but that factor was not unrelated to the stand Corbyn took on Brexit. The Tories were able to highlight Corbyn's various global allegiances to countries like Russia and Venezuela that had little good to say about Britain. Corbyn's old-style anti-imperialism undermined any attempt to appeal to British nationalism. Corbyn was also plagued by accusations of anti-Semitism in the Labour Party, some of which were justified. Laura Pidcock, an MP who lost her seat, summed up the problem with Corbyn's candidacy.

> When I knocked on your doors in 2017, so many of you talked about what a good guy he seemed, that he was on the side of the people. . . . In 2019, you seemed so much angrier about Jeremy Corbyn. I had a handful of angry people say "I would shoot him"

380   or "take a gun to his head" whilst in the next breath calling him
an extremist.

Finally, Labour may have suffered from being identified with
extreme positions on climate change, immigration, and gender identity. Two sociologists, Steve Hall and Simon Winlow, primarily
known for their work on criminal justice, put the problem in this way:

> Convincing an electoral majority in the grip of post-crash aus-
> terity that a progressive economic project based on public control
> of finance and investment is feasible would have been possible in
> an ambience of shared interests—prosperity, security, sustain-
> ability, and so on. Instead, the self-styled progressive liberal left
> relentlessly attacked the full spectrum of traditional institutions,
> beliefs, values, and identities.

After the election, there were troubling signs that the party's
new left had still not absorbed the lessons of Labour's defeat. In January 2020, as different candidates were vying to succeed Corbyn as
party leader, a heated controversy between a small, newly formed
transgender group and several venerable feminist groups made
headlines. Momentum and its candidate to succeed Corbyn threw
their support behind the transgender group, which was demanding
that the party *expel* the two feminist groups that wanted to be able
to limit their rape and shelter services to biological women. It was a
powerful sign of how much the Labour Party had become hostage to
a rarified cosmopolitan culture.

The question for Labour is whether it can develop a socialist
politics that retains the support and enthusiasm of millennials in
big metro centers and at the same time appeal to British voters who
don't live in London or a university town and don't have advanced
degrees and still carry with them a fondness for the British nation
and for a non-Marxist socialism. The response to Labour in the 2017
election and to its manifestos in 2017 and 2019 suggests that the

potential exists for a majority based on "shared interests" in "prosperity security, sustainability, and so on." But for Labour to succeed,
it has to frame these proposals in a way that respects and doesn't
denigrate British nationalism—a point that Jonathan Rutherford of Blue Labour made in his election post-mortem. "The democratic nation and its rule of law is the best means of safeguarding
our rights and freedoms," Rutherford wrote. "And the nation state is
still the best political unit to manage globalization in the interests of
a democratic polity."

At the end of January, Labour chose former Shadow Brexit Secretary Sir Keir Starmer as its leader. At first glance, he was a poor
choice. Starmer had been an outspoken proponent of "remain"
and of a second referendum—exactly the stance that had contributed to Labour's downfall. His choice appeared to reaffirm Labour's
abandonment of its older working-class roots and its embrace of
a London and university-based cultural insularity. But Starmer
attempted to revive the party's roots and to distance it from the
extreme stands taken by Momentum and its followers.

As a candidate for the leadership in January, Starmer made clear
he no longer opposed Brexit. "We are going to leave the EU in the
next few weeks and it is important for all of us, including myself, to
recognize that the argument about leave and remain goes with it,"
Starmer told the BBC. In September, as negotiations between the
Johnson administration and EU stalled, Starmer once again said, "I
don't think there's a case for reopening the issue of EU membership
of the EU. We have left. We need a deal."

Starmer repositioned Labour as a nationalist party. He rejected
demands from the Corbyn left that the BBC exclude two British
anthems, "Rule Britannia" and "Land of Hope and Glory," from its
annual eight-week music festival. In his speech to the annual Labour
conference in September 2020—dubbed "Labour Connected"
because it was conducted over Zoom—he spoke directly to the
voters who had deserted Labour. "We love this country as you do.
This is the country I grew up in. This is the country I will grow old

382 in." Glasman, the founder of Blue Labour, wrote that Starmer was "tapping into a form of modest Labour patriotism that had once had deep roots in the party and still has in the country."

Starmer also distanced Labour from the social and cultural controversies that had embroiled the party and isolated it from its working-class base. In January, Starmer had been the only one of the three leadership candidates not to endorse the transgender organization's call to expel the two feminist groups. In his address to Labour Connected, he described Britain as "a country in which we put family first." In June, he rejected calls by British supporters of Black Lives Matter to defund the police. And he expelled scores of members whose views of Jewry had gone beyond criticism of Israel into the netherworld of anti-Semitism.

But Starmer faces a formidable task winning back the Parliament in the next decade. Ousting Johnson and the Tories may prove difficult. After the election, Johnson chose not to ally his party to rightwing populists. He also drew selectively on Labour's tradition of economic nationalism. His budget included generous state aid to rebuild the industrial areas of England and money to repair the National Health Service. Johnson also promised to restore Britain's self-sufficiency in agriculture and to promote a campaign of "buy British." "The impression left," the *Guardian* wrote, "is that we are all Keynesians now." But Johnson stumbled in his handling of the coronavirus, and while he finally got a deal on Brexit with the EU, it, too, has met with criticism from supporters of leave and remain. Labour has made a comeback in the polls. It is conceivable, though not likely, that Labour, having revived its commitment to economic nationalism and shed its identification with the culture of Oxbridge, could be back as early as 2024, when the next general election is slated to occur.

Populism, Nationalism, and Socialism

This is Part Three in a trilogy that began with *The Populist Explosion* and continued with *The Nationalist Revival*. There is a connection among these subjects. The revival of populism, political nationalism, and socialism is a product of a breakdown in the consensus on the virtues of the free market and of globalization that had prevailed from the 1980s until the Great Recession. The pandemic and global recession are the severe blow to this older consensus. Here is how the rise of populism and nationalism bears on the rise of democratic socialism.

Populism

The rise of populism and of an us vs. them nationalism, which took place in the first two decades of the twenty-first century, are products of popular disillusionment with neoliberalism—with the promise of peace and prosperity under globalization and the free market. So, too, is the rise of a new democratic socialist politics in the United States and Great Britain. Populism, of course, is not itself a solution to the crisis created by the breakdown of the neoliberal consensus but the framework of a protest politics. Neither is the extreme nationalism of Trump or the AfD. They are part

384 of the breakdown of consensus. Democratic socialism, in some form, with or without the name, could be part of the eventual resolution of the crisis but only if socialists come to understand that they must develop a politics that addresses the uneven development of capitalism and the cultural differences that it has reinforced. That includes recognizing that nationalism, while abhorrent in its extreme forms, is an essential part of any resolution.

Populist appeals strike a chord with voters when politics and policies that have broadly united the electorate don't live up to their promises and when the dominant political and business leaders in Washington or London or Paris refuse to acknowledge that circumstances have changed. The populist parties and candidates are an early warning sign that a new direction and a new consensus is needed.

A populist campaign is particularly appropriate for a democratic socialist in the current post-Marxist era. The adversary is the same—the ruling class, the establishment—but what had been for socialists the widely accepted agent of change—the industrial working class—has been eclipsed by a diversified and stratified and sometimes very divided collection of wage and salary workers. They can best be described in the language of populism as "the people," "the 99 percent," or "working people." When some of the newly minted or old-time Marxists use terms like "class war" or appeal to a mythical "working class," they are evoking a theory of revolutionary change that 150 years have disproven. (My former colleague James Weinstein, who belonged to the Communist Party for a decade after World War II, used to tell the story of the Communist candidate for office in New York City who began his campaign speeches by addressing, "Workers and peasants of the Lower East Side.")

The virtue of Marx's theory of class was that it combined sociology and politics. The working class, which was just then emerging, was at once a mutually recognizable social group and a historical engine of change. It was a class *in itself* and *for itself*. But while academic sociologists and orthodox Marxists can make

elaborate sociological distinctions among and within classes in the
United States or Europe today, they carry little political weight. So,
too, does the pollsters' use of the term "working class" to refer to
voters with "some college" but not a four-year degree. (Junior college graduates, unite!)

Some socialists have picked up the term "professional-
managerial class"(PMC). In a debate in the New American Movement
in the early 1970s, Barbara and John Ehrenreich invented the term
to counter the view that post-industrial capitalism had spawned
a "new working class" that included upper-level-white-collar
workers. *Jacobin* used this term to distinguish supporters of Sanders
(the true working class) from Warren's backers (the PMC). But the
term is doubly misleading as a guide to socialist politics. It obscures
the leading role of nurses and schoolteachers—both of whom the
census classifies as professionals—in the labor movement and in
support for socialism in the United States today. The nurses' union
was one of the main supporters of Sanders's campaign. And it lumps
them or software developers or the other workers with advanced
degrees who make up a significant percentage of DSA's membership and Sanders's and Warren's donors in with corporate CEOs and
Wall Streeters who are generally opposed to socialist reforms such
as Warren and Sanders proposed in their campaigns. Populism has
reemerged on the left precisely because of the fatuity of attempts to
base a politics on a neo-Marxist class analysis.

Nationalism

In the United States and Great Britain, few on the left, let alone on the
socialist left, understand why nationalism is an integral part of any
socialist or economically progressive appeal. For orthodox Marxists,
their view of nationalism bears the stamp of Marx, Lenin, Trotsky,
and even Rosa Luxemburg: In his book *The Socialist Manifesto*, Sunkara quotes Luxemburg, "[The] Rights of Nations is nothing more
than a metaphysical cliché." Attacks against nationalism are rife in

socialist and leftwing journals. "There Is No Left Case for Nationalism," *Nation* senior editor Atossa Araxia Abrahamian declares. Blue Labour's support for national identity has been branded "bigoted" by its Labour foes.

In the United States, socialists and the left identify nationalism with Trump's America First—or even before that with support for unpopular wars in Vietnam and Iraq. In Britain, Labour Party intellectuals identify nationalism with UKIP and the European right. "There is a simple reason why pandering to nationalism will, in the end, always benefit the right: it is a tool employed by the ruling class to maintain their power and put blame for their failings somewhere else," Sabrina Huck writes in the party's unofficial website, Labour-List. In the United States, the disdain for nationalism extends to the sentiment of patriotism. "'Patriotism' is a Dead End for the Left," an article in *Jacobin* declares. In one Twitter poll conducted by a socialist writer, David Klion, only 12.3 percent of the respondents described themselves as "patriotic."

Strange as it may seem, a viable socialism must be nationalist. Its fundamental framework must be the nation and its citizens. For a democracy to function, its citizens must be clearly defined, their common commitment to the nation assumed. But socialists can be oblivious to this very simple idea. At the Labour Conference in Brighton, the "remain" faction proposed that temporary residents from other EU countries be allowed to vote in its national elections. That would be subversive to democracy.

Similarly, proposals for an advanced welfare state and a redistribution of wealth must rest on national boundaries. They must recognize that in order for a citizen to accept, for instance, "Medicare for All," they must be willing to pay high taxes to achieve coverage not only for themselves but for people they don't know and may never meet. If that latter group is not clearly defined and not limited to a nation's citizens—if, for instance, anyone who crosses the nation's borders can claim coverage, as some of the Democratic presidential candidates appeared to advocate during the 2020 primary—then many people won't support such proposals. Why should they pay their taxes to support people who don't share a common social and economic obligation to the nation?

Finally, where employment is not boundless, nations must protect the jobs of their workers by limiting immigration. If unions want to organize low-paid service workers, they cannot contend with a continuing surplus of immigrant workers eager to compete with those already employed. During the 2016 presidential campaign, when Sanders was rebuked by Vox editor Ezra Klein for opposing open borders, he replied, "No, that's a Koch Brothers proposal," referring to the rightwing business agenda of using unrestricted immigration and a labor surplus to drive down native workers' wages. Much of the plight of unskilled African American workers over the last 50 years was due to competition from unskilled immigrants. But America's socialist left is impervious to *any* restriction on immigration. "You can't talk about it," Dustin Guastella says.

When Sanders asked his supporters, "Are you willing to fight for that person who you don't even know as much as you're willing to fight for yourself?" the expected answer was "yes." But altruism has its limits. Our moral commitments go in concentric circles from family to friends to nation. They can extend to people of other nations, but not with the same intensity or commitment. Americans don't feel the same commitment to aiding the poor in Lahore (unless they happen to be Pakistani Americans) as they do to aiding the poor in Chicago. And the fact that they are willing to aid the poor in Chicago even if they live in Richmond, Virginia, shouldn't be trifled with by undermining our sense of common nationality. It's not just important for getting programs adopted; it's important for bridging the gap between America's disparate cultures and nationalities. Biden understood this in the 2020 election. Against Trump's exclusionary nationalism, he appealed for inclusive nationalism, a view of the "*United* States of America."

None of this is to say that socialists and the left can't support international cooperation to address problems that a single

388 nation cannot hope to address, such as climate change or the current pandemic, or that they can't support immigration or immigration reform. Or that socialists cannot be outraged by the Chinese regime's unconscionable treatment of the Uighurs. But when it comes to advocating a shift of power to labor and the expansion of democracy and equal rights, that must be done within the context of the nation. Much of the British Labour Party's failure under Corbyn lay in its abandonment of the party's commitment to economic nationalism and its equivocation on the subject of open borders. And American socialists—and shadow socialists—will not be able to escape their own cultural insularity until they come to terms with what their own national identity means to their politics.

Socialism

In his masterpiece, *The Economics of Feasible Socialism*, the late Alec Nove, a Russian expatriate who became a prescient expert on the Soviet economy, contended that the idea of socialism "should be conceivable within the lifespan of one generation—say in the next fifty years; conceivable, that is, without making extreme, utopian, and farfetched assumptions." Marx's own ideas seemed feasible in the 1880s—the industrial working class was expanding rapidly, along with the labor movement, and Europe had been riven by revolutions since 1789—but have proved to be utopian.

Socialists today who talk vaguely of an economy based on public ownership and control of the means of production—the standard Marxist formulation—are engaging in utopian thinking. When I pressed a young DSA member on the subject of how that would apply, say, to the computer industry, he replied, "I don't have an opinion." In *The Socialist Manifesto*, Sunkara used the model of a pizza sauce company that is transformed from owner-controlled to worker-controlled to illustrate the promise of socialism. That's the kind of argument by example that Robert Owen was making for what in retrospect were his relatively small textile plants. There already are and will be more worker-controlled enterprises, but it's not a

model that is easily transferrable to America's or Europe's large and
geographically dispersed corporations.

To be politically relevant, the left's idea of socialism must be
grounded in contemporary history. It need not, and can't be, an
inevitable outgrowth, but it has to be a *possible*—and in the eyes of
many—a *desirable* outcome. Citizens will not seek to replace capitalist with socialist institutions purely out of moral conviction.
They have to believe that purely market-based institutions have
dramatically failed to provide prosperity and well-being to workers
and consumers. And they might not seek the full socialization of an
industry. In many American industries, what is needed as a first step
is unionization or other forms of worker self-organization. That is a
prerequisite to any kind of worker co-determination on the ground
and to the creation nationally of what John Kenneth Galbraith called
"countervailing power." It's what Sanders in 1991 referred to as
"partnerships . . . between the private sector, the unions, the government, the working people."

In the wake of the pandemic and recession, the healthcare
industry certainly is a candidate for a partial public takeover. It has
clearly failed. So, too, are parts of the transportation sector. And as
the effects of climate change bear down, Americans, too, may finally
decide to increase public control over energy production and use.
Today's crisis has also laid bare the failure of the labor market to
provide equitable and needed outcomes. Many workers who are now
recognized to be "essential" to society, such as those in hospitals and
meat processing plants, barely can support families, while hedge
fund and real estate speculators, who do not make any contribution
to society's betterment, live in luxury.

By dramatizing the inequality of wealth and power, the pandemic and recession may have lent credibility to reforms that
might have seemed too radical for the public to contemplate. These
include some form of guaranteed annual income to cushion those
at the bottom from recession and depression and to sustain consumer demand; a massive investment in public welfare, including

390   schooling and healthcare (including universal, accessible health
insurance); a publicly subsidized and directed industrial policy
aimed at reviving American manufacturing, protecting the supply
chains of vital industries, converting to renewable energy, and chan-
neling the activity of the financial sector toward productive investment; universal access to broadband; and a radically redistributive
tax reform that undoes decades of regressive tax cuts on personal
and business income.

Many of these reforms would shift power from capital to
labor and make the country more democratic. They are currently
embraced not only by self-identified democratic socialists, but also
by "progressives" like Warren and Brown, by Biden in his rescue and
recovery plan and in Europe by part of the Green Parties and Social
Democratic Parties. And they are feasible within a generation as
the public has become aware in the wake of the Great Recession and
pandemic and recession of profound weaknesses in the economy
and the safety net. But while feasible, and possibly desirable for significant numbers of Americans, they are also likely to be resisted by
others. What will finally happen will be a product of politics.

The Polanyi Moment
We are experiencing a breakdown of capitalism similar to that which
Karl Polanyi described took place between the two world wars. In
the 1930s, protection against the vagaries of the free market and
the collapse of the gold standard came through state intervention
and the abandonment of the gold standard in favor of an economic
nationalism. At the extremes, it took two very different forms—
fascism in Central and Southern Europe and the New Deal in the
United States. In Europe, several forays to the left in France and
Spain were crushed by the right. Some countries, like Great Britain,
muddled through.

Today, the reign of globalization and market fundamentalism
is also breaking down and leaving the average citizen unprotected,
and perhaps with the onset of the pandemic, as much as during the

1930s. Add to that the threat of climate change. These menaces could justify massive state intervention and a dramatic shift away from private to public power. But as in the 1930s, the response to breakdown can take very different forms. In China, India, Russia, Turkey, Hungary, and Brazil, it seems to have already reinforced trends toward rightwing authoritarianism.

In Europe, the European Union, based on a promise of its upward economic convergence between North and South, and democratic convergence between East and West, is under stress, as countries in the prosperous North resist aiding those in the debt-stricken South, and as countries in the East, particularly Hungary and Poland, defy the democratic norms of the West. For the time being, France and Germany have been able to keep the peace, but in another variation of Jameson's quip, it is easier to see the end of the European Union than the end of European capitalism. How the countries of the European continent turn politically will depend on the fate of the EU.

In the United States, it also remains unclear what path the country will take. There is support among many Democrats for large-scale government intervention in the private market—and not just to deal with the pandemic and recession but to arrest the trends toward greater inequality, repair the safety net, and combat climate change. The clearest indication of that is in the change that came over the 2020 Biden campaign.

In a fundraiser held a couple months after announcing his presidential run, Biden assured wealthy donors that if he were elected, he wouldn't "demonize" them or threaten their standard of living. "Nothing would fundamentally change," he said. But during the campaign, and in the interval between the election and his inauguration, Biden showed that he appreciated the gravity of the challenge he faced. "I'm kind of in the position that FDR was," Biden told his biographer Evan Osnos. Biden and his advisors drew up ambitious plans that went beyond the immediate threat of the virus and of unemployment. He proposed massive government spending on infrastructure coupled with provisions that would require companies that receive funds to pay good wages and to allow unions to organize their workers. He proposed subsidies to multinational corporations that brought jobs back to the United States. He urged removing any tax incentives for companies to export jobs overseas. He also showed an understanding of how the uneven development of capitalism had divided the country politically. He proposed investments for the "forgotten" in rural America, including universal broadband and hospitals. These proposals made it into the extraordinarily ambitious rescue and recovery plans that Biden sent to Congress.

Biden's appointees also tilted leftward. The leftwing website The Intercept wrote, "In almost every spot so far named, Biden has chosen a person more progressive and less entrenched with Wall Street than the official who held the same position in 2009 under Obama." These included Yellen as treasury secretary and a former Warren aide as her deputy, two vigorous advocates of combating climate change—former secretary of state John Kerry as climate czar and Brian Deese as the head of the National Economic Council—two experts on income inequality, Jared Bernstein and Heather Boushey, for the Council of Economic Advisors, and a former union leader, Boston Mayor Marty Walsh, as Secretary of Labor.

Moreover, support for a new approach to capitalism was not limited to Democratic politicians and activists. In August 2019, the Business Roundtable, representing over 200 of America's largest corporations, issued a statement calling on corporations to reduce inequality and to heed the needs of stakeholders and not just shareholders. In September 2019, the *Financial Times* began a series of articles calling for a "reset of capitalism." Billionaire Ray Dallo, the highly regarded head of a leading hedge fund, Bridgewater Associates, declared in a speech at Harvard Law School that "capitalism needs to be reformed." Dallo also declared on the television show *60 Minutes*, "I'm a capitalist, and even I think capitalism is broken."

There are Republican politicians and intellectuals who have taken issue with what they call "market fundamentalism" and have

advocated a government "industrial policy" that promotes vital
industries. They include likely presidential aspirant Marco Rubio,
and intellectuals from a new journal, *American Affairs*, and a new
thinktank, American Compass. "With a sensible industrial policy,
Rubio wrote in the *New York Times*, "workers will take precedence
over short-term corporate gain." Rubio also signed a Labor Day
statement drafted by American Compass.

The United States may not, however, be ready for the kind
of clear break with a prevailing consensus that New Deal liberals, on the hand, and European fascists, on the other, made with
laissez-faire capitalism after World War II. There is still strong
opposition within the business community and the Republican
leadership to transforming the relationship between government
and the economy and to redistributing power and wealth. Republicans may acquiesce in huge spending bills to halt the pandemic and
speed the economic recovery, but not to measures putting the private economic under public control at the state or federal level. As
the rise of the Tea Party in 2009 showed, there is popular resistance
to increasing the power of government. And America's left has still
not built the popular organizations, including unions, that could
underlay in the states and nationally a genuinely democratic rather
than authoritarian response to the current crisis. The challenges the
country faces may well be comparable to those faced in the 1930s,
but truly dramatic change—whether on the left or the right—may
have to await neoliberal capitalism's next nervous breakdown.

Socialist Prospects

Over the coming decade, more young Americans will embrace some
version of democratic socialism. The 2020 election saw two new
socialists, Jamaal Bowman in New York and Cori Bush in St. Louis,
elected to Congress. If DSA can overcome its orthodox Marxism
and old left sectarian impulses, it should continue to grow. But it is
unlikely that a socialist presidential candidate will soon appear and be
as successful as Sanders was. With the median age of voters being 50,

394   too many older Americans outside college towns and post-industrial enclaves still continue to identify socialism with the Soviet Union or Cuba. And many still resist socialism simply as another instance of "tax and spend" and "big government" liberalism.

After the 2020 congressional elections, several Democrats from formerly Republican districts complained about being identified as "socialists" because of the party's association with Sanders and Ocasio-Cortez. Abigail Spanberger, who represented a longtime Republican suburban Richmond district and barely eked out a win in 2020, advised House Democrats never "to use the word 'socialist' or 'socialism' again." Ocasio-Cortez called her comments "irresponsible," but the Richmond congresswoman had a point. Many voters who were willing to accept Democratic healthcare reform proposals still bristle at the idea of socialism. Outside of college towns or post-industrial metro centers, it is very risky for a Democrat to run as a "socialist."

But as memories of the Soviet Union fade, and as the urgency of reforming capitalism and combating climate change grow, many Americans may find the idea and the term of *socialism*—with the connotation of putting the interests of "society" above those of private enterprise—the best way of describing the alternative to a failing free-market capitalism. The label "liberal" has become too closely identified with the extremes of social liberalism and identity politics. It has lost its mooring in New Deal economics. And "progressive" has always lacked content.

Of course, Americans could follow the lead of leftwing academics and decide to call their politics "social democratic," or they could devise an entirely new name. What matters most is not the movement's name but its collective aims. And these, the reclamation of public power over the direction of private enterprise and the rehabilitation of a decaying democracy, have become urgent in the wake of the pandemic, the economic recession, and climate change.

Nicholas Lemann and Jimmy P. So guided me through this and the prior three volumes. It has been a real pleasure to work with them. Camille McDuffie is a superb publisher and publicist. Miranda Sita prodded me to use social media and took very flattering photos of me. And my agent, Rafe Sagalyn, hooked me up with these people in the first place.

A host of friends helped me with the three small books on which this one is based—their names are inscribed in the back of those books. I should mention, though, that I have argued—and argue is the right word, since we often disagree—many of the points in these books with Michael Lind and Larry Lynn. My friend David Peck has weeded out bad wording in all three books and in the Introduction to this one. My wife, Susan Pearson, my daughters, Hilary and Eleanor, and my cat, Max, have kept my hopes alive for a better future through this awful year of 2020.

THE POPULIST EXPLOSION

I argue in *The Populist Explosion* that there is a significant strain of politics widely called "populist" that appeared in the United States in the 1880s and in Europe in the 1970s, and that it is different from conventional American liberalism, conservatism, European social democracy, and Christian democracy. In analyzing how it works, I was influenced by the late Ernesto Laclau's book, *On Populist Reason* (Verso, 2005). Laclau portrays populism as a *logic* that can be used by the left as well as the right, and he explains how the demands that populists make are different from those of other parties and candidates. There is also a useful anthology, *Populism and the Mirror of Democracy* (Verso, 2005), edited by Francisco Panizza, which includes essays by Laclau and Chantal Mouffe. Laclau's essay, "Populism: What's in a Name?" is a remarkably clear summary of his thesis, and Mouffe's "The 'End of Politics' and the Challenge of Right-wing Populism" counters the usual dismissal of populism by European intellectuals and politicians. (For a further discussion of Laclau and Mouffe, see my own essay on them in *Dissent*, Fall 2016.)

American historians have recognized that populism can appear on the left or right, from the People's Party to George Wallace. Michael Kazin's *The Populist Persuasion* (Basic Books, 1995) reflects this understanding. Kazin's treatment of populism as a "language" is similar to Laclau's view of it as a "logic." Most European studies focus on rightwing populism. That's partly because populist parties initially arose on the right there. And perhaps because of the memory of Hitler and Mussolini, many of these studies see Western European populism as a threat to democracy. I found Cas Mudde's *Populist Radical Right Parties in Europe* (Cambridge University Press, 2007) useful. I also liked Christopher Caldwell's *Reflections on the Revolution in Europe: Immigration, Islam and the West* (Anchor, 2009) as well as his essays on European populism in the *Weekly Standard*.

The key book to understanding American rightwing populism, from George Wallace through Donald Trump, is Donald I. Warren's *The Radical Center: Middle Americans and the Politics of Alienation* (University of Notre Dame Press, 1976). Warren, a largely unheralded sociologist who taught at Oakland University in Michigan, conducted extensive surveys of Wallace voters in the early 1970s. Warren discovered a strain of politics that blended right and left, which he called "middle American radicalism." It endures in Trump's support. Kevin Phillips is another invaluable analyst of American populism, from *The Emerging Republican Majority* (Arlington House, 1969) to *Arrogant Capital: Washington, Wall Street, and the Frustration of American Politics* (Little Brown, 1994). On Huey Long, I relied on Alan Brinkley's *Voices of Protest: Huey Long, Father Coughlin, and the Great Depression* (Knopf, 1982). On the Tea Party, I found Theda Skocpol and Vanessa Williamson's *The Tea Party and the Remaking of Republican Conservatism* (Oxford University Press, 2012) useful, as well a doctoral thesis by Emily Elisabeth Ekins, "Tea Party Fairness: How the Idea of Proportional Justice Explains the Right-Wing Populism of the Obama Era" (http://escholarship.org/uc/item/3663x343).

In describing the economic roots and ideology of neoliberalism, I was influenced by Robert Brenner's *The Economics of Global Turbulence* (Verso, 2006). The
crucial role played by Margaret Thatcher and François Mitterrand is described by
Peter Hall in *Governing the Economy: The Politics of State Intervention in Britain and
France* (Oxford University Press, 1986). In analyzing the Eurocrisis and the onset
of the Great Recession in Europe, I was also influenced by Hall's more recent
work, particularly an essay, "Varieties of Capitalism and the Eurocrisis," in *West
European Politics*, August 2014. I first became aware that the adoption of the Euro
was leading Europe into a cul-de-sac thanks to Paul Krugman's columns in the
New York Times. I became convinced of the special role played by German export
surpluses from the "Appendix" to Michael Pettis's book, *The Great Rebalancing:
Trade, Conflict, and the Perilous Road Ahead for the World Economy* (Princeton University Press, 2013). Pettis also has an interesting essay on Greece, Spain, and
the Eurozone crisis, "Syriza and the French Indemnity of 1871–73," on his blog
(http://blog.mpettis.com/2015/02/syriza-and-the-french-indemnity-of-1871
-73/). For other relevant books and articles, see my endnotes.

In following European Union politics, I found two websites invaluable: Social
Europe (socialeurope.eu) and Open Democracy (opendemocracy.net). Arthur
Goldhammer keeps up with "French politics" (artgoldhammer.blogspot.com)
and Michael Tangeman with Spain (progressivespain.com). One of the best
sources on leftwing populism in Greece and Spain is the *New Left Review*. Podemos's leader, Pablo Iglesias, was interviewed in the publication's May–June 2015
issue. The party's chief strategist, Íñigo Errejón, also conducted a dialogue about
populist politics with Chantal Mouffe in the book *Podemos: In the Name of the
People* (Lawrence & Wishart, 2016). I also benefited from James Galbraith's analyses of the Greek crisis, which was summed up in his recent book, *Welcome to the
Poisoned Chalice: The Destruction of Greece and the Future of Europe* (Yale University Press, 2016).

THE NATIONALIST REVIVAL

When I told my friend, the historian David Greenberg, that I was writing a book
on nationalism, he said, "See if you can write the book without using the phrase,
'What Benedict Anderson calls "imagined communities."'" I am guilty of only
one such reference. While I admire Anderson's book, *Imagined Communities*, I
am more inclined to the traditionalist school of analysis than to the modern-
ists like Anderson, Gellner, and Hobsbawm. I like Azar Gat's *Nations: The Long
History and Deep Roots of Political Ethnicity and Nationalism* (Cambridge, 2012),
Anthony D. Smith's *The Ethnic Origin of Nations* (Wiley, 1991), and Johan Huiz-
inga's essay, "Patriotism and Nationalism," in *Men and Ideas* (Princeton, 1984).
On what nationalism *means* today, I benefited from David Miller's *On Nationality*
(Oxford, 1997), Craig Calhoun's *Nations Matter* (Routledge, 2007), and Michael
Billig's *Banal Nationalism* (Sage, 1995).

In trying to understand American nationalism, I would recommend Michael
Lind's *Next American Nation* (Free Press, 1995), Eric Kaufmann's *The Rise and
Fall of Anglo-America* (Harvard, 2004), and (leaving aside his fears of a Hispanic
takeover of America) Samuel Huntington's *Who Are We?* (Simon and Schuster,

398 2004). On the UK and Brexit, I was influenced by David Goodhart's *The Road to Somewhere* (Hirst, 2017). On the origins of German nationalism, I learned from chapter four of Liah Greenfeld's *Nationalism: Five Roads to Modernity* (Harvard, 1992); on France, I liked David Bell's *Cult of the Nation in France: Inventing Nationalism 1680–1800* (Harvard, 2003); and on nationalism and immigration in France and Germany, Rogers Brubaker, *Citizenship and Nationhood in France and Germany* (Harvard, 1992).

On Poland, I recommend an essay by Leszek Koczanowicz, "The Polish Case," from *New Left Review*, November–December 2016, which brings out what is different about nationalism in Poland (or Hungary) from, say, nationalism in France or Germany. On Hungary I used Paul Lendvai's *Orban: Europe's New Strongman* (Hurst, 2017) for background. In following Hungary's twists and turns, Eva S. Balogh's email newsletter, *Hungarian Spectrum*, is invaluable. On Japan's nationalism, I learned from R. Taggart Murphy's *Japan and the Shackles of the Past* (Oxford, 2014) and Ian Buruma's *Inventing Japan* (Modern Library, 2004); on China, Howard French's *Everything Under the Sun* (Random House, 2017) and Richard McGregor's *Asia's Reckoning* (Random House, 2017); and on current U.S.-Russia relations, Samuel Charap and Timothy Cotton's *Everyone Loses: the Ukraine Crisis and the Ruinous Contest for Post-Soviet Eurasia* (Routledge, 2017).

On the current politics of nationalism, I recommend Jonathan Haidt's essay "When and Why Nationalism Beats Globalism," *American Interest*, July 2016; Wolfgang Streeck's "Germany, Refugees, and the British Vote to Leave" for the Sheffield Political Economy Research Institute, September 2016; Michael Lind's "The Case for Cultural Nationalism" in *National Review*, September 11, 2017; Michael Brendan Dougherty's "Confiscating the Nation," *National Review*, March 2, 2018; and Justin Gest's *The New Minority: White Working Class Politics in an Age of Immigration and Inequality* (Oxford, 2016). I also got a lot out of the website Social Europe and George Friedman's analyses on Geopolitical Futures.

On immigration, I would recommend David Miller's *Strangers in Our Midst* (Harvard, 2016), Reihan Salam's new book, *Melting Pot or Civil War? A Son of Immigrants Makes the Case Against Open Borders* (Penguin, 2018), and my own essay, "The Two Sides of Immigration Policy," *American Prospect*, Winter 2017. I recommended a lot of books on the EU and the Euro in the Further Reading section of *The Populist Explosion*, but I would add to these Yanis Varoufakis's *Adults in the Room* (FSG, 2017) and Wolfgang Streeck's *How Will Capitalism End: Essays on a Failing System* (Penguin, 2016). Dani Rodrik has been writing about globalization since 1997. I think his outlook is best summed up in *The Globalization Paradox* (Norton, 2011).

THE SOCIALIST AWAKENING

Many young people in the United States and Great Britain look favorably on socialism and even call themselves "socialists" without reading a word of Karl Marx's work. Ella Morton, the head of the Corvallis, Oregon, chapter of the Young Democratic Socialists of America, told an interviewer that she doesn't identify with the "economic part" of democratic socialism, but with the emphasis on "community bonds" and that she doesn't want to read Marx who, she fears,

would "ruin democratic socialism" for her. But for someone trying to understand capitalism and socialism on a theoretical basis, Marx's and Engels's works
are still the touchstone. The works I describe as "post-Marxist" arise out of an
engagement with Marx's thought.

Marx's great work is *Capital*, Vol. I, which lays out his theory of capitalism and
the transition from feudalism to capitalism. Marx describes the politics of the
transition to socialism in *The Communist Manifesto* and *The Critique of the Gotha
Program*. In "Socialism: Scientific and Utopian," Engels lays out his and Marx's
differences with Robert Owen and the utopian socialists.

Two works that weaned me from Marx's precise stages of history were Karl
Lowith's *Meaning in History* (Chicago, 1949) and Alec Nove's *The Economics of
Feasible Socialism* (Taylor and Francis, 1983). I began to think about the possibility of socialism occurring within capitalism when I read the concluding essay
of Martin J. Sklar's *The United States as a Developing Country* (Cambridge, 1992).
Sklar elaborates his theory in "Thoughts on Capitalism and Socialism: Realistic
and Utopian," in *The Journal of the Gilded Age and Progressive Era*, October 2003.

Erik Olin Wright and G. A. Cohen were hard-core Marxists who in the last
decades of their life broke with Marxist orthodoxy. In *Why Not Socialism?* (Princeton, 2009), Cohen makes a case for the moral basis of socialism. In *How to Be
an Anti-Capitalist in the 21st Century* (Verso, 2019), Wright argues for creating
socialist institutions within capitalism. Wright wrote a critical appreciation of
Sklar's theory of the "mix" of capitalism and socialism in *Telos*, Spring 2019.

I first read Karl Polanyi's *The Great Transformation* (Beacon, 1980) sometime
in the 1980s, and it had no impact on me. Under prodding from my friend Fred
Block, I tried again about five years ago, and I was astonished at how relevant it
is to understanding capitalism today. I highly recommend Block and Margaret
Somers's book on Polanyi, *The Power of Market Fundamentalism* (Harvard, 2016).
Robert Kuttner has a good summary of Polanyi's importance, "Karl Polanyi
Explains It All," in the *American Prospect*, April 2014.

A good history of American socialism is Michael Kazin's *American Dreamers*
(Random House, 2011). Jack Ross has written a comprehensive history, *The
Socialist Party of America* (Potomac, 2015), which goes from Debs to DSA. Nick
Salvatore's *Eugene Debs: Citizen and Socialist* (Illinois, 1982) is a superb biography.
I first learned about Debs and the Socialist Party from James Weinstein, *The
Decline of Socialism in America: 1912–1925* (Monthly Review, 1967). For Chris-
tian socialism and its influence, I recommend Gary Dorrien's *The Soul in Society*
(Fortress, 1995).

As readers will sense, my view of twentieth-century British history and of
the Labour Party was heavily influenced by David Edgerton's *The Rise and Fall
of the British Nation* (Penguin, 2018). I found Andrew Thorpe's *A History of the
British Labour Party* (Red Globe, 2015) useful. Rosa Prince's *Comrade Corbyn* (Biteback, 2016) tells the story of the former Labour leader. David Kogan's *Protest
and Power: The Battle for the Labour Party* (Bloomsbury, 2019) traces the conflict
between Labour's factions from the 1970s to the present.

400   NOTES

THE POPULIST EXPLOSION

CHAPTER ONE

44   **well ahead in polls:** "https://
www.noties.nl/v/get.php?a=peil.nl&s
=weekpoll&f=De+Stemming+van+10
+januari+2016. pdf.

44   **exclusively in all of them:**
For this analysis of language, see
Ludwig Wittgenstein, *Philosophical
Investigations*, Basil Blackwell, 1953,
Part I. For political language, the
lack of an "essence" is even more
obvious if you think of terms like
"liberal" and "conservative," and
their very different use from country
to country.

45   **"former against the latter":**
Michael Kazin, *The Populist
Persuasion: An American History*,
Basic Books, 1995, p. 1.

CHAPTER TWO

49   **presidential nomination:** http://
www.xojane.com/issues/stephanie
-cegielski-donald-trump-campaign
-defector.

49   **downscale white Americans:**
See http://www.politico.com
/magazine/story/2016/01/donald
-trump-2016-authoritarian-213533
#ixzz43pWmnAgK and http://www
.slate.com/articles/news_and_politics
/cover_story/2016/03/how_donald
_trump_happened_racism_against
_barack_obama.html.

49   **weakness as a front-runner:** See
http://www.bloombergview.com
/articles/2016-02-01/what-bernie
-sanders-gets-about-millennials.

52   **the legend goes:** McMath, p. 75.

53   **the gold standard:** Robert C.
McMath, Jr., *American Populism: A
Social History 1877-1898*, Hill and
Wang, 1992, p. 146.

54   **as "bourgeois":** Charles Postel,
The Populist Vision, Oxford University
Press, 2007, p. 208.

55   **John J. Ingalls wrote:** McMath,
op. cit., p. 135.

55   **"second Declaration of
Independence":** Postel, op. cit., p. 158.

56   **"cease in the land":** *The Populist
Mind*, ed. Norman Pollack, Bobbs-
Merrill, 1967, pp. 61–63.

56   **"despotism, and death?":**
The Populist Mind, p. 46.

56   **"moral and social lepers":**
Postel, p. 185.

56   **"Anarchists, and Communists":**
McMath, p. 69.

57   **"farmer deserves none":**
McMath, p. 182.

57   **"one word—nigger":** McMath,
p. 173.

57   **"foreign pauper labor":** http://
www.presidency.ucsb.edu/ws/?pid
=29586.

59   **"the people" together:** On
Long's life and politics, see T. Harry
Williams, *Huey Long*, Knopf, 1969.
Alan Brinkley, *Voices of Protest: Huey
Long, Father Coughlin, and the Great
Depression*, Knopf, 1982.

59   **"the ground he walks on":**
Brinkley, p. 29.

60   **"Mr. Rockefeller":** Brinkley,
p. 59.

60   **what he promised:** Brinkley,
pp. 72–73.

60   **"base your conclusions?":**
Michael Hiltzik, *The New Deal: A Modern History*, Free Press, 2011, p. 221.

60   **more than 7.5 million:** William Leuchtenberg, *Franklin Roosevelt and the New Deal*, HarperCollins, 1963, p. 99.

60   **politically volatile groups:**
Brinkley, p. 198.

61   **to the Republicans:**
Leucthenberg, pp. 99–100.

61   **Long had repeatedly raised:**
On whether Roosevelt and the Democrats in Congress were responding to Long and Coughlin, see Brinkley, pp. 79–81. Or Alonzo Hamby, *Man of Destiny: FDR and the Making of the American Century*, Basic Books, 2015, p. 238.

61   **"soaking the rich":** Frank Freidel, *Franklin D. Roosevelt: A Rendezvous with Destiny*, Back Bay Books, 1990, pp. 165–66.

61   **"economic royalists":** http://www.austincc.edu/lpatrick/his2341/fdr36acceptancespeech.htm.

62   **"outniggered again":** Marshall Frady, *Wallace*, New York, Dutton, 1968, p. 127. Wallace denied using the exact phrase, and another fellow politician said he used "out-segged." Stephan Lesher, *George Wallace: American Populist*, Perseus Books, 1994, p. 129.

63   **"the little businessman":**
Lesher, p. 390.

63   **"fleeing to Virginia":** http://www.ourcampaigns.com/CandidateDetail.html?CandidateID=4038.

63   **welfare, roads, and agriculture:** http://www.4president.org/brochures/wallace1968brochure.htm.

64   **"without paying taxes":**
Lesher, p. 474.

64   **"punks were in diapers":**
http://www.ourcampaigns.com/CandidateDetail.html?CandidateID=4038.

64   **"rich and poor simultaneously":** Donald I. Warren, *The Radical Center*, University of Notre Dame Press, 1976. p. 20.

64   **"have to pay the bill":** Warren, p. 21.

64   **"too big":** Warren, p. 73.

65   **George Wallace in 1972:**
Warren, p. 151.

65   **Warren's MARs:** Irving Crespi, "Structural Sources of the George Wallace Constituency," *Social Science Quarterly*, June 1971.

CHAPTER THREE

68   **free market liberalism:** There is a controversy about the use of the term "neoliberalism" that I would prefer to avoid. See http://coreyrobin.com/tag/neoliberalism/In the U.S. there are at least three uses of the term: 1) post-New Deal liberalism championed by Charles Peters of the *Washington Monthly* and his protégés that is wary of "big labor" and "big government" solutions and prefers means-tested over universal social programs. 2) Gary Hart's politics of 1984–88 that stressed achieving growth rather than equity through the use of an industrial policy that targeted high-tech industries; and 3) the dominance of Reagan's

402 Republicanism that accepted the existence of the safety net, but sought to lower taxes on business, remove regulations, free capital to move overseas, and allow immigrants to move into the United States. Democrats, including Bill Clinton, would accept some qualified version of this third version, as Labor's Tony Blair's New Labour would accept some version of Margaret Thatcher's neoliberalism. It's the third kind of neoliberalism to which I am referring in this book.

68 **automobiles, and refrigerators:** On global overcapacity in the '70s and beyond, see *The International Politics of Surplus Capacity,* ed. Susan Strange and Roger Tooze, Routledge, 1981.

69 **23.1 percent in non-manufacturing:** See Robert Brenner, *The Economics of Global Turbulence,* Verso, 2006, pp. 108–9 and Leo Panitch and Sam Gindin, *The Making of Global Capitalism: The Political Economy of American Empire,* Verso, 2012, p. 135.

69 **rates of profit:** For the "profit squeeze" theory that rising wage and benefit costs drove the neoliberal reaction, the classic explanation is Andrew Glyn and Robert Sutcliffe, *British Capitalism, Workers and the Profit Squeeze,* Penguin Books, 1972. Several economists applied this analysis to the U.S. For a recent example, see Panitch and Gindin, op. cit. The overcapacity and profit squeeze theses are sometimes presented as alternative explanations, but I think they both describe pressures that resulted in the end of the postwar boom in the U.S. and Europe.

69 **"labor unions, and the young":** John B. Judis, *The Paradox of American Democracy,* Pantheon, 2000, p. 11.

69 **American firms from expropriation:** I describe business's new lobbying offensive in *The Paradox of American Democracy,* chapter five.

70 **plants were undocumented:** *The New York Times,* December 12, 2001. In addition, immigration also exacted a cost in welfare spending for cities, states, and the federal government. According to a Center for Immigration Studies analysis, in 2012, between 62 and 65.6 percent of illegal immigrants received some kind of welfare assistance compared to 48.5 percent of legal immigrant households and only 30.2 percent of native-born households.

70 **38 percent in:** http://articles.latimes.com/1993-11-09/news/mn-54845_1_gallup-poll.

70 **32 percent for:** http://www.pipa.org/OnlineReports/Globalization/AmericansGlobalization_Mar00/AmericansGlobalization_Mar00_apdxa.pdf.

71 **"big government":** See Kevin Phillips, *Arrogant Capital: Washington, Wall Street, and the Frustration of American Politics,* Little Brown, 1994.

72 **rise in inequality:** See John H. Dunn, Jr. "The Decline of Manufacturing in the United States, and Its Impact on Income Inequality," *The Journal of Applied Business Research,* September–October 2012.

73 **white-collar jobs:** Peter Temin, "The American Dual Economy," *Institute for New Economic Thinking,* November 2015.

73 **bottom 70 percent:** http://www.urban.org/research/publication/growing-size-and-incomes-upper-middle-class.

73 **"wrong with the U.S. economy":** Daniel Yankelovich, "Foreign Policy after the Election," *Foreign Affairs*, Fall 1992.

74 **obtaining an early discharge:** On Perot's life, see Gerald Posner, *Citizen Perot: His Life and Times*, Random House, 1996.

74 **GM's management ignored him:** See Doron P. Levin, *Irreconcilable Differences: Ross Perot Versus General Motors*, Little Brown, 1989.

75 **"it's going to be too late":** Address to National Press Club, March 18, 1992.

76 **"make America work again":** Ross Perot, *Ross Perot: My Life and the Principles for Success*, Tapestry Press, 2002, p. 99.

76 **"industries of the future":** Ross Perot, p. 61.

76 **"biogenetics industry":** Ibid.

76 **"dictatorial":** Stanley Greenberg, *The Road to Realignment: the Democrats and the Perot Voters*, Democratic Leadership Council, 1993, pp. II-9.

77 **had a chance to win:** Posner, p. 322.

77 **"as liberal or conservative":** Frank Luntz, "Perovian Civilization," *Policy Review*, Spring 1993.

77 **"the radical middle":** Greenberg, pp. II-3.

77 **"worse now than in 1988":** http://www.cnn.com/ELECTION/1998/states/CA/polls/CA92PH.html.

77 **"a raw deal today":** Greenberg, p. III-11.

77 **trade loses more jobs:** Cited in Ruy Teixeira and Guy Molyneux, *Economic Nationalism and the Future of American Politics*, Economic Policy Institute. 1993, p. 29.

78 **"tougher U.S. trade stance":** Teixeira and Molyneux, p. 24.

78 **"rob us of American jobs":** *Washington Post*, September 9, 1991. John B. Judis, "The Tariff Party," *The New Republic*, March 30, 1992.

78 **"if not for its people?":** Buchanan, *Pittsburgh Post-Gazette*, November 28, 1995.

78 **"Robert Rubin's world":** Buchanan, *Arizona Republic*, February 9, 1995.

79 **"isn't really a country anymore":** John B. Judis, "Taking Pat Buchanan Seriously," *GQ*, December 1995.

79 **"peasants with pitchforks":** Tom Raum, "Leading a Revolution of Peasants with Pitchforks," Associated Press, February 18, 1996.

79 **real income had begun to rise:** https://www.census.gov/hhes/www/income/data/incpovhlth/1996/highlights.html.

80 **A steep recession followed:** John B. Judis, "Debt Man Walking," *The New Republic*, December 3, 2008, and Michael Pettis, *The Great Rebalancing: Trade, Conflict and the Perilous Road Ahead for the World Economy*, Princeton University Press, 2013.

404   80   **had backed McGovern in 1972:** See John B. Judis and Ruy Teixeira, *The Emerging Democratic Majority*, New York, 2002.

80   **new, enduring Democratic majority:** John B. Judis, "America the Liberal," *The New Republic*, Nov. 19, 2008.

81   **"prepare the nation for a new age":** https://www.whitehouse.gov /blog/2009/01/21/president- barack -obamas-inaugural-address.

81   **did not prosecute:** http://www .g-a-i.org/u/2012/08/DOJ-Report-8 -61.pdf.

81   **shake business confidence:** See Noam Scheiber, *The Escape Artists: How Obama's Team Fumbled the Recovery*, Simon & Schuster, 2011, pp. 170–8.

82   **growth of Medicare spending:** See Thomas B. Edsall, "The Obamacare Crisis," *The New York Times*, November 19, 2013 and "Is Obamacare Destroying the Democratic Party," *The New York Times*, December 2, 2014.

82   **"Chicago Tea Party":** See John B. Judis, "Tea Minus Zero," *The New Republic*, May 10, 2010.

82   **160,000 members:** Theda Skocpol and Vanessa Williamson, *The Tea Party and the Remaking of Republican Conservatism*, Oxford University Press, 2012, p. 22.

83   **"You are not entitled to what I have earned":** Skocpol and Williamson, p. 66.

83   **ACA as a redistributive transfer program:** Emily Elisabeth Ekins, "Tea Party Fairness: How the Idea of Proportional Justice Explains the Right-Wing Populism of the Obama Era," UCLA diss., 2015, pp. 74–75.

83   **"services by illegal immigrants":** Skocpol and Williamson, p. 71.

83   **took jobs from native-born Americans:** See Kazin, pp. 35–36.

84   **"sending him big checks":** John B. Judis, "David Brat and the Triumph of Rightwing Populism," *The New Republic*, June 11, 2014.

84   **from 2007 through 2011:** http://www2.itif.org/2015-inequality -rose.pdf.

85   **some college or a bachelor's degree:** https://web.stanford.edu /group/recessiontrends/cgi-bin /web/sites/all/themes/barron/pdf /LaborMarkets_fact_sheet.pdf.

85   **"The Economic Elite vs. the People of the United States":** For AmpedStatus.com's role see http:// www.washingtonsblog.com/2011/09 /a-report-from-the-frontlines-the -long-road-to-occupywallstreet-and -the-origins-of-the-99-movement. html. On the history of Occupy Wall Street, see Todd Gitlin, *Occupy Nation: The Roots, the Spirit, and the Promise of Occupy Wall Street*, It Books, 2012; Ethan Earle, *A Brief History of Occupy Wall Street*, Rosa Luxemburg Stiftung, 2012; Mattathias Schwartz, "Pre-Occupied," *The New Yorker*, November 28, 2011.

86   **finally undid it:** Jonathan Mahler, "Oakland, the Last Refuge of Radical America," *New York Times*, August 1, 2012.

CHAPTER FOUR

88 **"protest candidate"**: https://
www.washingtonpost.com/news
/post-politics/wp/2015/07/03
/bernie-sanders-seen-as-a-protest
-candidate-says-democratic-rival
-martin-omalley/.

88 **"Trump's campaign
is a sideshow"**. http://www
.huffingtonpost.com/entry/a-note
-about-our-coverage-of-donald
-trumps-campaign_us_55a8fc9ce4b0
896514d0fd66?section=politics.

88 **back into their politics
section:** http://www.huffingtonpost
.com/arianna-huffington/a-note-on
-trump_b_8744476.html.

89 **"personality not substance"**:
http://www.nytimes.com/2015/08
/23/us/politics/why-donald-trump
-wont-fold-polls-and-people-speak
.html.

89 **"Sanders's authenticity?"**:
Pablo Zevallos, *Politico*, February 12,
2016.

90 **recouped some of his losses:**
Michael D'Antonio, *Never Enough:
Donald Trump and the Pursuit of
Success*, Thomas Dunne Books, 2015.

91 **"I'm very pro-choice"**: "Inside
Politics," CNN, October 26, 1999.

91 **"liberal on health"**: Trump and
Dave Shiflett, *The America We Deserve*,
Renaissance Books, 2000, p. 212.

92 **"rebuild our own country"**:
http://www.npr.org/2016/ 04/01
/472633800/4-things-to-know-about
-donald-trumps-foreign-policy-
approach.

92 **criticized NATO:** http://www
.realclearpolitics.com/video/2016/03
/27/trump_europe_ is_not_safe_lots
_of_the_free_world_has_become
_weak.html.

92 **"police that deal"**: http://www
.slate.com/articles/news_and_politics
/politics/2016/01/donald_trump_is
_the_only_serious_gop_candidate
_who_hasn_t_promised_to_rip.html.

93 **"a bunch of saps"**: Associated
Press, December 2, 1999.

93 **"political hacks"**: Debate, June
28, 2015.

95 **"It's rigged against you"**:
https://www.donaldjtrump.com
/press-releases/donald-j.-trump-on
-the-stakes-of-the-election.

95 **"Enter by the law, or leave"**:
Trump, *The America We Deserve*,
p. 243.

95 **"Illegal immigration is a
wrecking ball"**: Trump, *Time to Get
Tough*, Regnery Publishing, 2015

97 **"anti-elite party of the working
class"**: D'Antonio.

98 **"two Ivy League contenders"**:
Trump, "What I Saw at the Revolution,"
New York Times, Feb. 19, 2000.

98 **"trying to stop me"**: http://
www.msnbc.com/msnbc/donald
-trump-hammers-home-anti
-establishment-message.

98 **didn't necessarily believe:**
Mary Jordan, "A Village named Syria
in the Heart of Virginia explains
why many will vote for Trump,"
Washington Post, May 24, 2016. Jordan
writes, "Several people said that it
made little sense to pay attention too
closely to election-year proposals
because candidates rarely deliver

406   when they are in office, especially if Congress is needed to approve a new measure. Richards, for instance, said she doesn't think a ban will occur, just as she knows that Mexico probably won't pay for the giant wall Trump talks about building on the southern border. But she said that no other candidate is telling her what she thinks: Just about anybody can set foot in the United States, and those days should end."

100   **"a widespread global depression"**: http://www.cnbc.com/2016/06/29/gop-donor-paul-singer-says-trump-would-cause-a-depression.html.

100   **The American National Election Studies**: http://www.electionstudies.org/.

100   **Pew Research Center in March**: http://www.people-press.org/files/2016/03/3-31-16-March-Political-release-1.pdf.

101   **leaving the Democrats in the '60s**: Some statistical sites claimed that Trump's supporters were not really "working class" because on some exit polls, they had an average income of $72,000, which is above the median income. But the principal test of whether someone is working class or above is usually education, and Trump's support is inversely related to the level of a voter's education. He does best among high school grads and voters with only some college. But his support is also proportional to age, and annual income rises with age, so the fact that Trump's supporters have a slightly above average income probably reflects their age rather than their social class.

104   **"nobody in the audience fainted"**: Sanders, "Fragments of a Campaign Diary," *Seven Days*, December 1, 1972.

104   **"Why Socialism"**: Albert Einstein, "Why Socialism," *Monthly Review*, May 1949.

104   **"I don't have the power to nationalize the banks"**: *Baltimore Sun*, December 23, 1981.

105   **"I'm a democratic socialist"**: Sanders with Huck Gutman, *Outsider in the House*, Verso, 1997, p. 29.

105   **"higher standard of living"**: Michael Powell, "Exceedingly Social, but Doesn't Like Parties," *Washington Post*, November 5, 2006.

105   **"two percent of the people"**: *Saint Albans Daily Messenger*, December 23, 1971.

106   **"buy the United States Congress"**: "The Rachel Maddow Show," MSNBC, April 15, 2015.

106   **"What Bernie Sanders Doesn't Understand About American Politics"**: Jonathan Chait, "What Bernie Sanders Doesn't Understand About American Politics," *New York*, January 27, 2016.

106   **"facile calls for revolution:"** "It Was Better to Bern Out," *The New York Times*, June 10, 2016.

107   **"eat out the heart of the republic"**: George E. Mowry, *The Era of Theodore Roosevelt*, Harper and Brothers, 1958, p. 101.

110   **84 percent from 2008 to 2014**: Judis, "The Bern Supremacy."

110   **among college students**: Abby Holterman, "Mental Health Problems

for College Students Are Increasing,"
Healthline, July 17, 2015.

110   **42 to 34 percent:** https://
today.yougov.com/news/2016/01
/28/democrats-remain-divided
-socialism/.

CHAPTER FIVE

112   **"three destroyers":** Jim Yardley,
"Europe on the March," *New York
Times,* May 24, 2014.

112   **"Henk and Ingrid":** *The
Changing Faces of Populism: Systemic
Challenges in Europe and the U.S.,* ed.
Hedwig Guisto, Stefano Rizzo, David
Kitching, Lexington Books, 2013,
p. 183.

113   **"demagogy, charismatic
leadership":** Cas Mudde, "Populism
in Europe: A Primer," *Open Democracy,*
May 12, 2015.

113   **"Exposing the Demagogues":**
Eds. Karsten Grabow and Florian
Hartleb, *Exposing the Demagogues:
Right-wing and National Populist
Parties in Europe,* Center for
European Studies, 2013. In spite of its
incendiary title, the book contains
useful scholarly studies of Europe's
populist parties.

114   **"virtuous circle":** J. Bradford
DeLong, "Post WWII European
Exceptionalism: The Economic
Dimension," NBER, December 1997.

115   **Comparing the period 1950 to
1973:** Nicholas Crafts, "Fifty Years of
Economic Growth in Western Europe,"
Stanford Institute for Economic
Policy Research, November 2003.

115   **a lowly 1.6 percent:** Eric
Hobsbawm, *The Age of Extremes:*

A History of the World, 1914-1991,
Pantheon Books, 1994. p. 406. My
account of Thatcher and Mitterrand's
policy experiments has been heavily
influenced by Peter Hall, *Governing
the Economy: The Politics of State
Intervention in Britain and France,*
Oxford University Press, 1986.

116   **"Initial characteristics"** ??
Tony Judt, *Postwar: A History of Europe
Since 1945,* Penguin Books, 2006, p.
542.

118   **"to change their minds":** http://
conservativehome.blogs.com
/centreright/2008/04/making-history
.html.

119   **actively recruiting guest
workers:** For these figures, see
Stephen Castles, "The Guest Worker
in Western Europe—An Obituary,"
The International Migration Review,
Winter 1986.

119   **3.4 million in France:** Hans-
Georg Betz, *Radical Right-Wing
Populism in Western Europe,* Palgrave
Macmillan, 1994, p. 73-4.

120   **numbers have continued to
grow:** Hans-George Betz, "The New
Politics of Resentment," *Comparative
Politics,* July 1993.

120   **by 268,902, or 520 percent:**
http://www.migrationpolicy.org
/article/denmark-integrating
-immigrants-homogeneous-welfare
-state.

121   **by 1991, it was 33 percent:**
Eurobarometer, June 1991, Brussels.

121   **took jobs away from natives:**
John Sides and Jack Citrin, "European
Opinions about Immigration," *British
Journal of Political Science,* July 2007.

407

408   121   **Mogens Glistrup founded in 1973:** Susi Meret, "The Danish People's Party, the Italian Northern League and the Austrian Freedom Party in a Comparative Perspective: Party Ideology and Electoral Support," Aalborg University, diss. 2010.

123   **"the most immigrant-obsessed party in Europe":** Christopher Caldwell, *Reflections on the Revolution in Europe: Immigration, Islam and the West*, Anchor, 2009, p. 316.

123   **"The gap was taken up by Søren Krarup":** Interview with author. On Krarup, I have relied on Susi Meret, op. cit., author's interview with Krarup's biographer Mikael Jalving, and John Terrell Foor, "State of Identity: National History and Exclusive Identity in Contemporary Denmark," Western Michigan University MA thesis.

124   **"Your Denmark":** translation by Cecillie Felicia Stokholm Banke.

124   **"You are not house-trained":** Translation by Jørgen Dragsdahl. Text can be found at http://www.stm.dk/_p_7628.html.

125   **inciting racial hatred:** Cas Mudde, *The Ideology of the Extreme Right*, Manchester University Press, 2000, chapter five. See also Paul Lucardie and Gerrit Voerman, "Geert Wilders and the Party for Freedom," *Exposing the Demagogues*.

126   **by 1999, 47 percent were:** See Reinhard Heinsich, "Austrian Right-Wing Populism," in *Exposing the Demagogues*, and Karl Aiginger, "The Privatization Experiment in Austria," *Austrian Economic Quarterly*, 4/1999.

127   **"irrational shifts in the market":** Cited in Donald A. Hempson Jr., "European Disunion: The Rise and Fall of a Post-war Dream," *Origins*, September 2013.

129   **"closed world of chancelleries":** Perry Anderson, *The New Old World*, Verso, 2009, p. 62.

129   **"The European Union will remain utopia":** Cas Mudde, *Populist Radical Right Parties in Europe*, Cambridge University Press, 2007, p. 159.

129   **"a new European superstate is not":** Mudde, p. 166.

CHAPTER SIX

132   **25.1 percent in 2012:** http://www.economicshelp.org/blog/1247/economics/european-unemployment-2/.

132   **cause of the deepening recession:** There is now an extensive literature on the causes of the Eurocrisis, and the explanation I offer here is a hybrid of several. See Peter A. Hall, "Varieties of Capitalism and the Eurocrisis," *West European Politics*, August 2014; Heiner Flassback and Kostas Lapavitsas, *Against the Troika: Crisis and Austerity in the Eurozone*, Verso, 2015; Engelbert Stockhammer, "The Euro Crisis and the Contradictions of Neoliberalism in Europe," *Post Keynesian Economics Study Group*, Working Paper 1401; Mark Copelovtich, Jeffry Frieden, and Stefanie Walter, "The Political Economy of the Euro Crisis," *Comparative Political Studies*, 2016; Servaas Storm and C. W. Naastepad, "Myths, Mixups, and Mishandlings: Understanding the Eurozone Crisis,"

International Journal of Political Economy 45, 2016; and Pettis, op. cit., Appendix.

For a narrative of the events, see Stathis Kouvelakis, "The Greek Cauldron," *New Left Review,* November–December 2011.

134 **"treasonous":** Ibid.

134 **Greece will be massively limited:** http://globalcomment.com /loansharking-greece-Syriza-the -troika-and-the-end-of-greek -sovereignty/.

136 **member of the European community:** For this history of Syriza, see Yanis Varoufakis, "Can Greece's Syriza Change Europe's Economy," *Boston Review*, December 3, 2013.

137 **rural voters:** Yiannis Mavris, "Greece's Austerity Election," *New Left Review*, July–August 2012.

137 **"the Greece of Democracy":** Yannis Stavrakakis and Giorgos Katsambakis, "Leftwing Populism in the European Periphery: the case of Syriza," *Journal of Political Ideologies*, 2014. The authors have precisely enumerated Tsipras's use of populist terms in his speeches.

137 **"acting like a model prisoner":** Varoufakis, op. cit.

138 **"the Troika is over":** Euractiv, February 12, 2015.

138 **"it wasn't the Greeks who did it":** Paul Krugman, "Killing the European Project," *The New York Times*, July 12, 2015.

138 **"simply appalling":** Flassbeck and Lapavitsas.

139 **"Berlin finance ministry":**   409
Interview with author.

140 **"A rupture is indispensable":** Interview with Stathis Kouvelakis, *New Left Review*, January–February 2016.

140 **"Spain is the problem, and Europe is the solution":** Cited in Omar G. Encarnacion, *Spanish Politics: Democracy After Dictatorship*, Polity, 2008, p. 32.

141 **inflation began to go down:** On these early years of the PSOE, see Paul Kennedy, "Spain: Exhaustion of the Left Project," *Parliamentary Affairs*, 2003(56), and Sebastian Royo, *From Social Democracy to Neoliberalism*, Palgrave Macmillan, 2000.

141 **"We are neither right, nor left":** Dan Hancox, "Why Ernesto Laclau Is the Figurehead, *Guardian*, February 9, 2015.

142 **energy of the Indignados:** On the history of Podemos, see Iglesias, *New Left Review* 72; Iglesias, *Politics in a Time of Crisis: Podemos and the Future of Democracy*, Verso, 2015; Giles Tremlett, "The Podemos Revolution," *Guardian*, March 31, 2015; author interviews with Fernando Roman and Segundo Gonzalez Garcia.

142 **"the principles of Groucho Marx":** Tremlett, op. cit.

142 **May 15 movement:** Iglesias, *New Left Review*.

142 **the "pink tide":** On the Latin American influence on Podemos, see Becquer Seguin, "Podemos's Latin American Roots," *Jacobin*, March 27, 2015. And on Latin American populism, see Carlos se la Torre and Cynthia J. Arnson, *Latin American*

410 *Populism in the Twenty-first Century*, Washington, 2013.

143 Ernesto Laclau: See Ernesto Laclau and Chantal Mouffe, *Hegemony and Socialist Strategy*, Verso, 1985; Ernesto Laclau, *On Populist Reason*, op. cit.; Íñigo Errejón and Chantal Mouffe, *Podemos: In the Name of the People*, Lawrence & Wishart, 2016. Laclau and Mouffe were also colleagues or mentors of several prominent leaders of Syriza, including economist Yanis Varoufakis and Rena Dourou, the governor of Athens. See Dan Hancox, "Why Ernesto Laclau Is the Intellectual Figurehead for Syriza and Podemos," *Guardian*, February 9, 2015.

143 "indebted to the work of Laclau": Jose Ignacio Torreblanca, *Storm the Heavens*, Debate Editorial, 2015, p. 33.

143 endorsed Laclau and Mouffe's view: Laclau and Mouffe, op. cit.

144 "stealing democracy from the people": Iglesias, op. cit.

144 "left and right metaphors": Íñigo Errejón, "Que es Podemos?" *Le Monde Diplomatique*, July 2014.

144 "their victory is easier": Pablo Iglesias, "Spain on the Edge," *New Left Review*, May–June 2015

144 "at the margins": Errejón and Mouffe, op. cit.

144 "social rights, and redistribution": "Understanding Podemos," *New Left Review*, May–June 2015.

145 "We want a welfare state": Interview with author.

145 "recover democracy and sovereignty": email interview with author.

145 unifying symbol: Writing in his role as political theorist in *New Left Review*, Iglesias described the strategic in Laclauian terms: "The task, then, was to aggregate the new demands generated by the crisis around a mediatic leadership, capable of dichotomizing the political space." "Understanding Podemos," op. cit.

146 "then we take Madrid": Lauren Frayer, "Spain's New Left-wing Party," *Los Angeles Times*, May 17, 2015.

146 from his Twitter feed: Cas Mudde, "Podemos and the Beginning of the End," *Guardian,* December 21, 2015.

146 "Spain is not Greece": *Guardian*, September 9, 2015.

147 middle-class support: Author's interview with political scientist Ignacio Sanchez Cueno.

147 Unidos Podemos: http://progressivespain.com/2016/03/09/podemos-conflict-boils-over-in-madrid-pointing-to-national-dispute-over-leadership-decision-making/.

148 "debt in the Eurozone area": http://www.izquierda-unida.es/sites/default/files/doc/50_Pasos_Para_Gobernar_Juntos_0.pdf (author's translation with the help of Google Translate).

148 "seals deal with communist group": http://elpais.com/ elpais/2016/05/10/inenglish/1462867217_272449.html.

148 192-page IKEA catalogue: http://lasonrisadeunpais.es/programa/.

149 would have done "even worse": http://www.comiendotierra

.es/2016/06/27/a-la-primera-no
-va-la-vencida/ and http://politica
.elpais.com/politica/ 2016/07/01
/actualidad/1467402 299_031801
.html.

149 **"fields remain immobile"**:
http://politica.elpais.com/politica
/2016/06/29/actualidad/1467185738
_087126.html.

CHAPTER SEVEN

152 **Explained Kenneth
Kristensen Berth**: Interview with
author.

153 **According to one newspaper
poll**: Alexander Tange, "Denmark
Considers Moving Migrants," *Reuters*,
January 21, 2016.

153 **said Rene Offersen**: Interview
with author.

153 **murders and rapes perpetrated
by recent migrants**: Alison Smale,
"Migrant Crimes," *The New York
Times*, May 21, 2016.

154 **nine of ten cities**: http://
www.bbc.com/news/world-europe
-36362505.

155 **male white working class**:
Robert Ford and Matthew Goodwin,
*Revolt on the Right: Explaining Support
for the Radical Right in Britain*,
Routledge, 2014. Also Ford and
Goodwin, "Understanding UKIP,"
The Political Quarterly, September–
October 2014.

155 **over 600,000 a year**: http://
www.bbc.com/news/uk-politics
-35658731.

156 **"push British workers out of
jobs"**: Ibid.

156 **"native employment rates"**:   411
https://www.gov.uk/government
/uploads/system/uploads/attachment
_data/file/257235/analysis-of-the
-impacts.pdf.

158 **less than $45,000**: http://www.
newstatesman.com/politics
/staggers/2016/06/how-did-different
-demographic- groups-vote-eu
-referendum.

161 **"world without pity"**: Marine
Le Pen, *À Contre Flots*, Editions
Jacques Grancher, 2006, author's
translations. For Marine Le Pen's
life, see Elizabeth Zerofsky, "Front
Runner," *Harpers*, May 2016; and
Stefan Simons, "Le Pen's Daughter,"
Der Spiegel, August 2006.

162 **"reinforced the caricature"**: Le
Pen, op. cit., p. 256.

162 **she broke publicly with him**:
"Chambres a Gas, Le Pen Persiste," *Le
Figaro*, March 24, 2008. The magazine
was *Bretons*.

162 **critical of Gollnisch's
comments**: "Marine Le Pen Reprend
ses Distances avec son Pere," *Figaro*,
April 24, 2008.

162 **"party like the others"**:
Alexandre Deze, *Le Front national: à la
conquête du pouvoir?*, Armand Colin,
2012.

162 **racists were not welcome in the
party**: Mathieu von Rohr, "Marine Le
Pen's Populism for the Masses," *Der
Spiegel*, July 7, 2011.

162 **"by all necessary means"**:
http://www.bbc.com/news/world
-europe-13206056.

162 **finally expelling him**: http://
www.bbc.com/news/world-europe
-34009901.

412   163   "among unassimilated children?": http://lelab.europe1.fr/debile-ou-degoutant-1403 (author's translation).

163   she explained to an interviewer: Russell Shorto, "Is This the Most Dangerous Woman in Europe," *The Observer*, June 26, 2011.

164   Philippot told *Le Monde*: "Florian Philippot," *Le Monde*, November 1, 2012 (author's translation).

164   referendum held on the Euro: http://www.frontnational.com/pdf/Programme.pdf (author's translation).

164   Le Pen's election brochure: http://www.frontnational.com/pdf/projet_mlp2012.pdf.

165   and Parisians: Nonna Mayer, "La Plafond de Verre Electoral Entame, mais pas Brise," *Les Faux-Semblants du Front National*, Presses de Sciences Po, 2015, p. 309.

165   "Merkozy": "Hollande contre Merkozy," *Le Monde*, June 2, 2012.

165   abandoned his promises: On Hollande's fall and the FN's rise, see Arthur Goldhammer, "As EU Technocrats Falter, the French Right Gains," *Boston Review*, December 16, 2015.

167   "reached very high levels": Pascal Perrineau, "Le Front National, une partie de plus en plus national," *Le Monde*, February 4, 2015.

167   Socialist Party support: Perrineau, op. cit.

167   "other public facilities": Interview with author.

168   Bouvet said: Interview with author.

168   Frédéric Martel: Interview with author.

169   Zemmour explained: Interview with author.

169   Sebastien Chenu: Interview with author.

169   Antoine Golliot: Interview with author.

170   "gay lobby": Sophie Pedder, "Marine Le Pen, L'Etrangere," *Economist 1843*, April–May 2016.

170   "buy it with francs or euros": Olivier Faye, "Au FN, le Sujet de l'identite," *Le Monde*, June 10, 2016, author's translation.

170   "Christians must stand up to resist Islam": *Briebart News*, July 26, 2016.

170   Bouvet says: Interview with author.

CHAPTER EIGHT

174   China's imports: David H. Autor, David Dorn, and Gordon H. Hanson, "The China Shock," Working Paper 21906, NBER, January 2016.

175   2.4 million jobs overseas: https://www. americanprogress .org/issues/labor/news/ 2012/07/09 /11898/5-facts-about-overseas -outsourcing/.

175   "determined more by immigration control": Ha-Joon Chang, 23 *Things They Don't Tell You About Capitalism*, Bloomsbury Press, 2011, p. 5.

176   Migrants made up 73 percent: Goran Adamson, "Migrants and Crime in Sweden in the Twenty-First Century," Society, 2020.

177 **"fulfill a redistributive role":** Wynne Godley, "Maastricht and all that," *London Review of Books*, October 8, 1992.

THE NATIONALIST REVIVAL

CHAPTER NINE

181 **myth that built the modern world:** "National Identity Is Made Up," Max Fisher, Josh Keller, Mae Ryan, and Shane O'Neill, *The New York Times*, February 28, 2018.

183 **concession of national sovereignty:** *Europe's Orphan: The Future of the Euro and the Politics of Debt*, Martin Sandbu, Princeton 2015.

184 **build more American oil refineries:** *Private Empire: ExxonMobil and American Power*, Steve Coll, Penguin, 2012.

CHAPTER TEN

190 **willingness to sacrifice:** *Nations: The Long History and Deep Roots of Political Ethnicity and Nationalism*, Azar Gat, Cambridge University Press, 2012.

192 **"noble-minded man":** "Seventh Address," *Addresses to the German Nation*, Johann Gottlieb Fichte, 1808.

193 **"sacred communion of citizens":** "The 'Sacred' Dimension of Nationalism," Anthony D. Smith, *Millennium: Journal of International Studies*, December 1, 2000.

194 **is a "novelty.":** *Nations and Nationalism since 1780*, Eric Hobsbawm, Cambridge University Press, 1992.

197 **poor potential Nigerian immigrant:** "Bernie Sanders's fear of immigrant labor is ugly—and wrongheaded," Dylan Matthews, Vox, July 29, 2015.

197 **"cosmopolitan ideal":** *The Elements of Politics*, Henry Sidgwick, 1891.

204 **huge Ford plant:** *The New Minority: White Working Class Politics in an Age of Immigration and Inequality*, Justin Gest, Oxford University Press, 2016.

206 **constructed a "word cloud":** "What mattered most to you when deciding how to vote in the EU referendum?" Chris Prosser, Jon Mellon, and Jane Green, British Election Study, July 11, 2016.

206 **"somewheres" and "anywheres":** *The Road to Somewhere: The Populist Revolt and the Future of Politics*, David Goodhart, Hurst, 2017.

CHAPTER ELEVEN

211 **82 percent were English:** *Our Foreigners: A Chronicle of Americans in the Making*, Samuel Peter Orth, Library of Alexandria, 1919.

213 **Israelish extraction:** *Genesis: Truman, American Jews and the Origins of the Arab/Israeli Conflict*, John B. Judis, Farrar, Straus & Giroux, 2014.

214 **legal immigrants:** "The Two Sides of Immigration Policy," John B. Judis, *American Prospect*, February 1, 2018.

215 **low-wage immigrants:** *We Wanted Workers: Unraveling the Immigration Narrative*, George J. Borjas, W. W. Norton & Company, 2016.

215 **against the waves of immigrants:** "Multiculturalism

414 in American Public Opinion," Jack Citrin, David O. Sears, Christopher Muste, and Cara Wong, *British Journal of Political Science*, April 2001.

218 **exclusionary nationalist sentiment:** "Varieties of American Popular Nationalism," Bart Bonikowski and Paul DiMaggio, *American Sociological Review*, September 8, 2016.

218 **Pakistanis and Iraqis on the border:** "Border Wars," John B. Judis, *The New Republic*, January 16, 2006.

221 **clerics cite biblical verses:** "Tea Minus Zero," John B. Judis, *The New Republic*, May 18, 2010.

222 **study of Tea Party blogs in 2010:** *The Tea Party and Reactionary Politics in America*, Christopher S. Parker and Matt a. Barreto, Princeton University Press, 2013.

223 **rife with conspiracy theories:** "Tea Party Movement Is Full of Conspiracy Theories," *Newsweek*, February 2, 2010.

223 **we were always winning:** *Fire and Fury: Inside the Trump White House*, Michael Wolff, Henry Holt and Company, 2018.

225 **white workers without a college education:** "Voter Trends in 2016," Rob Griffin, Ruy Teixeira, and John Halpin, Center for American Progress, November 1, 2017.

226 **"part of God's plan":** "Make America Christian Again: Christian Nationalism and Voting for Donald Trump in the 2016 Presidential Election," Andrew Whitehead, Samuel Perry, and Joseph Baker, *Sociology of Religion*, May 19, 2018.

233 **Internet startups in Silicon Valley:** "An Attempt To Measure What Silicon Valley Really Thinks About Politics And The World (In 14 Graphs)," Greg Ferenstein, The Ferenstein Wire, November 6, 2015.

CHAPTER TWELVE

241 **guarantee of secure employment:** "Varieties of Capitalism and the Euro Crisis," Peter Hall, *West European Politics*, August 14, 2014.

246 **672,000 applications for asylum:** "Fortress Europe: a Brief History of European Migration and Asylum Policy," Josi Seilono, University of Helsinki, 2016.

246 **highly segregated communities:** *Reflections on the Revolution in Europe: Immigration, Islam, and the West*, Christopher Caldwell, Anchor, 2009.

246 **welfare dependence:** "Immigrants and welfare programmes: exploring the interactions between immigrant characteristics, immigrant welfare dependence and welfare policy," Alan Barrett and Yvonne McCarthy, Oxford Review of Economic Policy, October 1, 2008.

252 **chastised by their rank and file:** "Why Sarrazin's Integration Demagoguery Has Many Followers," *Spiegel*, September 6, 2010.

256 **Neo-Nazi ideology:** "Gauland Apparently Employs Another Neo-Nazi," *Spiegel*, March 21, 2018.

256 **Once you've got weeds:** "'Revenge of the East'? How anger in the former GDR helped the AfD," Philip Oltermann, The Guardian, September 28, 2017.

257 **"Trianon was the cause":** "The DNA of the Hungarian Race Shows that It Is Chosen," Magdalena Marsovszky, *European Institute for Progressive Cultural Policies,* September 2000.

258 **extending beyond national borders:** *Orban: Europe's New Strongman,* Paul Lendvai, Hurst, 2017.

261 **phantasm that left a heavy imprint:** "The Polish Case," Leszek Koczanowicz, *New Left Review,* November-Decmber 2016.

CHAPTER THIRTEEN

269 **"regime change":** *The Folly of Empire,* John B. Judis, Oxford University Press, 2004.

271 **make and break such a promise:** "Deal or No Deal? The End of the Cold War and the U.S. Offer to Limit NATO Expansion," Joshua R. Itzkowitz Shifrinson, *International Security,* Spring 2016.

273 **"this is just wrong":** "Foreign Affairs; Now a Word From X," Thomas L. Friedman, *The New York Times,* May 2, 1998.

273 **"Russia did not exist":** *Everyone Loses: The Ukraine Crisis and the Ruinous Contest for Post-Soviet Eurasia,* Samuel Charap and Timothy Colton, Routledge, 2017.

276 **civilization and noncivilization:** *Everything Under the Heavens: How the Past Helps Shape China's Push for Global Power,* Howard W. French, Penguin, 2017.

276 **China's regional objectives:** *Asia's Reckoning: China, Japan, and the*

Fate of U.S. Power in the Pacific Century, Richard McGregor, Viking, 2017.

285 **not independent of net exports:** "Trump's Trade Chief Makes a Rookie Mistake," Noah Smith, *Bloomberg,* December 28, 2016.

CHAPTER FOURTEEN

289 **destruction of the labor movement:** *Has Globalization Gone Too Far?,* Dani Rodrik, Peterson Institute for International Economics, 1997.

292 **single hegemonic power:** *The World in Depression: 1929-1939,* Charles Kindleberger, University of California Press, 1986.

293 **revival of Keynes's proposal:** "High Wages Versus High Savings in a Globalized World," Michael Pettis, Carnegie Endowment For International Peace, April 3, 2018.

THE SOCIALIST AWAKENING

CHAPTER FIFTEEN

299 **In an October 2019 YouGov poll:** Fourth Annual Report on U.S. Attitudes Toward Socialism. Accessed at https://www.victimsofcommunism.org/2019-annual-poll.

302 **They included Philippe Buchez:** Gary Dorrien, *Soul in Society: The Making and Renewal of Social Christianity* (Fortress Press, 1995).

305 **Bernstein continued to embrace Marx's goal of socialism:** From Eduard Bernstein, *Evolutionary Socialism* (1899).

307 **Martin J. Sklar contended that the competitive capitalism**

415

416   **of Marx's day:** Martin J. Sklar, *The United States as a Developing Country* (Cambridge, 1992), p. 214.

307   **the first steps of progress along the long and difficult path:** Axel Honneth, *The Idea of Socialism: Towards a Renewal* (Polity, 2017).

307   **Alternative, noncapitalist economic activities:** Erik Olin Wright, *How to Be an Anti-Capitalist in the 21st Century* (Verso, 2019).

308   **"there is no single moment of transition from a profit-oriented economy to a socialist economy":** Fred Block, "Financial Democratization and the Transition to Socialism," prepared for workshop on "Democratizing Finance" at the University of Wisconsin, May–June 2018.

308   **"The moment anyone started to talk to Marx about morality, he would roar with laughter":** Quoted in Steven Lukes, *Marxism and Morality* (Clarendon, 1985), p. 27.

308   **"It is commonly true on camping trips":** G.A. Cohen, *Why Not Socialism* (Princeton, 2009).

312   **"What is now in crisis is a whole conception of socialism":** Ernesto Laclau and Chantal Mouffe *Hegemony and Socialist Strategy* (1985).

313   **appealed to socialist values as the means to unite a majority:** G. A. Cohen, "Back to Socialist Basics," *New Left Review*, September–October, 1994.

CHAPTER SIXTEEN

319   **"out of darkness into light":** Many of Debs's speeches are collected in an internet archive: https://www.marxists.org/archive/debs/index.htm.

320   **"They took their socialism like a new religion":** Cited in Michael Kazin, *American Dreamers: How the Left Changed a Nation* (Vintage, 2012).

322   **"Socialism is an eschatological movement":** See Daniel Bell, "The Problem of Ideological Rigidity," *The End of Ideology: On the Exhaustion of Political Ideas in the Fifties* (1960).

326   **in 1970 that there were 35,800 hippies in Vermont:** Cited in Harry Jaffe, *Why Bernie Sanders Matters* (Regan Arts, 2015).

326   **"The Revolution is coming, and it is a very beautiful revolution":** *Freeman,* November 1969.

326   **Sanders campaigned as a socialist:** *Seven Days,* December 12, 1972.

327   **"that idea suddenly becomes acceptable reality":** *Seven Days,* 1976.

327   **"No one gives a damn about your ideology":** Tim Murphy, "How Bernie Sanders Learned to Be a Real Politician," *Mother Jones,* May 26, 2015.

327   **"make it into a modern corporation":** Quoted in Jaffe, *Why Bernie Sanders Matters.*

328   **a "Eugene V. Debs type of socialist":** *Atlantic,* October 5, 2015 (publication of unpublished profile from 1985).

328   **"If you ask me if the banks should be nationalized, I would say yes":** *Baltimore Sun,* November 23, 1981.

328 "I'm not afraid of government control in economics": *Rutland Herald,* April 28, 1988.

328 "the guts to raise the issues that all of us know to be true": Speech reprinted in *Monthly Review,* November 1989.

329 "as it exists in countries such as Sweden": *Burlington Free Press,* October 16, 1990.

329 Asked to define his kind of socialism: *Rutland Daily Herald,* November 3, 1990.

329 "socialism doesn't mean state ownership of everything": Associated Press, November 7, 1990.

329 "democracy and socialism can exist in a compatible way": *Rutland Daily Herald,* June 8, 1988.

329 socialism as a command economy of nationalized firms was dashed: *Washington Post,* May 2, 2019.

331 "give workers an ownership stake in the companies they work for": "Corporate Accountability and Democracy," Bernie Sanders homepage. Accessed at https://berniesanders.com/issues/corporate-accountability-and-democracy/.

332 "it's too late to do anything inside the Beltway": Andrew Prokop, "Bernie Sanders's Political Revolution, Explained," Vox, January 28, 2016. Accessed at https://www.vox.com/2016/1/28/10853502/bernie-sanders-political-revolution.

332 historian Eric Foner penned an open letter to Sanders: Eric Foner, *Nation,* October 21, 2015.

333 the need to rein in the excesses of capitalism: See the campaign

memoir of Sanders aide Heather Gautney, *Crashing the Party: From the Bernie Sanders Campaign to a Progressive Movement* (Verso, 2018).

335 "we're talking about countries and systems that already exist": Nisha Stickles and Barbara Corbellini Duarte, "Exclusive: Alexandria Ocasio-Cortez explains what democratic socialism means to her," *Business Insider,* March 4, 2019. Accessed at https://www.businessinsider.com/alexandria-ocasio-cortez-explains-what-democratic-socialism-means-2019-3?utm_source=markets&utm_medium=ingest.

CHAPTER SEVENTEEN

339 43 percent of Democrats had a favorable view of socialism: Peter Moore, "One Third of Millennials View Socialism Favorably," YouGov, May 11, 2015. Accessed at https://today.yougov.com/topics/politics/articles-reports/2015/05/11/one-third-millennials-like-socialism.

340 47 percent preferred socialism: Data for Progress, *Progressive Future of the Party.*

341 those who thought of themselves as socialists were very likely to live in a city or suburb: Compiled by author from data sets provided by YouGov and Data for Progress.

341 voted for Democrats in roughly the same proportion: John B. Judis and Ruy Teixeira, *The Emerging Democratic Majority* (Scribner, 2002).

342 The rest of the alternatives were a grab bag: Frank Newport, "The Meaning of 'Socialism' to Americans Today," Polling Matters (Gallup),

418   October 4, 2018. Accessed at https://
news.gallup.com/opinion/polling
-matters/243362/meaning-socialism
-americans-today.aspx.

343   **Over half think it will pose a
"serious threat" in their lifetimes:** RJ
Reinhart, "Global Warming Age Gap:
Younger Americans Most Worried,"
Gallup, May 11, 2018. Accessed at
https://news.gallup.com/poll/234314
/global-warming-age-gap-younger
-americans-worried.aspx.

344   **gap in income between a male
high school graduate:** Kevin Drum,
"Chart of the Day: The College Wage
Premium over Time," *Mother Jones*,
August 9, 2019. Accessed at https://
www.motherjones.com/kevin
-drum/2019/08/chart-of-the-day
-the-college-wage-premium-over
-time/.

344   **Average student debt for the
young rose:** Kevin Drum, "Chart of
the Day: The College Wage Premium
over Time."

344   **One survey of 40 Uber drivers:**
Katie Wells, Kafui Attoh, and Declan
Cullen, "The Uber Workplace in D.C.:
Georgetown University," Kalmanovitz
Initiative for Labor and the Working
Poor, 2019.

345   **before they could afford
to buy a house:** Alexis Madrigal,
"Why Housing Policy Feels Like
Generational Warfare," *Atlantic*. June
13, 2019.

345   **According to a McKinsey
Study in 2013:** Accessed at https://
www.mckinsey.com/~/media
/mckinsey/industries/social%20
sector/our%20insights/voice%20
of%20the%20graduate/voice_of
_the_graduate.ashx.

347   **When Bhaskar Sunkara went to
his first DSA meeting in 2007:** "The
ABCs of Jacobin," *Columbia Journalism
Review*, January 2, 2019.

349   **DSA's membership of
approximately 70,000:** These
estimates are based on conversations
with David Duhalde, who was deputy
director of the organization, and had
access to the survey numbers, which
he quoted to me.

352   **"DSA should make it clear
that we will not endorse corporate
politicians":** Andrew Sernatinger,
"If Sanders Should Lose," *Medium*,
July 19, 2019. Accessed at https://
medium.com/@andrew.sernatinger
/if-sanders-should-lose-e1559c7
b2fd3.

353   **'What did you do in the war
against the neofascist Donald
Trump?':** Harold Meyerson, "What
the Socialists Just Did—and Why,"
American Prospect, August 9, 2019.
Accessed at https://prospect.org
/power/socialists-just-did-and/.

353   **"We believe Biden's anti-
Chinese xenophobic messaging
& the allegations of sexual
assault":** https://twitter.com/
DemSocialists/status/12602
44691888504834?s=20.

354   **political scientist Lee
Drutman found in his survey of
the 2016 election:** Lee Drutman,
"Political Divisions in 2016 and
Beyond," Voter Study Group, June
2017.

356   **"new breed of American
democratic socialists":** Joseph
Stiglitz, "A 'democratic socialist'
agenda is appealing. No wonder
Trump attacks it," *Washington Post*,
May 18, 2019.

357   "rethink the markets-first approach in favor of a pragmatic assessment": "New Rules for the Twenty-First Century: Corporate Power, Public Power, and the Future of the American Economy," The Roosevelt Institute. Accessed at https://www.new rules for the -21st-century.com/.

358   She's really a democratic socialist in some ways: Steven Rattner, "The Warren Way Is the Wrong Way," New York Times, November 4, 2019. Accessed at https://www.nytimes.com/2019/11/04 /opinion/medicare-warren-plan.html.

359   When one writer suggested that he sounded like Debs: George Packer, "The Throwback Democrat," Atlantic, February 7, 2019. Accessed at https://www.theatlantic.com /ideas/archive/2019/02/sherrod -brown-just-what-democrats-need -2020/582208/.

CHAPTER EIGHTEEN

363   they were not enamored of actual working-class ownership and control: "Socialism: the Fabian Essays," Boston, 1894.

363   "the pessimism of the revolutionaries": John Maynard Keynes, "Economic Possibilities for our Grandchildren," 1930.

364   "A mixed economy is what most people of the West would prefer": Quoted in David Marquand, Britain Since 1918: The Strange Career of British Democracy (Orion, 2009).

365   "owes much more to the teachings of Jesus": Tony Benn, "Revolutionary Christianity," Marxism Today, January, 1980.

366   Benn outlined a plan for "industrial democracy": Reprinted in The Best of Benn: Speeches, Diaries, Letters, and Other Writings (Hutchinson, 2014).

367   "brokers, jobbers, and the City's traditional merchant banks merged": BBC News, October 27, 2016.

368   "brought a deterioration in public-sector service standards and democratic accountability": Robin Blackburn, "The Corbyn Project," New Left Review, May–June 2018.

370   "I think it's called socialism": Quote from Richard Seymour, Corbyn: The Strange Rebirth of Radical Politics (Verso, 2016).

371   hoping to "break the grip of the Blairites": Quote from Richard Seymour: Corbyn: The Strange Rebirth of Radical Politics.

371   as "a coalition of idealistic youngsters": Conversation, September 12, 2015.

371   "moral sense of purpose rooted in Methodism": Rosa Prince, Comrade Corbyn (Biteback, 2016).

372   his positions were more in line with Benn's socialism: Quote from "John McDonnell: The Self-Made Socialist," Prospect, September 18, 2018.

375   "being a teenager in late capitalist Britain is now": Mark Fisher, Capitalist Realism: Is There No Alternative? (Zero Books, 2009).

377   Most scientists would regard 2030 as a radical and probably unattainable target: On the more standard view by social scientists and scientists, see https://www .foreignaffairs.com/articles/2020

420   -04-13/paths-net-zero and https://
prospect.org/greennewdeal/getting
-to-a-carbon-free-economy/.

379   **"When I knocked on your
doors in 2017":** Laura Pidcock, "Letter
to the People I Represented," *Medium*,
December 18, 2019. Accessed at
https://medium.com/@laura
.pidcock.mp/letter-to-the-people
-i-represented-406aea893243.

380   **"Convincing an electoral
majority in the grip of post-crash
austerity":** Steve Hall and Simon
Winlow, "Back to the Future: On
the British Liberal Left's Return to
Origins" (draft).

381   **"The democratic nation and
its rule of law is the best means
of safeguarding our rights and
freedoms":** Jonathan Rutherford,
"Blue Labour has been tragically
vindicated," *Medium*, December 14,
2019. Accessed at https://medium
.com/@blue_labour/blue-labour
-has-been-tragically-vindicated
-38022a970f9a.

382   **"is that we are all Keynesians
now":** "The Guardian View on
Boris Johnson's Budget: We Are All
Keynesians Now," *Guardian*, March 11,
2020. Accessed at https://www
.theguardian.com/commentisfree
/2020/mar/11/the-guardian-view-on
-boris-johnsons-budget-we-are-all
-keynesians-now.

CHAPTER NINETEEN

385   **It obscures the leading role
of nurses and schoolteachers:**
Meagan Day, "Bernie Sanders and
Elizabeth Warren Aren't Playing the
Same Game," *Jacobin*, August 2019.
Accessed at https://www.jacobinmag
.com/2019/08/bernie-sanders
-elizabeth-warren-democratic-party
-elite-2020-presidential-race.

385   **Sunkara quotes Luxemburg:**
Bhaskar Sunkara, *The Socialist Manifesto:
The Case for Radical Politics in an Era of
Extreme Inequality* (Verso, 2019).

386   **"There Is No Left Case for
Nationalism":** Atossa Araxia
Abrahamian, "There Is No Left Case
for Nationalism," *Nation*, November
28, 2018.

386   **Blue Labour's support for
national identity has been branded
"bigoted":** Chloe Chaplain, "What
is Blue Labour, the controversial
'culturally conservative' group calling
for support to shape the future of the
party?" *i*, December 16, 2019.

386   **"There is a simple reason why
pandering to nationalism will, in
the end, always benefit the right":**
Sabrina Huck, "Labour must reject
nationalism for an inclusive definition
of community," LabourList, March 3,
2020.

386   **only 12.3 percent of the
respondents described themselves
as "patriotic":** https://twitter.com
/DavidKlion/status/125802674512
8722432?s=20.

388   **"should be conceivable within
the lifespan of one generation":**
Alec Nove, *The Economics of Feasible
Socialism* (Allen & Unwin, 1983).

392   **began a series of articles
calling for a "reset of capitalism":**
"Financial Times Launches First
Campaign Since Global Financial
Crisis," B2B marketing, September 24,
2019. Accessed at https://www
.b2bmarketing.net/en/resources/news
/financial-times-launches-first
-campaign-global-financial-crisis.

Columbia Global Reports is a publishing imprint from Columbia University that commissions authors to do original on-site reporting around the globe on a wide range of issues. The resulting novella-length books offer new ways to look at and understand the world that can be read in a few hours. Most readers are curious and busy. Our books are for them.

Subscribe to Columbia Global Reports and get six books a year in the mail in advance of publication. globalreports.columbia.edu/subscribe

The Call: Inside the Global Saudi Religious Project
Krithika Varagur

Ghosting the News: Local Journalism and the Crisis of American Democracy
Margaret Sullivan

Carte Blanche: The Erosion of Medical Consent
Harriet A. Washington

The Agenda: How a Republican Supreme Court Is Reshaping America
Ian Millhiser

Reading Our Minds: The Rise of Big Data Psychiatry
Daniel Barron

Freedomville: The Story of a 21st-Century Slave Revolt
Laura T. Murphy